* Volumes with an asterisk following the title are a part of the NCRLL set: Approaches to Language and Literacy Research, edited by JoBeth Allen and Donna Alvermann.

(Continued)

STORYTIME

Young Children's Literary Understanding in the Classroom

LAWRENCE R. SIPE

Foreword by
P. DAVID PEARSON

Teachers College
Columbia University
New York and London

For My Mother

Os suum aperuit sapientiae,
Et lex clementiae in lingua eius.

Published by Teachers College Press, 1234 Amsterdam Avenue, New York, NY 10027

The author wishes to express gratitude for the use of the following:

Figure 3.1 was reproduced from *Secondary Worlds: Literature Teaching and the Visual Arts*, by Michael Benton (Buckingham, UK: Open University Press, 1992). Used by permission of the author.

Table 9.1 was adapted from "The Construction of Literary Understanding by First and Second Graders in Oral Response to Picture Storybody Readalouds," by Lawrence R. Sipe (2000) (*Reading Research Quarterly, 35*, 268). Used by permission of the International Reading Association (IRA).

Library of Congress Cataloging-in-Publication Data

Sipe, Lawrence R.
   Storytime : young children's literary understanding in the classroom / Lawrence R. Sipe.
         p. cm. — (Language and literacy series)
   Includes bibliographical references and index.
   ISBN 978-0-8077-4828-2 (pbk. : alk. paper) — ISBN 978-0-8077-4829-9 (cloth : alk. paper)
   1. Language arts (Elementary)—United States.   2. Reading (Elementary)—United States.   3. English language—Composition and exercises—Study and teaching (Elementary)—United States.   I. Title.
   LB1576.S457 2008
   372.6—dc22

                                                                              2007032358

ISBN 978-0-8077-4828-2 (paper)
ISBN 978-0-8077-4829-9 (cloth)

Printed on acid-free paper
Manufactured in the United States of America

15   14   13   12   11   10   09   08   8   7   6   5   4   3   2   1

Contents

Foreword

Our colleague Larry Sipe has given us a wonderful gift—a book that invites us to join him on a journey (at times it seems almost like a pilgrimage!) into the engaging world of children (and teachers) responding to literature. Once we accept this invitation, we are hooked. Sipe holds us spellbound by weaving his own tale about why it is so important for teachers to take the time to involve students in deep analyses and rich responses to the wealth of ideas and issues that await them in the pages of children's literature. In a policy world dominated by standards, assessments, fluency measures, and the rhetoric of science, this is a wonderful counterpoint—one that reminds us of why we teach reading in the first place.

Let me be clear: This is not a simple journey—certainly not an "If it is Tuesday, it must be Belgium!" jaunt through the world of children's literature. This journey requires longer stays at each important stop, as well as serious intellectual and aesthetic commitment on our part as readers. Sipe challenges us as often as he surprises or delights us with his insights about how and why children respond the way they do, how teachers can support response, and how his views about response both build on and move beyond earlier treatments of this rich and all too often neglected topic.

Who should read this book? Sipe contends that he has written it primarily for colleagues who want to share this journey with him—both practicing and novice scholars who have made a commitment to understanding how teachers can promote engagement with literature and why. He also believes that teacher educators will find a theoretical perspective along with compelling examples of children engaged in deep response that will allow them to provide guidance to novice teachers. And he believes that certain teachers will gain an appreciation for the sophisticated thinking that children, even young children, are capable of when we open our minds and conversations to a wide range of responses. I would go farther in recommending the book for teachers. I think that teachers who are committed to making literature a core part of their classroom curriculum will find in the book a set of theoretical ideas to accompany their commitments and activities. And those who are not currently committed will be swept away by the compelling examples of what children can do when they are invited by teachers to think great thoughts.

Why should you read it? Several reasons actually. First and foremost, because you will learn a new way of thinking about children's response to literature. Sipe is, as I will describe later, the master taxonomist, and he gives us a very useful set of categories for understanding and analyzing children's responses and the ways in which teachers can and do support them. Second, the numerous examples of children and their teachers talking about literature educate in their own right. They teach us much about the remarkable thinking that even young children can manage under the right conditions of teacher support. And the examples of teacher support in Chapter 10 would allow a thoughtful classroom teacher to build an entire theory of how to scaffold student response. Third, because as I alluded to earlier, all of us in the field of literacy education need a counterpoint to the current emphasis on "basic skills" in the national policy conversation. We need a reminder that reading is about thinking and that literature—perhaps especially children's literature— is an art form deserving of rich aesthetic response. And we need to see examples of classroom discourse in which students learn how to exercise agency and document their reasoning and teachers exercise professional prerogative befitting their stature.

Why do I like this book? There is much to like in Sipe's treatment of children's response to literature. First, I appreciated its dual grounding in (a) the long scholarly tradition of response to literature and (b) the real responses real students make to real literature under the guidance of real teachers; in short, Sipe demonstrates both respect and authenticity. Sipe's respect for the scholars of response who have come before him—Richards, Fish, Rosenblatt, Britton, Bleich, Langer, Bogdan, and others—is captured in his uncanny ability to capture the essence of each of these scholars. He even manages to place them on a useful continuum from an autonomous text (the meaning is really out there in the text) to an autonomous reader (the meaning in entirely what each reader says it is). Sipe demonstrates a comparable respect for teachers and students by using their conversations about stories (mainly readalouds) as the empirical bases of his theory of response. By traversing back and forth between theoretical and empirical poles, Sipe is able to craft a "story" that is responsive to both theory and evidence. There can be no higher standard for the credibility of scholarship.

Second, the book offers us a rich framework for understanding children's response to literature. Sipe has a penchant for developing taxonomies—category systems to help us build both a broad conceptualization of a domain along with careful distinctions among the elements of its infrastructure. These taxonomies (sometimes realized as continua) appear in virtually every chapter, so I cannot possibly preview them all. But I can use one as an illustration of his gift. In the final analysis, in Chapter 9, Sipe summarizes his 5 basic types of literary response (see Table 9.1): analytical (largely within the text), intertextual (reasoning across texts), personal (connecting experience to or from the text), transparent (moving into the text), and performative (using texts as platforms for creative expression). Not content with a single category system, he imposes yet another on top of the response types, which he labels as three basic literary impulses: the hermeneutic impulse, with its emphasis on a desire to "master the text," entails both analytical and intertextual responses; the personalizing impulse, with a focus on the desire to connect the text to our life experiences, entails only the personal response type; and the aesthetic impulse, which is driven by our desire to free ourselves from the bonds of reason and cognition, entails both the transparent (losing ourselves in text) and the performative (using texts for personal creations) response types. Taken together, these two category systems allow us as readers to appreciate both cognitive and aesthetic stances on integrating text and experience.

Third, the book shines a spotlight on some commonly overlooked aspects of response to literature. I was especially taken with the sections unpacking what we know as a field about the relationship between the imaginal and verbal representations in books. I also appreciated the emphasis on the parts of a book that come before and after the actual story—for example, the cover, the endpages, and even the role of the ISBN symbol! I found fascinating the transcripts in which students addressed the role of these features; their conjectures about the significance of space and color were quite remarkable. Sipe calls this peritextual (near or with the text) response, a term coined by Gerard Genette.

Fourth, Sipe writes in a style and register that is at once academic and accessible. Few scholars are able to do this—Stephen J. Gould's essays in *Science* come to mind as a notable exception. But Sipe manages to achieve this balance between erudition and transparency quite well. One never gets the feeling that he is "talking down" to his readers, nor does one ever get lost in opaque vocabulary or Byzantine syntax. This ensures that his book will travel well across audiences.

In the final analysis, I recommend this book because of my personal response to it. As I read it, I found myself in close conversation with Professor Sipe, sometimes affirming a point of agreement with an emphatic "*Yes!*" in the margin, or noting a quizzical, "Are you kidding?" At other times I questioned whether I had gotten it all wrong when I first discovered the comprehension processes some 40 years ago. But the highest recommendation I can make is that I learned so much—so very, very much—in reading what is a wonderful contribution to the profession. You will too!

P. David Pearson

Acknowledgments

I want to acknowledge the cooperation, support, and inspiration of a number of colleagues and friends without whom this book would have never been possible. First, I want to thank my Ohio State dissertation chair, Janet Hickman, and my dissertation committee (Diane DeFord, Karin Dahl, and Rudine Sims Bishop), as well as Evie Freeman, Barbara Lehman, Ken Marantz, Pat Scharer, and Roy and Thelma Wilson for helping me complete the first steps on the path to developing my passion for understanding young children's responses to picturebooks.

I am also grateful for the gracious cooperation of Tracey Bigler-McCarthy, Terry Miller, Jeff Bauer, Elizabeth Zack, Caltropia Wilder, and the young students in their classrooms. I have learned much from all of them, and their literary interpretive work forms the core of this book, as evidence of joyful teaching/learning and creativity.

My colleagues at the Graduate School of Education at the University of Pennsylvania (Susan Lytle, Morton Botel, Vivian Gadsden, and Maren Aukerman) have been greatly supportive in all my work, and never fail to be models of scholarship and intellectual stimulation. The staff of the Language and Literacy in Education Division, Penny Creedon, Lorraine Hightower, Suzanne Oh, and Mary Schlesinger, have been helpful in so many ways over the years.

Many members of the children's literature community at other universities —Janice Almasi, Mollie Blackburn, Tom Crumpler, Pat Enciso, Janet Evans, Doug Fisher, Lee Galda, Darwin Henderson, Christine Jenkins, Barbara Kiefer, Margaret Mackey, Jonda McNair, Beth Maloch, Miriam Martinez, Jill May, Lea McGee, Karla Möller, Perry Nodelman, Sylvia Pantaleo, Chris Pappas, Taffy Raphael, Nancy Roser, Frank Serafini, Kathy Short, Trika Smith-Burke, Laura Smolkin, Bill Teale, Shelby Wolf, Carol Wolfenbarger, and Junko Yokota—are generous scholars who have gifted me with many insights about literature written for children. Geoff Fox, Pam Barnard, and David Lewis, scholars from the United Kingdom, happily met through our involvement in the journal *Children's Literature in Education*, have also been another source of inspiration.

My family (my mother, Dorcas Transeau; my sister, Judy, and brother-in-law, Steven; and my nieces, Kate and Emily) have also helped me in many intangible ways, in addition to providing me with a place to write in peace and serenity.

Ray and Liz Bown generously lent me their summer cottage to work on the beginning stages of this book, in the pristine setting of the Newfoundland seacoast.

I owe a considerable debt of gratitude to the many master's and doctoral students in my courses and those who have served as master's and doctoral research assistants; I'm especially thankful to Anne Brightman, Gerald Campano, Deborah Cornatzer, Patricia Daley, Maria Ghiso, Gloria Johnson, and Angela Wiseman. A special note of thanks goes to Caroline McGuire, whose keen intellect and impressive computer skills made the final manuscript revisions a pleasure rather than a chore. I would also like to thank current and former doctoral students Donna Adomat, Diane Downer Anderson, Wanda Brooks, Susan Browne, Jenny Foight-Cressman, Darrel Steward-Hoagland, Susan Lea, Melissa O'Donnell, Mika Okawa, and Mary Beth Schaefer.

Chris Raschka, illustrator and author extraordinaire and a friend for many years, has my appreciation and gratitude for executing the beautiful cover for this book. I am very grateful to P. David Pearson, for agreeing to write the foreword.

Finally, I want to thank my editor, Carol Collins, for her graceful, incisive reading of the manuscript, which has been immeasurably improved by her guidance.

Introduction

For more than 30 years—as a classroom teacher, a coordinator of teachers' professional development, and a university professor—I have been intrigued by young children's understanding and interpretation of stories. Their talk about both the words and illustrations in picture storybooks has been a special fascination. For the past 12 years, I have been focusing my research on what happens when kindergarten, first-, and second-grade teachers read picturebooks aloud to their classes of youngsters, and have built a grounded theory of young children's literary understanding based on this work. The teachers I have observed have been chosen because they know and love literature for children. Moreover, these teachers know the value of allowing children to talk freely during story time, listening closely and attentively to what the children say, even when it may seem that they have gone off on a conversational tangent. Children who are accustomed to talking about stories with perceptive teachers say the most amazing things. Here is a vignette from a kindergarten classroom in which the teacher, Mr. Taylor, displays the front cover of Christopher Coady's (1991) version of *Red Riding Hood* to the class.

> MR. TAYLOR: What do you think this book—*Red Riding Hood*—
> might be about?
> KEYRON: Probably she read and she write a lot, and she live in the
> 'hood!

We might easily dismiss Keyron's comment as off task or simply one of those bizarre things young children sometimes come up with. And in the normal course of busy classroom time, this comment might be passed over in favor of a more sensible answer. However, because everything the teacher and children said during this readaloud was audiotaped and transcribed, we can take our time and consider this small exchange at our leisure.

First, a little context: Mr. Taylor's students are all children of color who live in a low-SES area of a large Northeastern city. Everyone in his class is eligible for the district's free lunch program. The class has had a great variety

1

of experiences with books, because this readaloud takes place in June, almost at the end of a school year where Mr. Taylor has read stories and discussed them with the children twice a day since September. Keyron is one of
the children who seems to know and remember a lot of stories. Both Mr.
Taylor and I (the university researcher) are positive that Keyron knows what
Red Riding Hood is about—he has heard other versions of the story. Keyron
is smiling very broadly when he makes this little comment, and the children
and the teacher laugh in response. But in this passing moment, they may not
realize the incredible, sophisticated *triple pun* that Keyron has just tossed
out of his head.

In a second or two, Keyron has done the following: he has taken the
three words—"Red," "Riding," and "Hood," and has—in the tradition of
deconstructive criticism—purposely misread them (de Man, 1982; Bloom,
2003). First, he has intentionally interpreted "red" not as a color, but as the
past tense of "read." Second, he has changed the voiced dental /d/ in "riding"
to the closely related *un*voiced dental /t/, producing "writing." Third, he has
playfully interpreted "hood" not as a cloak but as the shortened form of
"neighborhood." Fourth, he has put these three puns together in a sentence
that subversively answers Mr. Taylor's question. I dare any adult to come
up with a triple pun in a couple of seconds! This kindergartener's facility
with oral language—and playful literary interpretation—is well-nigh unbe-
lievable. In chapter 8, I describe Keyron's comment as an example of what I
call "Performative Response."

This book describes and interprets young children's understanding of
stories and presents a theory of this literary understanding that is based on
what they and their teachers said during more than a hundred readalouds of
picturebooks. It is meant to enable, above all, a sense of wonder: to allow
you to experience children's sophisticated and critical literary insight. The
art historian and aesthetic theorist Ernst Gombrich (1969) writes, "To marvel is the beginning of knowledge, and when we cease to marvel, we may be
in danger of ceasing to know" (p. 8). Although we may be skeptical that
children can be literary critics, this notion has been in currency for over
30 years, beginning with the publication of Glenna Davis Sloan's *The Child
as Critic* in 1975 (now in its 4th edition, 2003); and as children's literature
has assumed more prominence in many primary and elementary classrooms,
the issue of literary understanding by young children has also become increasingly important.

Here is another vignette that shows a marvelous child critic in action.
It's 3 months into the school year, and teacher Ms. Bigler-McCarthy is reading James Marshall's (1989) version of *The Three Little Pigs* to her class of
first- and second-graders, most of whom are from working-class backgrounds.
She shows the cover, which depicts the three pigs on a stage with brick-red

curtains drawn to each side, and reads the title. She then opens the book and displays the brick-red endpapers. Brad, a first-grader, says: "Well, it's like a curtain, like on the front cover, the curtain's open, the curtain's red, and, um, then the endpages, they're red, too, and it's like, like the curtain's closed, and you're gettin' ready for the play to start." And, indeed, the play *will* begin. The story will be told, and when it ends, the curtains will close again, with the endpapers at the end of the book. It's interesting to speculate on what Brad must know in order to make such an astonishing literary interpretive comment. Brad takes nothing for granted in the picturebook—not even the plain colored endpapers. Like Gerard Genette (1980) and other French critics, he knows that the *peritext*—all the parts of the book other than the printed text—carry meaning, too. He uses his knowledge of what a theater looks like before a play begins, and links this to the two visual experiences of the front cover and the endpages. He connects the teacher's reading of the picturebook with the performance of a play. He expects that everything in the picturebook will have meaning, in semiotic terminology, that all will function as *sign*, and that the signs will interrelate to one another and inform one another. For Brad, all the world's a sign, raw material waiting for his own construction of meaning.

Brad's comment was all the more marvelous to me because, less than a year before, in a seminar on picturebooks, I had heard a guest speaker, the professional illustrator Will Hillenbrand, use *exactly the same metaphor* of endpapers as the stage curtains for a book. And here was a first-grader inventing this refined idea!

As these examples indicate, my view of literary understanding (set forth in chapters 1, 2, and 3) is that it is a lot more complex than the traditional, somewhat constricted concepts of plot, setting, characters, and theme. These elements of narrative are important, and children do learn them through discussion with the teacher and one another, but the construct of literary understanding that this book advances is much broader and deeper than this. Also, literary understanding is not a matter of being able to parrot back details from the story, or being able to answer a barrage of questions from the teacher, or a test. It's a matter of engaging in literary meaning-making, of passionately interpreting stories with increasing sophistication, cognitive power, and delight.

LITERARY UNDERSTANDING: A NEGLECTED PART OF THE LITERACY LANDSCAPE

In comparison with the amount of research done on young children's learning sound–symbol correspondences and other elements of literacy learning, there is relatively little work on young children's literary interpretation of stories. The recently published *On Reading Books to Children: Parents and Teachers* (van Kleeck, Stahl, & Bauer, 2003), for all its comprehensiveness (16 chapters and 32 contributing authors), contains surprisingly little about children's literary meaning-making. The meaning-making it does include is usually limited to low-level labeling, simple retelling of plots, and "comprehension," conceived of as the answers to questions from a teacher or a standardized test. In the *Handbook of Early Childhood Literacy* (2003), Martinez, Roser, and Dooley write, "Much recent attention to young children's literacy has focused on their acquisition and understanding of the alphabetic nature of English—and on the instruction that ensures their ability to segment spoken language into phonemes and attach those phonemes to graphemes en route to independent decoding (e.g., National Reading Panel, 2000; Snow, Burns, & Griffin, 1998). Less attention (at least within recent reviews in the US) has focused on compiling evidence for the complexity of children's willingness and ability to make sense of their reading" (p. 222). Martinez, Roser, and Dooley also assert that "We are also at the very beginning point in understanding the nature of young children's textual knowledge (e.g., their knowledge of genre features, narrative devices, author and illustrator styles), how they acquire this knowledge, and how this knowledge impacts their construction of meaning" (p. 231).

Confirming this assertion from the world of practice, surveys of teachers (Lehman, Freeman, & Allen, 1994; Scharer, Freeman, Lehman, & Allen, 1993) indicate that "teachers expressed the belief that children's literature should be the primary component of a language arts program. Not surprising, however, there was little evidence that children's literature was being used for literary as well as literacy instruction" (Galda, Ash, & Cullinan, 2000, p. 374). In many studies of literature-based classrooms or of reading comprehension, "Literature is present, but often treated as invisible" (Galda, Ash, & Cullinan, p. 374).

This neglect of the literary understanding of young children is all the more striking, given the considerable amount of theoretical work (see chapter 1) that has been done on picturebooks, the principal format through which most young children experience literature. As I read this theoretical material, I am struck by the avoidance of actual, 21st-century children. Much writing about children's literature, specifically about picturebooks, makes little reference to real children and their literary interpretive skill.

In addition to writing in response to these issues, I'm also responding to certain disturbing trends in current educational practice: the move toward "teacher-proof" and scripted curricula; the shift toward an increasingly narrow view of what constitutes reading; the lack of recognition that talk about stories is critical; the reducing of reading stories aloud to 10 minutes a day in some curricula and eliminating it entirely in others; and ignoring the proper uses of real books.

THE MARGINALIZATION OF READING ALOUD TO YOUNG CHILDREN

Despite some disclaimers (Scarborough & Dobrich, 1994; Meyer, Wardrop, Stahl, & Linn, 1994), educational researchers and practitioners generally agree that reading stories to children and talking with them about stories is a very important factor in ensuring their development as independent readers and writers (Anderson, Hiebert, Scott, & Wilkinson, 1985; Johnson, 1992; Snow, 1983). This research base has been built up over the last 25 years. Despite this firm conclusion, there seem to be two major perspectives in the field of literacy that give scant attention to the importance of reading aloud to children, and to the development of literary understanding in general. On the one hand, reading aloud is barely tolerated by some and widely misunderstood by others as a waste of time (from those who urge a more explicit form of instruction in literacy); on the other hand, it tends to be ignored and considered a middle-class, elitist practice (from some researchers and theorists who valorize popular culture).

Those who argue that reading aloud is a waste of time are, in one sense, correct: as many researchers have observed, *most* reading aloud in classrooms is perfunctory at best and downright damaging at worst. To get the substantive talk and thoughtful literary interpretation we desire, teachers have to be serious and knowledgeable about literature, and be able to foster the development of children's higher-level literary interpretive skills. The teachers with whom I have chosen to work are decidedly *not* using readaloud time as a time-filler, or to settle children down, or as a means of teaching low-level comprehension skills; nor are they controlling the discussion to the extent that reading aloud results in endless (and boring) Initiation-Response-Evaluation chains (Mehan, 1979). These teachers truly listen to children and entertain the possibility of multiple interpretations, viewing the talk as "exploratory," to use Douglas Barnes's (1976) term, rather than "final draft talk."

From the perspective that reading aloud (and emphasis on literature in general) is a middle-class exercise, there may be a tendency to (unintentionally) create an artificial divide between "school-approved" literacy practices and children's literacy experiences out of school. Certainly, schools should be permeable to literacy practices from outside school, and teachers should not assume that there is only one path for all children to follow; however, this does not mean that in-school literacy practices are necessarily all inappropriate or stifling for children. Thus, I argue for a particular kind of reading aloud that is interactive and involves both active teachers and active students (Cazden, 1992) in the process of literary meaning-making. I also argue for a type of reading aloud that treats picturebooks as highly sophisticated aesthetic objects, rather than mere tools for teaching literacy. In other words, along with John Dewey, Eliot Eisner, Howard Gardner, Maxine Greene, and many others, I believe that the arts are critically important in young children's school experiences, and that, rightly approached, picturebook readalouds can contribute to the thoughtful, foundational (and critical) views of life that art has the potential to enable. As Nodelman and Reimer (2002) remark,

> Children's literature can be a powerful force in the lives of children. It can make them less innocent. It can make them conscious that there is more than one way of being normal. It can offer them the opportunity to experience and learn to enjoy a vast range of different kinds of stories, and so make it clear that the one story they so often hear from toys and TV is not the only possible or the only desirable version of the truth. (p. 149)

Thus, those who valorize popular culture and its literacy practices should not be too hasty to dismiss literature and reading aloud to children as an instantiation of mainstream ideology. I want to emphasize that when we read picture storybooks to children in the early years of school, we are doing much more than simply indoctrinating them into the world of school-based literacy. We are opening to them the richness, beauty, and fascination of subtle and fascinating stories and gorgeous visual art. We are expanding their aesthetic experience exponentially. This is decidedly *not* elitist—thousands of children's librarians over the past century who worked so diligently, especially for children who had little access to books, believed that children's literature was a source of immeasurable pleasure and a vehicle for expanding children's ideas about themselves and the world, as well as a means of developing and nourishing the ability to read and write independently. According to Fox (2003),

> Stories [and reading stories to children], storytelling, reading and writing, and role-play of all kinds particularly lend themselves to the maintenance of play-ful qualities. They are all forms of symbolic transformation, all involve imaginative activity, all are capable of giving pleasure and satisfaction, and many children undertake these literacy practices independently and voluntarily, and not only those from bookish backgrounds. (p. 193)

Yes—we must be inclusive as we invite children to further explore the world of literacy, and we must honor the varieties of literacy they bring with them into classrooms. However, we should not undervalue trade books and published literature. In responding to the perspective that may marginalize children's literature in order to valorize texts from popular culture and oral language (Carrington & Luke, 2003; Dyson, 1989, 1997, 2001, 2003), I would suggest that TV programs, videos, cartoons, cinema, advertisements, music, and other texts of popular culture are not only frequently tawdry and aesthetically inferior to picturebooks; they also glorify violence and continually reinscribe the culture of power's ideology of what is good and normal (as Nodelman and Reimer point out). Dyson, Carrington, and Luke seem to consider children's literature an example of the cultural hegemony. But reflect on the texts of popular culture—are they any *less* an example of the cultural hegemony than trade books? Also, children's literature can be one of the "textual toys" about which Dyson (2003) writes so eloquently; texts of popular culture are not necessarily more relevant or compelling than published trade books. Like Dyson (2003), I am wary of "tidy images of children on the literacy path (e.g., experiences with books, knowledge of letter sounds)" (p. 5). But, alas, the types of book experiences that result in aesthetic literary understanding are decidedly *not* among the "school-valued practices" of many school districts, schools, and classrooms today. Instead, there is a view of literature (if it is used at all) as mere fodder for the development of low-level "comprehension" and decoding skills. In other words, literary understanding is, in these times in the United States, not a "school-valued practice" any more than children's interest in the video games, TV, and cartoon characters that comprise the broad "voice-filled landscape" full of "textual toys" that is Dyson's focus.

Thus, I argue that we need multiple perspectives on literacy teaching and learning that include the power of literature for young children, without turning it into a mechanical tool for teaching children how to "do school" —perspectives that recognize the ways in which children may playfully interact with literature while at the same time contributing to their literacy learning, high-level cognitive abilities, and engagement with the imaginary worlds of stories so that they may develop more nuanced perspectives on real life, as well as a critical stance toward the status quo. According to some literary critics (Shklovsky, 1966), the central purpose of literature is to make the familiar strange and the strange familiar, thereby increasing our power to both critique the world we live in *and* to imagine other, more just and equitable alternatives.

On the other hand, we cannot claim, as William Teale (2003) reminds us, that reading stories to children is a panacea:

> We should never believe that the children in our early childhood classrooms will learn to read merely by being read to—no matter how high the quality of the books or how engaging the reading. There is much more to teaching children to read than simply reading to them. But reading to children *does* help

them develop the knowledge, strategies, and dispositions that are fundamental aspects of becoming literate. Read-alouds can easily become filler activities, which are done automatically and to not much effect. Like anything we do in our efforts to reach children, it is not the procedures of an instructional activity that make a difference; it is the principled way in which that activity is woven into the fabric of the classroom and addressed to the needs of the children that makes it significant. (pp. 135–136)

Martinez, Roser, and Dooley (2003) argue that classroom storybook readalouds are powerful paths to literary meaning-making. However, as Teale (2003) laments, ". . . the typical read-aloud leaves much to be desired" (p. 129). The mere act of reading a story aloud does not guarantee literacy development; instead, the quality of the interaction among the participants determines how children's growth in literacy is fostered (Meyer, Wardrop, Stahl, & Linn, 1994).

The classrooms in my studies are "sites of intensity," in Michael Patton's (1990) phrase, for the phenomenon I am studying. If you want to study surfers, you go to the beaches of Hawaii or Southern California. If you want to study young children's literary understanding, you go to classrooms where children and teachers love, know, and continually talk about books. If you want to study surfers, you go to places where there is a well-developed *culture* of surfing. If you want to study literary understanding, you go to places where there is a well-developed culture (Dixon, Frank, & Green, 1999) of literacy and literary appreciation, where teachers have taken great pains to develop a classroom literary "interpretive community" (Fish, 1980). If you want to study the potential of the fully developed art of surfing, you study the best surfers using the best equipment in places with the biggest waves. If you want to study literary understanding, you look for the best teachers, using the best-quality children's books, in classrooms where the presence of books and the love and appreciation of literature hit you like a wave as soon as you walk in the door.

WHY ANOTHER THEORY?

As I argue in the next few chapters, our current ways of understanding young children's literary interpretive skills are based on theories that either were not originally intended for young children (and thus may not be developmentally appropriate for them), or theories that rely on a rather narrowly conceived notion of what constitutes literary understanding. Also, these theories do not incorporate the visual aesthetic theory and the significant amount of theory specific to picturebooks that are necessary in order to fully describe young children's literary meaning-making, because picturebooks constitute the major format in which most young children experience literature. Finally, rather than theories that attempt to "cover the waterfront" from young children all the way to secondary and college students and adults, we need a theory of literary understanding that is specific to contemporary young children, and that is grounded in their responses to literature. This book aims to fill that gap.

Part I of the book describes picture storybooks as sophisticated aesthetic objects (chapter 1) worthy of children's literary critical abilities, and outlines various theoretical perspectives on children's literary understanding (chapters 2 and 3). Part II is the core of the book: my data suggest that children respond in five different ways during picture storybook readalouds; that these responses reveal that children are engaged in five different types of literary meaning-making; and that these five types of meaning-making are instantiations of five foundational aspects of literary understanding (chapters 4–8). In chapter 9, I relate these five aspects of literary understanding to one another, presenting a grounded theoretical model of the literary understanding of young children, and relating it to the broad and varied perspectives I outlined in the first section of the book. Part III deals with the various ways in which the teachers in the studies scaffolded the children's interpretation of stories (chapter 10). Finally, in chapter 11, I return to the wider question of the significance of young children's literary interpretation, other possible factors that may influence literary understanding, and implications for practice and further research.

AUDIENCE

I envision the readers of this book to be literacy researchers, theorists, and graduate students, particularly those concerned with literature for young children in schools of education, library science, and departments of English who seek a broad theoretical framework with which to understand, interpret, and conceptualize young children's rich and varied responses to literature, specifically picture storybooks. It is not a how-to guide; rather, it presents a theoretical framework that has important implications for how literature is "used" (I wish there were another verb!), discussed, and responded to in primary classrooms. It contains many excerpts of classroom discussions of literature by kindergarten, first-, and second-grade children with their teachers, to enable you to hear many real children's and teachers' voices, especially in Parts II and III. Because it is based on data from a number of classrooms (see Appendix A) and includes a wealth of examples of children's responses and teachers' scaffolding moves, I believe that field-based educators will find it useful for their own practice, through providing provocative and exemplary models of literature discussion, specifically about reading aloud to children and enabling their literary understanding. I also hope that the book will broaden practitioners' appreciation for (and understanding of) young children's marvelous abilities as literary critics.

Part I

Picturebooks and Literary Understanding

This part of the book begins by examining theoretical and research perspectives on the picture storybook, a form of literature present in virtually every primary grade classroom. In chapter 1, I discuss the constituent elements of the picturebook and their potential semiotic significance. Next, I draw on visual aesthetic theory to frame an examination of the various theories of text–picture relationships. I synthesize research about children's responses, including studies focused on children's interpretation of text sets, peritextual features, and postmodern picturebooks. I end the chapter with a review of the range of typologies researchers have developed to describe young children's literary meaning-making.

In chapter 2, I begin with the framework of a sociocultural constructivist view of teaching and learning, with implications for developing children's literary interpretive abilities. I then argue that the implicit view of literary understanding that is present in theories of reading comprehension, cognitive psychology, linguistics, and discourse processing, although useful, is somewhat narrow and confining, being limited to the traditional idea of the narrative elements of setting, character, plot, and theme. Finally, I move to various perspectives on literary understanding, including highly text-based approaches and perspectives offered by reader-based theories. These latter theories fall at opposing poles of what I conceive of as the broad range of the theories of reader response.

Chapter 3 considers a number of theories that seem to give equal power or authority to both texts *and* readers. In this chapter, the work of such literary luminaries as Wolfgang Iser, Louise Rosenblatt, James Britton, Michael Benton, Judith Langer, and Deanne Bogdan is explicated to provide additional lenses on young children's literary understanding. The chapter ends with a review of research about literary talk in the classroom, examining what happens when astute young readers and teachers interact with the sophisticated qualities of picture storybooks. The goal of Part I is thus to provide a multiplicity of theoretical and research-based lenses to understand these interactions. As Bertolt Brecht has suggested, "A man with one theory is lost. He needs several of them, or lots! He should stuff them in his pockets like newspapers" (as cited in Makaryk, 1993, p. viii).

1

Picturebooks and Children's Responses

Many years ago, in *Art as Experience*, John Dewey (1934/1987) lamented the isolation of art and aesthetic experience from everyday life, pointing out that art was literally put on a pedestal in museums and galleries. He proposed a return to the integration of art into daily life that had been an important characteristic of earlier ages. The picturebook, in addition to being the type of literature most commonly encountered by young children, also offers them a highly sophisticated visual aesthetic experience, making high-quality art present in tangible everyday activities. In this chapter, I focus on the literary affordances (Gibson, 1979) of this form as well as the ways in which young children engage with both words and images. There have been various theoretical definitions of picturebooks. Sutherland and Hearne (1977) suggest that "a picture book is one in which the pictures either dominate the text or are as important" (p. 158). Nodelman, whose *Words About Pictures* (1988) is one of the most comprehensive treatments of picturebooks, is satisfied with a very loose definition: "books intended for young children which communicate information or tell stories through a series of many pictures combined with relatively slight texts or no texts at all" (p. vii). A similar brief definition is present in Schwarcz and Schwarcz (1991), who comment parenthetically that the picturebook is the type of book "where text and pictorial narrations accompany each other, alternate, and intertwine" (p. 5).

Stewig (1995) follows Sutherland and Arbuthnot (1991) in distinguishing "picture books" (for example, alphabet, counting, and concept books) from "picture storybooks," because the latter have "a plot which tells a story" (p. 4). Stewig draws a further distinction between these two types of books and "illustrated books," in which "the illustrations are extensions of the text and may add to the interpretation of the story but are not necessary for understanding it" (p. 7).

Kiefer (1995) makes use of the illustrator Barbara Cooney's (1988) suggestion that a picturebook is like a string of pearls, where the pearls symbolize the illustrations, and the string symbolizes the verbal text. Kiefer points out that this analogy "supports the idea of the *interdependence* [italics in

13

original] of pictures and text in the unique art object that is a picturebook," as opposed to an illustrated book, "where the occasional picture is present to add to the words but is not necessary to our understanding of the book" (p. 6).

Marantz (1977), an art educator, likewise emphasizes the interdependence of illustration and verbal text, and adds that this interdependence extends to every part of the book: "A picturebook, unlike an illustrated book, is properly conceived of as a unit, a totality that integrates all the designated parts in a sequence in which the relationships among them—the cover, endpapers, typography, pictures—are crucial to understanding the book" (p. 3). Marantz goes on to assert that a picturebook must "tell a story" and that it is "much more a visual art object than a piece of literature." This particular definitional net excludes books like alphabet books or books of poetry, even though they are profusely illustrated. For Marantz, two of the crucial criteria are that the picturebook (1) is a unified narrative in some form; and (2) has a text (if it has a text at all) that would be incomplete without the illustrations. This definition is similar to the "picture storybook" defined above by Sutherland and Arbuthnot (1991). For the purposes of this book, I am using Marantz's definition: although I frequently use the term "picturebook," what I mean more exactly is "picture storybook." It is also important to note that picturebooks are less a type of literary genre than a type of form or format for a variety of genres, including fairy tales and folk tales, contemporary realistic fiction, historical fiction, contemporary or futuristic fantasy, and magical realism. Poetry, informational texts, and biographies are also available in picturebook formats; however, they will not be addressed in this book, as its focus is on picture storybooks.

EXAMINING PICTUREBOOKS

Many primary school educators are familiar with books like *Rosie's Walk* (Hutchins, 1968), one of the most popular picturebooks for young children. The first thing you will notice about these books is their brevity: generally, a picturebook is only 32 pages long. Occasionally, as in *Where the Wild Things Are* (Sendak, 1963), the number is extended to 40 (or more)—almost always multiples of eight because of the way the pages are printed on both sides of large sheets of paper and then cut, folded, and bound. In this limited number of pages, there is a small amount of text for each page (and occasionally no text at all), so that the illustrations take up a great deal of space in comparison with a chapter book. The entire text of *Rosie's Walk* has just 32 words; *Where the Wild Things Are* has 338 words, whereas at the end of this sentence in the chapter you are reading now, you will have reached 830 words! Indeed, some picturebooks (like David Wiesner's *Flotsam*, 2006) are virtually wordless, or employ quite sparse text (Ghiso & McGuire, 2005), like David Shannon's *No, David!* (1998).

Navigating picturebooks requires that we pay attention to every feature, from the front cover and the dust jacket to the back cover (see Appendix B for a glossary of picturebook terminology). We can't just skip to the first words of the story and begin reading; if we do, it's like arriving at the opera after the overture is finished (Moebius, 1986). Instead, we should carefully study both the words and pictures on the front and back covers to give us an idea of what the story will be like. We should remove the dust jacket (if there is one) to see if perhaps the inside board cover is different from the dust jacket (the books of illustrator Jan Brett are famous for creating this surprise). We should speculate (along with children) on why the illustrator, designer, or editor made these choices, communicating to children that every single detail of the book—down to the typefaces, the size and shape of the book, and the placement of the illustrations on the pages—is the result of somebody's calculated decision. This decision is the result of the cooperation among author, illustrator, editor, and designer (Solomon, 2003). In fact, it is this cooperation that ensures that every single aspect of the book works in concert.

Opening a picturebook, the first thing we see is the endpapers (sometimes called endpages), which contain much visual information. Are the front endpapers identical to the back endpapers, or are they different in subtle or dramatic ways? Why? What do the visual images or the choice of color tell us about the book we are examining? Even a plain colored endpaper is the result of a decision; why, for example, are the endpapers of Margaret Hodges's (1984) version of *Saint George and the Dragon* blue-gray in color? This somber color is appropriate for such a serious tale. In addition, the endpapers provide atmosphere in a literal sense, because following them, we have a half-title page with a border indicating a nighttime scene. Turning the page, we encounter the full title page, where the sky is still blue-gray, but the dawn is visible on the horizon. On the dedication page, the sun appears above the distant hills, and the sky is beginning to turn light blue. When the text of the story begins on the next double spread, the sky is bright blue, indicating that morning has arrived. Thus, this whole sequence, which begins with the endpapers, provides a prelude to the story that is both temporal and an indicator of mood/tone. We should encourage such speculations by the children; this helps to develop their critical and inferential thinking, and visual interpretation skills.

As the example above suggests, after the front endpapers, we encounter either the half-title page (with only the title of the book and perhaps an illustration) or the title page (with the full publishing information). What can these pages tell us? What about the dedication page, or the page with the copyright and ISBN information? It is only after examining all of these pages (as in listening to the overture of the opera, which alerts us to the various musical motifs to follow) that we are ready to actually begin the words of the story. And, like the overture, this experience will prepare us for the story in a number of ways. We will have some predictions about what the story will be about; we will also have a sense of the general tone or mood of the story—serious or lighthearted, sad or joyful. We will possibly have been introduced to the main characters and their interrelationships, the setting, and the literary genre to which the story belongs. As we read the story, we can confirm or disconfirm these predictions and expectations. Similarly, at the end of the story, we have the back endpapers to examine, as well as the back cover. In other words, literally from cover to cover, the picturebook is an art object, an aesthetic whole; every one of its parts contributes to the total effect, and therefore is worthy of study and interpretation. Sharing John Dewey's concern about the isolation of aesthetic experience from everyday life, I believe that high quality of art and design in picturebooks, which are such a common feature of many primary classrooms, can be critical in developing children's sense of visual aesthetics as well as contributing to their abilities in literacy.

READING THE SIGNS: SEMIOTIC PERSPECTIVES

A semiotic theoretical perspective (Eco, 1979; Kress & van Leeuwen, 2006; Scholes, 1982; Sebeok, 1994) on picturebooks seems natural and appropriate, given that semiotics assumes that language (written and spoken) is "only one subset of the many forms of communication used by humans to construct meaning about their world" (Rowe, 1994, p. 2). Picturebooks rely heavily on an illustrational sequence—a visual sign system—to convey meaning, as well as the sign system of the words. As a literary form, the picturebook has shown itself to be endlessly protean, sometimes including moveable parts (through tabs, flaps that can be lifted, pullouts, or pop-ups), lights, or sound (through small computer chips). All of these features constitute sign systems as well, so that in semiotic terms, a picturebook may be the locus for the interaction and combination of many sign systems. A picturebook is a "gesture towards semiotic repleteness," where at least two sign types (the words and pictures) "comment on each other" (Steiner, 1982, p. 144). In its multiplicity of signs, the picturebook finds its counterpart in the more technologically advanced forms of hypertext (Lemke, 1993), which in turn implies that there are many possible pathways through these manifold sign systems. A semiotic perspective provides a foundation for viewing children's literary understanding of picturebooks not as a deficient form of adult understanding, but the beginning of the same process of sign interpretation used by adults.

Finally, a semiotic perspective suggests that all the parts and characteristics mentioned above have the potential for conveying meaning (Nodelman, 1988): the overall size of the book; choice of colors; typefaces; the positioning, layout, and shape of the illustrations; even the publishing information— all of these can function as signs. Moebius (1986) has analyzed commonly occurring clusters of conventional signs in picturebooks. He refers to these clusters as "codes," arguing that reading the "visual text" of a picturebook involves learning the meaning of the various clusters of signs in the illustrations. Moebius identifies five groups of codes:

1. *Codes of position.* How high an illustration of a character appears on the page "may be an indication of an ecstatic condition . . . or dream-vision . . . or a mark of social status or power, or of a positive self-image," whereas "being low on the page is often by contrast a signal of low spirits, 'the pits,' or of unfavourable social status" (Moebius, 1986, p. 139). Figures that are depicted close-up and in the center of a page may have greater power or be more important in the story, whereas figures that are drawn at the margins or have relatively small size may be marginalized (both literally and figuratively). The more frequently a character appears on the same page (in, for example, a series of small illustrations), "the less likely that character is to be in control of a situation" (p. 140).

2. *Codes of perspective.* The perspective employed in an illustration engenders many meaningful associations. For example, Moebius asserts that if a horizon line is not showing in an illustration, this may indicate a complication or dangerous situation in the plot.

3. *Codes of the frame.* Moebius writes that "framed, the illustration provides a limited glimpse 'into' a world. Unframed, the illustration constitutes a total experience, the view from within" (p. 141). Similarly, Dooley (1980) suggests that frames often serve to convey the impression that we are looking through a window at the actions being depicted, and give us a more objective view. Illustrations without frames engage the viewer more directly, making the viewer more a part of the action. Doonan (1993) comments that the semiotic significance of illustrations that occupy the entire two-page opening (called a "double-page spread") in a picturebook and that have no frames at all, but rather "bleed" off every edge of the page, suggest "a life going on beyond the confines of the page, so that the beholder becomes more of a participant than a spectator of the pictured events"

(p. 81). Because the frame is the borderline between the illusion of the illustration and the reality of the physical page on which it is printed (Uspensky, 1973; Whalen-Levitt, 1986), "a bounded time and space between the real and imagined world, or a transition from the real world and the world of representation" (Harms & Lettow, 1989), occasions where a figure or object breaks the frame may blur the distinction between illusion and reality. The shape of the frame may likewise have semiotic significance: "A character framed in a series of circular enclosures is more likely to be secure and content than one framed in a series of utterly rectangular objects" (Moebius, 1986, p. 141).

4. *Codes of line and capillarity* include the meaning potential of various types of lines used by illustrators. "Thin, spare lines may suggest mobility and speed; thick, blurred or puffy lines, paralysis or a comfortable stasis" (Moebius, 1986, p. 142). An abundance of short cross-hatched lines ("capillarity") may indicate vitality or an excess of emotion or physical energy (as in many of the illustrations in *Where the Wild Things Are*, an exciting and adventurous book).

5. The *code of color* includes the traditional association of dark colors with sadness, depression, or fear, and bright colors with joy, confidence, or lightheartedness. Also, a given picturebook may have its own private system of color codes, where, for example, one character may be associated with a particular color.

A semiotic theoretical perspective on picturebooks, then, carries with it the implication that the literary understanding of picturebooks includes learning to read the visual text of the illustrational sequence according to the conventionally presented systems of codes, along with the verbal signs.

PERSPECTIVES FROM VISUAL AESTHETIC THEORY

Because the illustrations and illustrational sequence are so important in picturebooks, visual aesthetic theories provide valuable insights. Arnheim (1986, p. 306) has asserted that "the visual image always dominates the cognitive aspect of the experience" when presented together with either speech (as in film) or writing (as in picturebooks). Arnheim (1969) also argues that visual perception is the sensory equivalent of understanding on the cognitive level; in other words, we see what we learn to see, and the act of viewing a picture involves our active construction of its elements in a meaningful whole rather than a simply passive reception. Gombrich (1972) agrees, stating, "However automatic our first response to an image may be, its actual reading can never be a passive affair" (p. 86). If, therefore, the visual image always dominates the cognitive aspect of our experience, and if the perception of this visual image is not automatic, but learned and formed by experience, the full literary understanding of picturebooks includes learning the conventions and principles of visual art, at least implicitly.

Color, line, shape, and texture have been traditionally considered to be elements of visual design (Richard, 1969); Ocvirk (2006) adds "value," referring to the range of tones in either color or black and white. These elements comprise the artist's language or grammar in the sense that the artist uses them to communicate meaning in a nonverbal and visual manner (Cianciolo, 1984).

According to Ocvirk (2006), *color* has three aspects: hue, tone, and saturation. *Hue* refers to the different segments of the spectrum, allowing us to distinguish all that might be called red from all that might be called orange (though the distinctions are, of course, blurry, because the spectrum is a continuum). *Tone* refers to the amount of darkness or brightness of a hue, and can further be broken down into tint, with the addition of white (or water, in the case of watercolors) and shade (the addition of black). *Saturation* refers to the intensity or purity of a color—the most saturated colors have no addition of white or black. Artists' choices of hue, tone, and saturation have particular effects on viewers. For example, colors of high intensity, bright tone, and hues on the red end of the spectrum would be most appropriate for illustrating a cheerful or hopeful scene, whereas colors of low intensity, subdued tone, and hues on the violet end of the spectrum would be most appropriate for illustrating a dreamlike, sad, or fearful scene. These are the ways in which artists manipulate our attention and suggest symbolic meaning (Arnheim, 1974). Bang (2000) writes about the traditional associations of various colors with particular psychological states. Red, for example, suggests danger and high emotion such as fear or joy, and has associations with blood and fire. Much, if not all, of our associations with color are culturally bound; in other words, the same color can have a different meaning for different cultures.

The artist's *line* can vary greatly, and is perhaps the most powerful expressive tool in his arsenal. Randolph Caldecott, arguably the first picturebook artist, relied on pen-and-ink drawing for a flowing, expressive line that needed very little shading to communicate life and energy (Cech, 1983–84). The thickness of a line may suggest the degree of refinement or delicacy of the people portrayed (Golden, 1990). The smoothness or roughness of lines can suggest either serenity or anxiety, stasis or energy.

Arnheim (1974) believes that all *shape* is meaningful: "Form always goes beyond the practical function of things by finding in their shape the visual qualities of roundness or sharpness, strength or frailty, harmony or discord.

It thereby reads them symbolically as images of the human condition" (p. 97). Bang (2000) explains several general principles of shapes in pictorial art. Bang suggests that horizontal shapes give us a sense of "stability and calm," while vertical shapes are more exciting, and suggest energy. Diagonal shapes are the most dynamic of all, evoking a sense of motion or tension. Pointed shapes create more anxiety and fear because of their association with sharp objects, while rounded, curved shapes make us feel more comfortable and safe. The placement of the shapes on the page (one element of composition) is also important. According to Bang (2000), shape placement in the upper half of a picture implies freedom, happiness, triumph, or spirituality, while placement in the bottom half is a sign of greater "pictorial weight" or "down-to-earthness" and may also mean more threat or sadness. Placement at the center of the page is what Moebius (1986) calls the "ham factor" (p. 148). "Center stage" in an illustration is associated with greater importance, just as it is in the theater. The larger the object in a picture, the stronger it feels to us. In a well-composed picture, the artist leads the viewer's eye around the illustration from shape to shape through the overall arrangement of the shapes and their colors. Another factor is the number of shapes, which determines how busy or sparse the illustration appears. An illustration with fewer shapes tends to give the impression of calm or quiet.

According to Arnheim (1974), positioning a figure or shape on the left side of the picture gives it more weight and force, since we tend to "read" pictures from left to right. This is one of the factors in the balance of the picture, which consists of the various "weights" each shape has. Arnheim also suggests that a detail may acquire weight if it has "intrinsic interest." In a sequence of pictures, a detail acquires weight if it recurs, because "the meaning of an image is changed according to what one sees immediately beside it or what comes immediately after it" (Berger, 1977, p. 29).

On the flat, smooth, two-dimensional surface of a piece of paper or canvas, *texture* can only be suggested. Artists use various techniques to give the illusion of surfaces that are rough or smooth, delicate or sturdy. The artistic media an artist chooses have various potentials for indicating texture (Kiefer, 1995).

Value, referring to the range of different in the dark and light tones in an image, has symbolic associations. If there is only a small range of dark and light tones, and therefore little contrast, "the mood of the picture may be either serene or brooding" (Kiefer, 1995, p. 127). If the opposite case is true, and there is a wide range of tones and high contrast, an image will convey nervous energy or excitement.

These elements work together to produce a total effect that is usually referred to as *style*. Style is the "name we give to all the aspects of a work of art considered together" (Nodelman, 1988, p. 77). According to Novitz (1976), style can be defined on three levels. First, there is "pictorial" style: a recognizable style characteristic of a particular time or place, and consisting of generally accepted conventions for painting "called umbrella conventions" (p. 336). The Renaissance fascination with perspective and the Impressionist preoccupation with the immediate, unmediated light-saturated visual image would be examples of pictorial style. Second, there is "artistic" style, which involves "changes in emphasis or in subject matter but not in overall methods of depicting" (Kiefer, 1993, p. 76). Finally, an individual artist has a unique personal style, and some artists creatively employ very different styles for different projects. In picturebooks, artists may use both their personal style and make references to historic pictorial or artistic styles, as when Sendak gives a nod to the Impressionists in *Mr. Rabbit and the Lovely Present* (Zolotow, 1962) or the Northern Romantic style (particularly the work of Philipp Otto Runge) in *Outside Over There* (1981) and *Dear Mili* (Grimm, 1988). In *The Castle Builder* (1987), Dennis Nolan makes use of the pointillist artistic style of Seurat, though only in black and white, without color.

Gombrich (1969) argues that the history of art is largely the history of artists imitating the work of other artists. This is the way in which the conventions of pictorial representation—what Gombrich calls "schemata"—develop. Occasionally, a particularly imaginative artist will break out of the "prison of style" (p. 320), leading the way to a new set of conventions. DeLuca (1984) comments,

> The importance of artistic forbears and schemata may also, ultimately, make us a little more tolerant of the fact that after Sendak or Lobel, everything published seems to look like them for awhile. For an artist like Sendak changes the way children's book artists view their world. Clearly he has created some of the schemata that shape the field, much as Caldecott did for him. (p. 23)

Gombrich's argument suggests the need to consider how the style of a particular artist relates to the conventions or schemata that are available to her; and to understand the historical sequence of interrelationships of picturebook illustrators with one another and with the wider world of art. The implication of Gombrich's ideas for the use of picturebooks in educational settings is that children should be exposed to a wide range of artistic styles and media of presentation, and that children should learn to compare and contrast these styles, as well as to analyze the various elements (line, shape, color, texture, etc.) that comprise each style.

THE RELATIONSHIP OF TEXT AND PICTURES

The theoretical definitions outlined above consistently emphasize a unique quality of picturebooks: the illustration sequence and other visual matter play as important a role in the total conveyed meaning as do the words of the text. According to author Janet Lunn (2003), "the words and pictures have to be true partners" and "the best picture books are a good marriage of pictures and story" (p. 189). The verbal text and the illustrational sequence would each be incomplete without the other, and the total effect of the picturebook depends on the perceived interactions or transactions between these two parts. This idea was not always as readily accepted as it is today. Hall (1990) reports that "prior to the late 1970's, authorities were still of the opinion that 'the story is the tune, the illustration its accompaniment'" (p. 17). Now this musical metaphor would be changed—at least with respect to picturebooks—so that text and pictures are understood as the two equally important parts of a duet (Cech, 1983–84, p. 118) or as being in a "contrapunctal relationship" (Ward & Fox, 1984, p. 21) with each other. Other writers resort to theatrical metaphors; for example, Mini Grey's (2006) description of the "double act" provided by words and pictures. Thus, in a picturebook, the pictures (and other visual information) are absolutely necessary—as necessary as the words or even more so—in telling the story. The words of *Rosie's Walk* and *Where the Wild Things Are* alone would be incomplete and confusing without the pictures; and with no illustrations the books would cease to exist. On the other hand, texts like Rowling's *Harry Potter* books stand alone. Although we could imagine a profusely illustrated edition of these books with many pictures (and they would be inordinately long, indeed), none of these visual images would be crucial. Illustrations for *Harry Potter* are certainly pleasant, but inexpensive versions of the books without any pictures would still be complete in terms of Rowling's story. Thus, we must distinguish picturebooks (in which pictures are necessary) from illustrated books (in which pictures are optional and added on for enrichment).

Our society is word centered, and so are our schools. However, scholars such as W. J. T. Mitchell (1994) have observed that both academia and popular culture seem to have taken a "pictorial turn" (p. 11) and that the onset of various technologies—including television, cinema, and the Internet—and associated digital media have at least partially dislodged this complete dominance of the verbal (Barry, 1997; Kress & van Leeuwen, 2006). Nevertheless, though this dominance seems to be weakening, we still tend to privilege words over pictures. With a picturebook, this cannot be the case, because the words and pictures work together on an equal footing to produce a total effect.

In addition to the musical and theatrical metaphors for word-picture relationships described above, others have employed images from textiles; Moss (1990) writes of the "interweaving of text and pictures" (p. 21). Still others utilize images from physics and wave theory, using the idea of "interference," to describe how two wave patterns may combine to form a new and more complex pattern (Miller, 1992). Continuing the scientific meta-phors, Moebius (1986) refers to the "plate tectonics" of text and illustra-tions. Lewis uses at least two terms, "polysystemy" ("the piecing together of text out of different kinds of signifying systems," Lewis, 1996, p. 105) and "interanimation" (Lewis, 2001), referring to Margaret Meek's (1992) comment that the pictures and words on a page interanimate each other.

Lewis (2001) also proposes that we think of the "ecology" of picture-books in terms of the interdependence of text and pictures, as well as the flexibility of the relationships, which can change from page to page. Lewis argues that an ecological view of picturebooks also implies that neither ver-bal texts nor illustrations are univocal, and that there is a great deal of com-plexity and almost endless diversity, just as there is in a biological ecosystem. In other words, we are not just talking about text and pictures, but perhaps about a number of different texts and a number of different kinds of pic-tures, all in a complicated relationship with each other in the same book. Moreover, verbal texts have visual features, such as the size and character-istics of the typeface or illuminated letters, while illustrations may have speech balloons or other incorporated words; thus the distinction between words and pictures is not totally sharp. In addition, as I have mentioned above, some contemporary picturebooks incorporate more than words and pictures, add-ing movement in "pop-up" books such as those by Robert Sabuda (2003) in *Alice's Adventures in Wonderland* and *Mommy?* by Sendak, Yorinks, and Reinhart (2006); a kinesthetic experience (touching the raised lines of the spider's web in Eric Carle's *The Very Busy Spider*, 1984); sound in *The Very Clumsy Click Beetle* (Carle, 1999); and twinkling lights in *Winter's Tale* (Sabuda, 2005). All of these elements convey meaning and function in a complex ecological system of interdependence along with the words and pictures.

I argue (Sipe, 1998a) that "synergy" is a good descriptor of text–picture or multimodal relationships in picturebooks, because all the sign systems, together, produce an effect that is greater than the effect that either would produce alone, resulting in an aesthetic whole that is greater than the sum of the individual parts. I suggest that in semiotic terms, Siegel (1995) and Suhor's (1984) concept of "transmediation," "the translation of content from one sign system into another" (Suhor, p. 250), may be key in understanding picturebooks, because readers "must oscillate as it were, from the sign sys-tem of the verbal text to the sign system of the illustrations; and also in the opposite direction from the illustration sign system to the verbal sign sys-tem" (Sipe, 1998a, p. 102). In picturebooks with additional sign systems, this oscillation is even more complex.

As Mini Grey (2006) makes clear, words and pictures can have a vari-ety of relationships in picturebooks. They can each do a "different job," or tell different stories. How can we characterize these different jobs, and more fully understand their dynamics? A few theorists have attempted to deal with this issue in detail, notably Schwarcz (1982), Nodelman (1988), Golden (1990), and Nikolajeva and Scott (2000, 2001).

Schwarcz (1982) makes the point that the quantity of illustrations (in relation to the amount of the text) is an important factor. The relative proportions of text and pictures make up a "sliding scale," and in the picturebook the proportions are such that "composite verbal-visual narration" is possible (p. 11). Schwarcz conceives of two general categories of relationships between text and pictures: what he calls "congruency" and "deviation." In the category of *congruency*, the text and pictures are in a harmonious relationship. There is never simple redundancy, even in the situation where the illustration refers directly to the text. The illustrations may elaborate, amplify, or extend the situation described in the text. Sometimes the illustrations complement the text by "running ahead of the text and pushing the action forward" (p. 15). The text and the illustrations may also take turns in telling the story; this is what Schwarcz calls "alternate progress" (p. 15). In some cases, the pictures take over from the words entirely, continuing the story without any verbal accompaniment.

In *deviation*, Schwarcz's second category of relationships, the illustrations "veer away" from the text by opposing it in some way. Another type of deviation is what Schwarcz calls "counterpoint," when the illustrations tell a different story from the text. Part of the enjoyment of this type of story lies in the reader-viewer's perception of both stories at once.

In *Words About Pictures*, Nodelman (1988) devotes an entire chapter to exploring the relationship between text and pictures in the picturebook. He begins by pointing out that text and pictures don't simply mirror each other (p. 193), and that this can be proven by experiencing the verbal text of a picturebook without seeing the illustrations, or (conversely) by experiencing the illustrative sequence without the verbal text. If we do this, we begin to understand what each sign system supplies. The sequence of illustrations alone can be interpreted in many different ways; what the words do is to impose a particular, specific narrative on the illustrations. Nodelman refers to the intriguing implications of split-brain research for understanding texts and pictures as involving two different kinds of thinking, but points out that this research cannot be used to suggest that we process the text and pictures separately, because "placing them [words and pictures] into relationship with each other inevitably changes the meaning of both, so that good picture books as a whole are a richer experience than just the simple sum of their parts" (p. 199).

Nodelman lists three effects that words have on the picture sequence. First, "words can provide a cognitive map, a schema that we can apply to inherently unassertive pictures in order to determine the varying significance we might find in their details" (p. 213). In particular, the words inform us about what "emotional or narrative significance of visible gestures" (p. 215) to find in the illustrations. Second, the verbal text can specify particular cause-and-effect relationships, which would otherwise be vague in the illustrative sequence. Third, the words (and what the words are silent about) can tell us what matters and what does not matter in the illustrative sequence: what elements in the illustrations are important and what elements are incidental.

According to Nodelman, words and pictures have particular strengths and weaknesses in conveying information. "Words are best at describing relationships of details, pictures best at giving a sense of the whole" (p. 202). Also, "in picture books, the texts more significantly specify temporal information, just as the pictures convey the most significant descriptive information" (p. 214). Nikolajeva (2002) agrees, pointing out that if there is an illustration of a character, "the text usually does not have to supply any additional information [description] about the character's looks, or, if it does, we regard this as unnecessary duplication" (p. 184). Yet it is not as if there is a sharp dichotomy between the temporal nature of narrative and the spatial nature of the pictures. We get *spatial* information from both the pictures and the words (though in different ways); and we also get *temporal* information from both pictures and words. So, in understanding a picturebook, "we must integrate time and space, and two different versions of time and space, before we can understand the whole" (p. 200).

In Schwarcz's description (1982), the illustrations may "extend" the information given by the verbal text. Nodelman makes the opposite point: that what really happens is that the illustrations *limit* the words: "Many commentators say that the purpose of pictures in picture books is to 'extend' the text, but cognitive theories of perception suggest that extension may be the wrong metaphor. It would be more accurate to say that the pictures limit the text—and to add that the text also limits the pictures" (p. 220). Nodelman uses the example of a sentence from the first page of Nancy Eckholm Burkert's illustrated version of *Snow White and the Seven Dwarfs* (Grimm, 1972): "At a window with a frame of ebony a queen sat and sewed." What Burkert's illustration does is to both extend our knowledge of what the queen is like, exactly how and where she is sitting, and so on, *and* to limit our interpretation of the words by presenting this particular, specific queen, and no other. In the same way, the words limit the meaning of the illustrations. The sentence "At a window with a frame of ebony a queen sat and sewed" tells us what is important in the illustration, limiting our attention. What she is sewing, the particular style of clothing she wears, the other furnishings we glimpse in the room—all these are given subsidiary status by the words.

For another example of the idea of limiting, think about the beginning of *Where the Wild Things Are*, where Max is pictured wearing a white out- fit with a bushy tail, buttons, whiskers, and ears, while banging a nail into the wall to construct a makeshift tent. The accompanying text reads, "The night Max wore his wolf suit and made mischief of one kind . . ." Here, the picture limits the words by describing just what kind of mischief Max is perpetrating and what, exactly, his wolf suit looks like. Correspondingly, the words limit the picture by telling us that all this happened at night and that the human figure is a boy named Max (the gender of the figure in the illustration is ambiguous). The words also limit the picture by telling us what visual details we should pay attention to, out of the great array of possibili- ties. So the words tell us things that the pictures omit, and the pictures tell us things about which the words are silent: in a well-made picturebook, neither the words nor the pictures could tell the story alone.

Nodelman (1988) also suggests that words and pictures never tell ex- actly the same story, and are frequently in an ironic relationship with one another. For example, when Max meets the Wild Things, the text relates that "they roared their terrible roars and gnashed their terrible teeth and rolled their terrible eyes and showed their terrible claws"—pretty scary! However, the pictures don't match the words: the Wild Things are rather amusing, pudgy characters, more like stuffed animals than frightening monsters. So the words and pictures, in this case, are in an ironic relationship with one another.

In truth, Schwarcz's idea that pictures extend the text and Nodelman's idea that pictures and text limit each other may not be as oppositional as may first appear. Schwarcz (and others) who use the metaphor of extension mean that the illustrations add additional information; this is certainly the case. But it is also true that the illustrations make the words more specific— more concrete and particular. In this sense, the illustrations limit the mean- ing of the words.

Nodelman uses Barthes's (1985) idea of "relaying" to describe the pro- cess by which we relate the text and the pictures. Barthes, in writing about cartoons and comic strips, comments, "Here language . . . and image are in a complementary relation; the words are then fragments of a more general syntagm, as are the images, and the message's unity occurs on a higher level; that of the story" (p. 200; quoting Barthes, p. 30). Nodelman comments that "By limiting each other, words and pictures together take on a meaning that neither possesses without the other—perform the completion of each other that Barthes calls 'relaying'" (p. 221).

Golden (1990) describes a typology of the relationship between text and pictures that seems to be based on how much "work" the illustrations or the text do in conveying meaning. However, since this scheme depends mainly on the relative amounts of power the text and the illustrations have, Golden cannot attend to the dynamic way in which, as Nodelman puts it, "the words change the pictures and the pictures change the words" (p. 220). Thus, the relationship may not be so much a matter of a balance of power as it is the way in which the text and pictures transact with each other, and transform each other.

Nikolajeva and Scott's (2001) typology of word–picture relationships seems to be one of the most comprehensive and highly articulated. They suggest that there are five different ways in which text and pictures may relate in a picturebook, on a continuum ranging from virtual equivalence of words and pictures (which they term "symmetry") to an absolute "contradiction" between the words and visual images. There are three intermediate steps between these two extremes of the continuum: "complementarity" (words and pictures each contribute independently to one narrative), "enhancement" (words and pictures extend each other's meaning), and "counterpoint" (words and pictures tell different stories, which may be in an ironic relationship to one another). Nikolajeva (2002) also points out that in *omitting* information, words and images act in counterpoint: "For instance, in *Where the Wild Things Are*, the mother is presented in the text, but not portrayed in the pictures. By contrast, a vast number of picturebooks have secondary characters in the pictures, who are not mentioned in the book" (pp. 280–281). Additional complexity is provided by conceiving these five relationships as functioning "independently on the different levels of the picturebook narrative, such as plot, setting, characterization, perspective, and so on" (Nikolajeva, 2003, p. 238), thus giving us a rather dizzying number of possibilities.

An important implication of all this theoretical work for researchers and practitioners is that, since children are continuously shifting back and forth between words and pictures, their visual meaning-making may be frequently in tandem or integrated with their interpretation of the verbal text. Thus, it may be difficult to ascertain whether any particular comment or response is the result of their interpretation of the words or the pictures, since even quite young children have been shown to be capable of engaging in the dynamic process of "translating" from one sign system to the other. As readers/viewers, we are always interpreting the words in terms of the pictures and the pictures in terms of the words, in the intricate and recursive process of "transmediation" (Siegel, 1995; Sipe, 1998a; Suhor, 1984). This continual back-and-forth "relaying" (Barthes, 1985) between text and pictures means that the best and most fruitful readings of picturebooks are never straightforwardly linear, but rather involve a lot of rereading, turning to previous pages, reviewing, slowing down, and reinterpreting. Doonan (1993) suggests that there is an inherent tension in picturebooks: the words impel us forward to find out what happens, whereas the pictures invite us to savor and linger.

Finally, author/illustrator Steven Kellogg (2003) eloquently summarizes many of the possibilities for the interaction of multiple sign systems, suggesting that the artist "sets up relationships and tensions between the illustrations and the text, allowing magical discoveries and subtle revelations to emerge in the areas between. When this happens, there is an uncanny fusion of all the elements, and the dynamic new expression that is created introduces young readers to the world of art" (para. 10). All of these insights have important consequences for how educators use these books in classrooms. Children (and teachers) need time to examine and carefully interpret the ways in which words and pictures relate to each other in these aesthetically complex works of art.

RESEARCH ON CHILDREN'S RESPONSES TO PICTUREBOOKS

Given the amount of rich theoretical work outlined above, it is somewhat surprising that there is relatively little empirical research on children's responses to the illustrations and text–picture relationships in picturebooks. As Flood and Lapp (1995) observe: "Although educators have regularly recognized the importance of picture books in children's language and literacy development, the relationships between the pictures and the words (the language arts and the visual arts) have not yet been fully explored" (p. 9).

Meaning-Making with Sets of Picturebooks

Researchers have examined the ways in which children create meaning using several related books. Shine and Roser (1999), for example, studied preschool children's differential responses to four genres of picturebooks (fantasy, realistic fiction, informational books, and poetry). The children displayed different characteristic stances, according to the genre; in other words, their responses were demonstrably different for each genre. These researchers developed two principal categories for analysis: Focus of Talk and Type of Talk. Focus of Talk was further divided into Text as Experience, the response to the story as a lived-through experience (Rosenblatt, 1978/1994), and Text as Object, which reflected children's interest in the craft of the book, both in the verbal text and illustrations. In the first category, Text as Experience, among the seven subcategories was "text–illustration links," though children clearly used their integration of meaning from both words and pictures in all the categories. The second principal category for analysis was Type of Talk, which included the subcategories of "identify," "describe," "infer," "connect," "predict," "explore," and "narrate," all of which included children's use of illustrations along with verbal text. That children so young should have "developed a rich repertoire of expectations, tacit knowledge, and types of response to four kinds of texts" (Shine & Roser, 1999, p. 244) suggests that preschoolers, in addition to developing the ability to use the "elements of visual grammar" (Kress & van Leeuwen, 2006), have the ability to apply this visual interpretive knowledge to different types of texts.

In *Children Reading Pictures: Interpreting Visual Texts*, Arizpe and Styles (2003) reported on a 2-year study in seven schools with children ages 4 through 11 and diverse cultural and linguistic backgrounds. The researchers used two picturebooks by Anthony Browne, *The Tunnel* (1989) and *Zoo* (1994), and one picturebook by Satoshi Kitamura (*Lily Takes a Walk*, 1997). The data for this extensive study included interviews with the children (with reinterviews about the same books), group discussions, children's drawing in response to the illustrations in the books, and questionnaires about children's reading habits. The researchers' typologies of the children's visual responses are described in the section below dealing with categories of response. One important feature of the Arizpe and Styles study was their analysis of the drawings made by children in response to the picturebooks. The categories of analysis for the drawings were: (1) literal understanding (drawing events or people "to communicate story and content"); (2) the overall effect of the drawings, including "the aesthetics of the images and the colour, tone, form, and line" used by the children; and (3) the internal structure of the drawings, in terms of the "balance and the relationship between objects or characters and their relative scale" (p. 118). Also of note in this large study are comments of young children that display "what can only be described as intellectual excitement with the ideas raised by the book [in this case, *Zoo*] and aesthetic pleasure in the images" (Arizpe & Styles, 2003, p. 80). This focus on visual aesthetic pleasure and analysis distinguishes the study from other empirical work on children's responses to picturebooks. More specifically, children explored the perplexing and ambiguous features of the illustrations and discussed the way the illustrations made them feel, as well as the moral/ethical implications of the visual images (the animals' loneliness and the barrenness of their surroundings in the zoo). The children also analyzed the visual imagery, interpreting a close-up illustration of a gorilla with vertical and horizontal bars of the cage in front of him as "like Jesus's cross," and comparing the gorilla's eyes to a "grandpa's eyes," showing their awareness of the ways in which the illustrator humanizes the animals. These types of comments also revealed the children's empathy for the animals' situation. All of these responses were based almost solely on the children's visual meaning-making, which the researchers found deepened upon revisiting the story. Belfatti (2005), working with first- and second-graders, confirmed this impact of multiple exposures to *Zoo*, observing: "While at first students' responses centered on making predictions and personal connections with the text, later responses evidenced critical analysis of how perspective switches in *Zoo* blur the boundaries between human/beast and freedom/entrapment" (p. 1).

Peritextual Features of Picturebooks

As I mentioned at the beginning of this chapter, picturebooks do not consist merely of the words of the story and the accompanying illustrations; the format of the picturebook also includes the dust jacket, front and back covers, front and back endpapers, and title and dedication pages. These additional elements, commonly referred to as the "peritext," after the work of Genette (1997) and applied by Higonnet (1990) to picturebooks, afford rich opportunities for visual meaning-making. To date, only a few studies have concentrated on children's interpretive work with peritextual features. Pantaleo (2003a) studied the ways in which a class of first-grade children discussed the peritextual features of nine picturebooks. The children learned peritextual terminology (such as "endpapers" and "dust jacket"), and used peritextual elements to predict and to confirm their interpretations about characters, plot, setting, and tone of the books. Their talk about peritextual features was found to contribute significantly to their "aesthetic appreciation and cognitive and literary understandings of the books" (p. 74). Sipe and McGuire (2006a) examined kindergarten, first-, and second-graders' interpretations of just one peritextual element—the picturebook endpapers—in picture storybook readaloud discussions. They found that children were highly engaged in using the front endpapers for predictive purposes, and often assumed that the endpapers in some way were a prelude or preparation for the story. For picturebooks in which the front and back endpapers were different, children thought critically about why the designer or illustrator made this choice, and what semiotic significance the differences indicated. Children recognized that in some cases, the endpapers actually begin and end the story narrative, as in Steven Kellogg's (1991) version of *Jack and the Beanstalk*. Even for plain-colored endpapers, children wanted to speculate on why the color was chosen, attempting to connect the color to the book's design, content, or general tone. In a follow-up study, Sipe and McGuire (2006b) also analyzed readaloud transcripts from a combination first/second-grade class and a kindergarten class, focusing on the discussion of peritextual elements before the words of the story began. They found that there were nine main ways in which children responded in the initial peritextual discussion:

1. References to conventions of picturebook construction, production, and reading
2. Description

3. Interpretation and evaluation
4. Prediction
5. Attention to written language
6. Intratextual connections (making connections among various peri-textual features, such as the front cover and the endpapers)
7. Intertextual connections to books and other cultural products
8. Personal connections
9. "Performances" (using peritextual elements as a springboard for children's own creative purposes rather than for interpretation)

Postmodern Picturebooks

The label "postmodern" means a great many things to different people, but perhaps the most central assumption of postmodern literature is that the purpose of literature is not to seduce the reader into the illusion of having entered another world (Lewis, 2001), but rather to highlight the fact that the text is an artificial construction. In other words, the text calls attention to itself *as a text* rather than functioning as a transparent window into an imagined "secondary world" (Benton, 1992). In addition to describing these *metafictive/self-referential* elements (Stevenson, 1991; Waugh, 1984), I synthesized theoretical work on postmodern picturebooks (Goldstone, 1999; Kümmerling-Meibauer, 1999; Lewis, 1990, 1996, 2001; Nikola-Lisa, 1994; Paley, 1992; Trites, 1994) and identified five further common qualities of postmodern picturebooks:

- *playfulness* (the text as a playground for readers)
- *multiplicity of meanings* (multiple pathways through the text world because of nonlinearity of plot and a high degree of indeterminacy, nonresolution, and ambiguity)
- *intertextuality* (multiple types of texts and the juxtaposition of references to many other texts)
- *subversion* (mocking of literary conventions and a general tone of irony, parody, or sarcasm)
- *blurring distinctions* between high and popular culture, between authors and readers, and distinctions among traditional literary genres (Sipe, 2004)

These elements are noticeable in increasing numbers of picturebooks, most spectacularly and comprehensively in Jon Scieszka's (1992) bizarre sendup of traditional fairy tales, *The Stinky Cheese Man and Other Fairly Stupid Tales*. What has attracted the attention of researchers is that in addition to their frequently creative manipulations of the traditional picturebook format, these books seem to offer great promise for eliciting new and sophisticated types of responses from young children.

Pantaleo's (2002, 2003b, 2004a, 2004b, 2005) extensive research into young children's responses to postmodern picturebooks with multiple plots, multiple narrators, and metafictive devices provides strong evidence for the potential ability of young children to negotiate the layered complexities of these texts. The children in Pantaleo's studies constructed semiotic signifi- cance from visual details such as different type sizes; used illustrations to make connections among the multiple narratives; understood how the illustrations represented, complemented, extended, and sometimes contradicted the text; and used visual peritextual features of the books to predict the plot and to interpret the relationships among storybook characters. Pantaleo (2004a) noted that the skills necessary to interpret postmodern picturebooks are similar to those required for "web literacy": "attentiveness to information conveyed in the nontextual features, acquisition of multiple sources of in- formation, analysis of information, and associative processing" (p. 17).

The greater challenges presented by postmodern picturebooks may as- sist children in becoming more active sense-makers and critical readers. In a similar way, McClay's (2000) research with 20 children (ages 7, 10, and 12) and 25 adults reading Macaulay's (1990) *Black and White* demonstrated that the children could explore "multiple pathways through the text-world" (Lemke, 1993) of this challenging and ambiguous picturebook, which tells four seemingly separate stories, each with strikingly different illustration styles, which may or may not be related in a unified narrative. McClay found that the children's solutions to the problem of how to read such a text were, in general, more creative and flexible than the adults' attempts, and that, moreover, the children seemed to relish the challenges, whereas a number of the adults (mostly elementary school teachers) seemed to resist the idea that the verbal texts in this book are subordinate to the illustrations in construct- ing interpretations.

Typologies of Young Children's Responses to Picturebooks

A number of researchers have constructed typologies of children's responses to picturebooks. Working in kindergarten/first-grade, second/third-grade, and fourth/fifth-grade classrooms, Hickman (1979, 1981, 1983) studied the lit- erary response patterns of elementary school children. This study is note- worthy because Hickman "pioneered the study of children's responses to literature in naturally occurring contexts" (Martinez & Roser, 1991, p. 645). Although Hickman did not limit her study to picturebooks, many of the books to which children responded were in fact picturebooks, and many of the children's responses were connected to illustrations. Hickman defined response quite broadly as any behavior, verbal or nonverbal, that occurred in the classroom and showed a connection between the children and literature. Seven types or categories of response were noted:

1. listening behaviors such as applause or joining in refrains
2. contact with books such as browsing or keeping books at hand
3. acting on the impulse to share by reading together or sharing discoveries
4. oral responses such as retelling or freely commenting on stories
5. actions and drama
6. making things such as pictures or games
7. writing about literature or using literary models in one's writing

In several first/second-grade classrooms, Kiefer (1982) studied how children responded to the illustrations in picturebooks. By employing this naturalistic setting and using real trade books rather than isolated illustrations or illustrational sequences constructed for a research situation, Kiefer ensured that children's responses represented classroom experience rather than a clinical setting. She also wanted to focus on the aesthetic qualities of the children's responses rather than on their preferences for one medium over another. Kiefer adapted categories of the functions of language articulated by the linguist M.A.K. Halliday (1975) in order to describe four types of children's responses to picturebooks: informative, heuristic, imaginative, and personal. In *informative response*, children reported the contents of the picture or compared the picture to an aspect of the real world. In *heuristic response*, children wondered about events in the pictures, inferred the causes of pictured events or how illustrations were made, and predicted outcomes or events from pictures. In *imaginative response*, children entered the world of the book or created figurative language to describe it. In *personal response*, children associated their own experiences with the book, expressed their feelings about the book, or evaluated it. Kiefer found that the teacher's role was very important in helping children construct and negotiate the meaning of picturebooks. Books the teacher read aloud to the children achieved a special status in the classroom, and were more frequently sought by the children. The teacher's talk about the book often revealed nuances or special features that might be overlooked by the children. Also, the teacher enabled the children to make intertextual connections by modeling this activity, and probed children's responses by asking such questions as "How did that make you feel?" or "Tell me what you are thinking." Kiefer also found that response to picturebooks was an ongoing process, and that time was needed for children to fully develop their responses.

Drawing on both Kiefer's typology and on the work of Flinders and Eisner (1994) on the stages of the development of visual art criticism, Madura (1995, 1998) explored four patterns used by young children in talking about illustrations in picturebooks: description, interpretation, evaluation, and thematic issues. In these studies, there is evidence that children were "more attuned to the illustrator's rather than the author's craft" and were more likely to evaluate illustrations than text (Martinez, Roser, & Dooley, 2003, p. 224).

For child-initiated responses during readalouds in a second-grade class of working-class and lower-income children from diverse ethnic backgrounds, Maloch and Duncan (2006) found six types of spontaneous student responses: connecting (to personal experience, other texts, the world, future experiences, and shared experiences); predicting; clarifying information that was unclear or confusing; making observations about both text and illustrations; "entering the story world" by acting as if they were in the story or making suggestions about what they would change if they were the author; and offering suggestions about how the teacher should read the book or arrange the activity. This typology has significant similarities to the studies cited above, and seems to add an element of agency to the children's active participation, by describing children's ways of controlling the readaloud with the teacher.

Arizpe and Styles (2003), in the study described above, found that children in a wide age span from 4 to 11 displayed responses on 9 increasingly sophisticated levels of interpretation, ranging from "no explanation given," "mis-readings (wrong)," and "literal explanation" to "engaged description," "interrogation: superficial/engaged/anticipation," and "imaginative deduction" (p. 258). Arizpe and Styles also identified 15 "categories of perception" to classify children's responses, for example describing the relationship between text and picture; speculating about the artist's intentions; appreciation of visual features of the illustrator's craft such as color and pattern; and interpreting story characters' motives, relationships, expectations, and inner motives. Because of the wide age range on which they are based, it is unclear how these categories and levels of interpretation may apply to more narrow age ranges within this span.

One difficulty with all these typologies, as Martinez and Roser (2003) sagely observe, is that "the many separate systems for categorizing responses make it difficult to compare across studies" (p. 810). Ironically, the very strength of grounded theory (letting categories emerge from the data) also has drawbacks in terms of the applicability of the typologies to other studies and other situations. While it is true that qualitative interpretive research attempts to present description that is complete and nuanced enough for the readers of the research to make their own connections with other situations and contexts, the true challenge is to go beyond the "epistemology of the particular" (Stake, 1994, p. 240) into a generalizability that is nevertheless wary of the dangers of master narratives of any behavior, including children's literary and visual meaning-making. Martinez and Roser (2003) suggest that researchers "try more replications of their own systems across studies" (p. 810) as one way of remedying this problem. In applying my own typology to many studies, I have attempted to follow this suggestion. Also, whereas most of the typologies described above concern the responses of children from a wide range of ages, my own work has focused on the literary understanding of a much narrower band of age groups: kindergartners and first- and second-graders. The child participants in my studies have also represented diversity along several dimensions, including race, ethnicity, and socioeconomic status (see Appendix A). In these ways I have endeavored to address the difficulties inherent in generalizing qualitative research.

In the next two chapters, I lay out a theoretical foundation for the construct of literary understanding, and the various perspectives from which this important construct can be understood and applied to the ways in which young children interact with picturebooks.

2

Young Children's Literary Understanding: Either Text *or* Reader

This chapter and the next review theoretical perspectives and empirical findings from a variety of academic disciplines and subject matters, all of which contribute to a textured, multifaceted view of young children's literary understanding. I situate these theoretical perspectives within the broad framework of social constructivism and consider how each perspective would define literary understanding as it applies to young children in classrooms.

THE SOCIAL CONSTRUCTIVIST PARADIGM AND VYGOTSKY'S SOCIOCULTURAL APPROACH

The second half of the 20th century has seen the emergence of two basic shifts in the ways we view reality. What is known as the "social constructivist paradigm" (Schwandt, 1994) is a set of broad ontological and epistemological principles resulting from these shifts. One shift is a basic change from an objective view of reality to a subjective view (Bleich, 1978). The traditional, objective conceptualization of reality—what is "out there"—is that it has an objective organization and existence, and that through proper methods, we can discover its nature and structure. The observer is sharply differentiated from what is observed. In contrast to this view of reality, according to the social constructivist paradigm, reality is not found "out there," but rather socially constructed by groups of people. If reality is invented rather than found, then the sharp distinction between observer and the observed is blurred or rendered nonexistent (Gadamer, 1986). Constructivists thus speak of "knowledge production" rather than of the discovery of knowledge (Strauss & Corbin, 1998).

Another basic change or shift lies in the basic conceptualization of language, what Rorty (1967) calls the "linguistic turn." Traditionally, language has been seen as directly descriptive of (or transparent to) reality, in the sense

36

that language itself is merely a clear window through which we view reality. The work of de Saussure (1916/1983), Peirce (1931–1958), and others replaces this idea of the transparence of language with a view of language as a system of signs that has internal coherence but no *direct* correspondence with reality: "words mean what they do through their relations with each other rather than through their relationship to an extra-linguistic reality" (Blackburn, 1994, p. 256). Thus, from the point of view of social constructivism, language does not describe reality, but rather *in*scribes or constitutes reality (Berlin, 1986). We cannot get past language to some deeper, more "real" experience, particularly when we are trying to understand how human beings relate to each other. Thus, the way we talk and write about the human, social world actually creates that world (Lather, 1986). Moreover, language is freighted with the values and worldview of those who use it. Human thought dwells in the "prison-house of language" (Jameson, 1972), where meanings are socially constructed and therefore shifting and unstable. All knowledge is thus partial, positioned, and socially constructed.

From the perspective of the social constructivist paradigm, these shifts— to (1) the view of reality as invented or created by human beings, and (2) the view of language as the irreducible substratum of knowledge—suggest that for young children, *oral language in social settings* is a profoundly critical component of their cognitive development and one of the most important factors in their learning; this is one of the foundational assumptions of the work of Lev Vygotsky (1896–1934), a Russian psychologist who was particularly interested in child development, and whose theories of language and social interaction have become increasingly appreciated and utilized in the field of education (Berk & Winsler, 1995; Moll, 1990). Vygotsky's theory is often called the "socio-cultural" approach (Berk & Winsler, 1995; Wertsch, 1985) because it is concerned with how the surrounding social and cultural forces affect children's cognitive development. One of the unique qualities of his theory is that he did not conceive of thinking as being "bounded by the individual brain or mind" (Berk & Winsler, 1995, p. 12); rather, he felt that "the mind extends beyond the skin" (Wertsch, 1991, p. 90) and is irrevocably joined to other minds. Vygotsky therefore emphasized the social nature of cognition rather than its individual nature (as did Piaget). Vygotsky argued that "every function in the child's cultural development appears twice: first on the social level, and later, on the individual level" (Vygotsky, 1978, p. 57). In other words, children are exposed to and learn cognitive processes through social interaction, and *then* they internalize these cognitive processes.

This emphasis on oral language in social settings for children's cognitive development also led Vygotsky to focus on the role of adults and more capable peers in that development, because it is clearly those who are already expert in the use of language who can assist the child in developing it for her own. But what are the dynamics of this assistance? How does it occur? These questions led him to formulate a construct he called the "zone of proximal development," usually abbreviated as ZPD. For Vygotsky, the paradigm situation in children's development consisted of an adult and a child engaged together in some activity, and the ZPD explains the nature of this engagement. Vygotsky (1978) noticed that when we speak of a child's cognitive ability, we can define this ability in various ways, depending on whether or not the child is receiving assistance in a particular task. He therefore distinguished between two levels of children's abilities: the "actual" level (at which the child can function independently) and the "potential" level (at which the child can perform with the assistance of an adult or "expert other"). This potential level is always higher than the actual level, and there is always a certain distance or zone between them, which is the zone of proximal development. The ZPD *is the distance between the actual developmental level as determined by independent problem solving and the level of potential development as determined through problem solving under adult guidance or in collaboration with more capable peers*" (Vygotsky, 1978, p. 86, italics in the original). Learning is thus a matter of being able to do for ourselves what yesterday we could do with assistance, and this is how cognition develops. In further interactions, this sequence is repeated, and cognition is "ratcheted up."

Other theorists and researchers have refined this construct of the ZPD to further explain how the expert's assistance helps the child (Rogoff & Wertsch, 1984). Some researchers (Rogoff, Mosier, Mistry, & Goncu, 1993) use the term "guided participation" to describe the way in which the adult guides, supports, and challenges the child at the same time that the child is actively involved. Wood, Bruner, and Ross (1976) developed the term "scaffolding" to describe the ways in which adults attempt to sensitively support children, by giving directions, "talking them through" a sequence of actions, letting children do what they can, and supplying the more difficult parts of the task. In chapter 10, when I address teachers' roles in assisting children to develop literary understanding, I return to and refine the construct of scaffolding in the context of the picturebook readaloud in the classroom.

TALK IN THE CLASSROOM

Vygotsky's theory has clear relevance for the classroom situation, and for literary discussion in particular. In terms of Vygotsky's theory, the successful teacher is one who is able to identify the various ZPDs of the children in her class, to construct experiences that scaffold the children's developing abilities, and to arrange experiences that enable more capable peers to help with scaffolding. The theory suggests that learning occurs most powerfully in situations that are highly social, and in which children are engaged with one another and the teacher in meaningful activities where there is a great deal of talk.

Unfortunately, research has also shown that in actual classrooms, this type of situation is uncommon. Teachers tend to control talk rather rigidly (Green & Wallat, 1981; Wells, 1986). This has been shown to be true even for teachers identified as "good" teachers (Dillon & Searle, 1981). Several researchers (Bellack, Kliebard, Hyman, & Smith, 1966; Mehan, 1979) have identified a particular type of classroom discourse that is characterized by a sequence of three events. The first event consists of the teacher's initiation of a question or probe. The second event consists of the students' response to the teacher's initiating question. The third event is the teacher's evaluation of the response. The short description for this sequence is I.R.E. (Initiation-Response-Evaluation). It is clear that the first and third events are totally teacher-controlled, and that the students' involvement is sandwiched between them; in other words, there is one answer that the teacher is waiting for (O'Connor & Michaels, 1996), and I.R.E. "is not a structure in which teachers can be sensitive to student-directed work and inquiry" (Pappas, Kiefer, & Levstik, 1999, p. 43). Researchers have found that chains of I.R.E. sequences continually repeat in classrooms; in fact, they are "the hallmark of teacher-led discourse" (O'Connor & Michaels, 1996, p. 95). Whether learning occurs in this situation is seemingly less important than the execution of this "procedural display" (Bloome, Puro, & Theodorou, 1989).

Barnes (1976) argues that the oral language used to communicate in the classroom is the major factor in determining the actual curriculum that is being taught. He calls this the "hidden curriculum," in order to distinguish it from the curriculum that is written in instructional manuals and books. Problems arise when teachers assume that certain types of oral language interactions will occur without explicitly teaching the children what is expected. This can be a particular difficulty for children who come from homes in which these interactions have not occurred (Cazden, 1988; Tough, 1977). For example, Heath (1983) found that the African American children of low socioeconomic status in her study were not used to being asked questions to which the questioner already knew the answer; when these types of questions were frequently asked by their classroom teacher, these children were silent and withdrawn. Children from another cultural group were quite accustomed to this type of questioning, and readily adapted to the classroom discourse. Edwards (1979) notes that when teachers ask questions to which they already know the answer, they are constructing a situation in which they hold all the power because they are in a position to evaluate the answer.

Barnes also distinguishes between two types of language use in the classroom, "transmission" and "interpretation." As Dillon and Searle (1981) explain,

> In the transmission view, knowledge is seen as existing outside the learner, and teaching is seen as transferring a body of knowledge to the learner. In the interpretation view, knowledge is seen as being developed within the learner, and teaching is seen as giving students the opportunity to develop and express knowledge from a more personal perspective. (p. 312)

The implication of this research and theory for the storybook readaloud situation is that discussions of the book should not be rigidly controlled by the teacher, and that children should have the opportunity to relate personal experiences to the story. Also, teachers should be aware of the power relations involved in frequently asking questions to which they know the answer.

Researchers have also investigated the various routines of the classroom that are structured around certain oral language interactions. Gumperz (1986) calls such routines "speech events." Such events have norms or rules that are followed by the teacher and the children (Gilmore & Glatthorn, 1982; Green & Wallat, 1981). The storybook readaloud situation is one of these speech events, and children participate by speaking within the implicit and explicit norms of this speech event. What "counts" as literary discussion is determined by these norms.

COGNITIVE PERSPECTIVES ON CHILDREN'S COMPREHENSION OF NARRATIVES

From this broader conceptual background, the focus of this chapter now narrows to a discussion of the various perspectives that may be taken on children's experiences with stories. Theory and research from a variety of cognitively oriented disciplines inform our understanding of children's comprehension of narrative text. Since the early 1970s, a number of models of the structure of stories have been produced, variously called "story grammars," "story maps," or "story schemas" (Black & Wilensky, 1979; Brewer & Lichtenstein, 1981; Graesser, Golding, & Long, 1991; Meyer & Rice, 1984). These grammars or maps attempt to describe how narrative structures are represented in the mind; thus they are sometimes called theories of *narrative representation*. These theories of narrative are based on the more general principles of schema theory (Adams & Collins, 1979; Anderson, 1984; Anderson & Pearson, 1984), which posits the existence of cognitive structures called schemata that process and organize incoming information, and are themselves modified and refined by new information. Although schema theory has been challenged and refined during the last few decades (Paivio, 1986; Sadoski & Paivio, 1994; Spiro, Coulson, Feltovich, & Anderson, 1994), one of its major insights is still accepted. That insight is that what we bring to the act of reading (or to any experience) in the form of prior knowledge is an extremely important factor in how we understand that experience. New information is, as it were, filtered through our prior knowledge. In the case of story grammars or maps, researchers hypothesize the existence of schemata for stories, which allow us to understand the plot and to predict what will happen in the narrative. One important conclusion reached by researchers is that as complicated as all these models are, even young children may display a working understanding of story structure that is, if anything, in excess of the complex propositions and interrelationships in the models (Mandler & Johnson, 1977; Stein & Glenn, 1979).

Cognitive Flexibility Theory, developed by Spiro, Coulson, Feltovich, and Anderson (1994), refines our understanding of how schemata develop in "ill-structured domains" (such as the complex structures of narratives or the relationships between texts and pictures in picturebooks), by postulating that we build up knowledge gradually across cases by comparing and contrasting the cases, "criss-crossing" the knowledge domain, thereby arriving at higher levels of abstraction and more sophisticated schemata. Literary understanding, according to this theory, would involve exposure to many stories, preferably groups of stories that were cases of a particular genre or story type.

Some research has asked whether explicit instruction in story mapping would have a positive effect on the understanding of narrative; the evidence is fairly conclusive that such instruction is productive of greater understanding (Dimino, Gersten, Carnine, & Blake, 1990; Fitzgerald & Spiegel, 1983; Spiegel & Fitzgerald, 1986). Bauman and Bergeron (1993) were the first to study story mapping with children who were younger than grade three; they studied the relative effects of four different treatments of instruction in story mapping on first-grade children's comprehension of "central story elements." The study is thus notable for its focus on children in the emergent stage of literacy. Also notable is the researchers' use of children's literature in the form of picturebooks; previous studies had used abbreviated stories or stories written especially for the research. Bauman and Bergeron concluded that explicit instruction in story mapping is effective in helping first-graders to identify and understand "central narrative elements" such as characters, plot, setting, problem, and resolution (p. 407), as measured both by the children's answers on tests and by qualitative analysis of interviews of the children. However, diversity of response was not encouraged in the study: one of the comprehension questions was "What was the problem in the story?", which assumes that only one answer is acceptable.

Golden and Rumelhart's (1993) model of "story comprehension and recall" conceptualizes the reader's task as following the "narrative trajectory" of a story by mentally filling in the gaps in the narrative: "A story is represented as a partially specified trajectory in situation-state space, and thus, story comprehension is defined as the problem of inferring the most probable missing features from the partially specified story trajectory" (p. 203). The emphasis in this model is what is *not* in the story and what must be supplied by the active reader. Literary understanding, from the perspective of this model, consists in children's inferential filling in of the narrative gaps.

There seem to be several limitations to the research on story grammars, maps, and models. First, most of the models are based on very simple, short stories that were written by the researchers for the express purpose of developing and explaining the models. This means that the models are based on narratives that may not reflect the length or the complexity of trade books used in classrooms; therefore, the applicability of these models to children's understanding of the typical narratives used in classrooms may be questioned. Second, the models seem to assume the traditional view of literary understanding as consisting of the grasp of the "elements of narrative" such as setting, characters, plot, and theme. This traditional view may in actuality represent only one restricted aspect of children's literary understanding. Third, story grammar maps and models do not include attention to illustrations and the potential of illustrations for meaning-making by children. This is problematic because the great majority of narratives used in primary classrooms take the form of picturebooks, in which the illustrations play an equally important part with the verbal text. Thus, young children may be involved in a considerably more complex process (involving the coordination and integration of the sign system of the illustrations and the sign system of the verbal text, described more fully in chapter 1) than is contemplated by story grammars, maps, and models. Fourth, because of their focus on textual features rather than on the qualities of readers, story grammar maps and models do not explain how readers may have quite different but equally valid understandings and interpretations of the same text.

Miall and Kuiken (1994) have further critiqued story grammars and models of story comprehension by exploring the ways in which concepts from literary theory can expand, refine, and inform these text-based theories. One of these concepts is the idea of "defamiliarization," in which literary texts are viewed as different from other texts because of their degree of ambiguity. Literary texts have the possibility of a greater number of interpretations, and thus promote more personal and individual readings. Literature stimulates us to see and conceptualize in new ways; it is, as Shklovsky (quoted in Miall & Kuiken, 1994, p. 343) declared, the enemy of "habitualization," which "devours life," making us automatons as we merely go through the motions of life without savoring its experiences. Miall and Kuiken argue that story grammars fail to capture this aspect of literary experience. Most story grammars attempt to "economize comprehension, postulating that the mind takes the shortest route through the maze of meanings in a story" (p. 349), whereas defamiliarization theory suggests that literary texts are read in the opposite way, as the reader dwells on the ambiguities of the text. Miall and Kuiken conclude by commenting, "We read literary texts because they enable us to reflect on our own commitments and concerns; to discover better what they are, to reconfigure them, to place the ideas we have about our aims and identity in a different perspective. The differences between readers are thus not incidental to literary response, they are fundamental" (p. 351). On the basis of this theory, literary understanding consists of children's abilities to (1) suggest multiple interpretations and to (2) use these interpretations to think in new ways about their lives and the world—to defamiliarize life.

LITERARY PERSPECTIVES ON USING LITERATURE IN THE CLASSROOM

The previous section showed the kinds of perspectives and insights that cognitively oriented disciplines bring to children's understanding of stories. However, the literary qualities of the children's responses to and understanding of these stories are not the major focus of this research and theory. For a *literary perspective*, we naturally need to shift to *literary theories*, particularly those theories that deal with (1) the literary qualities of texts, as well as with (2) the literary qualities of readers' responses to literature. This section of the chapter deals with these two foci. First, text-based theory and research is presented, including various New Critical, Russian Formalist, and structuralist perspectives, as well as the perspectives of Archetypal Criticism. Then various types of reader-based theory are discussed. In this section, I discuss some of the reader-based theories that cede (1) most of the control to the reader or (2) most of the control to the text, which constricts the freedom of the reader. In the next chapter, the reader-based theories that seem to grant equal weight and importance to readers and texts are considered. In each case, the implications for the construct of literary understanding are laid out.

Text-Based Theory and Research

The work of Margaret Meek (1983, 1988) is important for its persuasive exposition of how the texts of literature for young children actually give beginning readers "untaught lessons" in reading. In her brief but extremely influential book, *How Texts Teach What Readers Learn*, Meek (1988) describes how *Rosie's Walk* (Hutchins, 1968), an easy text of high-quality children's literature in picturebook format, gives "lessons" in "authorship, audience, illustration, and iconic interpretation"—all part of the development of literary competence, but also crucial to reading. Meek explains that

> To learn to read a book, as distinct from simply recognizing the words on the page, a young reader has to become both the teller (picking up the author's view and voice) and the told (the recipient of the story, the interpreter). This symbolic interaction is learned early. (p. 10)

Young readers also learn from *Rosie's Walk* that there would be no story without them. This is because the words and the pictures work together in order to tell the story, and only the reader can use them to make sense of each other. Thus beginning readers learn their active role through the picturebook itself. Meek goes on to describe how literature provides beginning readers with the crucial lessons in narrative (of character, plot, action, conflict, and resolution) that teach "how texts work." The satisfactions of the narrative form are so great that children are driven to read and reread, even after they find out "what happens." One final point that Meek makes is that stories are members of a huge interrelated family; through literature, children learn intertextual relationships as well as the discourse conventions of various genres. The surprisingly wide range of these discourse types that young children learn is examined in some detail by Walmsley, Fielding, and Walp (1991) in their longitudinal study of second-graders' home and school literary experiences.

The work of Meek and others, then, points to the crucial importance of the *narrative structures* of literature in learning to read, and suggests that literary understanding consists primarily of learning these structures. The following clusters of text-based literary theories focus on the form and content of narrative texts.

New Criticism

From the 1920s until the 1960s, the field of English-speaking literary criticism was heavily dominated by an approach that focused almost solely on textual analysis. Known as "New Criticism," this approach reacted against the prevailing literary criticism that continued the Romantic tradition of viewing literary works as self-expression, and therefore concentrated on biographical and historical information about the author to the neglect of the text itself (Selden & Widdowson, 1993). American New Criticism emerged in the 1920s from the influence of English writers T. S. Eliot and I. A. Richards and achieved its greatest importance in the 1940s and 1950s. Richards is considered one of the originators of reader response criticism because he actually analyzed the responses of university undergraduates to poems. However, his work is New Critical in the sense that he considered that there was only one correct interpretation of the poems. John Crowe Ransom (1941), Cleanth Brooks (1939/1965; 1947/1968), Robert Penn Warren (Brooks & Warren, 1943), William Wimsatt, and Monroe Beardsley (Wimsatt, 1954) were some of the most influential figures in American New Criticism. The New Critics had a great concern for objectivity, and set about attempting to give literary criticism some of the characteristics of a science. They observed that the traditional trichotomy of literature—the *author,* the author's *text,* and the *reader* of that text—had only one element that was fixed, stable, and capable of objective investigation. That element was, of course, the text. The words of the text did not change (and the growing science of textual criticism ensured the "authenticity" of texts). The text was there—literally in black and white—and was therefore amenable to objective investigation in a way that the author and the reader were not. Authors like Shakespeare were dead, and had never commented in writing about their work. Other authors might have written about their work, but this evidence was usually scarce, spotty, and unclear. Contemporary authors might talk about their work, but it is well known that authors are extremely reticent and coy about explaining anything or pinning down a meaning. We could never determine authors' true intentions; what they said or wrote about their work might be ironic or even deliberately misleading. Therefore, the New Critics eliminated the author's part of the trichotomy.

By similar logic, the reader's part of the trichotomy was considered outside the scope of objective examination. The New Critics viewed readers with a great deal of suspicion and apprehension, for readers were even more destructive of the project to objectify criticism than authors. Readers were notorious for being incredibly diverse in their interpretations; I. A. Richards (1929/1964) had proved this with his study of university undergraduates, for even this homogeneous group had come up with wildly different readings of the same poems. To consider readers would therefore end in complete relativism and solipsism. These concerns were crystallized in two extremely influential essays by Wimsatt and Beardsley. The "intentional fallacy" (1954b) inveighed against any attempts to determine an author's intention; and the "affective fallacy" (1954a) recoiled from the prospect of using what readers said about texts as a basis for literary criticism. The text *alone* was considered worthy of investigation. Its form, its structure, and its use of image and irony could be analyzed. Since there was only one text, there could be only one interpretation, and close, careful reading would reveal it. While there might be disputes about interpretation, it was generally agreed that just as the text existed in its own right (as a "verbal icon" [Wimsatt, 1954]), so the purpose of criticism was to arrive at the meaning that was *already there* in that text. In a curious way, the New Criticism was quite democratic, for it assumed that great erudition about the history of literature and the biographies of authors was unnecessary. All that was needed was the text and a good dictionary. The text was stripped of context (to the point of not even providing the authors' names in some anthologies meant for the college classroom). Yet in another way, the New Criticism was autocratic: the instructor initiated the students into the techniques and procedures of analysis that would yield the correct interpretation. Along with a text and a good dictionary, a student needed the critical keys provided by the instructor.

In summary, New Criticism emphasized the text, rather than the reader or the author. The goal of reading was thought to be achieving the closure of objective understanding. The text was considered a message, and the reader's job was to decipher the message. There was a scientific objectivity about the whole process, since extraneous factors/variables (readers' backgrounds and the broader social and cultural context) were ignored. The focus was on the individual and the text, not on the world surrounding that relationship; and that relationship was unidirectional: from the text to the reader. The text "speaks" or transmits; the reader "listens" (receives) and understands. Various writers (Harker, 1992; Straw, 1990) have pointed out the similarities between the New Criticism and the behaviorist theories of reading that also focused on characteristics of the text, and that viewed reading as a matter of one-way transmission of meaning from author to reader through the text. There is one other way in which behaviorist reading theory and New Criticism are similar. Both are extremely tenacious because they extol the attractive vision of pristine objectivity and the possibility of certain knowledge. Currently, people who say that they have no articulated theory of reading are probably teaching reading with the theories of behaviorism; and people who say that they have no theory of literary criticism are probably teaching English using New Critical principles. On the articulated level, the behaviorist and New Critical principles still have many advocates in the academy. Indeed, most standardized tests of reading are based on New Critical principles, and most researchers who investigate "comprehension" are assuming that meaning resides exclusively in the text.

Although some contemporary literary critics (Eagleton, 1983) and others concerned with the teaching of English (Thompson, 1987) write of the New Criticism as if it were the Evil Empire, the New Critical insistence on the close, careful reading of texts has continued. Also, the New Critical language for talking about texts is still very much alive in the use of terms like "irony," "foreshadowing," and "plot complication and resolution," and the emphasis on the understanding of metaphorical language and unifying symbols in literary works. More contemporary literary theories tend to have foci other than the text; but when these theories do deal with text, they seem to use many of the concepts of New Criticism. Literary understanding, from the perspective of New Criticism, consists of extracting the (univocal) meaning of the text by explicating its structure, patterns, and unifying symbols, imagery, and themes. New Criticism (though hardly new anymore) is thus the implicit theory of literary understanding still prevalent in many primary, elementary, and secondary classrooms today.

Russian Formalism, Structuralism, and Narratology

Another group of text-based literary theories provides insights into how texts can teach what readers need to learn. The Russian formalists and the related critical school of structuralists, working at times with older forms of literature such as folk tales and classical myths, found ways in which these texts all had the same structures in terms of plot actions and characters' relationships with each other. These writers analyzed narrative in broad categories of sequence and in typologies of literary devices (for example, point of view). Particular texts were considered to be instantiations of these broad patterns. One important distinction was made by Shklovsky (1966) between *fabula* (story) and *syuzhet* (plot). Story referred to a series of events linked together in real linear time, whereas plot was defined as the artistic or literary rearrangement of these events, in a different order (as, for example, in the writing of a flashback in the course of a narrative, or in a character's narration of memories). According to Bressler (2007), story (*fabula*) "is the raw material of the story and can be considered somewhat akin to the writer's working outline. This outline contains the chronological series of events of the story" (p. 52). *Syuzhet* refers to "literary devices the writer uses to transform a story (the fabula) into plot" (p. 52). This may be a crucial distinction for children to learn if they are to follow a narrative, because the points in the narrative that depart from real chronological sequence may prove to be confusing to children. Thus, part of literary understanding is learning to make these distinctions between real time and narrative time.

Propp (1958) postulated that Russian folktales could be analyzed into a basic set of 31 "functions," or events that form the basis of the narrative. All of the functions are combinations of characters and the actions they perform. For example, function 25 is "A difficult task is proposed to the hero," and function 31 is "The hero is married and ascends the throne." Naturally, every folk tale does not contain all 31 functions; however, Propp posits that the functions describe the universe of possibilities in the folk tales, so that each folk tale is an instantiation of a certain number of functions. Although his analysis was based on Russian folk tales, Propp's system may have application to other folk tales and to other forms of literature as well (Selden & Widdowson, 1993, p. 110). Such work is valuable in relation to children's developing understanding of how stories (particularly traditional literature) work. Literary understanding, according to these principles, would be teaching children to make higher-level abstract generalizations about texts, involving such issues as "Who is the hero (or main character)?" "What trouble, conflict, or difficulty does the hero have?" "Who helps the hero solve his problem?" Children could then generalize across stories to find the commonalities.

Shklovsky (1966), whose work has already been mentioned, argued that the experience of life naturally dulls our senses and our feelings through repetition. We go through the motions of life, and because of its very familiarity, we tend to pay less attention. Shklovsky emphasized that the main purpose of literature is to allow us to acutely experience the freshness and vibrancy of life, through literary techniques and practices that "defamiliarize" life and make it strange and new again. One technique, for example, is to slow down the narrative by dwelling on a single moment with a great deal of descriptive detail; or, alternatively, to speed up the narrative by skipping over days or even months of time. This is closely related to Genette's (1980) ideas concerning pace or speed of narrative. Genette observes that narratives commonly either collapse time (with such transitional devices as "some days later . . .") or expand time (for example, by viewing a single dramatic moment, lasting only a few seconds, through the eyes of several characters in turn). Genette calls this the acceleration and deceleration of the narrative, and he further differentiates several types of these changes in speed. Real time is steady and predictable; narrative time is jerky, quirky, proceeding by fits and starts. We may be born (as Kant postulated) with an *a priori* idea of real time, but narrative time is something that clearly must be learned. There is almost no empirical research on young children's developing understanding of narrative time; however, we can assume that at least one aspect of literary understanding, for narratologists, would consist of knowing how stories represent the passage of time in quite different ways from our experience of time in real life as a seamless flow.

The narrative theorist Todorov (1977) posited that narratives contain 12 types of transformations (6 simple and 6 complex) that transform simple expository language (what Bruner (1986) called "paradigmatic" or "logico-scientific" language) into the language of narrative, widening the scope of meanings and "subjunctivizing" reality, or showing "an action or a state as conceived" by the characters in a story (Hade, 1988, pp. 312–313). For example, the sentence "John ate ice cream" is in the expository, paradigmatic mode; it simply makes a statement. A transformation of *mode* of this sentence would be "John might eat ice cream." A transformation of *intention* would be "John tries to eat ice cream." There are 10 other possible transformations in addition to these two. Hade (1988) used this system of "narrative transformations" worked out by Todorov to analyze the relationship between the text of a story and three children's retellings of the story. Hade's method was to analyze two stories that were read to the children (ages 3, 4, and 8), according to Todorov's system of transformations. Hade then also analyzed the children's several retellings according to the same system. His findings were that "the children are resonating syntactically to the language of the story," thus "making the language of the original texts part of their own story language" (p. 319). The implication is that the types of stories we read to children (or the stories they read) are formative of their concepts of narrative. Hade concluded that "Narrative transformations may be a structural tool that can enlighten the concept of 'a child's concept of story'" (p. 319).

Archetypal Criticism

Rather than seeing literary texts in lonely isolation, the literary theorist Northrop Frye (1957, 1964) explored the ways in which poems, novels, and plays represented the working-out of broad mythic themes that had perennial significance and meaning for the human race. Frye extended Jung's (1934–35) idea of archetypes—cognitive structures, themes, and concepts that Jung believed were part of the "collective unconscious" of all humanity—to the universe of literary discourse. According to Jung, the ancient myths and folk tales of all societies represent psychological states and symbols. One major product of the unconscious is the "hero myth" (popularized by Joseph Campbell, 1972), which recounts the resolution of struggle, coming-of-age, and other developmental themes. Frye used Jung's ideas to construct a typology of literature, identifying four basic narrative patterns or types, which embodied archetypal knowledge: romance, comedy, tragedy, and satire/irony. For Frye, literature (and other art) is what makes us uniquely human, providing us with meaning and the possibility of self-transformation. Frye's theories have been used extensively by two writers interested in children's acquisition of literary understanding, Glenna Davis Sloan (2003) and Kay Vandergrift (1980). The work of these two writers is described in chapter 3.

Whereas New Criticism tended to focus on each text as a unique entity, the major thrust of Russian Formalism, Structuralism, and Archetypal Criticism was to connect texts with each other by finding common patterns that united them. These last three movements in literary criticism represent the effort to discern the "grammar" and dynamics of narrative; to outline organizing principles common to particular genres and literary types; and to identify the ways in which literature reflects the universal human experience through the archetypal instantiations of values, goals, dreams, and character types. Thus, such theories value teaching children about the common content and structure of stories, so as to understand the underlying principles of all stories and the characteristics of literary genres.

Reader-Based Theories: Two Extremes of a Continuum

If the major assumption of the text-based theories is that there is objective meaning, structure, and content *in* the text (and that, therefore, there can be only one meaning for any one text), the major assumption of reader-based theories is that different readers will naturally and inevitably construct different meanings of the same text. One cluster of theories that focuses on the ways in which readers understand and interpret what they read is commonly called "reader response" (Beach, 1993; Marshall, 1993; Suleiman & Crosman, 1980; Tompkins, 1980). These theories have in common their emphasis on the role of the reader in constructing literary meaning. They also share the phenomenological assumption that what is perceived and who perceives it are inseparable (Nauman, 1994). Also, reader-response theories reject the idea of any single, univocal, objective meaning in a text, since all readers bring different experiences to a text and understand the text through their own unique cultural and psychological filters. All of this is not to imply, however, that reader-response criticism is monolithic. As Beach (1993) and Galda and Beach (2001) have shown, it is a house of many mansions. For this reason, I choose to describe it as a continuum, as shown in Figure 2.1, ranging from theories that understand the reader as dominated by the text to theories that assert that the reader functions in a totally autonomous way.

The two extremes of the continuum are discussed in this chapter, and those in the middle of the continuum in the next chapter. The extreme left-hand side may appear puzzling, since it describes a situation where the reader is dominated by the author or the text. Can this be *reader* response? Yet the focus of the theories on this end of the continuum is still *what happens in the reader's mind* as she reads. For example, the phenomenologist Georges Poulet (1980) believes that when we read, our minds are "taken over," *inhabited* by the author. We become a host to the author, who thinks (or rethinks) her thoughts through us: "This I, who 'thinks in me' when I read a book, is the I of the one who writes the book" (p. 46). Literary understand-

FIGURE 2.1. Continuum of Reader Response

| Reader as Author/ Text-Dominated | ------------+------------ | Totally Autonomous Reader |

ing, for Poulet, consists in being open to "possession" by the author; it reminds me of the film *The Exorcist*! In a curious way, the "Questioning the Author" techniques of Beck and McKeown (2006; Beck, McKeown, Hamilton, & Kucan, 1997), with their continual deferments to what the author wants us to think about a text, are implicitly based on this approach. This work also has an affinity for the criticism of E. D. Hirsch (1973), whose main thesis in *Validity in Interpretation* is that every work of literature has a univocal "meaning," determined by the author, which readers can discern by careful analysis. Hirsch asserts, however, that every culture and social context will ascribe a different "significance" to the text. Literary understanding, from these perspectives, consists of discerning the author's intention or pattern of thought: readers, active though they may be, are always controlled by the author; however, readers situated across various times, cultures, and social contexts may arrive at various types of significance for the same text.

Stanley Fish is another theorist whose early work (1967, 1970/1980) falls on this left end of the continuum. Fish is a fertile thinker, and has changed his approach significantly over a distinguished career as the *agent provocateur* of American literary criticism (Richter, 1989). In *Surprised by Sin: The Reader in "Paradise Lost,"* Fish (1967) brilliantly traces the moment-to-moment process of reading Milton's masterpiece. In so doing, of course, Fish challenged the New Critical "affective fallacy" by focusing on the reader of the poem (Fish himself) rather than the poem itself. Fish conceives of reading in linear terms: "The basis of the method is a consideration of the temporal flow of the reading experience, and it is assumed that the reader responds in terms of that flow and not to the whole utterance. That is, in an utterance of any length, there is a point at which the reader has taken in only the first words, and then the second, and then the third, and so on, and the report of what happens to the reader is always a report of what has happened to that point" (Fish, 1970/1980, p. 27). Fish seeks to describe "the responses of the reader in relation to the words as they succeed one another in time" (p. 27); and this moment-by-moment, play-by-play description of the effect that every new word or phrase has on what has already been read is what constitutes interpretation. (Fish emphasizes that his method of analysis slows down the process to a conscious level; and his description thus may have a surprising relevance to the reading process of beginning readers, whose processing is much slower than that of mature readers.) From this perspective, the text is no longer an object, but an event, "something that happens to, and with the participation of, the reader" (p. 25). Thus, although the text constrains the reader at every moment, it is the reader's processing of the text that is the focus of interest. Literary understanding, from this viewpoint, would consist of teaching children to think metacognitively about what they were reading moment by moment after each phrase or sentence of a story.

At the other extreme, the right-hand side of the continuum of reader-response theories, the opposite situation obtains. At this end, there is a cluster of theories that give almost total autonomy to the reader: the text, controlled by the reader, becomes merely "a vessel of associations helplessly open to the mastery of [our] response" (Grudin, 1992, p. 105). The most far-out of these positions are taken by David Bleich (1978, 1980) and Norman Holland (1968, 1975). Assuming the subjective nature of reality, Bleich (1980) writes that "It is true that there is often an illusion that a text acts on a reader, but it can hardly be the case that a text actually does act on the reader" (p. 145). Beyond seeing the same text and perhaps agreeing on the "nominal meaning" of words, "the only consensus about a text is on its role as a symbolic object, which means that further discussion of the text is predicated on each reader's symbolization and resymbolization of it" (p. 145), not on any illusory transaction. Discussion of reading means the sharing of one's own personal responses; and the pedagogical implication of this view is that the teacher (or professor—Bleich is primarily concerned with his own university teaching) needs to arrange a situation where literally any response is valued and accepted. However, his theory has application for young children as well. Following Bleich's theory, teachers would welcome all interpretations offered by children, even when these interpretations did not seem particularly grounded in the teacher's assumptions about the meaning of the story, and the teacher would encourage a lively exchange of these personal interpretations, without attempting to arrive at any consensus.

Norman Holland's position is similar, but he approaches the reader's autonomy from the perspective of psychoanalytic theory. His main concern is the emotional response that readers have to literature, and his earlier work (1968) takes a specifically Freudian view of how particular texts resonate with our basic fantasies and psychic conflicts. A bit later (1975), he examined the responses of five adult readers in detail, coming to the conclusion that what these people did when they read was to "read into" literature their basic personality structure or "identity theme." Since everyone's identity theme is unique and idiosyncratic, every reader's interpretation may also be unique. For Holland, what we find in a text is literally *ourselves*. Mailloux (1982) comments that for Holland, "All of us, as we read, use the literary work to symbolize and finally to replicate ourselves. We work out through the text our own characteristic patterns of desire and adaptation" (p. 25). Our interpretation of a text depends almost solely on the internal emotional structures we bring to it; thus, Holland's work has more than surface similarities to theories of reading that emphasize the reader's background of experience to the almost total exclusion of the words on the page. Koler's aphorism that "Reading is only incidentally visual" (quoted in Flynn, 1983, p. 42) reflects this type of thinking about the reading process. Practitioners who work with young children might use Holland's ideas to understand that when the children are talking about a story, they are really reflecting their own personalities, concerns, and preoccupations: literary understanding, then, becomes a form of self-examination and reflection.

Of course, the idea that each of us has a single identity has been challenged by postmodern thinkers (Derrida, 1976), who prefer the term "subjectivity" (Broughton, 2002). Subjectivities are ontologically unstable, and continually shift based on the sociocultural and linguistic contexts in which we find ourselves; thus to speak of a *single* identity, as Holland and Bleich do, is problematic. However, we do display patterns of behavior and attitudes with which we become comfortable, so it still may be possible to discern a child's "subjectivity theme" (Broughton, 2002, p. 4). Broughton is dealing with "early adolescent sixth-grade girls," but there is no reason to suppose that younger children would not display subjectivity themes as well. In this case, literary understanding would consist of a child's interpretation of a story based on her situated subjectivity at the time; thus, a child's set of school subjectivities might be quite different from her out-of-school subjectivities, and therefore she might interpret a story in a very different way depending on the sociolinguistic and cultural context of the interpretation.

I mentioned that a comparison between the earlier and later work of Stanley Fish reveals a significant shift in his thought about the relative importance of the text. In the collection of essays *Is There a Text in This Class?* (Fish, 1980), his perspective swings to the opposite side of the continuum, reflecting almost as extreme a subjective view as that of Bleich and Holland. For example, he asserts that there is no objective meaning in the text, referring in one essay (1980) to "affective criticism" as a "superior fiction," saucily declaring that "it relieves me of the obligation to be right (a standard that simply drops out) and demands only that I be interesting" (p. 180). The extreme relativism (not to say solipsism) that this view reflects was repudiated later by Fish himself, in another series of essays in the same book. Still maintaining that texts had absolutely no inherent meanings, he began to consider the reader not as a "sect of one," but in relationship to other readers. Meanings, he argues, are constructed by individuals in the context of the particular sociocultural "interpretive communities" to which they belong. This pivotal concept allows Fish to sit on both sides of the theoretical fence— to maintain reader autonomy while also avoiding the charge of interpretive anarchy. The interpretive community determines by what conventions and norms a work of literature will be interpreted; it sets the parameters, so to speak. So while there is obviously not total agreement among the members of any interpretive community, they all recognize a common set of rules for interpretation. (The knowledge of this set of rules, norms, or conventions is similar to what Jonathan Culler, 1975, calls "literary competence," though

Culler's is a more universal concept.) Thus, while Fish can assert on the one hand that "Interpretation is not the art of construing but the art of constructing" and declare that "Interpreters do not decode poems; they make them" (p. 327), he can also guarantee that meaning is not merely a matter of individual whim, but the result of the individual reader's membership in the interpretive community. It is important to note that the idea of an interpretive community is not limited to august bodies like the Modern Language Association. Indeed, one can simultaneously be a member of several interpretive communities, each with its own norms. In the classroom, the rules of the interpretive community will be reconstructed anew each year by the negotiation of the teacher and the children. Fish's concept of the interpretive community implies that what children think literature is and what they think is the "proper" way to respond to literature depends on the implicit definitions of their classroom communities. In other words, what is valorized in any particular classroom—what "counts" as response—may be quite different from what is valorized in another classroom. Thus, children's literary understanding is both enabled and constrained by the implicit and explicit rules of their classroom interpretive community. From this perspective, our view of literary understanding is quite pragmatic: it simply consists of what the classroom interpretive community has determined it to be.

3

Young Children's Literary Understanding: Between Text and Reader

Thus far, I've discussed examples of cognitively based theories of children's understanding of narrative, as well as the extremes of the reader-response theoretical continuum. In this chapter, I shift to a consideration of reader-based theories that are situated more toward the middle of the continuum: these theories attempt to strike a balance between the information in (and constraints of) the text and the prerogatives and control of the reader. The two theorists who have been most influential in the research on classroom response to literature in this middle area are Wolfgang Iser and Louise Rosenblatt.

THE MIDDLE GROUND: ISER AND ROSENBLATT

Subtitled *A Theory of Aesthetic Response,* Iser's *The Act of Reading* (1978) is the most complete exposition of his theory of reading literature. Unlike Bleich and Holland, Iser does not believe that "the text disappears into the private world of its individual readers" (p. 49). Reading does not lead to "daydreaming, but to the fulfillment of conditions that have already been structured in the text" (p. 50). Iser views reading as an "interaction" between the text and the reader: "Effects and responses are properties neither of the text nor of the reader; the text represents a potential effect that is realized in the reading process" (p. ix). Iser emphasizes the situatedness of reading in time, though his discussion is unlike Fish's relentless unidirectional progress through a text. Iser sees the reader having a "wandering viewpoint," which not only focuses on varying characters and what they know compared to what the narrator is telling us, but also wanders back and forth between the memories of what has already been read and the reading of the moment, revising these memories as new information is added while reading. The reading process is conceived of as essentially recursive, with "a continual interplay between modified expectations and transformed memories" (p. 111). Another important concept in Iser's theory is the idea of "indeterminacies" or "gaps" in the text. No text, no matter how detailed, can describe every action, situation, or character in exhaustive detail. One of the reader's main jobs is to fill in these gaps by inference. Iser says that "The gaps function as a kind of pivot on which the whole text–reader relationship revolves" (p. 169). As the readers fill in the gaps in the text, they must assure that their ongoing gap-filling is consistent with the information they have encountered previously in the text; and readers may revise their inferences as they come upon new information. Iser calls this whole process "consistency-building," and it bears a great deal of similarity to Piaget's important concepts of assimilation and accommodation, in the constant process of revising expectations in the light of new knowledge (Piaget, 1985). The reading process involves anticipation, frustration, retrospection, reconstruction, and satisfaction. Iser's notion of gap-filling also resembles Golden and Rumelhart's (1993) idea of a story as a "partially specified trajectory" and the reader's job of supplying "the most probable missing features" of that trajectory (p. 203).

For Iser, then, meaning is not in the text, but created by an active reader, who nevertheless follows the instructions of the text that acts as a framework or schema upon which the reader builds a meaning. In the balance between the reader and the text, Iser gives perhaps slightly greater weight to the text, since it is the text that provides the reader with the "set of instructions" she needs to make meaning. Iser even goes so far as to speak of the "implied reader," by which he means the one that is established by the text itself, through the "response-inviting structures" in the text. On our continuum, then, Iser would probably be placed slightly to the left of center. Therefore, teachers whose view of literary understanding followed Iser's tenets would (1) give slightly more credence to the power of the text, while at the same time honoring children's interpretations; (2) encourage children to adopt a "wandering viewpoint" by asking children what various characters might be thinking in the same situation, asking what the teller of the story (the narrator) knows that the characters do not know, or asking what one character knows that another character does not know; and (3) help children fill in the "gaps" in the story, by talking about what the story does *not* tell us.

The work of Louise Rosenblatt (1938/1996, 1964, 1978/1994, 1982, 1985, 1986, 2004) has been largely ignored by other literary theorists, but of all the theorists I have discussed, she is the most important for current literacy research and pedagogical practice. Long before the term "reader-response" criticism was coined (and during the ascendancy of New Criticism), Rosenblatt was a pioneer in emphasizing the importance of the reader (Clifford, 1988). Her perspective on reading is that it is a "transactional" process involving the reader and text as equal partners; and of all the theorists, she is probably the one who approaches most closely the exact middle of the continuum. She insists that her theory has "always kept both reader and text in focus" (1985, p. 103); in fact, she does not like being called a reader-response theorist because that label implies that she privileges the reader over the text. Whereas Iser uses the metaphor of a "set of instructions" for the text, Rosenblatt's (1978/ 1994) metaphor gives a bit more authority to the reader: she calls the text a "blueprint, a guide for the selecting, rejecting, and ordering of what is being called forth" in the reader's mind (p. 11).

Rosenblatt's insistence on the transactive nature of the reading process bears fruit as she discusses the *stances* readers may take toward any text. She describes two basic stances, which she calls "efferent" and "aesthetic." These two stances constitute the opposite ends of a continuum rather than a dichotomous pair. When readers adopt an efferent stance, they are reading for the purpose of taking some information away from the text. (The term "efferent" is derived from the Latin *effere*, meaning "to take or carry away.") Therefore, efferent reading is focused on what happens *after* the activity of reading. Rosenblatt gives the example of reading the instructions on a bottle of prescription pills when someone has taken an overdose. The reader of these instructions cares nothing for the "experience" of reading; reading in this case is simply the means to a (very urgent) end. On the other hand, when we read a play or a novel or a poem, it is precisely this lived-through experience that is important. Our focus is on this experience with the text during the act of reading, rather than on any information we might use after reading. When we do this type of reading, we are adopting what Rosenblatt calls the "aesthetic" stance. One of Rosenblatt's great insights is that the "literariness" of texts is really an illusion; literariness resides not in the text, but in the reader, as the reader chooses the aesthetic stance. It is quite possible (and, in some English classes, unfortunately all too common) that poems, novels, and plays may be read purely efferently, that is, for the information we may acquire from them: for the purpose of analysis of literary form, or for the ethical or thematic "message."

Any reading situation, for Rosenblatt (1982), "falls somewhere on the continuum between the aesthetic and efferent poles; between, for example, a lyric poem and a chemical formula. I speak of a *predominantly* efferent stance, because according to the text and the reader's purpose, some attention to qualitative elements of consciousness may enter. Similarly, aesthetic reading involves or includes referential or cognitive elements. Hence, the importance of the reader's *selective* attention in the reading process" (p. 269; italics in original). Rosenblatt believes that both efferent reading and aesthetic reading should be taught. However, "Contrary to the general tendency to think of the efferent, the 'literal,' as primary, the child's earliest language behavior seems closest to a primarily aesthetic approach to pleasure" (p. 271). Children have an "affinity for the aesthetic stance" (p. 272), which suggests that aesthetic reading should be a very important component of early school experiences.

Rosenblatt (1986) remarks that the "physical text is simply marks on paper until a reader transacts with them," bringing to the text "a unique reservoir of public and private significances, the residue of past experiences with language and texts in life situations" (p. 123). In other words, of itself, the text has no meaning; the reader makes the meaning in the process of transaction. In so doing, the reader creates what Rosenblatt (1978/1994) refers to as the "poem," by which she means the lived-through aesthetic experience evoked by the text. The poem is not an object, but an "event in time" (1964, p. 126), an "experience" (p. 127). In this respect, her thought is very similar to that of Fish, with his emphasis on the experience of reading moment by moment. She calls the poem "an occurrence, a coming-together, a compenetration, of a reader and a text" (p. 126).

For Rosenblatt (1938/1996), the immediate, personal response of the individual reader, uninfluenced by the teacher, is the crucial *beginning* of the literary experience: "Without linkage with the past experiences and present interests of the reader, the work will not 'come alive' for him, or rather, he will not be prepared to bring it to life" (p. 112). However, this personal response is not the end of the literary experience. The teacher has a critical role to play, as well as the whole interpretive community. The teacher must order the classroom environment so that individual response is elicited and encouraged, but this is only the beginning. Students must discuss their personal responses, and in so doing, they will discover that others have very different responses. This will drive them back to the text, and they will modify and refine their response as a result. At this point, background information of all types—information about the author, the author's historical milieu, the genre to which the text belongs, and formal and structural aspects of the text—may be brought to bear on the response, which will then be further modified. It is a distortion of Rosenblatt's position to assert that she is encouraging interpretive free-for-alls, though she does insist that the students should be initially free to respond individually and idiosyncratically: "Though a free, uninhibited emotional reaction to a work of art or literature is an absolutely necessary condition of sound literary judgment, it is not, to use the logician's term, a sufficient condition" (p. 75). Nor does she believe that every response is equally valid: "There is, in fact, nothing in the recognition of the personal nature of literature that requires an acceptance of the notion that every evocation from a text is as good as every other. . . . The aim is to help the student toward a more and more controlled, more and more valid or defensible, response to the text" (p. 281).

Unlike most reader-response critics, Rosenblatt (perhaps because of her years of postdoctoral work in anthropology) pays some attention to socio-cultural context, by asserting that reading occurs "between a particular reader and a particular text at a particular time, and under particular conditions. All of these factors affect the transaction" (1986, p. 123). She believes that readers who have similar social and cultural backgrounds will be able to arrive at similar (though not necessarily identical) interpretations. These backgrounds limit the range of responses that are possible, just as the blueprint of the text "limits or controls" response (1978/1994, p. 129). In the classroom, teachers who adopt Rosenblatt's view of literary understanding would emphasize and honor children's initial aesthetic responses to a story and then, through discussion and reference back to the text of the story, encourage children to modify, refine, and extend their understanding of the story by being influenced by the other children's interpretations as well as by the reference back to the story itself. Literary understanding, from this theoretical perspective, consists of a sequence, from the "lived-through" experience of the text (a totally private aspect of sense-making) to discussion, debate, and the creation of public aspects of sense-making (Rosenblatt, 2004), ideally through discussion with others—others whose cultures, ethnicities, and races may be quite different from the reader's.

BRITTON'S PARTICIPANT AND SPECTATOR STANCES

James Britton is another theorist who is much more appreciated in the educational community than in the literary community. Drawing on the work of the psychologist D. W. Harding (1962) as well as the linguistic perspectives of Halliday (1975), Britton (1984, 1993) attempted to describe the difference in the stances we take when we read literature and when we read (or use) expository language (for example, contracts or any formal discourse). Britton calls these two stances (or roles) the *participant* and the *observer* or *spectator*. According to Britton (1993), "language in the role of participant designates any use of language to get things done, to pursue the world's affairs, while language in the role of spectator covers verbal artifacts, the use of language to make something, rather than to get something done" (p. 28). When we use language as participants, we are using *transactional* language, and when we use language as spectators, we are using *poetic* language. Britton (1993) conceives these two types of language as lying on opposite sides of a continuum, and further defines *expressive* language as lying midway between them. Britton has stated that his participant stance is similar to Rosenblatt's idea of efferent stance, and that his poetic stance is similar to her idea of aesthetic stance. Rosenblatt (1985) disagrees, pointing out that the transactional language and poetic language associated with the two stances implies that there are texts that are in themselves transactional and texts that are in themselves poetic. Rosenblatt believes that any text can be read efferently or aesthetically, and that the difference is in the stance of the reader, not in any qualities of the text. For example, when an insomniac keeps a book of recipes at her bedside to peruse during sleepless nights, she is probably reading from an aesthetic stance—to have a lived-through imaginative experience of the way the food will taste and look. If the same person were to be reading that recipe book in order to make something for dinner, then her stance would shift to the efferent end of the continuum, because the purpose of reading would be to take something away, in this case something to eat! The recipe book is an example of a text that Britton would call transactional language, to be read from the participant stance; Rosenblatt, however, insists that the recipe book—or any text—can be read both aesthetically or efferently, as this example shows.

In addition, Rosenblatt (1985) points out that "Emphasis on the 'spectator' aspect does not do justice to the total transactional (in my sense) relationship with the text" (p. 102). In the participant stance, readers read in order to learn something that will be of use to them in the real world, whereas in the spectator stance, the reader uses language to make a storyworld, without any thought of any real-world consequences or outcomes. Britton's use of the term "transactional" for participant or efferent reading is a source of confusion, because Rosenblatt uses the term "transactional" to mean the transaction between the reader and the text, whereas the same term for Britton means a particular kind of language that might be used in a common transaction, for example buying something from a store. For Britton, literary understanding means children's developing awareness of the differences in poetic (literary) and transactional (everyday) language, and adopting the spectator stance that is appropriate to poetic language.

For Britton, the poetic language that is characteristic of literature is not to be treated as if the reader were actually participating in the events of the narrative, but from the spectactor stance. This idea invariably causes confusion in my courses on literary theory, because students think that participating in a work of literature (in the sense of Rosenblatt's lived-through experience) is a positive thing, whereas Britton means something quite different: participatory language is the language we use when we go to the bank or buy groceries. On the contrary, the spectactor stance is not an uninvolved attitude toward literature, but can involve deep emotional reactions and personal connections; nevertheless, Britton insists that it's not the same kind of emotional reaction or personal connection that we would have if we were actually participating in an event. We can read about a traffic accident and experience sympathy, horror, and the like as *spectators* might experience these emotions; but if we are actually in a traffic accident, our experience as actual *participants* is quite different. We may disagree with Britton on this, but it is important to understand his point. Britton believes that it is simply naïve to conflate our literary experiences with the experiences of real life. Along with Harding (1962), he believes that literature does not provide us with vicarious experience, however impassioned or emotionally involved we may be in a literary text. Part of literary understanding for Britton, therefore, is for children to realize that the language of stories and the language of "real life" are quite distinct.

I now consider other reader-based literary theories, theories that are not usually mentioned in discussions of reader response, but which nevertheless focus on what happens in the reader's mind.

BENTON'S CONSTRUCT OF THE SECONDARY WORLD

All of us have had the experience of becoming "lost in a book." As Victor Nell (1988) beautifully comments in his study on this phenomenon,

> Reading for pleasure is an extraordinary activity. The black squiggles on the white page are still as the grave, colorless as the moonlit desert; but they give the skilled reader a pleasure as acute as the touch of a loved body, as rousing, colorful and transfiguring as anything out there in the real world. . . . These are the paired wonders of reading: the world-creating power of books, and the reader's effortless absorption that allows the book's fragile world, all air and thought, to maintain itself for a while, a bamboo and paper house among earthquakes. (p. 1)

Although this is a common enough experience among readers and listeners, it is only recently that it has begun to be theorized and taken seriously as an important element of the reading process. The theorist who has most extensively considered the "world-creating power of books" is Michael Benton (1979, 1992; Benton, Teasey, Bell, & Hurst, 1988). In elaborating his concept of the "secondary world," Benton draws on Suzanne Langer's (1953) belief that when we read literature we are engaging in "virtual life" or "virtual experience." He also refers to Winnicott's (1974) construct of the "third area," which exists between the "personal or psychic reality that is biologically determined for each of us and the actual world that is our common property" (Benton, 1992, p. 23). However, the major inspiration for Benton's theory is the metaphor of literature as a "secondary world" developed by both J. R. R. Tolkien and W. H. Auden. Tolkien (1938/1964) felt that the "willing suspension of disbelief," by which Coleridge had described the reader's acceptance of an author's imaginative re-creation of reality, was an inadequate description of what happens when we read:

What really happens is that the story-maker proves a successful "sub-creator." He makes a Secondary World which your mind can enter. Inside it, what he relates is "true;" it accords with the laws of that world. You therefore believe it, while you are, as it were, inside. The moment disbelief arises, the spell is broken; the magic, or rather art, has failed. You are then out in the Primary World again, looking at the little abortive Secondary World from outside. (p. 36)

Auden (1968) writes of the dual desire that everyone feels of knowing "the primary world, the given world outside ourselves in which we are born, live, love, hate and die, and the desire to make new secondary worlds of our own or, if we cannot make them ourselves, to share in the secondary worlds of those who can" (p. 49). Benton (1979) attempts to describe the psychological dynamics of this secondary world. He argues that it is

1. *active*, "making meaning from signs," because "when we are engrossed in a book, we are conscious not of words on the page, but of meanings made" (p. 73)
2. *creative*, because the reader is just as much a "sub-creator" (in Tolkien's terminology) as the author, making a "novel within the novel" by her reconstruction of the novel as it is read
3. as *unique* as each performance of a play or a piece of music is unique, because all readers bring different experiences to a text, and each reader, constantly changing herself, produces a unique reading each time a text is reread
4. *cooperative*, since "the experience of reading fiction is a compound of what the text offers and what the reader brings" (p. 74)

The affinities of this description of reading with Rosenblatt's transactional views are clear. Rosenblatt, too, says that the text is "marks on a page" until the reader breathes life into them; that the lived-through experience is unique to each reader; and that the text is a blueprint, as important to the meaning the reader constructs as a musical score is to the symphony that we hear.

Benton describes the secondary world as having the structure of three dimensions, which are analogous to the three dimensions of the primary (physical) world. As shown in Figure 3.1, he diagrams these three dimensions as a coordinate system with three axes, suggesting that at any moment of reading, our reading process can be located on a point mapped by the intersection of the three axes in psychic space, just as any point in physical space can be located by three coordinates.

One dimension is the *psychic level*, which can range from conscious to unconscious (from responses we control to responses we cannot control because we are not consciously aware of them). Benton agrees with the common view that reading and writing "involve a mixture of conscious and

FIGURE 3.1. Structure of the Secondary World

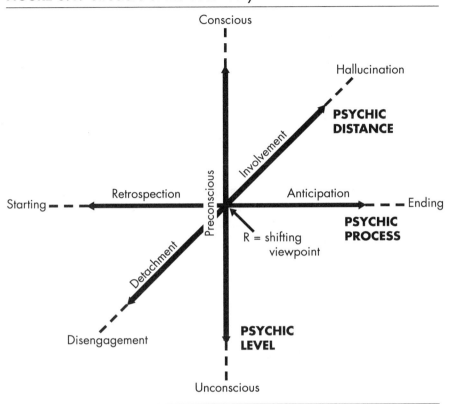

Reproduced with permission from Benton (1992), p. 26.

unconscious ideas" (1992, p. 27). The second dimension is *psychic distance*, ranging between detachment and involvement, and describing our degree of engagement with the text. When we are totally engaged in the secondary world of the text, our state is similar to hallucination (1992, p. 28). The third dimension is *psychic process*, encompassing our retrospection (or looking back on actions and situations we have already read about) and anticipation (looking ahead to predict what will happen). This is similar to Iser's concept of the "wandering viewpoint." The intersection point **R** marks what is happening at any moment of reading. **R** shifts constantly as

> we vary in our degree of involvement in and detachment from the story world [our psychic distance], the degree to which the story engages our conscious and unconscious mind [our psychic level], and the degree of anticipation of what is

going to happen based upon our retrospective knowledge of the story so far [our psychic process]. (1979, p. 78)

Benton further describes the reader's progress through a story as having four characteristics. This progress is:

1. *anticipatory*, because the main thrust of the reader's attention is in the forward direction
2. *dialectical*, in the sense that the reader is also constantly assimilating and accommodating new information in light of the old, previously read information, making hypotheses and either confirming or disconfirming them
3. *conventional*, because the reader's knowledge of the conventions of a particular genre will influence the types of predictions that are made
4. *analogical*, because of "our tendency to compose stories structured upon the ones we read (or upon parts of them) which give us an opportunity to relive or alter our actual experience, or act out dramas revolving around our wishes and fears"

(1979, pp. 80–81)

Benton's is a truly elegant theory, but it deals with such an interior experience that it is difficult to know how we would employ it as a conceptual tool in research. Nevertheless, we must try, because, as Benton himself says, "If we want to fathom the process of 'storying,' we need to develop new methodologies which genuinely take account of the insubstantial nature of the fictions we construct in imagination as we read" (1979, p. 73). This is a tall order. It has been shown that children display a great range of verbal and nonverbal responses to literature (Hickman, 1981; McGee, 1992a; Morrow, 1988). As we will see, however, researchers on response generally rely on what children *say* or *write* after their experience of listening or reading. This may provide an index or a simulacrum of their aesthetic experience, but can we get any closer? The research of Enciso (1992) suggests an ingenious solution to this problem. Enciso studied the literary experience of three fifth-grade girls by employing a "symbolic representation interview" (1992, p. 78). Immediately after reading, a child would engage in an "introspective recall" (Benton, 1988, p. 26) of her reading experience. This was followed by the child's creating cutouts that represented the characters in the story as well as cutouts that represented the reader's own experiences. Then the child would read the story, using the cutouts of the characters and reader. This was followed by creating cutouts for the author of the story and the narrator. The story would then be reread, using all the cutouts of the characters, reader, author, and narrator. During the reading and rereadings of the story, the child would verbalize her thoughts while she moved the cutouts to show the relationships and experiences she had perceived. This provided a window on the storyworld the child created as she read—a window that enriched and extended oral response to include visual representation. In analyzing this rich data, Enciso used the work of Benton, Iser, and Rosenblatt in interpreting the child's transactions with the text. Indeed, the entire study was framed theoretically on the literary theoretical constructs of transaction, stance, and the secondary world. Literary understanding, from Benton's perspective, would therefore involve the reader's movements along the three dimensions of the secondary world, as well as actively being a subcreator along with the author, while cooperating with the text and the author's intentions.

Before I leave Benton's theory, I want to point out the similarities between his concept of entering the secondary world and the psychologist Mihaly Csikszentmihalyi's (1998) concept of "flow." Csikszentmihalyi asserts that some of the most satisfying moments of our lives are when we experience a concentration or preoccupation that takes us away from the workaday, moment-to-moment time that we experience, and into another dimension, as it were, where one moment may feel as if it is eternal or transcendent, and where a long period of time may feel as if it has transpired in an instant. Csikszentmihalyi calls this experience "flow"; it may happen when engaging in some physical activity, or some intellectual activity (even when writing a book on literary understanding!), or both. The experience of reading literature is, for many people, an experience of flow. Benton's theory of the secondary world limns the dimensions of this flow experience in literary reading. In terms of psychic distance, a reader experiencing flow is situating herself toward the "hallucination" end of that dimension; in terms of psychic level, a flow experience in reading is situated on the "unconscious" end of that dimension.

LANGER'S MODEL OF ENVISIONMENT

The work of Judith Langer (1990, 1995) provides another perspective on the ways in which readers may engage with a text and enter the text-world. Langer describes four changing, constantly shifting relationships of readers (of a wide range of ages, from young children to high school students) to texts. She also asserts that these four relationships or stances are employed by readers regardless of the type of text they read (both narrative text and informational, expository text). "Being out and stepping in" refers to the reader's first approach to the text, and the reader's mobilization of prior life experiences to understand it. In this stance, readers establish the context for their reading. At any moment of difficulty or confusion, readers may revert to this stance. In the second stance, "Being in and moving through," readers feel comfortable and immersed in the text, and begin to construct meaning.

The third stance, "Being in and stepping out," refers to the stance readers assume when making connections between their own lives and the lives or characters in the story, or between some experience or feeling expressed in the story and a similar experience or feeling in their lives. The fourth stance, "stepping out and objectifying experience," refers to the ways in which readers stand back and make judgments about their own understanding. In this stance, readers reflect on their own experience with the text and the emotions or understandings it evoked for them. They evaluate how accurately they have read the text, and make literary judgments. Langer and Close (2001) compare the whole process to that of a student who moves to a new school, assuming an outsider's perspective at first, and gradually fitting in by knowing more and more information until she is able to reflect on her own experience and accommodate to the new setting.

Langer emphasizes that the reader's experience does not follow a linear progression through these stances, but is recursive and iterative, shifting back and forth from moment to moment. In this way, Langer's model is similar to Benton's idea of the reader's constant shift between reflection on what has been read and anticipation or prediction of what will happen. The very fluidity of the categories, however, makes the application of these stances to specific situations somewhat problematic; for this reason, perhaps, there has been little research based on the model. Nevertheless, each of Langer's four stances involves a different aspect of literary understanding. In the first stance, literary understanding involves activating a tentative schema (our prior knowledge that will be useful for interpreting the story). In the second stance, our literary knowledge is akin to Rosenblatt's idea of the lived-through moments, where it is not so much literary understanding that is important, but rather literary experience. For the third stance, literary understanding consists of the personal connections we make between the events or characters of the story and our own lives. In the fourth stance, our literary understanding consists of analysis, reflection, and consideration of the ways in which the story has shifted our views of what life is like or could be like.

BOGDAN'S THEORY OF READER STANCES

Deanne Bogdan (1990) writes about readers' responses in a new way that seems to extend and refine Rosenblatt's ideas about the stances readers may assume when they read literature. Bogdan bases her approach on Frye's (1957) assertion that the form and content of literature are distinct and distinguishable, observing that "Content draws us in; form distances us. It is through the push-me-pull-you of content formalized that the vicarious nature of literary experience is possible and pleasurable" (p. 117). Bogdan argues that the full experience of a work of literature—what she calls the "apprehension of total form"—involves both understanding the form and experiencing the content. Readers can do this in one of two ways: "the short easy way or the long hard way" (p. 119). The easy way comes unsought, and cannot be prepared for or taught, as the reader "perceives/receives the literary object through direct insight as a kind of gnostic vision" (p. 119). Bogdan names this rare transporting experience *stasis*. The hard way (and the way readers must travel most often) is "the lower road of interpretive inquiry, the road that oscillates between engagement with the text and detachment from it" (p. 119). This is called *dialectic*. In engagement, we feel the emotional power of the content of the text, and this is similar to Rosenblatt's idea of the aesthetic experience. In detachment, we are able to think about and understand the literary form of the text; this is similar to one type of efferent stance—the type that engages in literary analysis. Bogdan argues that both engagement and detachment are necessary in order to achieve the apprehension of total form. She acknowledges the "virtual psychological impossibility of simultaneously participating in [aesthetic stance] and being consciously aware of experience [the efferent stance]" that is the gift of stasis (p. 120). She then comments,

> The reader's habitual mode of responding to literature is some form of imbalance between thought and emotion: we either overintellectualize, lacking feeling—or sentimentalize, lacking truth. . . . To strike a balance would be akin to coalescing Louise Rosenblatt's two kinds of reading, aesthetic and efferent (1978), thus enabling the reader to bring away from the reading the consciousness of the poetic experience itself. (pp. 120–121)

But this is the rare gift of stasis, and cannot be planned. The long, hard way is the way of dialectic, which involves the sequence of participating in literature and *then* reflecting on our experience, and it is this way that teachers should employ in the classroom: we simply can't stand around and wait for the lightning of stasis to strike us and our students.

Bogdan argues that stasis and dialectic are the two paths to "full response"—the apprehension of total form. But there are lesser, incomplete responses that are apprehensions of "partial form." Bogdan identifies three of these incomplete responses: *stock response*, *kinetic response*, and *spectator response*.

- A *stock response* "interprets and values a text solely according to whether the work in question seems to reinforce or countervail the welter of ideas, values, and feelings that go to make up the reader's conscious or unconscious worldview" (p. 124). It "reduces the meaning of literature to its extraliterary terms, usually some historical, moral, or social analogue of the work itself" (p. 124), and assumes that the point of literature is to deliver a message or make a social/moral point. Literary understanding, from the point of view of stock response, is understanding the message or moral of a story, as well as seeing the similarities and differences between the text-world and the reader's own world.

- *Kinetic response*, on the other hand, views the purpose of literature as providing emotional gratification—to "further the reader's enjoyment" (p. 127). It "raises the pleasure principle to a critical axiom of literary interpretation; that is, the reader evaluates the work according to whether it packs a whollop or falls flat" (p. 126). Literary understanding, from the perspective of kinetic response, is a reader's reflection on the emotions evoked by the story. Thus, readers evaluate a piece of literature on the basis of whether or not it "hits" them with pleasurable emotion.

- *Spectator response* is solely concerned, like the New Critics, with literary analysis. It produces "indifference to the emotional and imaginative dimension of a literary text" (p. 128), like T. S. Eliot's "lemon-squeezer" school of literary criticism. (Here it should be noted that Bogdan's use of the term "spectator stance" is entirely different from Britton's; in fact, the two uses of the term are almost opposites. By "spectator stance," Britton means an aesthetic engagement in a text, whereas Bogdan is referring to an objective, analytical stance.) Spectator response results in the type of literary understanding that has already been described as characteristic of New Criticism: discerning the patterns, images, structure, characterization, plot, setting, and theme of a text.

Bogdan argues that each of these three forms of response is incomplete, but in a different way: "Each of these three responses isolates and reifies one aspect of a full literary response: stock response, the search for truth; kinetic response, desire; spectator response, knowledge about literature" (p. 129). Bogdan feels that it is the job of the teacher to understand what type of partial responses the students are making, and to augment them with one another. For example, if students are only making spectator responses, Bogdan would suggest that teachers encourage expressions of how the story made the students feel emotionally and personally (kinetic response) and what social message or moral the students could glean from the story, as well as how the ideologies conveyed in the text compared or contrasted with the students' own ideologies and worldviews (stock response). The point is that the astute teacher will augment each stance with the two other stances, thereby achieving the possibility of the students' apprehension of total form.

Bogdan's theory has been explicated at length because it provides a powerful way of conceptualizing the combination of both literary experience and literary analysis—a way that the aesthetic-efferent continuum does not provide for. For Bogdan, the true aesthetic experience involves (in Rosenblatt's terms) both aesthetic *and* efferent stances. But whereas Rosenblatt speaks of the reader's continual back-and-forth movement along a linear continuum with two end points, Bogdan's theory attempts to introduce three aspects of literary understanding, and how they interact. In this way, it extends and modifies Rosenblatt's ideas, possibly providing a more refined perspective on the issues of literary response and understanding.

CAN'T WE JUST ENJOY LITERATURE?
THE THEORIZATION OF PLEASURE

At this point, you may be weary of theory, and be wondering why we just can't read a story, think about it, and *enjoy* it with children! It is fitting to end this section on literary theory with a consideration of pleasure, an aspect of the experience of literature that has so far been addressed only obliquely. Here, though the experience of pleasure is certainly one of the chief reasons we read or listen to literature, the theoretical guides are few. Touponce (1996) argues that New Criticism completely ignored pleasure, conflating it with the perception of "formal patterns of meaning" (p. 177). Likewise, Touponce complains, reader-response theories (which we might have reasonably expected to develop a theory of pleasure) ignore it almost as steadfastly as the frosty New Critics. Iser (1978), for example, conceptualizes the reader's task as an active (we might say relentless) search for meanings that will complete the indeterminacies of the text, and dismisses literature that does not make the reader do this highly cognitive work as "light reading." Of Rosenblatt, Touponce remarks, "While not negative about pleasure, Rosenblatt is so wary about discussing it that she keeps the word constantly in quotation marks, noting that 'attempts to define aesthetic pleasure by specifying its peculiar sources in the text have been inconclusive.' For Rosenblatt the reader's main purpose is to participate as fully as possible in the potentialities of the text" (Touponce, 1996, p. 177), and she seems simply to conflate pleasure with the "lived-through experience" of aesthetic reading, just as the New Critics conflated it with analysis.

Roland Barthes' *The Pleasure of the Text* (1975), brief and quirky as it is, takes a head-on approach to literary pleasure. Barthes distinguishes between two types of texts: texts of *plaisir* (translated in English as "plea-sure") and texts of *jouissance* (usually rendered as "bliss"). We feel pleasure when we can easily master a text; Barthes writes that pleasure is linked to a "comfortable practice of reading" (p. 14). This kind of text reinforces our cultural and social expectations—"it comes from culture and does not break with it" (p. 14). Texts of bliss, on the other hand, unsettle our comfortable assumptions and jar us, opening up new vistas of experience. The text of bliss takes us out of ourselves, whereas the text of pleasure confirms and reinscribes our feelings, attitudes, and values. We master texts of pleasure, and the plea-sure is in the mastery; but we *are mastered by* texts of bliss. In this way, the experience of reading texts of bliss is similar to Poulet's idea of being inhab-ited, possessed, or mastered by the author, who rethinks his thoughts through us as we read. Indeed, Barthes remarks that "The text is a fetish object, and this fetish desires me" (p. 27). This is pleasurable, because it frees us from ourselves momentarily and propels us into strangeness and uncertainty. Barthes says that the impulse to reread is driven by the experience of texts of bliss.

Rosenblatt (1978/1994) criticizes Barthes for locating pleasure in the text rather than in the reader; according to McCormick (1988), Barthes' categories can be more heuristically applied to the reading experience than to the text. In any case, many of Barthes's statements clearly seem to refer to the reader. For example, he asserts that "pleasure can be expressed in words, bliss cannot" (p. 21). Teachers who followed a Barthian model of literary understanding would be interested in children's expression both of pleasure and bliss; in other words, they would encourage children to talk about what made a story familiar, as well as what made the story new and mysterious. Because bliss cannot be expressed in words, teachers might encourage non-verbal response, for example drawing or painting, as well as acting out the story wordlessly or with movements and gestures. Likewise, they would be tolerant of responses that might at first seem off the wall or off task, and value the playfulness with which young children approach stories.

RESEARCH ABOUT LITERARY TALK IN THE CLASSROOM

The chapter now focuses on empirical research on talk about literature in the classroom, research that has employed some of the literary theoretical perspectives outlined in the last section. Generally, though, this research applies the work of relatively few literary theorists: Nauman (1994), in a study of the research on reader response to literature, found that Rosenblatt, Iser, and Fish were the most commonly cited theorists, and that references to other theorists were rare. This section is divided into four parts: research on reader stance; research on literature discussion groups; research related to the ways in which children may be taught to be literary critics; and research on picture storybook reading that focuses on children's literary understanding.

Reader Stance Research

Stance is a feature of the reader, not the text, and it refers to the particular set of assumptions and expectations a particular reader has of a particular text at a particular time. The research that clusters around *reader stance* makes direct use of the work of James Britton (Galda, 1982, 1990) and Louise Rosenblatt (Cox & Many, 1992; Many & Wiseman, 1992; Wiseman, Many, & Altieri, 1992).

Though it does not concern young readers, Galda's work on stance (which utilizes Britton's concept of the spectator role of the reader) is important for both the investigation of individual differences in stance (1982) and the longitudinal perspective it provides on stance (Galda, 1990). The 1982 study, with three fifth-grade girls, showed that children of the same age and reading ability differed widely in their ability to assume the spectator stance toward the novels they read. For example, "All three participants recognized the alternate interpretations of reality offered in the texts, but only Anne [one of the participants] accepted them as valid" (p. 18). The other two children were, in Aidan Chambers's (1985) terminology, "unyielding" readers, unable to accept any interpretation other than their own. Anne was also able "to read for more than plot," understanding and appreciating the author's craft. Galda suggests that the ability to assume a true spectator stance to literature is connected with the development of the Piagetian stage of formal operations. If this is true, then emergent readers would be cognitively incapable of assuming the spectator role. This, however, is disputable. Chambers (1985) gives many examples of very young children whose responses indicate that they have assumed the spectator role.

Another of Galda's studies (1990) investigated the development of the spectator stance across time (2 years for one group of fourth- through ninth-graders and 4 years for another group, beginning in fourth grade and ending in seventh grade). Utilizing Applebee's (1978) system of analyzing responses, Galda found that the children's evaluative responses were mainly categoric (closely tied to personal experiences and linked to categories like "adventurous and exciting") in the fourth grade and more analytic (concerned with understanding how a literary text works) in the upper grades. There was also a difference in responses to different genres: students responded to fantasy with more categoric responses and to realistic fiction with more analytic responses. Generalization responses (Applebee's highest stage, in which there is preoccupation with the ways in which the text changes how one understands the world) were present only at the eighth- and ninth-grade levels. This also has important implications for emergent readers, because it suggests that generalization response does not occur until children are much older. However, young children may be capable of some degree or level of generalization.

Other research tends to utilize Rosenblatt's efferent–aesthetic continuum rather than Britton's, and it, too, is primarily concerned with upper-elementary children. One notable exception is the work of Many and Wiseman (1992) and Wiseman, Many, and Altieri (1992) with third-graders, which studied the effects of different teaching approaches on students' responses to children's literature. The study conducted by Many and Wiseman had three treatment groups: "literary analysis" (focused on the identification and interpretation of literary elements during and after the reading of a story); "literary experience" (focused on providing a lived-through experience and personal reaction during and after the reading of the story); and no discussion after the reading of the story. All three groups were asked to "write anything you want about the story we just read" (p. 269), and the written products were analyzed. The literary analysis group tended to write more responses having to do with literary elements, and the literary experience group tended to write responses that indicated that they had entered the storyworld. The group with no discussion tended to write a simple retelling of the story.

The Wiseman, Many, and Altieri study (1992, p. 285), also using third-graders, used three instructional approaches: "student-centered" (consisting of "free discussion with no guidance from the researchers"); "teacher-guided aesthetic treatment" ("centered on the students' thoughts and their reactions to the story"); and "teacher-guided aesthetic approach followed by literary analysis" (which employed an aesthetic treatment followed by discussion that dealt with both literary analysis and personal reaction to the story). As in the Many and Wiseman study, children in all treatment groups were asked to write anything they wanted about the story they had just heard and discussed, and the written products were analyzed using a scale of level of aesthetic response. The results indicated that

> Subjects in the student-controlled discussion groups were more likely to focus on literary analysis and seldom produced responses categorized as purely aesthetic. In contrast, those in the aesthetic or aesthetic-analysis probe groups produced a high concentration of aesthetic responses which explained their feelings or described real life happenings or people or other literary characters that reminded them of story events. (p. 286)

There were no significant differences in the responses of the aesthetic and aesthetic-analysis groups, suggesting that "students who analyzed how the literary elements affected their own experiences as they read were just as likely as students in the purely aesthetic discussion group to respond from an aesthetic stance" (p. 287). The results thus suggest that discussion aimed at furthering the analytic aspect of literary understanding at least does not harm literary experience.

One difficulty with some of this research is that Rosenblatt herself never writes of "aesthetic response" (as it appears in the quote above), seeing the aesthetic experience instead as the lived-through experience *during* reading. Even discussion after the story is read is at one remove from the aesthetic experience, and writing after the discussion is at two removes. Another problem is that responses considered efferent are often of several types. One type might be a statement suggesting literary understanding (for example, "the characters were well-developed"); and another type might be a response suggesting a purely efferent stance, such as "the character was tall and had red hair." Thus, the research tends to lump together (1) efferent responses to efferent questions like, "What facts did this poem teach you?" or "What color of hair did the main character have?" and (2) responses or questions that appropriately "organize and elaborate" children's "ongoing responses," by pointing out literary elements that would increase children's abilities to listen or read aesthetically. The research on stance frequently attempts to discuss "response" without reference to the analytical modes of literary understanding, thereby making the implicit argument that response would be somehow sullied by teachers' attempts to "organize and elaborate" that response. This implicit argument probably represents an overreaction to the New Critical emphasis on textual analysis to the exclusion of any consideration of the reader. But that is precisely what it seems to be: an *over*reaction, which some of the stance research tends to perpetuate. The research suggests that the question is not whether teachers should assist children in developing literary understanding, but rather how *explicit* that assistance should be. This question is addressed by research reviewed in the next two subsections.

Classroom Conversations about Literature

There is a growing body of research (Commeyras, 1994; Eeds & Wells, 1989; Gilles, 1994; McGee, 1992a, 1992b, 1992c; McGee, Courtney, & Lomax, 1993, 1994; Raphael & McMahon, 1994; Roller & Beed, 1994; Scharer, 1992; Wiencek & O'Flahavan, 1994) and research-based pedagogy (Chambers, 1993; Daniels, 2002; Eeds & Peterson, 1991; Peterson & Eeds, 1990; Roser & Martinez, 1995; Short & Pierce, 1990) on how teachers and children engage (or could engage) in discussion about literature in the classroom. Virtually all of this work has relied heavily on the theoretical underpinnings of reader-response criticism, primarily the work of Rosenblatt and Iser. Most of the research (and much of the pedagogy) has dealt with children in the upper elementary grades (grades four to six) or older. For example, the work of Eeds and Wells (1989), which was a stimulus for much subsequent research, concerned fifth- and sixth-graders. Eeds and Wells argue that much classroom discussion of literature is in the form of "gentle inquisitions," with the teacher probing for understanding of what is read in an efferent manner. What they propose is a form of discussion they call "grand conversations," focusing on child-centered talk and personal response that reflects aesthetic reading. They found that relatively untrained undergraduate student teachers could hold successful grand conversations with small groups of children. One of their important findings was that "the elements of literature can be expected to emerge naturally as children and teacher talk about the book together because talking about a book necessitates a discussion of character coping, time, place, theme, mood and language as they are contained within and evoked by the work" (p. 23). In other words, in socially constructing a meaning of the story, relating the book to their personal experience, and engaging in hypothesis-testing about character or action, many elements of the analytical aspect of literary understanding were a natural part of the process.

Eeds and Wells encouraged the student teachers who conducted the discussions to feel free to point out literary elements when they felt there was a "teachable moment" for them. Their findings thus support the idea of the interwoven nature of literary experience and literary understanding. Moreover, the active involvement of the teacher in the construction of literary understanding is also supported. Other researchers (Scharer, 1991, 1992) have more specifically studied the teacher's role in literature discussions, finding that it is often very difficult for teachers to make the transition from the gentle inquisition to the grand conversation approach. Knobel (1993) has reported that students frequently respond to the teacher rather than to the text, despite the teacher's efforts to value the students' responses. One of her conclusions is that "teachers need to be aware of how their own meanings and interpretations of reality may affect, and sometimes conflict with, their students' meaning making and reality construction in relation to literature and reader response" (p. 302). The importance of the creation of a noncompetitive community of learners where the response of each person is valued— largely the responsibility of the teacher—has also been investigated (Scharer & Detwiler, 1992; Short, 1990).

Some writers have made suggestions about the content and organization of literature discussion groups. Chambers (1993) has proposed a "framework" of questions designed to encourage children to share their personal enthusiasms about a book; to share "puzzles" or difficulties they had in understanding the book; and to share "connections": patterns that they have discovered within a book or intertextual connections with other books. He warns that the framework is not to be used mechanically, and that "It is *not* intended that readers of any age should be given lists of questions and be required to answer them one after another either in speech or in writing" (p. 87; italics in original). Chambers's question framework has three parts, including "basic questions" such as *Was there anything you liked/disliked about the book?*; "general questions" such as *When you first saw the book, even before you read it, what kind of book did you think it was going to be? Is it what you expected, now that you've read it?*; and "special questions," such as *Which character interested you the most?* (pp. 87–90). Other writers (Daniels, 1994) have proposed that children in a literature discussion group or a storybook readaloud could take on specific roles that would help focus the discussion and give each child a sense of purpose. Most writers, however, do not advocate the assigning of particular roles, possibly fearing that this procedure would inhibit response, as Daniels himself has acknowledged in his more recent work (2002).

The success of this approach (variously called "grand conversations," "literature discussion groups," "literature circles," or "booktalks") with upper-elementary and secondary students has led researchers to investigate the use of the approach with younger children. McGee (whose work is cited above) is one of the few researchers who has studied the grand conversations of young children, as well as the role of the teacher in these conversations. McGee audiotaped and transcribed the discussions of first-graders following the reading of picture storybooks. Following Rosenblatt's transactive model and Iser's interactive model, McGee (1992c) noted that "Readers' responses can be expected to reflect a continuum having at one end responses to the readers' personal experiences and emotions evoked by reading and at the other end responses that reflect attention to the text" (p. 178). McGee's coding of children's responses ranged from "reader-bound" to "textbound" statements to reflect the range and focus of children's comments. McGee (1992b) noted three types of talk structures: "mucking about" (sharing of ideas that were seemingly unconnected); "weaving through" (in which children returned to a previous idea in nonsuccessive turns); and "focusing in" (where succeeding turns seemed to build on each other as the children continued to talk about the same idea). In her version of grand conversations, McGee and the other teachers who led the discussions made a point of not adding any interpretive comments. Midway through the discussion, however, the teachers asked an "interpretive question" that they had prepared beforehand. It was found that this question played an important role in the conversations, eliciting "a higher percentage of interpretive responses" (1992a, p. 186) as well as eliciting more "focusing in on sustained inquiry about a common idea" (1992b, p. 21).

In a further study (McGee, Courtney, & Lomax, 1994), which focused on the role of the teacher in book discussions of first-graders, McGee and her colleagues found that teachers played several roles, including that of *facilitator* (by managing turn-taking, for example); *helper/nudger* (by summarizing, restating, or asking for clarification); *responder* (by introducing, expanding, or elaborating of topics); *literary curator* (by extending literary understandings during teachable moments); and *reader* (by reading the story). Of particular interest is the literary curator role, which seemed to be exercised seldom, yet which clearly had the same positive effects as the interpretive questions. In one example, McGee (1995, p. 17) reports two children responding efferently to the fantasy story *Hey, Al* (Yorinks, 1986) by saying, "I think it's all silly," and "Birds can't talk, except parrots." In this case, the teacher took the opportunity (a teachable moment) to explain that "This kind of story is called a fantasy," and that "Anything like that can happen in a fantasy." What is fascinating is the response of a child after the teacher's brief explanation. The child commented, "I don't think I would like to be a worm on that island, then they would eat me!" The child used this literary understanding provided by the teacher to extend her lived-through (aesthetic) experience of the book by thinking about the implications of being a worm on the island.

McGee's work is also notable for its use of literary theory in her discussion of the creation of the "interpretive community" (Fish, 1980) where readers negotiate meaning by arguing persuasively for their interpretations, and where consensus is reached by this interplay of opinions. She describes this interplay, and comments that the results of her studies "support that first graders are literary critics who are capable members of interpretive communities" (McGee, Courtney, & Lomax, 1993, p. 22).

Children as Critics

McGee's assertion that first-graders are literary critics may seem a bit far-fetched to some. However, the idea that children—even very young children—can be critics has been in currency for about 20 years, and has received continuing attention (Chambers, 1985; May, 1995; Sloan, 2003; Stott, 1983, 1987; Vandergrift, 1980). Chambers (1985) poses the question, "But are children critics?" and comments that for most teachers,

> Criticism is regarded as an unnatural, specialist and adult activity for which you need training, as well as a perverse taste for pleasure-destroying analysis. Criticism, it seems, deals in abstractions, unfeeling intellectualism, cold-blooded dissection. You can't do criticism with children, and if you try you only put them off literature altogether. Many colleagues, it turned out, had been put

off by what they thought of as criticism during secondary school and college literature courses. (p. 144)

Chambers goes on to write that "We asked the question in the first place because our work persuaded us that children have an innate critical faculty" (p. 144) that can be guided and formed by a sensitive teacher. Chambers believes that much of what we call criticism amounts to the discovery of patterns—"of language, of narrative 'codes,' of plot events, of images, of character, and the rest" (p. 147)—and that human cognition is essentially a matter of finding patterns. Finding patterns is the making of meaning, and "when we make meaning we experience pleasure" (p. 147). Chambers (1985) takes Iser's idea of the "implied reader," the abstract reader that the text assumes—the "reader-in-the-book"—and relates it to real child readers. He argues that child readers are often "unyielding" readers, expecting the story to have a one-to-one correspondence to their own experience, and that they reject stories that do not have this correspondence. After continued experiences with stories, and with the help of a teacher who fosters literary understanding, however, a child can yield to the story and experience it from the "inside," becoming the embodiment of the text's implied reader. Chambers places special emphasis on the active involvement of the reader in filling in the "gaps" or "blanks" in the text, and in understanding the point of view from which the story is written. If abilities like these are fostered, children's critical faculties can be developed from a very early age.

Many of these writers believe that some form of explicit teaching about literary elements, genres, or forms is appropriate, in order to help children develop literary understanding in tandem with literary experience. Stott (1983, 1987) and Landes (1983) have proposed curricular models for learning literary criticism or "critically aesthetic" reading in the elementary grades, and have tested these models with children. Stott (1987) developed and implemented a "spiralled sequence story curriculum" over a period of 5 years with second-graders, and eventually worked out a curricular sequence for children through the elementary years. The general goal of the curriculum, which is based on structuralist principles and some of the archetypal criticism of Northrop Frye, "is to introduce the children to the basic elements and methods of literary analysis, it being my firm belief that the individual who has a fuller understanding of any story can enjoy it much more" (Stott, 1987, p. 165).

Landes (1983) describes how she worked with second-graders in a curriculum that was designed "to take them beyond literacy into literature" (p. 161). She provides a page-by-page analysis of how the children learned to appreciate the literary qualities of Beatrix Potter's *The Tale of Peter Rabbit* (1902/1987). When she read a coarse adaptation of this classic, in which "it seemed as if the author had noted every literary aspect of Potter's language and illustrations and then set about to remove them" (p. 163), the children were surprised and then annoyed. They much preferred Potter's sophisticated language and illustrations to that of the adaptation, and could give good reasons for their preferences. By so doing, they demonstrated their literary critical abilities.

Sloan (2003) uses the work of Northrop Frye as the overarching theoretical frame for her conception of "the child as critic." Echoing Frye's suggestions in *The Educated Imagination* (1964) about what children should be taught about literature, Sloan emphasizes the importance of learning myths, legends, and Bible stories so that children may acquire knowledge of the archetypal characters, symbols, themes, images, and motifs that recur throughout all of literature. She believes that although the experience of literature begins with personal response, the experience should not end there. She asserts that it is "pointless" to ask children questions like "Would you do as X [a story character] did? Would you like to have X as a friend?": "While literature relates to each one's life experiences, these relations cannot be the basis for systematic criticism" (p. 118). She emphasizes that there are no right or wrong answers to questions about literature; her lists of suggested questions (pp. 119–124; 128) include questions like, *What is the basic shape of the story? Who is the main character?* Sloan suggests that children can be taught some basic conventional patterns of stories (for example, the home-away-home or circle story, in which the characters leave home, have a series of adventures, and return to the same place they began). She suggests that children's literary understanding can be increased by introducing them to Frye's four basic narrative types (comedy, romance, tragedy, and irony/satire).

Vandergrift (1980) also recommends Frye's approach, suggesting that children can learn to use an understanding of narrative types to read with increased perception and to write more effective stories themselves. Vandergrift suggests drawing "story lines" to follow the increasing drama or emotional level of the story characters; she also places a great deal of emphasis on children being exposed to a variety of literary genres because, in Frye's conceptualization, all literature is part of a comprehensive system. Even though Frye's ideas have been critiqued as being grounded exclusively in Western European literary and cultural traditions, this does not negate their value as a heuristic for children to use in their reading and writing.

May's (1995) work on children as critics emphasizes the need for teachers to learn literary theory so that they can apply its principles to their teaching:

> Adults can determine how much children will learn about their stories, and they can help children communicate about the stories they share. Those adults who want children to discover how a story works for themselves will collabo-

rate with them to construct new meanings for the literature they share. Since these adults must initiate the discussions, they must know about story structure and critical theory. Unfortunately, since teachers have rarely studied critical theory they often don't emphasize methods of reading that encourage collaborative learning. (pp. 14–15)

May believes that if teachers do not disclose the "common framework of interpretive skills used by all good readers," the children are in a situation where they "are being forced to respond to patterns in texts without understanding that literary appreciation depends upon knowing about literary or writerly structures" (pp. 15–16). May's book includes several short studies by teacher-researchers on the ways in which they use children's literature to increase children's literary experience and understanding. These studies provide empirical evidence for her claim that teachers who know literary theory will be able to help emergent readers and writers to develop a sense of story and to learn to take a critical, interpretive stance toward literature.

Storybook Reading and Literary Understanding

In the Introduction to this book, I argued that the voluminous research on storybook reading is rarely concerned with children's literary understanding. Instead, the overwhelming bulk of this research addresses questions related to other aspects of children's developing literacy: their growing attention to the visual features of print; the effect of hearing literature read aloud on children's own writing; their oral language development and acquisition of "book language"; or the particular types of teacher readaloud styles that may be most powerful for the children's later development as independent readers. There is, however, one notable exception to this generalization. *The Making of a Reader*, Marilyn Cochran-Smith's (1984) well-known longitudinal study of the literacy learning of preschool children, was focused on the storybook readaloud sessions that were a daily occurrence at the preschool that was the site of her research, and these children's abilities as literary critics. Cochran-Smith uses literary theory extensively in her construction of a theoretical frame for examining these readaloud sessions. Among the constellation of literary theorists she cites are Roland Barthes, Wayne Booth, Jonathan Culler, Wolfgang Iser, Hans Robert Jauss, and Gerald Prince; and she weaves important insights from these theorists together with the more usual theoretical sources of emergent literacy in a fascinating way. Also intriguing are the ways in which she *modifies* some of these insights in applying them in the context of the literary development of three-, four-, and five-year-olds. Cochran-Smith refers to two of the five codes (or sign systems through which a narrative is made understandable) utilized by Barthes

(1974) to analyze a short story by Balzac. Barthes's "cultural" code refers to the broad cultural and social knowledge that most adult readers access unconsciously while reading. This is precisely the type of knowledge that young children lack, and that the story readers supplied while reading. Another Barthian code, the "hermeneutic" code, refers to the puzzles, enigmas, or questions that are raised by the text, and that are later resolved or answered. The story readers mediated this code for the children as well, by referring to the way previous incidents answered the questions that had been posed (implicitly or explicitly) by the text.

Booth's and Iser's concept of the "implied reader" is brought to bear during Cochran-Smith's analysis of the roles played by the story readers (the adults who read the stories aloud to the children). Authors of the books used for readalouds had obviously never met the particular children in the preschool. The authors had written these books with an "implied reader" in mind. On some occasions, the children (the real reader-listeners) had the same characteristics as the text's implied readers. At other times, however, there was information that the fictional implied reader possessed that the real children lacked. Cochran-Smith found that one of the main roles played by the story readers was that of mediator between the implied reader of the text and the real child listener-readers in front of her. This was one of the main ways in which the story reader helped the children to make what Cochran-Smith (1984) refers to as "Life-Text" connections: "reader exchanges aimed at helping children use their knowledge in order to make sense of literature" (p. 183). Cochran-Smith does not employ another concept of Iser's, the idea of the reader's "wandering viewpoint." It is, however, clear from her descriptions of the story readers that they mediated the story for the children not only by bridging the distance between the children's knowledge and the knowledge assumed by the text's implied reader, but also by directing the children's attention to past occurrences in the narrative and connecting them with the actions of the moment, and by discussing what various characters were feeling and/or knew. In these ways, the story readers were helping the children to see that the reader must employ a wandering viewpoint while reading, as well as facilitating their construction of that viewpoint for themselves.

Cochran-Smith also makes use of Culler's (1975) idea of "literary competence," which is the knowledge of literary conventions that both authors and readers must share in order for readers to make sense of what they are reading. She modifies this idea to include two broad categories of literary conventions: book conventions and genre conventions. Book conventions include the ways in which books "work": the meaning of the cover, the title page, and the sequence of the pages; the process of turning pages; and the use of speech balloons to indicate what a character is saying are all examples of conventions that children must learn, and part of their literary compe-

tence. Culler's concern is with genre conventions: with the norms and expectations surrounding particular types of literature, like realistic novels or
folk tales. In talking about genre conventions, Cochran-Smith employs Jauss's
concept of the "horizon of expectations" that is adopted by readers when
they pick up a book of a certain type. When we read a folk tale, for example,
our horizon of expectations will lead us to assume that the plot will begin
very quickly, with little character-building or establishment of a setting; that
the protagonist may receive help in the form of magical aid from some super-
natural being; that the story will resolve happily; and so on. This horizon of
expectations has been built up over the many years that the folk tale has been
told or written. Young children's experience with all genres is limited, and
Cochran-Smith found that the story reader helped them to begin to build a
horizon of expectations for the different genres of stories that were used for
readaloud time. Cochran-Smith's work demonstrates that hearing stories read
aloud may be the very crucible in which children's literary awareness is forged,
and that literary theory may allow the development of exciting new perspectives in this vitally important area.

In concluding this first section of the book, I have summarized theory
and research concerned specifically with picturebooks, the principal form in
which young children experience literature. I have also explicated a multifaceted view of young children's literary understanding, based on many theories from a variety of disciplines, and noted that most research on child
response to literature has utilized relatively few theories. Thus, this first section lays the foundation for my own grounded theory of literary understanding, which will be presented in Part II.

PART II

Five Aspects of Literary Understanding and Their Interrelationships

In this part of the book, I describe five types of response children made while they listened to the picture storybooks their teachers were reading aloud; these types of response arose, as conceptual categories, from my analysis of all the children's talk in the transcripts. I understand these five types of response as distinct aspects of their evolving literary understanding. The five kinds of response are:

- Analytical
- Intertextual
- Personal
- Transparent
- Performative

In the case of Analytical response, a large amount of the data fell into this category, so I further subdivided it into five subcategories. Chapter 4 deals with the first of these subcategories (1A), Making Narrative Meaning. In chapter 5, I turn to the other subcategories of Analytical responses. In chapters 6 and 7, I write about Intertextual and Personal responses, respectively. In chapter 8, I deal with the last two aspects of literary understanding, the Transparent and Performative. Finally, in chapter 9, I relate the five facets or aspects of literary understanding to one another to present a grounded theory of young children's literary meaning-making. In the course of the presentation of the theory, I also place it in relation to other theoretical perspectives on literary understanding, building on the foundation established in Part I.

4

Introducing the Categories of Response and the First Type of Analytical Response

In this chapter, I first offer an overview of the five major conceptual categories of children's responses, which suggest five types or aspects of literary understanding. After the overview, I turn to the first conceptual category, Analytical Response, which is further subdivided into five subcategories because of its complexity and importance. The rest of the chapter is devoted to the first of these five subcategories of the Analytical: Making Narrative Meaning.

THE CATEGORIES OF CHILDREN'S RESPONSES

Category 1: The Analytical

This category includes all responses that seem to be dealing with the text as an opportunity to construct narrative meaning. Children made comments that reflected an analytical stance. For example, they discussed the structure and meaning of the verbal text; the illustration sequence; the ways in which the verbal text and pictures related to each other; conventional visual semiotic codes; and the traditional elements of narrative (setting, characters, plot, and theme), as well as narrative techniques such as foreshadowing and the manipulation of narrative time. Also included in this category were responses that addressed the book as a made object or cultural product, analysis of the specific language used in the story, analysis of illustrations' design and semiotic significance, and the relationship between fiction and reality. This category was by far the largest, comprising approximately 73% of the children's conversational turns in the coded data.

Category 2: The Intertextual

This category reflected the children's abilities to relate the text being read aloud to other cultural texts and products: other books, the work of other artists and illustrators, movies, videos, advertisements, TV programs, or the writing or art of classmates. In this category, the text seemed to be viewed in relation to other texts, serving as an element in the matrix of interrelated cultural texts. This category comprised approximately 10% of the children's conversational turns in the coded data.

Category 3: The Personal

In this category, children connect the text to their own personal lives. There were two directions to these responses: from their lives to the text, and from the text to their own lives. A life-to-text connection was one in which the children utilized some experience from their own lives to understand or illuminate the text being read aloud. A text-to-life connection was one in which the children used the text in order to understand or illuminate something in their own lives. In addition to life-to-text and text-to-life connections, there were several other ways in which the children personalized stories. The responses in this category were thus essentially personal in nature, and the text seemed to act as a stimulus for a personal connection. This category comprised approximately 10% of the children's conversational turns in the coded data.

Category 4: The Transparent

Category 4 includes responses suggesting that the children had entered the narrative world of the story and had become one with it. The world of the text, for the moment, seemed to be identical with and transparent to the children's world. Verbal responses in this category were rare, providing only tantalizing glimpses of what was probably happening inside the children's minds. This category comprised only approximately 2% of the children's conversational turns in the coded data.

Category 5: The Performative

In this category, children's responses indicate that they are entering the world of the text in order to manipulate or steer it toward their own purposes. In Category 4, the children were, so to speak, manipulated by the text; in Category 5, responses suggested that the text was being manipulated by the children. The text seemed to function as a platform for the children's own creativity or imagination, or the text became a playground for what I called a "carnivalesque romp." The children took some situation or event in the book and used it as the basis for a flight of their own imagination, a type of playful performance or "signifying" (Gates, 1988). This category comprised approximately 5% of the children's conversational turns in the coded data.

Taken together, these five categories and the patterns of their interrelationships describe what constituted literary understanding for children as suggested by their verbal responses: what they (and their teachers) had constructed as the appropriate ways of displaying literary competence. The children analyzed the text; linked the text with other texts and cultural products; formed relationships between the text and their own lives; entered the world of the text and allowed it (momentarily) to become their world; and used the text as a platform for their own creativity.

EXAMPLES OF THE FIVE CONCEPTUAL CATEGORIES

The following lengthy vignette is an excerpt from the transcript of the read-aloud of *Amazing Grace* (Hoffman, 1991) in Ms. Bigler-McCarthy's first- and second-grade class. This excerpt was chosen because it provides examples of each of the five categories of the children's talk within a small number of conversational turns. *Amazing Grace* is the story of an African American girl who wants to be Peter Pan in her school play. Some of her classmates discourage her, claiming that she can't be Peter Pan because she is a girl, and because she is black. Grace's grandmother, however, takes Grace to the ballet to see an African American ballerina dance the lead role in *Romeo and Juliet*. Grace, heartened by this experience, auditions for the part of Peter Pan and is chosen to play this lead role.

The text of the book (which the teacher reads) is in **bold** font, the category of each response is indicated by the numbers in brackets, and the conversational turns are numbered consecutively, beginning with 100, for easy reference as I interpret them following the transcription. The term "opening" indicates that a page has been turned, and refers to the sequence of double-page spreads, with the "first opening" designated as the double spread on which the text of the story begins. (This designation is necessary because the pages in picturebooks are rarely numbered.) The underlined opening designation includes a description of the illustrations for that double-page spread. A question mark indicates that I could not tell who was speaking. (For a complete description of all the transcription conventions, refer to Appendix C.) Julie, Sally, Gordon, and Terry are the child participants. Charles, the fifth child in this small group, was absent for this readaloud.

Tenth opening—right-hand page shows Grace in eight different
    dancing poses (an example of what Joseph Schwarcz [1982] calls
    "continuous narration")
100   TEACHER: [reading; text of story in bold font] **After the ballet Grace played the part of Juliet, dancing around her room in her imaginary tutu. I can be anything I want, she thought.**

101 [4] GORDON: Oh yeah, yeah, right [sarcastically, under his breath]
102 [3] JULIE: My sister used to do that—ballet.
103 [5] TERRY: Ballet, ballet! [singing and moving his body to and fro]
104 TEACHER: Why do you suppose there are so many pictures of Grace?
105 [1] SALLY: Because they want to:
106 [1] JULIE: She's practicing all of her moves:
107 [1] SALLY: They want to show how she moves.
108 [1] GORDON: This one's the same as this one [pointing to one picture at the top of the page and one at the bottom]. Oh, no, not exactly.
109 TEACHER: Similar, yeah.

Eleventh opening—illustration shows Grace dancing while her classmates watch

On Monday the class met for auditions to choose who was best for each part. When it was Grace's turn to be Peter, she knew exactly what to do and all the words to say—she had been Peter Pan all weekend. She took a deep breath and imagined herself flying. When it was time to vote, the class chose Raj to be Captain Hook and Natalie to be Wendy. There was no doubt who would be Peter Pan. Everyone voted for Grace. "You were fantastic!" whispered Natalie.

110 [5] GORDON: "Grace, oh Grace, you were great!" [high falsetto voice]
111 [3] TERRY: I've got a secret to tell you, [teacher], but don't tell anybody else. [Speaking in a low voice] I like to play ballet at home.
112 TEACHER: Oh, that's nice, ballet is fun.

Twelfth opening; left-hand illustration shows Grace as Peter Pan, dancing in a pale green costume, while the right-hand illustration shows the faces of Grace, her mother, and her grandmother

113 [2] SALLY: That doesn't look like any Peter Pan I've seen.
114 [2] TERRY: Yeah, it looks like the Joker.
115 TEACHER: **The play was a big success and Grace was an amazing Peter Pan. After it was all over, she said, "I feel as if I could fly all the way home!"**
116 [5] ?: [high whistling sound in a falling pitch, like an airplane]
117 [1] GORDON: [frustrated] Why don't they put arrows on who's Nana and who's not?

118 [1] SALLY: You don't need to, because Mama looks younger, and Nana's older [pointing to right and then left figure above Grace]

119 TEACHER: Do you think that the kids in the classroom changed their minds about who could be Peter Pan?

120 [5] TERRY: Yeah, I want to be Peter Pan, pleeeease!

121 [1] SALLY: Because Grace put her mind to it, I guess, and she, and she got chosen.

This vignette was chosen because all five types of child response were represented over the course of the discussion of these three openings. The following sections elucidate each type of response in turn, with line references to specific instances of the children's talk.

1: Analytical Responses

At 105, 106, 107, 108, 117, 118, and 121, the children are focused in various ways within the text, intent on analyzing and interpreting it. At 105, 106, and 107, the responses of Sally and Julie are answers to the teacher's question about the multiple images of Grace on the page. Sally and Julie are interpreting these images as indications of Grace's movements as she dances. At 108, Gordon questions whether two of the images are identical, deciding that they are slightly different. He is responding to the meaning of details in the illustration. At 117 and 118, Gordon and Sally have a conversational exchange that identifies characters in the illustration. At 121, Sally makes a generalizing or quasi-thematic statement that summarizes a great deal of the story: Grace "put her mind to it," and achieved her goal. All of these responses are examples of Category 1, the Analytical, and most function primarily to make narrative meaning from the words and pictures. All are focused within the text and interpretive in intent.

2: Intertextual Responses

At 113 and 114, Sally and Terry make implicit comparisons between the image of Grace as Peter Pan and other cultural products. Although it is not clear whether Sally is referring to a movie, a play, or other illustrated books, she is obviously making a comparison with several other texts, in the broad sense of that word. Terry's intertextual link is a bit more explicit; later in the transcript, he repeats his observation that Grace looks like the Joker, adding "I hate Batman." So we know that this link is to the appearance of the character of the Joker in the television or movie version of *Batman*, or possibly a comic book. These two responses are examples of Category 2, the Intertextual.

3: Personal Responses

At 102 and 111, Julie and Terry make connections between the text and their own lives. Julie remembers that her sister had studied ballet, and Terry shyly reveals that he likes to pretend to be a ballet dancer at home. These responses are examples of Category 3, the Personal.

4: Transparent Responses

At 101, Gordon's comment ("Oh, yeah, yeah") suggests that he is in the world of the text, and that he is talking back to it. Grace has just thought, "I can be anything I want," and Gordon replies pessimistically. The fact that he speaks under his breath suggests that this is an automatic response that is not intended for an audience. It is an example of a response that was coded as Category 4, the Transparent. For the moment, Gordon's world and the world of the text are identical. Another way of conceptualizing this is to use the metaphor of transparency: Gordon has mapped or transposed his world on the world of the text, and made his world transparent to the text world.

5: Performative Responses

At 103, 110, 116, and 120, Terry's and Gordon's responses are examples of Category 5, the Performative. They are using the text as a platform for their own expressive creativity. Terry's singing response at 103 ("Ballet, ballet!"), while swaying his body back and forth, is a miniature *sprezzatura* performance. At 110, Gordon takes on the role of the story character Natalie, speaking in the high falsetto voice in which boys often imitate girls. At 116, a child I could not identify provides sound effects for Grace's exuberant feeling that she could "fly all the way home." At 120, Terry comically inserts himself into the story, pleading, "I want to be Peter Pan, pleeeease." These responses, in various ways, manipulate the story and use it as a springboard for a performance. Thus, this excerpt provides examples of each of the five categories of children's talk during storybook readalouds.

ANALYTICAL RESPONSE 1A: MAKING NARRATIVE MEANING

In this first subcategory of the Analytical response, children made extensive use of the traditional elements of narrative: setting, plot, characters, and theme. The children described, evaluated, speculated, or made inferences about the actions or characters or other plot events; predicted the plot of the story; or provided alternative suggestions for the plot. They made comments about the structure of the story, comments that involved several incidents or episodes, and also made thematic or quasi-thematic statements about the story. They questioned the text in an effort to understand what was happening in the narrative. They described or wondered about the *external* character-istics of characters: their appearance, location, identity, or their relationships with each other. The children also described or wondered about the *internal* characteristics of characters: their feelings, thoughts, personalities, or capa-bilities. They also speculated on what characters could have or should have said or done in the story. They used the illustrations to interpret the verbal text of the story, and the verbal text of the story to interpret the illustra-tions. The children made summarizing or quasi-thematic statements about the story, demonstrating their ability to understand the story as a whole, not just a collection of details. They employed specific pieces of their general background knowledge for interpretive purposes; attempted to interpret events or objects symbolically; and made general evaluative comments about the story. They grappled with the way in which the narrative of the story was different from (or similar to) the real passage of time. The responses in this subcategory comprised over half of the responses in Category 1: literary analysis was clearly of prime importance in the children's developing liter-ary understanding. This subcategory is complex, representing a variety of ways in which the children made narrative meaning.

Peritextual Analysis

In traditional novels for adults, the text itself is the only important thing, and readers usually consider other physical aspects of the book—its size and shape, the cover, front matter, and title page, for example—as relatively unmeaningful necessities that can be skipped in order to get to the "real book": the author's words. Genette (1997) and other critics have referred to all of these peripheral features of a book—everything other than the words of the text—as the peritext, explained in chapter 1. The use of "peritext" in this study refers to any part of a picture storybook *other than* the sequence of double-page spreads that contain the verbal text of the story and the ac-companying illustrations. Any print or illustrations on the front and back covers; dust jacket, including the end flaps; endpages; half-title and title pages; and dedication page are all included in this designation.

The children considered the peritext just as much of a source of poten-tial meaning as the verbal text of the story. This may have been the result of the teachers' actions in sharing a book: they never omitted giving the chil-dren the time and the opportunity to consider all of a book's peritextual fea-tures. As a result, parts of a picturebook that might have been passed over by less astute adults were scrutinized and interpreted very carefully by the children. Brad's comment about the endpages of *The Three Little Pigs* (Marshall, 1989) functioning as the stage curtains for a play has been mentioned in the Introduction to this book; it is a prime example of a sophisticated interpretation of a peritextual feature. In semiotic terms, Brad interpreted the endpages as a sign: as possessing the potential for meaning in relation to other signs. Brad's interpretation was confirmed as a possibility after the reading of the book was completed and the teacher showed the class the back cover, which depicts the backs of the three pigs, onstage again. In subsequent readalouds, the teacher adopted Brad's terminology, frequently saying, "The curtains are closed; we're waiting for the play to start" as she showed the front endpages; when she reached the end of the book, she showed the back endpages, remarking, "So the curtains close, and the play is over."

Children often made predictions about the plot, characters, setting, tone, and theme of the picturebook by peritextual analysis. This was especially true in Mrs. Martin's class, where she began each readaloud with a close examination of the front and back covers and endpapers, inviting the children to predict what the story would be about. Prediction concerned both the literary genre to which the picturebook belonged as well as specific actions in the plot. In *The Adventures of Sparrowboy* (Pinkney, 1997), several children noted that the title on the cover looked "like a comic," and Katrin proclaimed, "He's a superhero!" Kevin made an even more precise connection: "Superman's name is like that." Certainly, the thick block letters arranged in a slight curve on the front cover do suggest a connection to comics, specifically to Superman. Thus, from the front cover alone, the children were able to place this story in the literary subgenre of a superhero comic story. This interpretation was confirmed when the children saw the layout of the illustrations as comic book "cells" (McCloud, 1994) and the use of comic book terminology, such as "ZAP!"

During the reading of *Wings* (Myers, 2000), Mrs. Martin showed the front and back covers to the children, and they made the following predictions based on this visual and verbal information:

100   BELLA: I think it's about when some people, he was flying away.
101   JOE: I think people don't like him and then he flies away.
102   NAISHA: He's trying to fly, he's trying to fly from his mommy and daddy.
103   AMANDA: It's about a little boy and he's flying somewhere so he could be with an angel.
104   MARTIN: I think, um, um, he is flying away to, um, mom and dad.

105   TEACHER [showing back cover]: And on the back it just is
        another little hint about the story. It says, **Let your spirit soar.**
106   ?: Let your spirit soar, my soul . . . let your spirit fill my soul!

At 100, Bella predicts that the boy "was flying away," and at 101, Joe
amplifies on this, commenting that it's because "people don't like him" that
he is flying away. This is actually quite a prescient comment on Joe's part:
Ikarus Jackson, the boy with wings, is rejected or insulted by many children
during the course of the story. Naisha (102) and Martin (104) make opposite predictions: either the boy is flying *away* from his "mommy and daddy"
or he is flying *to* them. Amanda (103) connects flying and wings with being
an angel, which injects some spiritual significance into the discussion. When
the teacher shows the back cover (105) with its prominent words, "Let your
spirit soar," a child I unfortunately could not identify (106) makes another
spiritual connection, possibly to a hymn. In this passage, the children are
already making some important observations about the theme of the story:
it will, indeed, be about being rejected, as Joe observes, and it will be about
how not to allow being different to harm one's soul.

In Ms. Bigler-McCarthy's class, Gordon was a child who was particularly intrigued with the semiotic significance of endpapers (termed "endpages"
in this class). He assumed that there was always a reason for the choice of
their color or design. During my one-to-one readaloud of *Changes* (Browne,
1990) with him, Gordon wondered about the endpapers, which are painted
a light tan with small darker brown spots.

GORDON: Hmm. I wonder if they chose different kind of endpages. I
        wonder why they did choose this. Wait, let's look through the
        book, we might notice something like this. [he pages through the
        book, coming to an illustration of a wall that is a similar color]
        That's sort of the same texture here.
TEACHER: Yeah, it is, sort of.
GORDON: Maybe it is the same, but only. Maybe the walls are the
        same. [turns back to the endpages]
TEACHER: So the endpages represent, maybe, the walls?
GORDON: Maybe. Dots on 'em. Probably you can't just see that
        stuff. All the little dots and scratches. All the little dots, rock, in
        the wall. Or the ground. It makes you feel like you're on the
        ground, or something.

Discussion about the peritext also seemed to enable the understanding
of structure and form in stories. After the reading of *The Napping House*

(Wood, 1984), Kristin pointed out that unlike most picturebooks, the front endpages were different from the back endpages. In fact, the front endpages of this book (a dark blue-gray) contrast markedly with the back endpages (which are azure blue). The following discussion ensued:

> SALLY: That makes sense, because it's dark when the story starts, so there's a darker endpage, and it's lighter when the story ends. So the endpage is lighter, back there.
>
> GORDON: Yeah, that makes sense! Darker, then lighter. That's different, like most books, the endpages're the same on the front and the back.
>
> TEACHER: Yes, that's very interesting, it is one of the few books I've seen where the endpages are different at the beginning and the end, and it's certainly a good choice the illustrator made. Brad?
>
> BRAD: The flea is the alarm clock in this story!
>
> ??: Yeah, it is!
>
> TEACHER: What an interesting idea, Brad. Tell me more.
>
> BRAD: Well, the flea wakes 'em all up, they're all sleeping, and the flea's their alarm clock because he wakes 'em up.
>
> ?: Brrrriiiiing! [imitating alarm clock] Time to wake up, all you guys!

In this excerpt, Sally and Gordon made structural comments about the story based on the information provided by the peritext. It may also be that Brad's generalizing statement (that the flea acted as the alarm clock in the story) was triggered by this discussion. Structural information is information that lets children think about the story as a whole rather than as separate, specific parts. This may have sparked Brad's thinking in general terms about the story as well, and stimulated his comment about the flea. Brad's statement, in turn, seems to have stimulated the amusing response that closes the excerpt.

In Mrs. Martin's kindergarten class, the children were also exposed to a picturebook where the front and back endpapers are different: *Come On, Rain!*, Karen Hesse's (1999) story about the stifling heat of the city during the height of summer, and the shower of rain that cools everything off. The front endpapers of this picturebook are bright red, and the back endpapers are a soothing blue. After she read the title page, Mrs. Martin opened the book and showed the children the red endpapers:

> 100   TEACHER: Why do you think it's red? I don't know why it's red, I'm just asking you what you think.
>
> 101   ANTOINE: 'Cause I like that color.
>
> 102   ?: Little Red Riding Hood! Because of Little Red Riding Hood!

103   TEACHER: Oh, maybe Little Red Riding Hood is going to be in
      here; we've been reading a lot of *Little Red Riding Hood*s
104   TERRELL: Because of the paint [the title on the front cover
      appears painted in red].
105   TEACHER: Oh, because the title is red and you think it just
      goes nicely with it? I was just thinking that to myself. Maybe
      that's the reason. Let's read.

Mrs. Martin then read the first opening of the story, which describes
the "endless heat" and describes the protagonist's mother: "Mama lifts a
listless vine and sighs. 'Three weeks and not a drop,' she says, sagging over
her parched plants." Amanda then had an idea:

106   AMANDA: Um, I know why the endpages are red. Because it's
      hot and then at the last end pages, they gonna be blue because it
      rains!
107   TEACHER: Oh! They're gonna be blue at the end, because it
      rains! Oops! Maybe! That was a real good thought. . . . Let's see.

At the end of the story, Mrs. Martin showed the back endpages:

108   TEACHER: And here we see . . .
109   MANY CHILDREN: Blue endpages! Yay! [applause]

From 100 to 105, Mrs. Martin entertains several possible interpretations about the choice of red for the color of the front endpapers. After the
first opening has been read, Amanda (106) offers another interpretation,
associating red with the stifling heat and (perhaps) blue with rain; the teacher
acknowledges this idea (107). When she reaches the end of the story, after
the rain has cooled everything off, Mrs. Martin (108) turns to the back endpapers, and the children express their delight (109). As in *The Napping House*,
the different colors for the front and back endpapers—an important part of
the peritext—indicate the general sweep of the narrative (from darkness to
light in *The Napping House*, and from heat to coolness in *Come On, Rain!*).
      In addition to setting the tone or mood of a story, plain-colored end-
papers can also refer more specifically to elements of the story, such as particular characters or events in the plot. Such an interpretation was made by
Mrs. Martin's class when they responded to *In the Rainfield, Who Is the
Greatest?* (Olaleye, 2000), an African folk tale in which human figures representing Wind, Fire, and Rain hold a contest to see who has the most power.
On the front cover and throughout the story, Wind and Fire are represented
as men, whereas Rain is represented as a woman with lavender skin. At the

end of the story, when Rain triumphs, the children discussed the significance of the lavender endpapers, with Donna suggesting, "Maybe cause the lady [the illustrator, Ann Grifalconi] liked the color purple and she put it on there because Rain was the best girl." Here, Donna insightfully connects Rain's victory to the prominent place given to the lavender color in the endpapers. She understands that the endpapers gesture toward the answer to the question posed in the title of the book. In another readaloud, *Wilhe'mina Miles: After the Stork Night* (Carter, 1999), Mrs. Martin showed the dark purple endpages, and the children interpreted their significance:

> AALIYAH: Because the, um, on the front cover that was a purplish-blue. That's the sky.
> JOE: Um, this is dark and that's dark.
> AALIYAH: Because it happens at nighttime.
> TEACHER: Right, a lot of this story takes place at night.

Some picturebooks use the peritext to begin the narrative. In Steven Kellogg's (1991) version of *Jack and the Beanstalk*, for example, the front endpages show the giant, having descended from his sky-castle in a tornado, stealing gold, the singing harp, and the hen that lays the golden eggs from a pirate ship. The title page continues the story, depicting the giant's return to his castle via tornado; the sinking pirate ship; and our first sight of Jack, who is looking at a procession of a king and queen and their retainers on horseback. On the dedication page, Jack is shown offering a bunch of flowers to the daughter of the king and queen, the princess he will marry at the end of the story. Thus, the peritext of this book supplies a great deal of background information and preliminary narrative before the verbal text begins. All of these details were noted by the children. Robert noticed that "the story shows how the giant got the gold." Don said, "First the giant steals the gold from the pirates, and then, Jack steals the gold from the giant."

Also present on the endpages, title page, and dedication page of Kellogg's *Jack and the Beanstalk* are images of a hot-air balloon with a bearded man in a star-studded robe. This man is also depicted on the first and second openings. On the first opening (the beginning of the verbal text), the man holds a book in which he is painting. The arrangement of golden blocks on this small book is identical with the arrangement of the large golden text blocks on the opened book we hold in our hands. The implication is that this wizard is writing the story. On the second opening, the wizard is depicted as the one who sells the magical beans to Jack. It was not until the teacher had completed reading the story that Don discovered the meaning of this figure, and the part played by him in the story:

Hey, that guy is writing the book! This [pointing to the golden rectangular block on the left-hand page of the book the wizard is holding] is this [pointing to the rectangular block on the left-hand page of the book itself]. And this [pointing to the square block on the right-hand page of the book the wizard is holding] is this [pointing to the square block on the right-hand page of the book itself]! He's probably an artist, maybe a magician, too!

Don then turned to the end of the book, pointing out that the wizard was also depicted on the back endpages: "He's here again at the end. And the book says 'finished.' [The small book the wizard is holding has the word 'finis.'] He made the book. He's the magician, the guy who made the whole entire book!" Then he made another discovery. Excitedly turning to the second opening, Don pointed out the wizard again, commenting, "Hey, he's *also* the guy who sold the beans to Jack!" Don's series of discoveries demonstrates the potential of the peritext in refining and extending the children's understanding about the narrative. It also demonstrates the way in which illustrations alone can carry the story line, and children's understanding of this concept.

Other peritextual features of picturebooks include moveable parts (through tabs, pullouts, and pop-ups), lights, or sound. The latter two features are accomplished through the use of computer chips. In Eric Carle's (1995) *The Very Lonely Firefly*, the solitary firefly finds a group of friends at the end of the story. As the reader turns to the last page, a microchip is activated, and the fireflies' many yellow lights literally begin to flash. During one of the small-group readalouds of the book, Ms. Bigler-McCarthy's children were delighted by this surprise:

TRUDY: It's like they're playing music. It's like music you can see.
KENNY: A musical firefly chorus!

Although there was no audible music, Trudy perceived the flashing lights as "like music you can see," interpreting one sign system in terms of another. Kenny's comment, "A musical firefly chorus!" also interprets the visual experience of the many fireflies in terms of a musical group: the fireflies flash their lights together, just as a group of people might produce the sound of music with one another. We can only marvel at these children's sensitive and poetic interpretations of these peritextual features.

Structural Analysis

Structural comments by the children indicated that they could step back from the particular episode or illustration that was being discussed at the time and adopt a more inclusive perspective. The common element of threes in fairy and folk tales is an example of a structural feature that was familiar to the children. This feature was so familiar to Kenny (one of Ms. Bigler-McCarthy's first-graders) that he insisted that his own written story (which adapted *The Three Billy Goats Gruff*) conform to the pattern in even minor details. As he wrote about the "snapping" bridge that the goats crossed, he commented, "We have to put in three 'snaps' because it's a folk tale." During the reading of James Marshall's (1988) version of *Goldilocks and the Three Bears*, Sean noted that the illustrator had included many patterns of three, including three toy blocks for Baby Bear. During the readaloud of *The Three Bears* (Galdone, 1985), Gordon stated that "It keeps on repeating itself after a few pages. The print copies itself." During a rereading of *The Napping House* (Wood, 1984), the children made several general statements about the structure of this book, which is a cumulative tale. They noticed that "it gets smaller and smaller" because each of the successive characters is smaller than the one before, but also that each page contains "more and more" text. An unidentified child summarized, "The words go from small to big, and the animals go from big to small."

The children invested a great deal of energy in piecing together the actions of the plot and in understanding the cause-and-effect relationships involved. During the reading of Hyman's (1983) version of *Little Red Riding Hood*, the teacher suggested that the wolf wanted Red Riding Hood for supper. Krissy agreed, commenting, "'cause he was so hungry," but disagreed about the meal: "No, *breakfast*, 'cause they just woke up." In this case, Krissy was correct; in this version of the story, Red Riding Hood's mother sends her on her way "early in the morning," and the clock in Grandmother's house indicates that the wolf is caught and killed well before noon.

A good example of the children's use of prediction is Charles's comment after the children noticed that a black cat is following Red Riding Hood or appears close by her in all the illustrations: "The cat must be there, whenever, the cat, whenever Red Riding Hood's at the house, and like the wolf, eats the grandma, that cat'll go on back and say *Meowww* to her mom, and her mom call hunter, to the hunter." Charles predicts that the cat will be involved in the rescue of Red Riding Hood and her grandmother; this is indeed the case in this version of the story, although the cat meows to the hunter directly, rather than going back to Red Riding Hood's mother. What is especially interesting about these comments is that they are based solely on the illustration sequence: the words of the story mention nothing at all about a cat.

The children also made alternative suggestions for the plot. At the point in the *Red Riding Hood* story when Red Riding Hood first speaks to the wolf in the forest, Sally felt that "She should have ignored him." Gordon disagreed, feeling that this strategy would not have worked:

GORDON: No, he wants answers.

CHARLES: He'd probably say, "Answer me, or I'll chop you to bits."

Chains of Speculative Hypotheses

These structural and predictive comments at times turned into much longer sequences. The children's speculations about characters' thoughts, feelings, and actions or other events of the narrative were characterized by the persistent generation of hypotheses, which either predicted what might happen or attempted to explain something that already had occurred. The discussion often formed a series of comments in which the hypotheses built on and refined each other. These hypotheses could sometimes be confirmed by the story; mostly, however, they represented gaps in the text and illustrations upon which the children could only speculate.

In Mrs. Martin's class, there was a lengthy discussion (and many predictive hypotheses) during the readaloud of James Marshall's *Red Riding Hood* (1987) about Red Riding Hood's possible responses to the sly wolf's invitation, "Good afternoon, my dear . . . Care to stop for a little chat?":

100   NAISHA: She's gonna say no.

101   LAMAR: 'Cause her mom said don't talk to strangers.

102   YASMIN: 'Cause her mom's gonna give her a whoopin'.

103   TEACHER: What do you think; is she going to stop and talk to the wolf?

104   AALIYAH: Yes.

105   AMANDA: I think she is definitely going to do it.

106   TEACHER: Let's see what she does. [reading] **"Oh gracious me," said Red Riding Hood. "Mamma said not to speak to any strangers"**

107   BELLA: *He's* a stranger.

108   KEVIN: He's an enemy!

109   AALIYAH: And her mom said don't hang around with strangers.

Several themes emerge in this discussion, which actually went on for quite a while longer. First, the children point out that Red Riding Hood's mother told her specifically not to talk to strangers, and the wolf is a stranger, even an enemy (101, 107, 108, 109). Yasmin (102) points out the consequences of disobeying her mother. Some children don't believe that Red Riding Hood will talk to the wolf (100); others think that she will (104, 105).

During the small-group readaloud of *Bad Day at Riverbend* (Van Allsburg, 1995), the children generated a chain of descriptive, explanatory hypotheses about the "slime" that covers more and more of the environment in the book. The illustrations in this clever and self-referential picturebook resemble those in a coloring book; they consist of black outlines printed on off-white paper. During the course of the book, the inhabitants of the frontier town of Riverbend are tormented by the appearance of what is described as "shiny, greasy slime" of various colors, which is printed over the black-and-white drawings. The ending of the book suggests that this slime is actually the scribbled crayon coloring done by Van Allsburg's little girl Sophia, to whom the book is dedicated, and who appears in a photograph with her father on the back of the book's dust jacket. As the reading of the book progressed, the children generated no fewer than 13 related hypotheses about the nature and effects of the slime; these hypotheses are extracted and listed here in the order of their appearance:

1   KRISSY: I wonder why the author choosed to scribble. And I just see that he kind of went out of the lines. It looks like it has marker on it.

2   KENNY: They wanted to show you what it looks like if you scribble.

3   BRAD: Um, maybe some, maybe like a wild [thing] attached to them or something.

4   KRISSY: I think it could be like, if there was, it could be like, um, like those sticky, those sticky and slippery sticks, and they get sticky on your hands, and stuff. They're sort of like all kinds of colors, and then they get mixed up on people and stuff.

5   JIM: Maybe it's sticky slime, like, like it gets stuck on them.

6   KENNY: It's slime, I know it, because it said.

7   KRISSY: Oh, I know what this could be! It could be like somebody, somebody, like attacked, the coach, and after that, maybe they attached [sic] it, they attached [sic] the horse, and tried to get the world destroyed.

8   KENNY: It's because maybe they fell on the sticky stuff on the ground, because it's on the ground.

9   JIM: Maybe it's the rainbow. It could have been the rainbow, kind of hit him, and then colors came out.

10 KENNY: Maybe the sunlight spits out the stuff, like it spits out, like spits, and then it gets on, gets on the person.

11 TRUDY: Maybe it's water, and the water turns to colors.

12 KRISSY: Maybe the sun got really sweaty, the sun got sweaty, really hot, and then maybe there was this, there was this rainbow that came, and had these strings, and after that, after that, um, maybe the sweaty stuff came down off the sun, and maybe it got mixed up with the stringy stuff, and turned into colors.

13 KENNY: Maybe the sun, like the rainbow was out, and then the sunlight hit it, the rainbow, and it, like the colors melted on them.

Here we see the children engaged quite intensely in constructing a chain of speculative reasoning that eventually grows to the point of articulating a scientific theory involving sunlight, water, and the rainbow (lines 10–13). They engaged in the process of assimilation to and accommodation of each other's theories. They readily abandoned this carefully erected edifice when they saw the last page of the book, with its illustration of a little girl and crayons. This was a case in which the information in the text provided at least a partial disconfirmation of their reasoning.

Another series of speculative hypotheses was provoked by Mickey, during the readaloud of *Cinderella* (Galdone, 1978), at the point in the story where the prince sends his courtiers to find the owner of the slipper that has been left behind by his beautiful dance partner. Mickey asked, "Why doesn't the slipper disappear?" Why, indeed? Presumably the slipper was part of all the magically produced clothing and accoutrements, which the fairy godmother had warned would disappear at midnight. Why shouldn't the slipper disappear along with everything else? This question represents what Iser (1978) would call a gap or indeterminacy in a text: the text does not tell us, and the illustrations do not help us, either. On this occasion, the children tenaciously generated no less than 10 hypotheses. Some children thought it had to do with the size of the slipper; maybe it was too small to be affected by the magic. Others suggested that the material—glass—had something to do with its permanence. One particularly intriguing hypothesis might be called the "Energizer Bunny" theory: maybe the fairy godmother's magic wand ran out of power! Several children built on the idea that the fairy godmother's intention had something to do with it, eventually arriving at the conclusion that the godmother had planned all along that Cinderella would marry the prince, and that therefore the slipper had to remain in order to provide a way of identifying her. These hypotheses could be neither confirmed nor disconfirmed by the text, but the speculation was considered meaningful in its own right.

Both these examples of hypothesis generation arose from questions formulated by the children. Both examples also indicate the impressive amount of interpretive energy the children were willing to expend in answering these questions.

Analysis of Storybook Characters

Another important aspect of making narrative meaning involves the analysis of storybook characters' actions, feelings, thoughts, intentions, and the ways their external appearance may give us information about these elements. In the *Poetics*, Aristotle (1997) calls "plot" the "imitation of human beings-in-action," so plot and character are inextricably connected; by devoting a separate section to children's interpretations of storybook characters, I do not mean to imply that these interpretations functioned in isolation, but rather to highlight the importance of analysis of character in literary understanding.

Details in facial expression fill in aspects of the story often omitted by the words, and allow for the uncovering of multiple layers of character development and plot. For example, the incredibly detailed illustrations in Maurice Sendak's *Outside Over There* (1981) add depth and richness to the sparse text. Sendak's first and second openings offer the book's first text: "When Papa was away at sea, . . . and Mama in the arbor . . ." The illustrations do far more than disclose location; the facial expression of the mother creates a window to her state of mind. Examining this illustration within the context of the words prompted the following discussion in Mrs. Martin's kindergarten class:

> TEACHER: How do you think Mama feels right now?
> JOE: Sad!
> TEACHER: Why do you think she's sad?
> JOE: Because she want to go on the boat!
> TEACHER: Because she wants to go on the boat with who?
> JOE: With Daddy!
> TEACHER: With the daddy, her husband, sure! Deshawn?
> DESHAWN: She's sad because she couldn't go because they are taking away her house.
> TEACHER: They're taking away her house? Okay. And I see the baby is crying—and there is the little girl holding her and Mama is looking very, very sad.
> VIOLET: She's sad because she thinks her man died!

This rich conversation emanated from a careful analysis of the illustrations in conjunction with the text. Mrs. Martin does not ask students where the parents are, but instead poses deeper questions about the character's feelings.

Mrs. Martin also encouraged children to speculate on what a character might be thinking. In a reading of *Where the Wild Things Are* (Sendak, 1963), when Max returns to his "very own room" after his adventure, the children made the following responses:

> AALIYAH: He's thinking!
> JOE: [He's thinking that] the wild things be outside!

NAISHA: Now he's hot and . . . he's hungry.
AMANDA: He's saying, "I've been out for so long . . . I'm ready for some chow!"

In the readaloud of *There's an Alligator under My Bed* (Mayer, 1987), Katrin speculated that the boy in the story was "dreaming" that there was an alligator under his bed. Later in the story, when the boy calls his mother and father to see the alligator, Mrs. Martin observed:

TEACHER: His mom looks a little annoyed. Why do you think she's annoyed?
AALIYAH: Because she don't see no alligator.
VIOLET: His mom thinks that there's not this alligator under the bed and there really is.
YASMIN: She thinks that he is lying.

This is an example of the children's ability to interpret a situation from two different characters' perspectives: the mother's and the boy's.

In Paul Galdone's version of *The Three Bears* (1985), Goldilocks is shown missing a tooth. When Ms. Bigler-McCarthy shared this book with her first/second-graders and asked her students to estimate Goldilocks's age by studying the illustration, Gordon answered, "Let's *make* her our age!" By incorporating this important detail of young children's lives, the illustrator allows for a bond to form between text and readers because of children's strengthened visual identification with the protagonist. This is one possible reason for Galdone's decision to depict Goldilocks with a missing tooth—to help readers identify with the character and be drawn into the imagined world of the story. By making Goldilocks about five or six years old, Galdone also gives the character innocence, setting her prior to society's "age of reason." Goldilocks then is not merely a spoiled girl who samples the property of others, but is instead endowed with a childlike innocence that excuses the self-centeredness of her actions.

A character's clothing or hairstyle can also help readers interpret personality and identify more closely with certain characters. In David Delamare's version of *Cinderella* (1993), there is an illustration of several dancing couples at the ball, but Cinderella is at the forefront and the only character looking directly at the reader. The other characters have elaborate, mannered hairstyles. By contrast, Cinderella wears a simple, more natural hairstyle. Also, Cinderella's ball gown is unpretentious and elegant, while the stepsisters' dresses have garish colors and patterns. This choice of clothing suggests the coarseness of their personalities, whereas Cinderella's attire suggests her gentle purity.

In Ms. Bigler-McCarthy's class, Joey, a first-grader, responded to the illustration of the ball by asking, "Why do they all have funky hair except Cinderella?" When the teacher asked the other children for their ideas about that question, Julie posited that perhaps it was the illustrator's intent for readers to identify with Cinderella: "Probably the illustrator wants me to like Cinderella—and the other people look stupid." The children understood that through his artistic choices in depicting clothing and hairstyle, the illustrator has made Cinderella look like a more contemporary young woman, thereby eliciting more sympathy from modern readers, whereas the illustration creates emotional distance between the stepsisters and readers.

Characters can also suggest the literary genre to which the story belongs. *Swamp Angel* (Isaacs, 1994) is a tall tale with a larger-than-life heroine. The framed cover art shows a couple at the bottom of the page looking upward; looming above them is a gigantic young woman, holding up the book's title with one hand and supporting the book's frame with the other. She is bent over to fit within the confines of the frame, and her upper back and the top of her head are not visible. This image prepares readers to predict the plot and to understand the nature of the story as a tall tale. The children in Ms. Bigler-McCarthy's class responded to the cover in this way:

CHARLES: She's too big for the picture!
JULIE: She's bent over; she's trying to get out!
TEACHER: This is one way the illustrator shows that this girl is very, very tall.

The grouping of characters also provides clues about how they relate to one another, as illustrated in the opening images of Beatrix Potter's *Peter Rabbit* (1902/1987). In her introduction of the rabbits, Potter portrays Mother Rabbit, Flopsy, Mopsy, and Cotton-tail clustered together in a solid mass. Peter, however, stands apart, facing away from his family. His placement in the illustration foreshadows the events of the story, contrasting Peter, who will shortly go exploring in Mr. McGregor's garden, with his obedient siblings. The detail was noticed by a first-grader in Ms. Bigler-McCarthy's class:

JUDY: Peter's turning away—he's already thinking about getting into trouble.
TEACHER: He's not paying attention to his mother like Flopsy, Mopsy, and Cotton-tail, is he?

Here, the position of the characters embodies the events of the text and allows the children to make predictions about Peter's personality and the action of the story. Judy's comment, which suggests her prior familiarity with the story, nevertheless interprets Peter's intentions from the very beginning of the tale.

Summarizing, Thematic, and Quasi-Thematic Statements

Mrs. Martin's kindergarten class made quasi-thematic statements most often in response to the teacher's invitation about the "message" the author wanted to convey. *In Something Beautiful* (Wyeth, 1998), for example, a little girl finds several things about her neighborhood that depress and sadden her, but she also finds many things that encourage her and cause her to feel happy to live there. At the end of the reading, Mrs. Martin specifically referred to what the girl had learned:

> TEACHER: Why do you think the author wrote this book? When somebody writes a book there's usually some kind of message in the story. What do you think she wanted to tell people who were reading this book?
> YASMIN: That you can like yourself!
> AMANDA: And that you have to love yourself.
> TEACHER: Yes, even if you live in a place where it's not beautiful outside, right?
> AMANDA: You can still love yourself.
> TEACHER: You can love yourself, and you can make your place beautiful.

In Ms. Bigler-McCarthy's class, Jim, a first-grader, made responses that were often characterized by a reflective and ruminative approach (he spoke rarely, but always insightfully) that used active listening to draw together many threads of the story and the discussion, as shown in his tendency to generalize and to make thematic or quasi-thematic statements. He often made summarizing statements that encapsulated much of the plot. For example, he generated more thematic and quasi-thematic statements than anyone else in the class. During a discussion concerning the choice of the author-illustrator of *Ira Sleeps Over* (Waber, 1972) to show a teddy bear in color (brown) on an otherwise black-and-white page, several children offered possible reasons, but only Jim's was related to the storyline as a whole:

> GORDON: 'Cause it's brown.
> JOEY: 'Cause probably the author did it, probably.
> TEACHER: Yeah, the author-illustrator did that.
> GORDON: 'Cause it's brown, it's supposed to be brown.
> JOEY: Because it's dark.

TEACHER: Jim, what do you think?

JIM: 'Cause everyone's talking about it and that's like what everything's about.

TEACHER: Ah, did you guys all hear that? Jim, would you say that really loud, again?

JIM: Everybody was talking about it, and the story's about it, the whole story's about the teddy bear.

It was characteristic of Jim that his response had to be encouraged by the teacher during this whole group readaloud; it was also characteristic that it indicated that he had thought about the whole story. This generalizing tendency or predilection to take a broad perspective was a constant pattern in Jim's responses. His feeling, in the small-group readaloud of *Fly Away Home* (Bunting, 1991), that an illustration of the bird was repeated on the back cover because "it was important to the boy" represents this tendency to put together details in the story so as to see their general significance. The reading of *Where the Wild Things Are* (Sendak, 1963), the whole-group readaloud during which he made the most responses, included a discussion of the increasing size of the illustrations as Max's fantasy grows in the first half of the book, and the decreasing size of the illustrations as Max returns home from his adventure with the Wild Things. The discussion proceeded as follows:

[Teacher shows the illustration sequence quickly, paging through the book]

KENNY: Bigger and bigger.

KRISSY: And then it's going to fill up the whole page [during the Wild Rumpus episode].

GORDON: 'Cause the trees are gettin' bigger and bigger and bigger.

TEACHER: Why do you think it's so small here, with all the white around [showing first opening] and here [showing sixth opening] is when Maurice Sendak chooses for the illustration to fill the whole page? What happens on this page? Bill?

BILL: Because most of it gets really small, and then, bigger and bigger, and that's because the trees are getting bigger.

JIM: Um, because some jungles are that big, and um, that's what the whole thing's about, 'cause it's where the wild things are, and, and that place is important, 'cause that's where the wild things are, and he wanted to get it bigger, so you could see more.

This comment was typical, in that Jim was concerned with "what the whole thing's about"—rather than being caught up in the details, he attempted to put these details together.

The details in *Changes*, one of Anthony Browne's (1990) most surreal picturebooks, are quite seductive. However, although Jim enjoyed all the transformations of furniture and other objects into animals, he did not lose sight of the main point of the book, which concerns the even greater changes that will be experienced by the main character of the story when his mother and father bring his new baby sister home from the hospital. Of the 10 children to whom I read this book, Jim was the only one to make a voluntary unsolicited quasi-thematic statement about it: "Mom gets pregnant, that's why things are going to change, 'cause he ain't gonna be the only kid now, in that house."

Summarizing statements were a specialty of Jim's. In Steven Kellogg's (1985) *Chicken Little*, Foxy Loxy dreams of all the wonderful meals he will have when he catches the feckless fowl. Foxy Loxy does not realize any of his culinary fantasies, however; he is caught and put in jail, and his diet is "green bean gruel and weed juice," which we see him pouring out of his cell window on the back cover of the book. Jim's incisive comment about the whole story was this: "All the things, he like really wished in his head, they didn't happen. And all the things he didn't wish, they happened."

Peggy, another first-grader in Ms. Bigler-McCarthy's first/second-grade class, was another child who specialized in quasi-thematic statements, which she displayed in the readaloud of *The Whales' Song* (Sheldon, 1990). This poetic, fanciful picturebook is about a young girl, Lilly, who is told by her grandmother that whales can "sing," and that once the grandmother heard them calling her name. Lilly's great-uncle Frederick thinks this is all hogwash, but Lilly goes down to the ocean's edge and waits. Great-uncle Frederick comes down to fetch her, grumping that she's wasting her time. However, that night she hears something that sounds like her name, and rushes down to the shore again. The whales are near shore, and are truly calling her name. As the children were discussing the ending, Peggy made a comment that summed up the story on a highly abstract level:

PEGGY: Can I share the secret?
TEACHER: Yeah, you can share what you think the secret is.
PEGGY: You should stand for what you believe in, because it might come true.
TEACHER: I think that's a really nice way to put it all together, Peggy.

The idea of a book's "secret" was not a common way of referring to a book's message or theme in Ms. Bigler-McCarthy's class, and it is interesting that Peggy used this word in the context of the discussion of *The Whales' Song*, which is a book with elements of the magical and mysterious. Peggy managed to gather many threads of the story together in this succinct statement.

Perception of Flashbacks and Other Narrative Manipulations of Time

Very few of the picture storybooks the children heard had to do with complicated temporal moments. Fairy tales and folk tales take place in some unspecified, vague "once upon a time," and other stories (for example, *Wilhe'mina Miles: After the Stork Night*, Carter, 1999) are historical fiction, set firmly in the past. Some fantasies, like *Cosmo and the Robot* (J. B. Pinkney, 2000), take place in the future. Memoir, however, is narrated in the present, yet the remembered incidents take place in the past. Examples of books with this temporal complication in the studies were *When I Was Young in the Mountains* (Rylant, 1982) and *Bigmama's* (Crews, 1998); in both books, the narrator, who is an adult, is reminiscing about his or her youth. Ms. Bigler-McCarthy's first- and second-graders had no difficulty in grasping the concept of memoir in Cynthia Rylant's autobiographical *When I Was Young in the Mountains*; they realized, in Alice's words, that "the author is writing about when she was a little girl; she's telling the story." Julie amplified on this: "Yeah, it's like if I wrote about when I was a little tiny baby." Because Rylant's book is a series of reminiscences, each beginning with the phrase, "When I was young in the mountains . . .", this narrative structure seemed helpful in interpreting the temporal differences between when the story was written and the past events it recounted. In Donald Crews's memoir, *Bigmama's*, there is no such repetitive narrative structure, although there are certain clues that Mrs. Martin's kindergartners noticed, which they used to understand that the story took place in the past. Bigmama lives in a house with no running water; instead there is a pump, and there is an "outhouse" instead of an indoor bathroom. However, the indication that this story is a memoir comes only on the last page, when the narrator (Crews himself) is pictured as an adult. The teacher read the last words of the story:

> TEACHER: **Some nights even now, I think that I might wake up in the morning and be at Bigmama's with the whole summer ahead of me.** Who is this talking like that? He says, **"Sometimes even now."** Do you think this story happened now or a long time ago?
>
> DONNA: Now.
>
> TEACHER: Now? What do you think, Amanda?
>
> AMANDA: A long time ago, because all those things are not like now.
>
> TEACHER [nodding]: And there's another clue. When it says, **"Some nights even now . . ."** Look at this person. **"I think that I might wake up in the morning and be at Bigmama's with the whole summer ahead of me."** Who is that man?

KEVIN: I think it is the grandpa.

TEACHER: You think it is the grandpa? That's a good guess, Kevin. Who do you think it is?

EDWARD: Jesus.

Clearly, despite the teacher's assistance, the children did not understand this more complicated memoir, in which the revelation that the narrator is an adult occurs at the very end of the story. Edward's interpretation of the adult as "Jesus" is understandable (Crews has a good-sized beard); and Kevin's suggestion that it is the "grandpa"—Bigmama's husband—is also sensible; yet the temporalities of the narrative were not grasped.

However, Mrs. Martin's class did understand the idea of a flashback. In *The Old Dog* (Zolotow, 1995), beautifully illustrated by James Ransome, a young African American boy grieves for his dog, who has died. He remembers many happy hours he spent with his dog, and at one point in the story, there is a close-up illustration of the dog itself, with nothing else in the background. Edward commented, "That's not the dog now. He [the boy] is remembering." Thus, Edward not only perceived that the illustration was a flashback to the time when the dog was alive; he also realized that the illustration was a depiction of a memory. I conclude that although there were very few books in which the temporality of the narrative was not straightforward, these young children were beginning to sort out the complexities of narrative time. In the theoretical terms of narratology, they were learning the difference between story occurring in linear time (*fabula*), and plot (*syuzhet*), which employs narrative devices such as flashbacks (Bressler, 2007).

Literary Critical Resistance to Stories

As children broadened and deepened their responses to literature, they constructed their own increasingly sophisticated criteria for analytically evaluating stories. They thus occasionally resisted a story because they saw it as somehow flawed; they critiqued faults in the author's craft. They were developing their own ideas of what made a story good and what rendered a story bad. Children in Ms. Bigler-McCarthy's class complained that *The Boy Who Ate Around* (Drescher, 1994) "just didn't make sense." When asked for more clarification, Mike said, "Well, it's like there are a whole lot of parts, but I can't figure out how it all goes together." Mike was raising a question about the lack of a coherent structure. Similarly, children objected to the didacticism of the overt ecological message in Chris Van Allsburg's (1990) *Just a Dream*, calling it "cheesy." They felt that "The author is, like hitting you over the head with it [the message]." Another objection of these children was that the illustrations in *Just a Dream* didn't match the words: "The illustrations look too realistic—they should be more dreamy, more weird, like in a dream."

Children's comments occasionally reflected their literary critical resistance to the moral, message, or theme of the story. One of the most striking instances of this type of resistance occurred at the conclusion of Christopher Coady's (1991) dark and sinister version of Red Riding Hood. Coady, following Perrault (1993), ends the story with the death of both Red Riding Hood and her grandmother, and adds a moral, which Perrault included for all his literary fairy tales. In this case, Ms. Bigler-McCarthy read the conclusion:

> **From that day until this, the sad story of Red Riding Hood has been a lesson to all children. This cautionary tale is meant to make them frightened of creatures like wolves, who can be pleasant and charming when other people are nearby. But these creatures can be very dangerous indeed, as Red Riding Hood unfortunately found out.**
> CHARLES: She didn't learn anything; she was *dead*!

Thus Charles resisted this moral, as it made no sense to him. I'm reminded of Huckleberry Finn's comment that he was "all in a sweat" to find out about "Moses and the Bulrushers," until he found out that Moses was dead, commenting, "I don't take no stock in dead people"! These comments show that these young children were capable of giving reasons for their evaluation of a story as imperfect.

5

Other Types of Analytical Response

Since approximately 73% of the children's responses to picturebooks fell within the Analytical category, I decided to undertake another level of analysis to further differentiate the various types of responses within this large category. This more finely grained analysis resulted in five subcategories for Category 1. In chapter 4, I explained the first subcategory: Making Narrative Meaning (1A). The rest of the Analytical subcategories are:

1B. The book as made object or cultural product
1C. The language of the text
1D. Illustration analysis
1E. The relationship between fiction and reality

ANALYTICAL RESPONSE 1B: THE BOOK AS MADE OBJECT OR CULTURAL PRODUCT

In this subcategory of responses, the children discussed the author and the illustrator as the makers of the book, questioning their decisions and choices. Children in all the classes learned the terms "author" and "illustrator" quickly and easily, as well as the cases in which one person was both the author and the illustrator: "It means she wrote the words and drew the pictures, too." A commonly heard question began, "I wonder why the illustrator [or author] . . ." Evaluations of an author's or illustrator's work—Krissy's great enthusiasm for Jerry Pinkney's accomplished watercolors, or Charles's appreciative comment upon seeing the front cover of *Chicken Little* (Kellogg, 1985), "Steven Kellogg, he gettin' right good!"—were also included in this subcategory. The children also discussed the awards or medals the book had won. The catalyst for this type of discussion was usually the silver or gold Caldecott medallion on the cover of books that had been designated Caldecott honor books (silver) or had won the Caldecott Award (gold). Talk about the publishing information (date of publishing, versions of the book in hardcover or paperback, and the mechanics of editing and publishing) was also included in this subcategory.

In Mr. Taylor's kindergarten class, the children at first charmingly called the Caldecott medallion on the front cover of a picturebook the "quarter": "Look, Mr. Taylor, it won a quarter!" Even when they had learned the proper name, they mischievously insisted on this usage. In Mrs. Martin's kindergarten class, some of the children learned the labels "Caldecott Medal" and "Caldecott Honor" within a few weeks. Others took longer, but still knew the meaning of the round object on the front of the book. For example, in discussing *Yo! Yes?* (Raschka, 1993), Mrs. Martin pointed out the silver medallion:

> TEACHER: Who can tell me something about this?
> ISAAC: It means the book is special.

The children also noticed the gold medallion on *Where the Wild Things Are* (Sendak, 1963): "It got a *gold* Caldecott—that means it's the best!"

In all the classes, teachers used the trade edition of the picturebook if at all possible, so they could remove the dust jacket and ascertain, with the children, whether the board cover was the same as the jacket. Children quickly learned the name "dust jacket" or "dust cover," as well as the "endpages." Learning this metalanguage for talking about picturebooks—these terms as well as "double-page spread," "cross-hatching," "full bleed," and many others (see the Glossary in Appendix B)—appeared to be primarily a matter of the teacher's modeling it a number of times, followed by the children proudly using the language for themselves. It seemed that this meant more than simply learning labels; knowing the terms drew the children's attention to the elements of picturebook design and production, and therefore helped them to look more closely and perceptively at these features (Sipe, 1998b). This subcategory is distinguished from the discussion of peritextual elements in Category 1A in that in instances of Category 1B, the children's interest in these features had more to do with their understanding of the design of the picturebook than with prediction about the story.

An interesting example of author-illustrator talk occurred during Mrs. Martin's reading of *The Colors of Us* (Katz, 1999). In this book, the author and the illustrator are the same person; moreover, the dedication page reads, "To all the kids in the world, especially my beautiful daughter Lena." The story itself begins, "My name is Lena, and I am seven, and I am the color of cinnamon." Then the narrator (Lena) says that her mother is an artist. In other words, Karen Katz, the author/illustrator of the book, dedicated the book to her own daughter, and it is her daughter who narrates the book. Amazingly, Lakia caught on to this relationship:

LAKIA: Turn back, turn to this page. I think she was doin' the
     picture.
TEACHER: She is doing the picture! She's painting the picture. But her
     mommy said that all the browns were different and then she
     went and saw her whole neighborhood and she saw that every-
     body really was a different color.
LAKIA [insistently]: I was sayin' the *illustrator* who makes the book.

Mrs. Martin had momentarily misunderstood Lakia's point; the teacher
thought "she" referred to Lena, but Lakia was pointing out that it was
the illustrator (Lena's mother) who "makes the book." This became clear
later on:

LAKIA: Her mom wrote the story.
TEACHER: For who?
LAKIA: Her [pointing to the picture of Lena].

Thus, Lakia had worked through this complicated relationship among author, illustrator, and narrator.
     Examples of subcategory 1B from Ms. Bigler-McCarthy's class include
the following, all excerpted from the transcript of the readaloud of *Little Red
Riding Hood* (Hyman, 1983).

[Teacher shows the front cover, which has the silver Caldecott
     medallion.]
PEGGY: It got a Caldecott Honor. [Award talk]
??: Yeah, a silver. [Award talk]
KENNY: It's second best. [Award talk]
TEACHER: Yes, if the medal is silver it means it was a Caldecott
     Honor, like Peggy said. If the medal is gold, it means it was the
     number one. So it's a Caldecott Honor book; that means its
     illustrations are considered some of the very best illustrations in
     that year in a picturebook.
MICKEY: What year was it illustrated? [Publishing talk]
TEACHER: Where could I find that out?
MICKEY: In the back, in the copyrighting. [Publishing talk]
Title page. On the right-hand page is the title and publishing informa-
     tion; on the left-hand page, an illustration of a little girl in a red
     cape, sitting on a bench beside her house, reading a book. The book
     she is reading is *Little Red Riding Hood*, and it is just possible to
     see that the book she is holding in her hands has the same front
     cover as the book we, as readers, are holding in our hands.

TEACHER: It was her favorite story, she drew a picture of herself as
Red Riding Hood reading it.
GORDON: She, um, probably, um, she's probably reading the same
book. She probably read the book after she got done with it.
After she got done writing it. [Author/illustrator talk]
TEACHER: She probably read her book after she got done writing it?
MICKEY: They probably got done, when they were all done with the
book, they probably sent it back to her so she could look at it.
[Author/illustrator talk and publishing talk]

In Ms. Bigler-McCarthy's class, Jim was concerned with doing things
correctly himself, and so it was perhaps natural that he would be concerned
about how illustrators and authors accomplished their tasks. During the
reading of *Where the Wild Things Are*, Jim had an answer for Krissy's question, "I wonder why the author did not put a picture on the last page":

I know something for Krissy's question. Because, maybe some books
need time, and maybe he had wrote the words, and he was about to
do the pictures, but maybe, maybe he was out of time, and he had to
get the book in to the publisher. Maybe some books have time to get
it done, maybe he, like needed a lot of time because he, like, tried to
do it neat, but when he was finished the last page, when he wrote the
words, it looks like the publisher said it's all the time he had, and he
had to return it now, and he didn't have time to finish it.

Here, Jim's own concerns about his schoolwork (to be neat and efficiently
finished)—part of his "identity theme," in Norman Holland's phrase—seemed
to be transferred to Maurice Sendak's publishing deadline.
    In these excerpts, the children are talking about the medal that was
awarded to the book; about the book as an object that is made by other people
(the author and the illustrator); and about the process of publishing it. For
the children, then, one aspect of literary understanding was knowledge about
how books were made and the people who made them. They also spoke about
the copyright, the date of publishing, and the meaning of these concepts. The
children became fascinated with the small © before the publishing date; they
always looked closely for it. After the teacher and I explained what "copyright" meant, Alice, one of Ms. Bigler-McCarthy's first-graders, brought her
math homework paper to me with a small copyright symbol by her name at
the top and said, "Look, Mr. Sipe, I copyrighted my homework!" Another
surprising but quite consistent response was children's constant amazement
and delight that many picturebooks they heard read aloud were published
in New York: cheers and applause followed the teacher's reading of this fact

in almost every readaloud. In Ms. Bigler-McCarthy's class, Kenny questioned this: "Why is everything published in New York?," which gave the teacher the opportunity to explain that New York, for the United States, is the center of the publishing world. This led to an interesting discussion about how books are published, and the difficulty and time involved in this process.

ANALYTICAL RESPONSE 1C: THE LANGUAGE OF THE TEXT

In their comments that fell into this subcategory, children displayed an interest in or awareness of the visual features of print. Their curiosity and interest, natural in emerging readers, led to attempts to read the text. Also included in this subcategory were occasions when the children imitated the language of the story by repeating it, questioned the meaning of a word or phrase, provided suggestions for alternative wording, described or evaluated the language of the story, or attempted to prove a point they were making by referring to the specific language of the text. All of these responses were grouped in this subcategory because they suggested a careful focus on the language of the text itself.

In Mrs. Martin's kindergarten class, it was common for children or the teacher to question the meaning of a word or phrase. The first sentence of *Outside over There* (Sendak, 1981), "When Papa was away at sea and Mama in the arbor . . . ," was puzzling to the children. Mrs. Martin pointed to the illustration and explained that "an arbor is a place where flowers grow and she's sitting there," but some of the children were obviously unused to calling a father "Papa":

TEACHER: Who got on the boat and went away?
DESHAWN: The man!
TEACHER: And who is the man?
DESHAWN: Grandpop!
TEACHER: What's Papa another name for?
AMANDA: Daddy! [laughter]

In another Sendak book, *Where the Wild Things Are* (1963), during the Wild Rumpus scene, Kevin commented that "He [Max] got a crown on his head!" and Amanda commented, "And he's got scepter," a word that most of the children did not know. Amanda explained, "It's this stick that kings and queens have . . . they hold it when they sit in their chairs and when they stand up." Amanda also explained the meaning of a puzzling phrase during the reading of *Come On, Rain!* (Hesse, 1999), at the end of the story when the rain has cooled the city:

TEACHER [reading]: **I hug Mamma hard, and she hugs me back. The rain has made us new.** What do they mean by that?

ANTOINE: 'Cause they been playing around all the time.

TEACHER: Playing around all the time, what do they mean that the rain has made us new?

AMANDA: We were a little grumpy when it was hot; now we feel much better.

An example of subcategory 1C from Ms. Bigler-McCarthy's first/second-grade class, drawn from the transcript of the readaloud of the Hyman (1983) version of *Little Red Riding Hood*, is the following:

TEACHER [reading]: **One day the grandmother sewed a red velvet cloak with a hood, and gave it to Elisabeth for her birthday. It looked so pretty, and she liked it so much, that she would never wear anything else, and therefore everyone called her Little Red Riding Hood.**

TRUDY: But she doesn't ride anything.

CHARLES: What about "hood"? The last one's "hood." She got a hood on.

PEGGY: Maybe it's a hood for riding horses, or a bike or horses.

TEACHER: That's interesting; sometimes they would wear capes like that when they rode horses.

In this excerpt, the children are questioning the meaning of the word "riding" in the story, and together with the teacher reach the conclusion that "riding" is a modifier of "hood," so that it is a hood used for riding. The children sometimes suggested alternative wording for the story, as the next vignette demonstrates:

TEACHER [reading]: **"You'll have to lift the latch and let yourself in, dear," the grandmother called out. "I'm feeling too weak to get out of bed."**

PEGGY: She could have said, "feeling too nauseous."

Out of all the children in Ms. Bigler-McCarthy's class, Terry was the child who was most concerned to "prove" statements by referring back to the exact language of the text. For example, as the teacher read *Mufaro's Beautiful Daughters* (Steptoe, 1987), an African *Cinderella* variant where there are only two daughters (an obedient one and a haughty one), there was a dispute about which girl was being depicted in one of the illustrations:

TEACHER: Which one do you think, by looking at the way their mannerisms are captured, what makes you think that's Nyasha [pointing to girl on the right, with her hands clasped] and this is Manyara [pointing to girl on left, with raised elbow and hand on cheek], by looking at them?

KENNY: It's because Manyara is mean, and so she made her look mean, and Nyasha is nice, and she made her look nice.

TEACHER: And by the way the illustrator has drawn her [pointing to Nyasha] to look calm and her [pointing to Manyara] to look a little bit more boastful. It kind of captures that in the picture.

GORDON: In the front page, it's Manyara.

TEACHER: Yes [turning to front cover], she's kind of showing off a bit, isn't she? Yes, Terry?

TERRY: Turn to the other page [teacher turns back]. Yeah, that page right there [to second opening]. Read that page.

TEACHER: Right now? [reads] **Manyara was almost always in a bad temper. She teased her sister whenever their /father's back was turned**

TERRY: See, it says Manyara// was always in a bad temper, then you know that that's her right there because she looks mad [pointing to illustration of girl directly beneath the text the teacher has just read].

Thus, Terry insisted that the dispute be resolved by reference to the actual language of the text. There were many instances in the data of Terry's tenaciousness in this regard.

The examples for this subcategory demonstrate that for the children, literary understanding included a close examination and appreciation of the specific language an author had chosen to use in a story.

ANALYTICAL RESPONSE 1D: ANALYSIS OF ILLUSTRATIONS AND OTHER VISUAL MATTER

In this subcategory, the children's responses indicated an analytic approach to the illustrations. Although the children frequently made comments based on their transmediation of both text and illustrations (these were included in Category 1A, Making Narrative Meaning), there were responses that were clearly *only* about the illustrations or other visual matter. By this, I do not mean to imply that the children were acquiring this information purely for its own sake; certainly, their visual analysis was a critical factor in their understanding of their interpretation of the whole picturebook. However, I believe it is useful to consider visual analysis separately, in order to point out how much the children relied on it in their meaning-making: Responses within this subcategory comprised approximately one-quarter of all the coded data in all 5 categories. Children discussed the artistic medium or media that may have been used to produce the illustration. They described the arrangement of the illustration or the illustration sequence, by referring to double-page spreads, borders, or the physical arrangement of the words and the pictures on the page opening. They constructed semiotic significance for various illustrational conventions and codes, such as the code of color, conventions for portraying movement or shadows, and the portrayal of illusion of space through perspective and point of view. They also made comparisons across illustrations and described the details or general background of illustrations.

Illustration Layout, Design, Media, and Style

The layout, design, use of media, and style of illustration were a continual source of speculation and interest in Ms. Bigler-McCarthy's class. During the readaloud of the Hyman (1983) version of *Little Red Riding Hood*, the following conversation occurred:

> KRISSY: On the inside of the endpages, there's . . . [pointing]
> MICKEY: I think she means a border. [illustration layout and arrangement]
> GORDON: It's on, all over, on all the pages. [comparison across illustrations]

At the beginning of the reading of the Coady (1991) version of *Red Riding Hood*, the children speculated about the artistic medium used to produce the illustrations:

100 KRISSY: I like the pictures.
101 TEACHER: Krissy, you like the pictures?
102 KRISSY: Yeah, ### it looks like watercolors.
103 ALICE: No it isn't.
104 TEACHER: Alice, you say no it isn't. What do you think it is?
105 ALICE: It could be tissue paper.
106 TEACHER: It's not as light as tissue paper or watercolor, is it? I think it's more like a paint called acrylics or oils. And that ###
107 KRISSY: And that [pointing to the front cover, making several short, jerky motions] makes it scratchboard.
108 ?: It's got like scratches all over.
109 ?: Scratchboard!

110   TEACHER: Oh, it does have a texture like scratchboard.
111   KRISSY: You scratch it, like Sally did, and like Jerry Pinkney [she means Brian Pinkney].
112   TEACHER: That's scratchboard. Scratchboard is different-looking than this. I'll get an illustration with scratchboard for you, too. This is oils or acrylic, and when you paint with oils or acrylic, it's a real thick paint, even thicker—
113   ?: I still think it's scratchboard.
114   TEACHER: Well, no, that's just the brushstrokes. But it's even thicker than like the tempera paint that we paint with. We don't have oils and acrylics in here.

In this excerpt, we see the children's familiarity with various illustration techniques, as well as their puzzlement about Christopher Coady's illustrations. The illustrations do indeed have a pronounced "scratchy" look: the paint is applied so thickly that not only the individual brushstrokes are visible, but the lines from the hairs on the paintbrush are noticeable as well. Krissy, who was fascinated with illustration technique and loved the dappled impressionistic watercolor style of Jerry Pinkney, at first suggests that the illustrations are in watercolor (102). Alice disagrees (103), and suggests tissue paper (105). This hypothesis was not unrealistic, for the children had seen illustrations made with tissue paper that were highly textured, with crinkled or crumpled surfaces that suggested brushstrokes. Ms. Bigler-McCarthy makes her own suggestion at 106, only to be interrupted by Krissy, who is sure it's scratchboard, the major medium used by Brian Pinkney (107). Children I couldn't identify tenaciously agree (108, 109, 113). At 111, Krissy points out that her classmate Sally had used scratchboard technique in one of her homemade books, and, confusing Jerry Pinkney (the father) with Brian Pinkney (his son), gives an example of a professional illustrator who uses this technique. Although the children's hypotheses are not correct, this excerpt demonstrates their fascination with illustrational media.

This fascination continued throughout the school year. One especially fruitful line of investigation was Krissy's interest in the watercolor style of Jerry Pinkney (mentioned above), which at times resembles the Impressionists' use of dappled color and depiction of shimmering, light-drenched surfaces. This led Ms. Bigler-McCarthy to bring in a book of Impressionist paintings, and the children were especially taken with the dots of carefully juxtaposed colors employed by Seurat. Much later in the year, the children were viewing *The Sweetest Fig* (Van Allsburg, 1993), where the illustrations have a highly grainy, textured look. Mickey observed, "That looks like the dot guy—what's his name, Seurat?" The children had truly "learned to see" and had become highly sensitive to illustrational style.

Making Meaning from the Visual Text

The children used visual information extensively in making meaning. Although the words of the story were important to them, the children showed a disposition to consider all the features of the book as potentially meaningful. Arnheim (1986, p. 306) has asserted that "the visual image always dominates the cognitive aspect of the experience" when presented together with either speech (as in film) or writing (as in picturebooks); this was certainly the case in my data. In this section, several aspects of this visual meaning-making are considered.

Conventions for Portraying Movement

Since illustrations are static, illustrators have had to evolve certain conventions for portraying movement. For example, the same figure can be shown in several successive poses in what Schwarcz (1982) calls "continuous narration." The seventh opening of *The Tunnel* (Browne, 1989) contains four illustrations in a horizontal sequence that depict a little girl crawling through a tunnel. The first three illustrations (viewing from left to right) show the girl in various crawling positions, and the fourth shows only her legs on the right side of the illustration. In my one-to-one readaloud of *The Tunnel* with Kenny, he commented, "She's going, like, she's that far [pointing to the first picture] and she gets closer [pointing to the second picture] and closer [pointing to the third and four pictures]," indicating that he realized that the sequence of illustration was depicting movement. He also used this knowledge to extend and amplify the text for this page:

> TEACHER [reading]: **The tunnel was dark, and damp, and slimy, and scary.**
> KENNY: And long.

This excerpt shows the way a child used the visual information in the illustrations—the horizontal sequence of pictures stretching across both pages of the double spread ("continuous narration")—to supplement the verbal text with the observation that the tunnel looked long. In other words, Kenny made meaning from the illustrational sequence on the page and integrated it with the information provided by the words.

Another example of "continuous narration" to portray movement is found in the 10th opening of *Amazing Grace* (Hoffman, 1991), which features a sequence of illustrations of Grace pirouetting in her room, pretending to be a ballet dancer. Each of the eight images depicts Grace at a different point in her dance, and their alignment creates a representation of the twirling and movement of the dance. The images of Grace even include the swishing of her skirt and the turning of her feet. Thus, the illustration captures the flow of Grace's private dance and makes more visible her energy, "grace," and determination—all essential traits of her character. In response to this illustration, a first-grader commented:

DIANE: It looks like a movie!

TEACHER: Yes, it does. Sometimes, illustrators choose to show action by making a series of pictures like this, so it seems like the character is moving.

If the illustrator is trying to suggest quick movement, part of the figure may be depicted as blurred. In *The Tunnel* (Browne, 1989), the little girl becomes frightened and begins to run. The illustration for this episode of the story depicts the girl on the far right side of the page, with one leg stretched forward. The back of her red coat and her white stockings are horizontally smudged or blurred. This page is wordless; the illustration covers the entire page. Part of the text of the previous opening reads, "But now she was very frightened and she began to run, faster and faster . . ." During my one-to-one readaloud of *The Tunnel* with Julie, I read this text and then turned the page, showing the illustration of the girl. Julie commented, "She's starting to run faster and faster." When I asked, "How can you tell?" Julie replied, "Because, the red is kind of getting off her dress." In this case, Julie used her knowledge of one convention for depicting movement to confirm the information in the text.

The children sometimes referred to the blurring that indicated movement as a "shadow." In my readaloud of *The Tunnel* with Terry, he attempted to explain *why* the viewer might interpret such a blurring or shadow as movement. Adults would probably be hard-pressed to provide such an explanation, and Terry struggled valiantly:

TERRY: I wonder sometimes why, when they run so fast that it becomes like you can't see it too good. Well, when they run so fast, I think, well there's two reasons I want to say, one is probably, um:

TEACHER: There's two reasons why it looks like this [pointing to the blurry part] when they're running?

TERRY [nods]: One is that they're right here [pointing to the blurry part], and they're running faster, like where they're going [pointing to the right side of the girl, which is not blurry], and also, I think—*I can think about it but I just can't say it!* . . . they're running so fast that they're probably showing their shadow, like, um, here [places hand on left part of page and moves it to the right] they are, and they're running so fast from there, and then you can see a little bit of them . . . a little bit of them are showing right over here [pointing to the blurry part], and then, it would go away.

Terry clearly knows that blurring in an illustration can indicate fast movement, but he wrestles with the clumsiness of words to express this understanding. In chapter 10, which concerns the scaffolding provided by adults and expert peers, it will be shown that one method of scaffolding was to provide words—terminology—that assisted children in saying what they knew, and also allowed them to understand more by providing tools for thought.

The Portrayal of the Illusion of Space

One of the most serious challenges faced by illustrators is the depiction of three-dimensional space on a flat two-dimensional surface. This is not only a matter of perspective (the technical rules that enable the illusion of three dimensions) but also of point of view. Point of view refers to the illustrator's manipulation of where the viewer seems to be located in relation to the scene being portrayed. Thus, an important part of the children's meaning-making with illustrations was an awareness of these aspects of the portrayal of the illusion of space.

During the readaloud of *Owl Moon* (Yolen, 1987), there were two illustrations that called forth a discussion of illustrational point of view. One illustration (on the 12th opening of *Owl Moon*) shows an owl sitting on a tree branch. The figure of the owl takes up most of the illustrational space. The children and the teacher considered how to interpret this portrayal:

?: It looks like he's really close!
?: But that's not how close he is, because he's above them.
TEACHER: Yes, he was further away, maybe something like this [holds the book over her head, showing the illustration, in imitation of the owl's position].
?: I can stare like that, real hard.
TEACHER: Probably he was further away, maybe even higher, up like this [stands on her chair, holding the book over the children's heads].

In this excerpt, the children notice that the owl looks very close, but also point out that the owl is actually far away because it is positioned above the viewer. The teacher makes this clear by physically positioning the book above the children's heads.

The other discussion during the readaloud of *Owl Moon* that tried to make sense of illustrational point of view occurred as the children were looking at the 15th opening, which is a side view of a little girl and her father walking up a slight incline. They are depicted rather far away from the viewer, because the figures are small. In back of the figures is the dark green of an evergreen forest. In the foreground is snow, so approximately the bottom third of the illustration is taken up with white snow. Gordon commented that "the snow seems to get bigger and bigger," moving his finger from left to right. The teacher asked the children, "Do you remember what it feels like to walk in snow this deep? What does it feel like? Show me what it looks like when you walk in deep snow." The following discussion suggested that the children were grappling with the difference between a true side view (in which case the strip of white in the bottom third of the illustration would be interpreted as the depth of the snow) and a side view that also included the depiction of a great deal of foreground:

> DON: It feels like you're sinking.
> TEACHER: Show me.
> JULIE: Like in quicksand.
> DON: [gets up and moves feet up and down very slowly]
> TEACHER [speaking while Don is walking]: And you walk, and it feels so tiring, it takes so much work to walk in the snow, doesn't it?
> SEAN: Snow makes you feel heavy.
> TEACHER: I think that's kind of how Jane Yolen wanted you to feel. She wanted you to feel like you were walking in snow when you read this page. I think that's why she made so much white at the bottom.
> PEGGY: But that's not how deep the snow is.
> TEACHER: No, it's not that deep, is it, Peggy?
> PEGGY: It's just like you're seeing it from here.

Here, with the teacher's help, the children talked about the effect that such a large amount of foregrounding may have on the viewer: it calls to mind the difficulty of walking in deep snow. Peggy reminded the group, however, that the bottom third of the illustration shouldn't be interpreted as the depth of the snow. Immediately after the discussion in this excerpt, Terry suggested that the reason "the snow's bigger on that page" was that "'Cause if the snow wasn't that big, probably it, probably you wouldn't be able to see the words on the snow. There wouldn't be any room for the words." In other words, Terry was commenting on the *practical* reason for the depiction of a large amount of foreground: the necessity for illustrations that cover a page to include parts that are light enough to provide a space for the printed text.

The Semiotic Significance of Color

Color is used by illustrators in various ways, including the suggestion of mood or emotion. This semiotic significance of color was explored by the children during the reading of Christopher Coady's (1991) version of *Red Riding Hood*. Coady follows Charles Perrault's (1993) version of *Red Riding Hood*, which ends abruptly and shockingly with the death of Red Riding Hood; in this version, no woodsman comes to save either the little girl or her grandmother. Coady's illustrations are correspondingly dark and foreboding. The title page of this book contains an oval illustration of a bare tree, with a full moon behind it. The tree branches and the lower border of the illustration are tinged with red. The following is a portion of the discussion about this page:

> 100   SEAN: At first, there's some red strokes over the moon [pointing to the title page vignette].
> 101   TEACHER: Some red strokes over the moon.
> 102   SEAN: And down here, too [pointing to the bottom curve of the vignette].
> 103   TEACHER: Yes, red strokes over the moon, and over the picture here, red strokes of paint. Nicole?
> 104   NICOLE: Because it's Red Riding Hood.
> 105   MICKEY: Because when, um, the hunter cuts him open, there's blood in the story.
> 106   TEACHER: Do you think that might be something we call foreshadowing, to let you know? Foreshadowing is what allows you to predict what might happen. Because when the illustrator and the author give you little clues to foreshadow what will happen next, and to let you know what will happen next. Julie?
> 107   JULIE: It is October because the leaves are not on the tree.
> 108   TEACHER: And look at that moon: a full moon.
> 109   CHARLES: It's a warning of blood from the wolf that's going to eat the grandma.

The discussion shows that the children were learning how to "read" the visual metaphors in illustration: the visual text. Red can suggest excitement and joy, but it can also be a sign (in the semiotic sense) for danger, warning, or blood. The association of red with blood in Coady's version of *Red Riding Hood* continued throughout the book. The children were building this association as they commented that there's "more and more red" in the illustrations as the story progressed. By the end of the story, the association was so strong that their response to the last illustration, showing the empty, rumpled bed with a red bedspread, was one of horror: "Look at the bed! It's full of blood!"

Another measure of the effect of these illustrations was the lack of audience participation during the dramatic series of conversational exchanges between Red Riding Hood and the disguised wolf in most versions of the story, which usually begin, "Oh grandmother, what big eyes you have." During the readalouds of several other (cheerier) versions of the story, the children invariably chimed in at this point, gleefully saying the words along with the teacher. This was not the case during the reading of the Coady version of *Red Riding Hood*; the teacher read alone, with total silence from the children. Afterward, the children discussed the other ways in which the illustrator had achieved the effect of "scariness." They pointed out that the illustrations are dark, and seem to get darker as the story progresses. The teacher pointed out the odd perspectives Coady had chosen to use, and suggested that these strange points of view reminded her of a "funhouse, a scary funhouse." Don compared the illustrations to *"The Twilight Zone."* Thus, there is proof that the children were successful in interpreting the general tone of the story; and they had primarily used the illustrations to arrive at this interpretation.

Similarly, Charles made a spontaneous association of the color red with the emotion of fear during the reading of *3 Billy Goats Gruff* (Dewan, 1994). The illustration on the left-hand page of the seventh opening of this book depicts a frightened little billy goat, with the black shadow of the troll behind. The background of the illustration is dark red. Charles asked a question and then answered it himself: "Why is it red back here? Oh, I know why, because he got so frightened."

One of the most complex discussions about the semiotic significance of color took place during the readaloud of *The Whales' Song* (Sheldon, 1990), a magical contemplative story that was described in chapter 4. Trudy mentioned that the illustrations were "dark," and the teacher asked why the illustrator might have chosen to use dark colors:

JULIE: Because the whales are blue.
TEACHER: Umm. What else?
KENNY: 'Cause it's really slow, and it's dark illustrations.
MICKEY: Because it's a relaxed book, and it's slow, like the ocean.
KENNY: The, um, the darker the color is, the slower the words are.

The teacher then asked Kenny to point out a specific page where this was so, and he asked her to turn to the opening where the whales are calling Lilly's name. When the teacher showed the illustration, Kenny said:

KENNY: Can you read it over again? And in, can you read it in a slow voice? 'Cause it's slow, and it seems like it, like the colors are slow, and the words are slow, too.

TEACHER: So with the colors being slow, and the words being read slowly, how does it make you feel?

KENNY: Relaxed.

The teacher then read the text for that page in two ways: quite slowly and dreamily, and in a fast, clipped manner. Peggy volunteered to read the passage for the third time with her interpretation, and also read slowly and deliberately. The children unanimously agreed that the slow reading matched the mood of the story best.

The illustration that was the focus of this discussion is painted almost monochromatically, with various shades of blue. In this excerpt, we see the children making a rather sophisticated association of dark colors (and particularly blue) with slowness and relaxation. In Coady's *Red Riding Hood*, the dark colors suggested fear or unease to the children, but they were also able to perceive another semiotic dimension to dark colors. These examples demonstrate that the children were using the illustrations to interpret the text, and the text to interpret the illustrations. They used the illustrations to interpret the text when they suggested that the teacher read it slowly and calmly; and they used the text to interpret the illustrations when they interpreted the colors as indications of slowness rather than of fear or unease. Again, the general tone of the story—contemplative, reflective of an interior experience—was interpreted by the children mainly through the illustrations, particularly the color palette the illustrator had chosen.

For the children, then, an important part of the literary understanding of picturebooks was an appreciative comprehension of the form and content of the illustrations, and in learning the language of visual analysis, which both enabled and expressed this understanding.

ANALYTICAL RESPONSE 1E: RELATIONSHIPS BETWEEN FICTION AND REALITY

Finally, in this last subcategory of analytical responses, the children grappled with the various ways in which the story (both the verbal and visual texts) related to what they understood as "real life." Examples of this subcategory include Charles's speculation that the wolf must not have chewed when he swallowed Red Riding Hood and her grandmother, because otherwise they would not have had whole bodies when the hunter cut the wolf open and saved them. This is an application of real-life eating to the eating that happens in the story. When Krissy questioned, "Was Red Riding Hood a real people?" she was also wrestling with the relationship of the story to reality. This question launched a discussion about the origins of folk tales (reminiscent of the rationalist explanations for the ancient myths), which included the speculation that perhaps real children were eaten by wolves, and that the story may have been an attempt to warn children of the dangers of going into the forest alone. "Don't talk to strangers" was another conclusion reached by the children, and in this case, they were nearing Charles Perrault's (1993) warning to young women of the French court in one of the first literary versions of the tale. At the close of this version, Perrault cautions, "Not all wolves walk on four feet," and asserts that despite their handsome appearance, some men are just as voracious as wolves.

Children tended to resist stories when there was a perceived conflict between the world of the story and children's understanding of reality. It's as if they were saying, "That's not the way life is." In my studies, kindergarteners almost never exhibited this type of resisting response based on the distinctions between fiction and reality; they tended to accept the storyworld without question, despite any fantastical elements. However, first- and second-graders quite commonly did address these distinctions, and seemed to be in the process of constructing a complex understanding of the relationship between fiction and reality. A first-grader's (Sally's) objection to *3 Billy Goats Gruff* (Dewan, 1994)—that trolls do not exist—suggests this child's struggle with the goal of making distinctions between what is make-believe and what life is really like. (Notice that the objection is to trolls, not to goats that talk: goats, at least, are real animals, and animals that talk are a very common element of children's literature.) Similarly, upon observing the illustration of Scieszka's (1992) Stinky Cheese Man (with olives for eyes and a strip of bacon for a mouth), a second-grader I could not identify scornfully observed, "Bacon can't talk, anyway!" These types of comments indicate that there is no analogue in a child's experience to the events or characters in a story (Cai, 2002), or that the story contradicts the previous experience or worldview of the child. The comments also suggest the children's assumption that stories should be about the "real world." This sense of what the world is like is, of course, partly formed by a children's developing ideology in conjunction with experience; young children are formulating implicit rules about the distinctions between reality and fiction. (Adults may struggle as well: witness the comments of many people for whom, as the catastrophes of 9/11/2001 unfolded on their television screens, it seemed as though they were watching a disaster movie rather than real events.)

For some children, this concern seemed to be more paramount than for others; it was especially true for Sally, the first-grader in Ms. Bigler-McCarthy's classroom who stated flatly, "there is no such thing as a troll"—at two points in the story. In *Chicken Little* (Kellogg, 1985), she observed that "the sky can't fall," and that a parachute was much too small for the large hippo who had bailed out of his helicopter. This concern, however, did not seem to interfere with her appreciation of stories. Rather, it seemed to be one of her ways of exploring the intricacies of the fiction/truth connection.

The children's struggles with fiction and truth were evident not only in fantasies like *Red Riding Hood*, *3 Billy Goats Gruff*, and *Chicken Little*; this effort surfaced even more acutely in the more complicated relationships between realistic fiction and reality. In a way, "realistic fiction" is an oxymoronic term: events are "made up," yet they could be real, and there is thus a hybrid nature to this literary genre, similar to historical fiction, where real historical events are melded together with characters, dialogue, and parts of the plot that are plausible, but never really happened. The best example of the children's grappling with the oxymoronic qualities of realistic fiction occurred during the readaloud of *Fly Away Home* (Bunting, 1991), the story of a homeless boy and his father who, upon the death of the boy's mother and the resulting family economic crisis, are reduced to living in an airport. The airport is warm, safe, and has washing and eating facilities, and if they keep moving from terminal to terminal, the security staff does not notice them. That a boy and his father actually might live like this may seem improbable, but such unfortunate things do happen. The boy is the first-person narrator, and the story is not presented as a fantasy, either in the verbal text or the illustrations. Charles, however, had a hard time believing it, and his disbelief sparked a discussion about the nature of the relationship between stories and reality.

100   CHARLES: This ain't true.
101   SALLY: It could be.
102   CHARLES: Nuh uh.
103   SALLY: Yes, it could.
104   GORDON: It is possible. It is *possible*.
105   TEACHER: Do you think there are people who might not have a house because they might not have enough money?
106   CHARLES: I don't think so.
107   GORDON: Yeah, people in the desert, they don't have no home, they:

108 CHARLES: But I saw this movie about the desert; they make home, outta branches, and stuff.

109 GORDON: But what if there is no branches? What if they didn't find any bushes?

110 TEACHER: What if people right here in [the city] didn't have any money?

111 TERRY: They'd probably have to die.

112 CHARLES: But they let people that don't got no money, or nothing, they stay in a hotel, for free.

113 SALLY: My grandma, she met a woman who lived in the back of, of a gas station. And she gave that woman some money for something to eat.

114 CHARLES: I still don't think it could be real. 'Cause it's a cartoon.

[Pause]

115 CHARLES: It couldn't be by anybody. It would be by nobody.

116 GORDON: But it /could be by somebody.

117 CHARLES: If it was by the author// and the um, illustrator, it wouldn't be right there, it would be just by whoever wrote the book, like right there, there would be no illustrator [pointing to the front cover, and the names of the author and illustrator].

118 GORDON: It could be by, it could be real, because they could've told the author about their adventure, or something, and then the author wrote about it, and written the story down, and then, it could be possible, Charles.

119 TERRY: They told the story, and the author knew, and then he write it down. And then the illustrator, he probably knew, and then he drew the pictures. What he thought it would look like.

Charles states several reasons why the story can't be real. First, he disagrees with the teacher's suggestion (105) that insufficient money might make people homeless; he argues (112) that people who don't have money get to "stay in a hotel, for free." Charles has a good point; in at least some cities, so-called "welfare hotels" house indigent people. Second, Charles (114) argues that "It's a cartoon," by which he may mean that the illustrations are not photographs, which would indicate realism. At 115 and 117, Charles gives his third reason. His logic seems to be that the fact that there's an author and illustrator listed on the front cover means that the story can't be real. I believe that he is stumped by the fact that it's the *little boy* who is narrating the story. Indeed, the little boy and his father (and perhaps all the characters in the book) are likely not real in the sense that these particular people exist and live in airports; it is more likely that Eve Bunting, the author, has produced a fictional story, and that the characters are composites constructed from her research on homeless people. So in one sense, Charles is right: the story isn't real, though it presents the truth. Sally, Gordon, and Terry all try to counter Charles's arguments. At 118 and 119, Gordon and Terry speculate on how the book was actually written and produced: perhaps the people who had the "adventure" told their story to the author, and the author wrote it down. Then the illustrator studied the story and drew the pictures, not the way it actually was, but the way "he thought it would look like." Here, Gordon's (118) reference to the story as an "adventure" is quite significant: it suggests that he is simultaneously conceiving of the story as "possible," and yet merely a piece of fiction; if he had seen a documentary film about homeless people, he would be unlikely to call it an "adventure."

Charles's recalcitrance thus provided the impetus for the children to do some very hard thinking about the ways in which realistic fiction is both real *and* fictional. This sophisticated excerpt was constructed with only minimal input from the adult.

The aspect of the children's literary understanding that is highlighted by this last subcategory is their awareness that reality and story are not entities that are hermetically sealed off from one another, but that interact in complex ways. The children's discernment of the relationship between the storyworld and the real world (and their grappling with the intricacies of that relationship) was revealed by their simultaneous acceptance and rejection of the secondary world (Benton, 1992).

In all these subcategories of the Analytical Category presented in this chapter and chapter 4, the children stayed *within* the story (in the sense of being text-based) and interpreted it, paying attention to the author/illustrator's craft. They also considered the storybook as a made object; paid close attention to the language of the text; analyzed the form and content of the illustrations; and attempted to relate the story to reality. The type of literary understanding represented by all these responses was a close reading of the text valorized by the New Critics. In the next chapter, I discuss instances of the children's moving *outside* the story to make literary meaning, bringing to bear other texts that assisted them in their interpretation.

6

Intertextual Responses: How Stories "Lean" on Stories (and Other Texts)

When the children were making Intertextual responses, the subject of this chapter, they shifted their focus from within the text to its relationship with other texts they knew. The word "text" in this sense refers to any other cultural product involving language and/or visual art: a television program, a song, a billboard, a video or movie, a painting, the artwork or writing of other classmates, and even (in one instance) a T-shirt. They contextualized, placing the text at hand in a conceptual matrix of related texts. In most cases, these intertextual links were hermeneutic in intent: the children used them to interpret the story. The aspect of the children's literary understanding that is highlighted by this category is the knowledge that stories do not stand alone; that stories (as Jane Yolen puts it) "lean on other stories" (Yolen, 1981).

THREE TYPES OF INTERTEXTUAL CONNECTIONS

Intertextual connections did not invariably have the same purpose or function. Rather, these connections represented different levels of complexity. Children forged three types of intertextual connections, each progressively more abstract: *associative links*, *analytical links*, and *synthesizing links*.

Associative Links

Associative links were characterized by an unelaborated statement of likeness. The language utilized by the children followed the pattern of "That is like _____" or "That reminds me of _____." The subject of the link could be either the picture or the story. In Mrs. Martin's kindergarten class, during the reading of *Strong to the Hoop* (Coy, 1999), the story of a small boy who plays basketball with some much older boys and helps win the game, Naisha commented, "This is just like *Love and Basketball*," a movie that begins when two 11-year-olds meet and share their longing to play basket-ball, in emulation of one of the children's fathers. In similar manner, Kevin commented during the reading of *Anansi and the Moss-Covered Rock* (Kimmel, 1988), "I saw a movie of that spider. I have it at home." During the discussion following Ms. Bigler-McCarthy's reading of *Owl Moon* (Yolen, 1987), Alice made a connection between an illustration (on the 13th opening of *Owl Moon*) of an owl flying with its wings outstretched and an illustration in *Owl Babies* (Waddell, 1992), which also depicts an owl in flight. Alice looked for *Owl Babies* on the bookshelf, found it, and showed the class that the two illustrations were indeed similar. When Ms. Bigler-McCarthy read *The Rough-Face Girl* (Martin, 1992) to the class, the children quickly realized that it was a variant of the *Cinderella* story, commenting that it was "like" *Cinderella*. In this Native American variant, "a poor man had three daughters. The two older daughters were cruel and hard-hearted, and they made their youngest sister sit by the fire and feed the flames" (Martin, 1992, unpaged). The younger sister is burnt and scarred from her work, and she is tauntingly called the "rough-face girl" by her sisters, just as Cinderella receives her name by sleeping on the hearth in the cinders.

Analytical Links

Analytical links were characterized by making an intertextual association and then going on to describe the similarities or differences in the texts, what might be called "intertextual analysis." A simple example of this type of analysis is the comment of a child I could not identify during Mrs. Martin's reading of *The Three Little Javelinas* (Lowell, 1994), a Southwestern variant of *The Three Pigs*: "It's just like *The Three Pigs*, except he doesn't build his house out of straw" (the first javelina builds his house of tumbleweeds, more appropriate to the Southwestern context). During the readaloud of *Silver Rain Brown* (Helldorfer, 1999), children commented on its similarities to *Wilhe'mina Miles: After the Stork Night* (Carter, 1999), pointing out that both stories centrally involved a woman who was having a baby. They also connected the story with *Come On, Rain!* (Hesse, 1999), mentioning that both stories take place in the city, in stifling summer heat. In the readaloud of *Uptown*, Brian Collier's (2000) celebration of Harlem, the illustration of the landmark Apollo Theater prompted several children to connect the illustration with their experience of seeing performances at the Apollo on television—as Donna said, "It's on TV; it's a place to see singing and dancing." Another simple example of an analytical link is Julie's comment about *The Rough-Face Girl* in Ms. Bigler-McCarthy's first/second-grade class: "Where she was doing her chores, it was like *Cinderella*, 'cause Cinderella has chores also."

These examples demonstrate relatively simple intertextual connections. However, this intertextual analysis could become quite complex, as in the following vignette from the transcript of the readaloud of *The Three Little Javelinas* (Lowell, 1994), the *Three Pigs* variant mentioned above. Mrs. Martin explicitly invited and furthered this analysis:

100 TEACHER: So, who can tell me if these stories were alike? Who can tell me if these are similar? Similar means kind of alike. Not exactly alike, but somewhat alike.

101 YASMIN: They both have pigs, and they both have clothes on.

102 ISAAC: Probably because both of the wolves got burnt in the story.

103 TEACHER: Right. One wound up in a kettle and the other one ended up in the stove.

104 EDWARD: They don't have a mom.

105 ANTOINE: This [he points to the Marshall version, which the teacher has placed on the easel beside *The Three Little Javelinas*] says, "I'll huff and I'll puff and I'll blow your house down."

106 JOE: They did not build the houses out of the same stuff.

107 BELLA: And the girl made it out of blocks! Bricks! [adobe bricks]

108 TEACHER: So what's different about these three pigs? There's something really different about these three pigs and these three pigs. [Still comparing this book with the Marshall version]

109 AMANDA: One is hairy and one is plain and pink.

110 TEACHER: And what else is different?

111 DEAN: They got horsey clothes one [*Javelinas*] and they don't [Marshall].

112 TEACHER: That's right. These are pigs that live out west [*Javelinas*] and these are pigs that maybe live around here [Marshall].

113 MARTIN: Yeah, they live around here. They play in mud.

114 NAISHA: This can't be the same thing because it's no girl pig and it doesn't have no umbrella in there [the umbrella keeps the sun from beating down on the javelinas].

115 TEACHER: Thank you. There's no girl pig in this one. The only one here [in the Marshall version] is the mom. She sends them off. Mrs. Pig is sending her piglets off. But here, this one is a girl. And, who was the one that had the strongest house?

116 MANY CHILDREN: The girl!

117 YASMIN: Because she's smart!

118 EDWARD: They have fur and the other ones don't.

119　TEACHER: That's right. These are javelinas, they are furry and they are related to pigs.
120　ISAAC: That story, it sound different because they don't really look like pigs and the other pigs do.
121　TEACHER: Yes, these don't really look like the kind of pigs that we are used to seeing. But they are definitely related to pigs because they have the same kind of noses.
122　DEAN: Probably they dressed up like pigs!
123　JOE: I think that they [the javelinas] are black and the other pigs [in the Marshall version] are white.

In this excerpt, Mrs. Martin worked hard (at 100, 108, and 110) to encourage the children to identify differences and similarities between the two tales, and to keep the intertextual analysis going. She also explicated or amplified on the children's responses (at 103, 112, 115, 119, and 121). As the result of her efforts, the children were able to identify no less than a dozen similarities and differences. Also, although Mrs. Martin did not choose to follow up on Joe's comment that the javelinas are black and the "other pigs" in the Marshall version are white, there's an implicit racial intertextual analysis here, or at least a partial perception of the diversity that is characteristic of traditional stories, but that published picturebook versions of these tales have only recently begun to represent.

Another example of an extended intertextual analysis occurred in Ms. Bigler-McCarthy's class during the reading of *The Rough-Face Girl* (Martin, 1992), a Native American variant of *Cinderella*. In this exchange, Mickey refers to the Invisible Being, whom all the young women in the village want to marry, a clear parallel to the prince in the European versions of *Cinderella*.

100　TEACHER: Now, Mickey, all along through the story you kept saying that this was similar to another story that we had read. Could you tell me more?
101　MICKEY: *Cinderella*, cause, um, the two sisters, the two sisters were mean. And, but in the middle I noticed it wasn't, it wasn't like *Cinderella*, kind of.
102　TEACHER: How so?
103　MICKEY: Because she asked the father, her father, and that wasn't there, but I think it's a little bit related because, I think kind of the father is like the fairy godmother.
104　TEACHER [nodding]: Giving her the things that will help her become the wife of the Invisible Being. Are there any other connections, Mickey, to *Cinderella*, other than the father and the fairy godmother and the sisters?

105   MICKEY: Because only the rough-face girl could see the thing, the invisible person, and um, only the slipper fit Cinderella.
106   TEACHER: Um. Charles.
107   CHARLES: It is *kind* of like *Cinderella*.
108   TEACHER: Tell me more.
109   CHARLES: 'Cause, like, Cinderella is the only one that dress raggedy, so does the girl in the book [the rough-face girl] and the Invisible Being's, um, sister is like the fairy godmother.
110   TEACHER: The invisible being's sister is like the fairy godmother; I'm interested in that thinking. Tell me more.
111   CHARLES: The invisible being's sister's like the fairy godmother, she gives the rough-face girl the pretty clothes.
112   TEACHER: She does make things possible for her, doesn't she? She makes it possible to live happily ever after.
113   CHARLES: Like, the sister probably has a wand or something and she lost it, and she can make magic.

At 101, Mickey begins the intertextual analysis by comparing the two cruel sisters in *The Rough-Face Girl* to the stepsisters in *Cinderella*. He also begins to tease out the differences. Cinderella's father is hardly present in the European version of the tale, but the father of the rough-face girl figures in the plot of this Native American variant because he gives the rough-face girl clothes to wear to meet the Invisible Being. Therefore, Mickey thinks that the two stories are "a little bit related" because the father in *The Rough-Face Girl* is parallel to the fairy godmother in *Cinderella* (103). Also, the Invisible Being is only visible to the rough-face girl, and Mickey makes a sophisticated connection between the uniqueness of the slipper and the uniqueness of being able to see the Invisible Being (105). At 109, 111, and 113, Charles argues that there is a character who is a better candidate for a fairy godmother figure in *The Rough-Face Girl*: the sister of the Invisible Being. In the story, the Invisible Being's sister tells the rough-face girl to wash in the lake; through the washing, the rough-face girl becomes magically beautiful. The sister also gives regal garments to the rough-face girl. Charles points out that because the sister "can make magic," and because she gives "pretty clothes" to the rough-face girl, she is a more suitable fairy godmother than the rough-face girl's father.

Synthesizing Links

Synthesizing links were characterized by using multiple intertextual links to make generalizations and draw conclusions about sets of stories. For example, the children began to notice that the front and back covers of picturebooks often depict the main character and other characters in the story. Further-more, they noticed that the front cover often depicts the "good" character and the back cover depicts the "bad" character. The children in Ms. Bigler-McCarthy's class reached this general understanding by the intertextual links they made among several books. They noticed that the versions of *Red Riding Hood* by James Marshall (1987) and Christopher Coady (1991) and the version of *3 Billy Goats Gruff* by Ted Dewan (1994) all conformed to this pattern. In the Marshall and Coady versions of *Red Riding Hood*, Red Riding Hood appears on the front cover and the wolf is depicted on the back cover; in the Dewan version of *3 Billy Goats Gruff*, the three billy goats appear on the front cover and the troll appears on the back.

This use of intertextual links to make generalizations was a powerful interpretive strategy, and is discussed in a separate section below, along with several other ways in which intertextual links figured in the children's devel-oping literary understanding.

The three types of intertextual connections—associative links, analyti-cal links, and synthesizing links—represented three levels of increasing cog-nitive complexity. These levels seem to have built on each other; associative links enabled analytical links, and analytical links enabled synthesizing links. At the same time, it must be noted that the verbalizations of the children are not a transparent window onto their cognitive processes. In other words, an associative link may have included the (unverbalized) analytical process, or even the synthesizing process; we ultimately have no way of knowing whether, at any given moment, a child was merely making a simple associative con-nection between texts or whether she was also mentally comparing and con-trasting them or generalizing at the level of synthesis.

THE ROLES OF INTERTEXTUAL CONNECTIONS

In addition to having three levels of cognitive complexity, the children's intertextual connections were utilized to make a number of interpretive moves. That children made frequent intertextual connections was interest-ing, but even more important was what the connections allowed the chil-dren to *do* interpretively. There were at least eight ways in which intertextual connections were utilized by the children:

1. The children *interpreted imagined or real personal experiences* (which had been shared by the children as they personalized a story) in the light of intertextual connections. In Mrs. Martin's class, during the reading of *Up-town*, Bella commented, "I was in a show in the Apollo [theatre] when I was

four—I was singing and dancing." This was unlikely, but Bella was interpreting her own experience in the light of the talk about the highly popular televised shows at the Apollo that had been sparked by the illustrations and description of the Apollo Theatre in *Uptown*. Similarly, Naisha used the metaphorical language for skin color of *Shades of Black* (Pinkney, 2000) to playfully tell Mrs. Martin, "You, you're white just like an ice cream cone," interpreting Mrs. Martin's own skin color, using the same type of language as this picturebook, which has photographs of children with a broad range of skin tones.

During the reading of *Ira Sleeps Over* (Waber, 1972) in Ms. Bigler-McCarthy's class, as the children were discussing Ira's pillow fight with his friend Reggie, Kristin made a personal link that Joey connected to another text:

> KRISTIN: One time, um, I was jumping on my bed when my mom
>   was getting pajamas for me, and I fell off and I broke my head
>   on the windowsill, right on the corner, and I had to go to the
>   hospital and get stitches.
> JOEY: Like *Five Little Monkeys* jumpin' on the bed!
> TEACHER: That's what I was thinking, Joey [laughing]. No more
>   monkeys jumping on the bed!
> DON [chanting]: No more Kristin jumping on the bed!

2. The children used intertextual connections *to make symbolic interpretations of visual elements of the text*. For example, Trudy made a particularly striking symbolic interpretation during the small-group readaloud of *Fly Away Home* (Bunting, 1991). This book, a piece of realistic fiction mentioned in chapter 5, tells the story of a homeless little boy whose mother has died and who lives with his father in an airport. The boy (who narrates the story) notices a bird that has become trapped in the airport and tries unsuccessfully to escape. Finally, the bird manages to fly out through a door that is momentarily open. Most adults would probably take the view that the bird functions in the story as a metaphor for the plight of the boy and his father: they, too, are trying to escape from the necessity of living in the airport. An illustration of the bird also appears on the back cover, and the following exchange occurred as I was probing Jim's statement that "it looks like he [the bird] was important to him [the boy]":

> TEACHER: Do you think the bird might be special to the boy, maybe?
> TRUDY: The bird could be watching over the boy, maybe it's his
>   mother, turned into a bird.

TEACHER: I love it. I never thought of it before. It's kind of like the
bird is, the bird is his mother's spirit, maybe, and she's watching
over him?

JIM: Yeah, it's like he wants his mother.

TEACHER: And when the bird gets out of the airport:

TRUDY: Maybe she goes to watch over the dad. I knew it might be
his mother because on *Married with Children*, Bud turns into
another dog. 'Cause he has been bad.

JIM: It looks like the bird is flying to heaven [showing 7th opening,
with illustration of the bird in the distant sky]

The situation comedy *Married With Children* is an unlikely intertextual
connection to enable such a beautiful idea, but fortunately we do not have
to make any inferences about the source for Trudy's symbolic interpretation;
she tells us herself that it was inspired by a transformation of one of the
characters in the show. This unlikely juxtaposition demonstrates that children can find popular cultural texts just as powerful a source of ideas as well-
wrought picturebooks. In this vignette, the intertextual connection also seems
to function as an enabler of Jim's extension of Trudy's idea, as he adds a
confirmation of Trudy's hypothesis about the symbolic identity of the bird:
it seems to be "flying to heaven."

3. One of the most common patterns associated with intertextual connections was their function in *assisting children to predict what might happen
in the narrative*. In Mrs. Martin's kindergarten classroom, the children used
intertextual knowledge to make predictions about the plot and characters
during the readaloud of *The Hatseller and the Monkeys* (Diakite, 1999), a West
African folk tale that bears a striking resemblance to *Caps for Sale* (Slobodkina,
1947), which the class had heard previously. Just a few pages into the story,
when the hatseller, BaMusa, takes a rest under a mango tree, he falls asleep:
"Little did BaMusa know that the fruit from this tree attracted monkeys.
BaMusa's snoring alerted them to his company." At this point, Amanda commented, "This is just like *Caps for Sale*!" and proceeded to find that book from
the classroom library and to show the similar illustration of the hatseller asleep
under a tree. This sparked a series of predictions about what was going to
happen, based on the children's knowledge of *Caps for Sale*:

EDWARD: I think that the monkeys are going to climb down the tree
and get the hats.

YASMIN: I think that the monkeys are going to eat the stuff from the
trees.

TEACHER: You might be right. There are mangoes in the tree and mangoes are a delicious fruit.

When the teacher read that the monkeys were attracted to the colorful hats and took them back up the tree, Amanda cried, "I knew it!"

TEACHER: You've never heard of this book before?
AMANDA: No, but I knew the monkeys were a copycat!

Later in the story, when the hatseller yells at the monkeys, they yell back; Khalil commented, "They're copying off him." And when the hatseller finds a stone and throws it into the tree, the monkeys reply by picking mangoes and throwing them down at BaMusa. After eating the mangoes, BaMusa "could think clearly." At this point, Mrs. Martin commented,

TEACHER: Now he knew what he wanted to do. What do you think that was?
MARTIN: He's going to climb up the tree and get all his hats.
YASMIN: He's going to throw his hat off.
TEACHER: He's going to throw his hat off? And then what is going to happen?
YASMIN: And then the monkeys will throw their hats off.

These predictions were clearly based on the children's knowledge of the (parallel) plot of *Caps for Sale*. However, the teacher also encouraged the children to analyze the differences between the African tale and the European tale, asking, "How was it different?" The children came up with some important differences:

YASMIN: Different caps and different trees.
AMANDA: They [in *Caps for Sale*] didn't have colored hats.
KATRIN: The man says "Caps for sale!" And the other one said, "Hee manu . . ."
SEVERAL CHILDREN: "Hee manum ninkoi kadi sa!"
TEACHER: And he [pointing to the European tale] was saying, "Caps for sale!"
AMANDA: He said in American [pointing to *Caps for Sale*] and he said in African [pointing to *The Hatseller and the Monkeys*].
EDWARD: This man is white and that man is black [pointing to both books].
AMANDA: And they have different clothes.

In addition to demonstrating the use of intertextual connections to make predictions, this example shows the importance of having the classroom's collection of books near at hand, so that the children could easily find the book to which they were making a connection.

During the reading of one of the opening pages of *The Whales' Song* (Sheldon, 1990), a piece of magical realism about a young girl who is fascinated with whales and who hears them calling her name, the children in Ms. Bigler-McCarthy's class made various predictions about what gift a whale might give:

> TEACHER [reading]: "But why did they swim to you, Grandma?" asked Lilly. "How did they know you were there?" Lilly's grandmother smiled. "Oh, you had to bring them something special. A perfect shell. Or a beautiful stone. And if they liked you, the whales would take your gift and give you something in return."
>
> KRISSY: I wonder what a whale might give you.
>
> TEACHER: What do you think a whale might give you, Krissy?
>
> KRISSY: A shell.
>
> BILL: Give you a shell back. Because in *Free Willy*, when this one guy dropped his balloon, um, Willy dived in after it, and he put it in his mouth, and he swimmed back up, and he opened it up, and he took his hand, and put it in and pulled it out.

Bill's prediction that a whale might "give you a shell back" is informed by his connection to the movie *Free Willy*, and is another instance of the power of popular culture in the children's thinking, and their (and their teacher's) willingness to use any text to interpret the text at hand.

4. Closely related to the ability to predict was the function of intertextual connections in the children's *creation and modification of schemata for stories*. Cognitive Flexibility Theory (Spiro et al., 1994) suggests that we create schemata for understanding our reading (and presumably texts we listen to) by "criss-crossing" or building up our knowledge across cases, and by linking this knowledge together. According to this theory, schemata are extremely fluid, continually changing as new information modifies the receptive cognitive structure. This fluid nature of children's schemata was evidenced during Mrs. Martin's reading of *Leola and the Honeybears: An African American Retelling of Goldilocks and the Three Bears* (Rosales, 1999). In the story Leola, an African American little girl, meets a weasel in the forest who threatens her; this is the reason she enters the "charming little inn" of the Honeybears, who are out "catch[ing] a mess of catfish." Children recognized that

the introductory addition of the threatening weasel was similar to versions of *Red Riding Hood*, where Red Riding Hood meets the wolf in the forest. In fact, the children at first interpreted the weasel as a wolf. "The two stories are mixed up," exclaimed Yasmin, demonstrating that her schemata for both *The Three Bears* and *Red Riding Hood* were developed well enough to understand the presence of elements of both stories in *Leola and the Honeybears*. When the teacher finished reading the story, the children returned to this melding of tales, as Isaac pointed out that other versions of *The Three Bears* "don't have that part where that thing come by and wanted to eat her." The children also recognized that a blonde European girl is not a necessary component of a *Three Bears* variant, through several unidentified children's comments that Leola should be called "Blackie Locks." This intertextual connection expands the schema of traditional tales to include races and ethnicities other than European characters; it's similar to the children's understanding that the main character in *Caps for Sale* (and its variant *The Hatseller and the Monkeys*) and the pigs in different versions of *The Three Pigs* could be white or black, as Joe observed in *The Three Little Javelinas*.

However, it was the ending of *Leola and the Honeybears* that expanded, refined, and changed the children's schema for the *Three Bears* tale most significantly. In *Leola and the Honeybears*, the bears, having returned and discovered all the damage done by Leola, are not angry or disturbed for very long. They forgive Leola readily, give her a basket of food, and ask "Miss Blackbird" to see that she gets home safely. This ending is quite different from more common versions of *The Three Bears*, where Goldilocks escapes quickly, leaving the bears to deal with the damage she has caused. At first, the children's predictions about the ending conformed to their previous schema for *The Three Bears*:

AALIYAH: They gonna say, "Get out my bed!"
NAISHA: Um, she gonna jump out the window.
ISAAC: I think they gonna say, "Get out of my house right now!"

However, the gentle tone of the story and the illustration of the friendly bears with Leola was enough to alter their schema:

YASMIN: They gonna say, "You can stay, Blackie Locks."
KEVIN: I know what they can say, um, you stay til the weasel goes back home.
MARTIN: I think the bears, I think the bears gonna let her out the window.
TEACHER: They're gonna let her out the window?
MARTIN: Uh-huh. Or, or, or share with her.

TEACHER: Let's see. [reading] As the tears flowed down Leola's face, Mama Honeybear saw that she was only a youngster, "She's only a little girl!" . . . no different than her own Lil' Honey. Soon, all was forgiven.

Thus, the children had assimilated what they could of *Leola and the Honeybears* into their schema for *The Three Bears*, and accommodated the new information in this African American variant to produce a new schema, which included a much happier alternative ending.

During the readaloud of *The Rough-Face Girl* (Martin, 1992) in Ms. Bigler-McCarthy's class, intertextual connections figured largely in the discussion of two general characteristics of fairy and folk tales: the opposition of good and evil and the frequent metamorphosis of characters. These two characteristics are important elements in our schemata for these tales (Kiefer, Hepler, & Hickman, 2006). The children and the teacher first discussed the general observation that good always wins over evil in fairy tales. Kenny commented that "That one [*The Rough-Face Girl*] was, that one was happily ever after, and in *Cinderella* it was happily ever after, and in *Snow White* it was, too." Charles objected, pointing out that in *The Swan Princess* (Singer, 1994), one of the main characters dies. The teacher returned to Kenny's comment:

TEACHER: Do you think it's fair to say, Kenny, that a lot of fairy tales end happily ever after? Not all of them.
SEAN: Not all of 'em, but some of 'em.
?: Like *Batman Forever*, it did, 'cause:
?: Batman never dies.
TEACHER: Do you think Batman is a fairy tale?
??: Yes! No! ### [great uproar]
SEAN: But it has a happy ending.
MICKEY: *Lon Po Po* isn't a happy ending. 'Cause the wolf dies.
TEACHER: It all depends on whose point of view you're looking at, the wolf or the children's, doesn't it?

This lengthy discussion continued with observations by the children that the wolf in *Red Riding Hood* dies, but since he is obviously evil, this confirms the hypothesis that good always wins in fairy tales. However, other children pointed out that in *The Three Bears*, Goldilocks is the bad character, and that she seems to get the better of the situation. No less than eight texts were used in this discussion, which tested and refined and (for some children) seemed to change the portion of their schema for fairy tales, which required good invariably to triumph over evil.

The other common feature of fairy tales that received attention in this discussion was the metamorphosis of characters. In *The Rough-Face Girl*, the face of the Invisible Being appears in one illustration as a pastiche of elements in the natural world: the Being's eyes are birds, and a rainbow and clouds outline the rest of his face. In another illustration, the Being also appears as an ordinary (though handsome) man. The children discussed these transformations by comparing them to the metamorphosis of characters in three other texts: *The Lion King* (in which Simba's father shows himself to Simba in the sky); *The Frog Prince*; and *The Swan Princess*. These intertextual references allowed them to reach the conclusion that the Invisible Being could assume many shapes, changing back and forth from one form to another.

These examples demonstrate that the children's knowledge of (and discussion about) the characteristics of literary genres like fairy tales rested upon the bedrock of their intertextual connections. Moreover, the concept of genre assumes some cognitive structure that allows us to classify and group stories as members of this or that genre, by linking together many individual stories. The examples also show the children in the process of modifying and refining their fluid schemata as well as building up their "intertextual histories" (Cairney, 1992). (This process is shown in greater detail in the following section, "The Power of Text Sets.")

5. Just as intertextual connections enabled the children to build up schemata for stories, connections between illustrations in different texts allowed them to *construct and refine their ideas of illustration style*. They could recognize the distinctive styles of particular artists: the scratchboard of Brian Pinkney, Eric Carle's collage, the watercolor style of Jerry Pinkney, or Tomie dePaola's soft colors and rounded outlined shapes. This recognition was made possible by their exposure to many texts illustrated by these artists, and in some cases, to their hands-on experience of experimenting with the technique themselves. In fact, in Mrs. Martin's class, once the children had heard several stories illustrated in Brian Pinkney's accomplished use of scratchboard, Mrs. Martin and I brought in some blank scratchboard from an art supply store, and the children delightedly made art, in Edward's excited comment, "the way Brian Pinkney does!" Having had this experience, they began to overgeneralize, suggesting that all the picturebooks we read were done in scratchboard! This points to the importance of allowing children to try out many illustration media and techniques. However, they definitely became experts on scratchboard, and were easily able to identify a new Brian Pinkney book from across the room.

Their intertextual connections to the work of their classmates and their own artwork also helped the children to talk about illustrational style. During the small-group readaloud of *Amazing Grace* (Hoffman, 1991), the end-papers stimulated the following discussion:

KENNY: That looks like chalk, like Mickey made for his book.
KRISSY: That's not chalk!
KENNY: Yeah, cause you like sketch with a, you can sketch it
        with, um:
KRISSY: It looks like water paint. Because of the white spots, that's
        why.
KENNY: Yeah, but he coulda gone like this and like this [imitating
        sketching, making little dabs in the air] and then dip it in water.
BRAD: Or maybe he can take a piece of chalk and put it in water:
KRISSY: You scrape it!
BRAD: Scrape it in water, and then, and then, and then, dip the
        pages, sliding, sliding, and when it's done it looks like that
        [pointing to the endpage].

In this excerpt, the children's own artistic products and those of their classmates (like Mickey's book) enable them to talk about the possible ways in which the endpapers were illustrated. Brad and Kenny described the technique (marbleizing, taught to them by Ms. Bigler-McCarthy) of scraping colored chalk in a pan of water and then carefully "sliding, sliding" a piece of paper through the water to pick up the chalk powder. This technique produces an effect that is indeed quite similar to the endpages in *Amazing Grace*, though it is probable that Krissy was correct about the use of watercolor.

6. Intertextual connections were utilized in order to *interpret story characters' feelings, motivations, or actions*. During the small-group readaloud of *Amazing Grace* (Hoffman, 1991), Trudy used her intertextual knowledge to understand Grace's motivation to be Peter Pan in the school play: "Um, there *is* a girl who plays Peter Pan, 'cause I got a tape of it, I got both tapes." Historically, in fact, most stage performances of *Peter Pan* have utilized a young woman to play the part of Peter. It is likely that Trudy had a copy of the filmed version of one of these performances (possibly the famous performance by Mary Martin); and she also had another tape (since she had "both tapes"), possibly the Disney cartoon. Trudy's intertextually based reasoning is that it is in the realm of possibility that Grace could play Peter, because there is another text in which a female does just this.

7. Intertextual connections allowed the children *to position themselves above the dynamics of the narrative*: to stand outside and above it, as it were,

in order to take on new perspectives in relation to the story. Babette Cole's (1987) *Prince Cinders* is a gender-reversed spoof of the traditional Cinderella story, in which the protagonist is a young prince who has to do all the housework while his older, bigger, and hairier brothers go to the Palace Disco with their girlfriends. A fairy promises to make him big and hairy like his brothers, so that he can go to the disco, too. However, she's rather inept, and Prince Cinders is changed by mistake into a big, hairy gorilla. Outside the disco, he meets Princess Lovelypenny, who is frightened by the gorilla, but just at this moment, the clock strikes midnight and Prince Cinders changes back into himself. The princess thinks that he has saved her from the gorilla and falls into love with her rescuer, but Prince Cinders is too shy to talk to the princess, and runs away so hastily that he loses his trousers in the rush. The trousers in this story function like the slipper in the European version of *Cinderella*, in that the princess "decrees that she will marry whoever fits the trousers lost by the prince who saved her from being eaten by the Big Hairy Monkey." At this point during the small-group readaloud of the story, Krissy, Trudy, Jim, and Brad begin to connect *Prince Cinders* intertextually with three other texts: the traditional version of *Cinderella* (Galdone, 1978); *Ugh* (Yorinks, 1990), a Cinderella variant in which the role of the slipper is played by a newly invented bicycle; and *Princess Smartypants*, another book by Babette Cole (1986), in which a liberated princess is successful in *not* marrying a prince, by kissing him and turning him into a frog:

100 KRISSY: Oh, it's like, um, Miss, what is it?
101 JIM: *Cinderella?*
102 KRISSY: No.
103 JIM: [*Princess*] *Smartypants?*
104 KRISSY: No, it's *Ugh. Ugh*. It reminds me of *Ugh*. Whoever, whoever, rides this bike, bicycle, they get to be king.
105 BRAD: /It's just like *Cinderella*, too.
106 TRUDY: It's like *Princess Smartypants//* and *Cinderella*, too.
107 TEACHER: Why is it like *Cinderella?*
108 TRUDY: Because she, uh, had the slipper, and had to try it on, and:
109 KRISSY: And he had to put on the pants:
110 JIM: Trousers.
111 BRAD: Let's hope she does not kiss his pants!

This four-way comparison led to Brad's wry comment (111), "Let's hope she does not kiss his pants!" Brad used the group's intertextual connections (101–110) to position himself so that he could, as it were, speak above all the characters' heads, to speak even above the narrator's head, to survey them all from a superior position—a position or stance of irony and humor. Also, the way his comment begins—"Let's hope"—includes the other children in this sly and knowing perspective.

8. Last, intertextual connections frequently *begat other intertextual connections*. It seemed that when a child (or the teacher) referred to the contextual matrix, this opened up a conceptual path on which other children might travel (though the adults may not have been able to understand all the links). In the example presented above during the reading of *Prince Cinders*, as well as the earlier vignette about a girl playing the part of Peter Pan, one intertextual link led to another. The process gathered momentum like a rolling snowball, until a critical mass was reached that frequently enabled the children to achieve a higher level of interpretive understanding or predictive power. In Mrs. Martin's class, during the readaloud of Galdone's (1985) version of *The Three Bears*, Kevin playfully stitched two stories together, which set off a barrage of intertextual connections:

> KEVIN: Goldilocks and Red Riding Hood they was talking on the phone . . .
> TEACHER: Goldilocks and Red Riding Hood were talking on the phone?
> KEVIN: Yeah, and wolf was at the uhm, went to the uhm, was in the Three Little Bears' house . . . And, and Goldilocks was in there . . . came by and walked up and didn't know that no one, that the wolf wasn't there.
> TEACHER: Oh, that was a really mixed-up fairy tale, wasn't it? Amanda?
> AMANDA: It's like that nursery rhyme. [singing] "Sing a song of six pence, a pocket full of rye . . ."
> TEACHER: [puzzled] Ok, what about it?
> AMANDA: Well, it got, "the queen was in the parlor . . ."
> TEACHER: The queen was in the *parlor*. That's what she was in, in the parlor, which is like the living room. Good that you remembered that that word was in there [the text previously mentions Goldilocks entering the "parlor"].
> UNIDENTIFIED CHILD: I seen that cartoon before/I seen the same cartoon//
> TEACHER: You saw the same cartoon he did? Ok. Yasmin?
> YASMIN: Uhm, oh, *Rugrats* do the same thing as *The Wizard of Oz* . . .

Thus, Keith's intertextual stitching of two stories seemed to open the floodgates for children's intertextual connections: there are no less than six in this brief excerpt. Neither Mrs. Martin nor I could figure out what the *Rugrats* (a cartoon series) and *The Wizard of Oz* were doing in this conversation; the children had "left us in the dust," as Newkirk and McClure (1992) remark in *Listening In: Children Talk about Books (and Other Things)*.

In summary, then, the role of intertextual connections was foundational and pivotal for many interpretive moves. As Charlotte Huck has remarked, "Thinking is linking." The children used intertextual links to interpret personal experiences that had been brought forward during the readaloud; to make symbolic interpretations of elements of the text; to predict what might happen in the narrative; to create and modify their schemata for stories; to interpret story characters' feelings, actions, or motivations; to position themselves outside and above the dynamics of the narrative; to build up and refine their concept of illustration style; and to make chains of other intertextual connections which raised the discussion to a higher cognitive level.

THE POWER OF TEXT SETS

Literary competence (Culler, 1975) has a quantitative element, in that the more stories we know, the greater number of critical tools we can bring to bear on any particular story. There may be specific experiences that increase the number of intertextual links dramatically (Sipe, 2000). For example, in Mr. Taylor's kindergarten classroom, I audiotaped picture storybook readalouds 13 times at fairly regular intervals during the school year. During the first four readalouds, the number of intertextual connections did not increase significantly: (4, 6, 0, 4). However, during the fifth readaloud, there were 45 intertextual connections, and the number of these types of connections remained significantly high for the rest of the readalouds. What caused this dramatic rise? Mr. Taylor and I theorized that because the fourth readaloud was the Galdone (1975) version of *The Gingerbread Boy* and the fifth readaloud was the Egielski (1997) version of *The Gingerbread Boy*, it was easy and natural for the children to make intertextual connections: they wanted to compare and contrast the two versions of the story they had heard. Once they had this experience, this seemed to jump-start the children's making of intertextual connections. In other words, once they added the idea of intertextual connections to their implicit concept of literary understanding, this idea became a part of their literary tool kit, and they continued to make use of this tool for the rest of the year (see Sipe & Bauer, 2001, p. 339), not only making these links among variants of the same story, but generalizing this ability to make intertextual connections in virtually every story they heard.

One of the other supplemental studies for this book (Sipe, 2001a) confirmed the hypothesis that variants of stories increase not only the quantity of children's intertextual connections, but also the level of cognitive abstraction suggested by these connections. The study involved a teacher (Mrs. Zigler) reading five picturebook variants of the *Rapunzel* story to a combined class of first- and second-graders, and analyzing the way the children linked the variants through intertextual connections. Such a group of variants of the same story is called a "text set" (Harste, Short, & Burke, 1988; Short, 1992). I chose the *Rapunzel* story because it is not as well known as some other traditional tales (for example *Red Riding Hood* or *The Three Little Pigs*), and thus, because of the unfamiliarity of most of the children with the story, I started, as it were, at a baseline of zero for children's knowledge (they did, of course, have some knowledge of the general structure of fairy tales, but not the specific knowledge of the Rapunzel story). I could then trace the ways in which the children gradually built up an understanding of the structure and content of the story as the variants were read and discussed. The variants were by Zelinsky (1997), abbreviated R1; Grimm (1997), illustrated by Dusikova, called R2; Berenzy (1995), R3; Grimm (1992), illustrated by Heyer, R4; and Stanley (1995), R5. The Zelinsky version was read first in order to begin with what we felt were the most artistically accomplished illustrations (it won a Caldecott Medal). The Dusikova, Berenzy, and Heyer versions were read second, third, and fourth because such an order exposed children to the greatest variety of changes in plot actions and details. This was desirable because we wanted to afford the children the opportunity to discuss both similarities and differences across all the texts. For example, in the Zelinsky version, Rapunzel has twins after a wedding ceremony in the tower. In the Heyer version, there is no wedding, and there is no mention of a child or children. In the Berenzy version, there is no wedding ceremony in the tower, but Rapunzel does bear children. The Stanley version (called *Petrosinella*, a Neopolitan variant of the story) was read last in the sequence because although recognizable as a Rapunzel variant, it contains several features not found in the other four variants; thus, we felt it was the most challenging version.

I found that the children made a great number of intertextual connections among the variants. This in itself was not surprising, because the readalouds were conducted over a relatively short period of time (8 weeks); in other words, the children were able to remember the previous variants and wanted to compare/contrast them without any explicit direction from the teacher. Another unsurprising finding was that the intertextual connections as a percentage of the total of the children's conversational turns for each readaloud was quite low for the Zelinsky readaloud (3%), presumably because the children had little knowledge of the Rapunzel story. Then, with the second version (Dusikova), the percentage of intertextual connections jumped dramatically to 56% of the conversational turns, and remained relatively high for the rest of the readalouds (41% for Berenzy, 28% for Heyer, and 46% for Stanley). In other words, the children were quite actively engaged in making intertextual connections among the readalouds after their experience of the first variant.

However, what *was* significant was that the *quality* of the intertextual connections increased in cognitive sophistication and abstraction over the course of the study. For example, in the first several readalouds, the children primarily made intertextual connections on the level of the *specific language* used in the stories ("this time he didn't say 'Rapunzel, Rapunzel' or whatever; and this is a 'witch,' not a 'sorceress.'"). They also used their knowledge of the previous versions to make predictions at the level of the *story plot* ("She's going to take her and put her in the tower"; "She's gonna say, 'I want your baby.'"). Also, they compared and contrasted the *illustrations* ("When it shows the picture of the kids, Rapunzel has the [grownup] kids; in the other stories they were wrapped up in blankets and they were babies").

Another type of intertextual connection was what I name "schema-building—'They all'" responses, because these responses frequently began with the words, "They all . . ." These types of responses indicated that the children were making high-level connections across several stories, and were beginning to build a cognitive schema for the *Rapunzel* story in general: "All of them start with a woman and a man who want a baby." "All the stories, usually like *Cinderella* and *Snow White* and lots of stories, start with 'Once upon a time.'" "In the others, they don't say that she made the tower; it was just there." Schema-building responses did not occur at all in R1. For R2, the percentage is 6%, but it is at R3 that this response was the greatest at 17%. This type of response was maintained with a slight decrease to 14% in R4, and dropped to 9% in R5. This suggests that the children were beginning seriously to build a schema in R3, and that they continued to construct schema knowledge for the rest of the readalouds.

The most sophisticated intertextual connections were what I name "schema-building—'Alternatives'" and were characterized by children's suggestions for alternatives to the plot or expressed preferences for one version over another:

DAVE: Isn't there any Rapunzels where the dad, his wife dies and he has the baby with him and then he goes down and gets the child, and he likes the rapunzel [the herb]?

TEACHER: Well, you know, I have not read a version like that, but you could certainly write one.

Other examples of this response expressed preferences, based on the knowledge of several versions:

MEGAN: I like it [*Petrosinella*] because there was more magic in it and there was another witch, and it never told you the mother was married; it just started in the garden.

SUSIE: I like at the end when they get married it doesn't mention her mother at all, and when a girl gets married her mom is usually there.

LENA: I like this one [*Petrosinella*] because there's like more detail and it's like more exciting.

"Schema-building—Alternatives" responses did not occur at all in R1 or R2. In R3, there was a minuscule percentage of these types of responses (2%), and there were none in R4. However, in R5, the last readaloud, 9% of the responses were in this category. This suggests that by the last readaloud, the children had enough control over the *Rapunzel* schema to suggest alternatives to the plot sequence. Their *Rapunzel* schema, in other words, was so well developed that they may be said to have owned the story, and gave evidence of this ownership by proposing to add other variants and expressing their preferences.

The analysis of these readalouds suggests that the children were able to build up knowledge across cases, in the complex domain of story schemata. This type of abstract knowledge is a necessary prerequisite for coming to understand what makes it necessary for a story to be recognizable as a *Rapunzel* variant, and what is of secondary importance. Children's knowledge of literary genres is likely built up in this way as well. By hearing many stories of the same type or genre, children may arrive at an increasingly abstract conception of what constitutes fairy tales, realistic fiction, historical fiction, contemporary fantasy, or other genres and subgenres.

INTERTEXTUAL RESISTANCE TO STORIES

I found that if young children already knew a story (for example, *Cinderella*), they might object if the teacher read a new version of the story that was different from the familiar story in some details or plot elements. This is a type of intertextual response because it is a matter of children's connections between a text they already know and a text that is new to them. Those children for whom the Disney cartoon movie is the original version of the story may question illustrated literary versions and variants from diverse cultures, like *The Rough-Face Girl* (Martin, 1992), *Yeh-Shen* (Louie, 1982), or *Mufaro's Beautiful Daughters* (Steptoe, 1987). The first version of a story that children hear tends to become the Ur-story by which every subsequent variant is judged (Sipe, 2002b). Children in Mr. Taylor's kindergarten classroom were incensed that Richard Egielski's (1997) version was entitled *The Gingerbread Boy* rather than *The Gingerbread Man*—"Not boy—man!" they shouted. In Paul Galdone's (1975) version, they also objected to the Gingerbread Man's taunting refrain, "Run! Run! Run! Catch me if you can!" because it did not exactly match the words they were used to ("Run, run, as fast as you can!"). For these children, the language of the story of the Gingerbread Man was immutable, and divergence from this familiar language was not acceptable. The children were saying, in effect, "That's not how the story goes!" In other cases, children rejected variants of stories on the level of genre, disputing the legitimacy of parodies of fairy tales, for example. A few children in Ms. Bigler-McCarthy's first/second-grade class thought that the stories in *The Stinky Cheese Man* (Scieszka, 1992) were "stupid" and "silly." They had a good point: the full title of the book is *The Stinky Cheese Man and Other Fairly Stupid Tales*!

However, I also found that as children were exposed to multiple variants of the same story, as in the *Rapunzel* study just mentioned, they rather quickly moved beyond this type of intertextual resistance: the objections simply dropped away. Children modified their internal schema for a story, becoming more flexible and accepting of differences. Thus, they constructed an understanding of stories as what the French literary critic Gerard Genette (1998) refers to as "palimpsests" (after a term for a vellum manuscript that has been used and reused by partially erasing the previous writing). With an immersion in many variants of the *Rapunzel* tale, the children were not responding solely to the textual features of the book at hand, but the various instantiations to which they had already responded. Text became intertext. They did not experience one text of *Rapunzel* in isolation; rather, *Rapunzel* became for them a layered set of multiple texts. Children understood that stories can be transformed (Sipe, 1993), and that they, too, could take a story and change it, producing their own version: they could add the latest layer to the rich palimpsest. Thus, a sense of authorship and ownership of literacy can develop from this type of intertextual response.

7

Personal Response:
Drawing the Story to the Self

The universal impulse of readers to link the events or characters in a narrative with their own lives was confirmed by my data: about 1 out of every 10
of all the children's conversational turns represented this personalizing connection. In this category, the text seemed primarily to act as a stimulus for
what Cochran-Smith (1984) calls "life-to-text" and "text-to-life" connections. The children connected their lives with some element of the text or used
knowledge gained from a text to inform their lives. The chapter also includes
several other ways in which the children drew the stories to themselves.

LIFE-TO-TEXT CONNECTIONS

Life-to-text connections were associated with an element of interpretation,
but they seemed primarily to represent a drawing of the story toward oneself. For the children, as for all of us, there seemed to be a pleasure in perceiving the ways in which the story (or details of it) mirrored their own lives.

Simple Connections to the Children's Lives

The simplest of these connections was an unelaborated statement of recognition that a detail of the story was similar to an aspect of the child's own
life. In Mr. Taylor's and Mrs. Martin's kindergarten classes, children seemed
to especially enjoy character names that were the same as theirs or the names
of friends: "I know somebody name Christopher!" (during the reading of
Christopher Coady's [1991] *Red Riding Hood*); "I got a cousin named Richard!" (during *Hey, Al* [Yorinks, 1986]). Children in Mr. Taylor's kindergarten
classes also expressed simple pleasure in the mention of favorite colors ("that's
my favorite color—blue!" during *Hou Yi Shoots the Suns* [Jiannan, 1996]).
Latoya was thrilled to note that "My cousin got that shirt that the Ginger-

bread Boy got on!" in the version of the story by Richard Egielski (1997). In Mrs. Martin's class, during the reading of *The Colors of Us* (Katz, 1999), which celebrates the great range of human skin colors, children delightedly compared their complexions to those of characters in the book: "That looks like me, like the creamy peanut butter!" "I look like that girl—the 'brown cupcake' girl!" "Me and Vi and Lakia is that one!" During the reading of *The Napping House* (Wood, 1984) in Ms. Bigler-McCarthy's first- and second-grade class, the teacher read about the various characters "thumping" and bouncing on a bed; first-grader Nicole offered, "Miss Bigler, I did that on my old bed." At this point, Nicole seemed less interested in interpreting the story than in simply taking pleasure in seeing the characters of the story doing what she had done.

What good, then, are these simple personal connections if their primary purpose is not hermeneutic or interpretive? It may be that they represent the very beginnings—the crucial foundation—of an impulse which, as children grow older and develop more sophisticated literary interpretation, will become increasingly important for both their enjoyment *and* their understanding. How can stories affect us, move us, delight or sadden us; how can they cause us to reflect deeply on our own lives in thoughtful ways if we do not first have the groundwork of these seemingly trivial personal connections? If children draw the story to themselves in these easy and down-to-earth ways, and are not discouraged by their teachers, they may develop the ability to make much more important and meaningful connections as they become more astute and sensitive readers.

Elaborated Life-to-Text Connections

The children could also elaborate on their life-to-text connections, as Juan demonstrated during Mr. Taylor's reading of *The Tunnel* (Browne, 1989). In the story, a brother attempts to frighten his sister at night. Juan connected with this experience, and explained it: "My brother, every time I go to sleep, my brother creep under my bed and try to scare me, but I clock him on the head with a shoe for messin' with me!"

In Ms. Bigler-McCarthy's class first/second-grade class, Kenny demonstrated the same type of elaborated life-to-text connection during the reading of *The Napping House* (Wood, 1984), which is a gentle fantasy in the form of a cumulative tale about an increasing number of characters (humans and animals) that go to sleep on a "cozy bed":

> TEACHER [reading the sixth opening; depicts an old woman, a child, a dog, and a cat all sleeping on top of each other in a bed]: **And on that dog there is a cat, a snoozing cat on a dozing dog on a**

dreaming child on a snoring granny on a cozy bed in a napping house, where everyone is sleeping.

KENNY: Hey, that's just like at day care, at snacktime, we, we all napped for two hours.

TEACHER: In the day care, everyone was asleep like that?

KENNY [nodding]: Two hours.

TEACHER: Two full hours, you had to sleep?

KENNY: Uh huh. I used to play in the cot, though.

TEACHER: When did you use to go to day care?

KENNY: I still go to day care. I go to day care right now. Um, since it's in [name of nearby community]? The days that we don't have school, we go to day care.

Here Kenny's connection, with the teacher's encouragement, turned into an evocation of his past daily routine and his schedule on "the days that we don't have school." Again, although these experiences obviously assisted Kenny in understanding and interpreting the visual image and text, the primary function for the child seemed to be to provide a pleasant personal detour from the story line (sanctioned and assisted by the teacher), which was enjoyable in its own right.

Telling Stories "on" the Story

Kenny's personal connections often went even further, turning into full-fledged stories with beginnings, middles, and ends, as the following excerpt, also drawn from *The Napping House* readaloud, demonstrates. Kenny's story was sparked by the movement of the flea in the seventh opening of the book. Unfortunately, he was so excited that some of his words were unintelligible:

KENNY: Well, I saw this ### once, and I took a magnifying glass, and I looked down there, and there was tons of fleas. And then I got a bucket, I mean I got a little like #, and ### couldn't get out, with no holes, because if I put a hole in it, they get out, but no holes, um, they, um, then I caught 'em? And I put one in my house?

TEACHER: The fleas? You put the fleas in the house? Oh boy!

SEAN: Oh yeah! [in a dubious tone]

KENNY: And then my brother, my sister, my sister had a fork, and she put holes in it, and the fleas ran all over the house.

TEACHER: And then what?

KENNY: Then, everybody was itching.

TEACHER: What did your mom do?

KENNY: Well, she, my dad, when he opened the door, he had a thing
of them, and ### and my punishment was putting fleas down my
underwear! And my mom spanked me, and I couldn't sit down
for a week!

For Kenny, then, stories seemed to provide an opportunity to become a
storyteller; they seemed to be part of his individual response style. And, like
all well-told stories, it was difficult to ascertain how much of his plots were
based on personal experience and how much was pure fancy. We all assumed,
however, that Kenny's day-to-day life was not quite as crammed with drama
as his stories. (During the readaloud of *Jack and the Beanstalk* [Kellogg,
1991], he declared that his father had been taken up into the sky by a tornado, only to be set down again unharmed.)

In one of the supplemental studies for this book (Sipe, 2002a), urban
kindergarteners in another classroom displayed a similar propensity for telling such "stories about the story" as they heard *The Tale of Peter Rabbit*
(Potter, 1902/1987) read aloud by their teacher. The following story was
sparked by the teacher's reading that Peter was "trembling with fright" after
almost being caught by Mr. McGregor. The numbered sentences and phrases
refer to parallel elements in *The Tale of Peter Rabbit*, and the ellipses refer
to pauses, not omissions in the child's speech.

TEACHER: Have you ever been so frightened by something that you
would start shaking and be nervous?
TANISHA: (1) Well, one day, my mom, she had told me not to go
somewhere. One day my mom had told me not to go where my
next-door neighbor's bar because she was going to put some
more # through it, and (2) I had went in there and (3) I had
grabbed a lot of carrots and I had gotten full. So Mrs. Mc . . .
um . . . so Mrs . . . um . . . whatever, she had caught me and I ran
and (4) jumped in a pool. And I went to my house and I jumped
in a pool and she . . . and (5) I sneezed and she caught me 'cause
I was allergic to pool water and she had caught me. I was
allergic to the chlorine that they put in the water.
TEACHER: The chlorine, mmm hmm.
TANISHA: Yeah, I was allergic to chlorine, and when I got in the pool
I sneezed and swum out of the pool and I ran across the street
and . . . and I ran across the street and I had got scared that (6)
she had tried to, um, catch me so she could kill me and eat me,
and I was, like, You can't do that, because if you do that, God
won't forgive you.
TEACHER: God won't forgive you.

TANISHA: (7) And then I had ran 'cause I wasn't going to get hurt, and (8) my mother put me to bed without no food. And then . . . she, he . . .

TEACHER: She put you to bed without what?

TANISHA: Without my dinner. And then the next morning I did it again.

TEACHER: Oh, OK. Well, we're going to go on. But you were frightened. That's a good example, OK.

TANISHA: (9) And then I got scared, and I had got the shivers.

In this fascinating little story, the child used at least nine of the plot elements of *Peter Rabbit*. She situated herself as Peter, and alternated between first- and third-person narration. Like Peter, she:

- is warned by mother not to go some place clearly off-limits: a bar (1)
- goes anyway (2)
- eats carrots and gets full (3)
- jumps in water [a pool is a fine substitute for a watering can!] (4)
- sneezes (5)
- reports that the next-door neighbor was trying to kill her and eat her (6)
- escapes (7)
- is put to bed by her mother (8)
- is frightened and shivering (9)

A number of features of the child's story are obviously not in Potter's story: the allergy to chlorine as the cause of the sneeze; the admonition that "God won't forgive you"; being caught; going to bed without any food as a punishment (a more stringent variation on Peter's illness and inability to join in the supper); and doing "it" again the next morning. In these ways, Potter's tale is modified, extended, and injected with elements of the child's own experience and life. It's a "remix" (Dyson, 2003) that "signifies" on the original story. Tanisha has also indicated a possible sequel to Peter's adventure; just as she "did it" again the next morning, so perhaps will Peter!

In the kindergarten classrooms where *Peter Rabbit* was read, children forged several links between their own lives and Peter's experiences; in other words, they constructed their own relevance for the story for themselves. They spoke of disobeying their own parents and the consequences; losing their own clothing (as Peter often does); and being chased (though by older children or dogs, not Mr. McGregor). They also made some very touching personal connections between Peter's family and their own families. They discussed how Peter was, in Kareem's words, a "chip off the old block" because Peter's father had also gone into Mr. McGregor's garden and had been "turned into a pie" by Mrs. McGregor; this led several children to speculate that Peter's father was a ne'er-do-well whose actions had hurt his family:

MARCUS: Well, his dad didn't care—he was bad and he got into
      trouble and got killed, and then Peter's mom had to take care of
      all of 'em.
LATOYA: My dad's in jail, but my grandma takes care of us, too.

In this brief exchange, we see children thinking about Mrs. Rabbit as a single mother—burdened with sole responsibility for four offspring (Flopsy, Mopsy, Cottontail, and Peter), one of whom is recalcitrant and headed for certain trouble like his absent father. In contrast to Mrs. Rabbit's isolated situation, however, children pointed out the strong extended family supports in their own communities.

Personal Connections to the Book as a Physical Object

A special type of life-to-text connection took place with well-loved stories that were old favorites with the children. *Where the Wild Things Are* (Sendak, 1963) was one of these stories: according to what they reported, the great majority of the children in several classes had heard this book read aloud several (or many) times before, and a little less than half had a copy of the book at home. The following excerpt is taken from the beginning of the transcript of the readaloud of this book to Ms. Bigler-McCarthy's class:

TEACHER: You know what? This book, I had this book when I was a
      little girl.
?: I have a small one of it.
?: I have a video.
KENNY: I have a bendy book [paperback edition] of it.
TEACHER: You have a videotape of this?
JIM: When I was six years old, I went to this library that looked like
      the airport?
TEACHER: A library looked like the airport to you?
JIM: Yeah, it kinda looked like it, and I went into the library shop
      and I bought that. That's where I got it.

Examples from Mrs. Martin's classroom include children's celebration of the presence of books and literacy activities from outside school: "My sister got that book." "I have that book at home." "My uncle draws pictures for books." "I got this book at my day care." In all these instances, the children are not making connections with the story line, characters, or details of the text, but with the book—the physical object—itself. Such a popular and well-known book as *Where the Wild Things Are* is a protean text; as the children knew, it is available in a great variety of forms and formats. Jim even remembered where he bought his copy—at a "library that looked like the airport"—much as adults of a certain age might personalize President Kennedy's assassination by remembering exactly where they were when they heard the news.

Questioning the Story from Personal Experience

Yet another type of life-to-text connection began with questioning the story line. This type of connection was much more clearly interpretive. During the reading of *Where the Wild Things Are* (Sendak, 1963) in Ms. Bigler-McCarthy's class, the following exchange occurred:

> TEACHER [reading]: **His mother called him "WILD THING!" and Max said "I'LL EAT YOU UP!" so he was sent to bed without eating anything.**
> PEGGY: Just for saying, "I'll eat you up"?
> TEACHER: Well, that's not very nice to talk back to your parents, is it?
> JOEY: I always go, "I don't wanna do that!"
> TEACHER: Really? You should respect your parents and say, "OK."
> [Pause]
> [unintelligible; several children talking at once]
> TEACHER [pointing to Max's frowning facial expression in the illustration]: Look at him. Looks like he feels like you might feel, Joey, when you say that.
> JOEY: I, I, um, I was *that* close to not eating.

In this excerpt, Peggy's questioning of the text (how can Max's mother send him to his room for what Peggy considers such a minor infraction of the domestic rules?) is the catalyst for Joey's memories of similar struggles of will between himself and his parents. Peggy's question is interpretive in nature, and Joey's identification with the character of Max almost certainly allows him to interpret this episode of the plot in a profound way.

During the reading of *Something Beautiful* (Wyeth, 1998) in Mrs. Martin's class, a story about a young child's encounters with sad and disturbing features of her urban neighborhood (including graffiti and homelessness), a poignant discussion ensued when the teacher read the third opening of the story. The children questioned the text, resulting in a powerful personal connection by Kevin:

TEACHER [reading]: **Where I walk, I pass a lady whose home is a big cardboard carton. She sleeps on the sidewalk wrapped in plastic.**

AALIYAH: I think if somebody sleeps on the sidewalk, they don't have a house.

TEACHER: Why do you think she's there? Violet?

VIOLET: She maybe died.

AMANDA: Because nobody will want her, somebody threw her out of her old house, and maybe she lived where that person lived, and then they kicked her out.

ISAAC: Maybe they, um, she didn't have no food and that box thing, and maybe she didn't eat, the only thing she did is slept, um, every night and every daytime . . . maybe she didn't have no food to eat and maybe she just died.

NAISHA: How did she live on the ground?

TEACHER: She does, she lives in that cardboard box right there on the ground. Do you think she wants to live there, Kevin?

KEVIN: No, because every time when me and my mom go to the [doughnut shop], we see people on the ground, um, and they be sleepin' and they look like they don't have no food. And this guy is laying on the ground and came in the [doughnut shop] and he went over in the corner and then laid down in the street.

TEACHER: And how did that make you feel? When you see that, how does that make you feel?

KEVIN: It make me sad.

Something Beautiful also engaged Mrs. Martin's class in a serious discussion about the destructive actions of people in their own neighborhoods, and the children's own futures. In the story, the little girl sees some graffiti on the side of a building, prompting Khalil to remark:

KHALIL: 'Cause I know that some people, like some bad boys, go down and write on the doors and then they get in their cars and then they mess with the police. And they make the police get lost!

TEACHER: They chase them and they make the police get lost. 'Cause they're slick, but they are bad boys. You don't want to be a bad boy, right?

KHALIL: I'm gonna be a bad boy when I grow up though.

TEACHER: You are? Why?

KHALIL: I want to be like my big brother!

At this point, Mrs. Martin clearly felt that she had to deal with Khalil's perception of his future:

TEACHER: Aw, but you don't want to do that! You want to be, you want to be, I know sometimes when we say "bad," it means "good," but you want to grow up to be, maybe you might want to be a teacher? Or a doctor? Or maybe you could be a policeman and you could help people.

Here, Mrs. Martin's language indicates her deep distress; however, she was not going to let this go: she continued to refer to this issue as the story progressed. When the little girl in the story goes to school, we see that her teacher is an African American man, and Mrs. Martin returned to her concern about Khalil's statement that he was "gonna be a bad boy when I grow up":

TEACHER: So here she is, she's at school with that teacher, and look at him; he looks so handsome, and so smart! And he's teaching the little children . . . He's not running around in hot cars and getting into trouble, he's in school being a man!
SEVERAL CHILDREN: [laughter]
TEACHER: *Excuse me*, this is a man! Those other boys are boys, those are bad boys, they didn't grow up to be men; they are still little boys up here in their head.

After Mrs. Martin read the next page of the story, where the little girl begins to discover positive things about her neighborhood, it was clear that the children were still thinking about their futures:

LAMAR: I want Khalil, he'll be writing on the door [graffiti] and I'll be locking Khalil up.
TEACHER: Well, I don't think Khalil is going to do that when he grows up. Khalil is going to become a man, not a little boy.
KHALIL: I changed my mind!
TEACHER: Oh, I'm glad, I'm glad to hear that! I'm glad you changed your mind!
KHALIL: I'm going to be a police when I grow up.

TEXT-TO-LIFE CONNECTIONS

Connections from "the other direction"—from text to life—were rare, but when they occurred, they were obviously deeply meaningful for the children. These connections formed the basis for informing and possibly transforming the children's lives. In other words, the emphasis was not on interpreting the story or making an associative link (however elaborate), but rather using the story as a form of (vicarious) experience to assist in understanding or dealing with life. For example, Khalil's last comments (above) about changing his mind and wanting to be a policeman suggest that he was making use of the story (and the discussion) to understand his own life and possibly to envision his future differently.

In Ms. Bigler-McCarthy's class, the reading of *Princess Furball* (Huck, 1989), a variant of the *Cinderella* story, to the whole class provoked a very serious discussion about death. The frontispiece for this book (or, as Robert put it, "the bit that happened before the writing starts") is an illustration of a funeral procession with figures in mourning garb carrying a bier through a graveyard. The children had glanced at it and interpreted it as a funeral early in the discussion. As the teacher's reading of the verbal text began, they realized that this illustration depicted the funeral of the mother of the princess—"Princess Furball"—who is the principal character in the story, identifying the small child in the funeral procession as the younger Princess Furball. The children asked the teacher to turn back to the illustration on the left-hand side of the title page, which shows a portrait of the dead queen, with the young princess standing beside it. At the end of the story, there is an illustration of Furball with her own children. At this point, Alice commented that "Now her children look like she did when she was little. And she looks like her mother." Don further developed the connections between the illustrations by pointing out that the governess "who took care of Furball when her mother died" in the frontispiece is also depicted on the dedication page, watching while the princess and other children play together.

The discussion about these illustrations provided the impetus for the children to share some of their fears about death and their memories of people they knew who had passed away. In a lengthy discussion, the children talked about various reasons why people die, and the teacher pointed out that "Dying happens to every single thing that's alive." Mickey told the story of a mechanic, a friend of the family, who had died of a heart attack and was cremated: "You get burned into ashes, and that's all that's left." Terry recounted the story of a relative who died of a stroke, commenting that "He was smoking a lot." The teacher shared her feelings about her grandfather's death. Children spoke of visiting their grandparents' graves and placing flowers there, and Mickey shared his disappointment that he had never known one of his grandparents (who died before he was born) and his jealousy of his older brother, who had known this grandparent. Immediately after this discussion, both the teacher and I noticed that the children seemed remarkably calm; it is possible that this experience had functioned as a catharsis for their personal anxiety about grief and death.

OTHER PERSONAL CONNECTIONS

Life-to-text and text-to-life connections did not exhaust the types of personal connections the children made; there were several other ways in which the children personalized stories.

Connections to Play

Characters in stories elicited children's connections to their own play and pretend experiences. For example, during the readaloud of *The Adventures of Sparrowboy* (Pinkney, 1997) in Mrs. Martin's class, there was quite a lengthy discussion of the various superheroes the children pretended to be, and what they had done to rescue people in distress or rectify wrong. The following is a short excerpt:

> KEVIN: I used to pretend that I was Batman, Batgirl, and Supergirl; I ask my mom can I be a hero.
>
> TEACHER: Amanda, did you ever pretend you were a superhero? You know, girls can be superheroes because I sure pretended all the time.
>
> AMANDA: Superwoman and Kelsey from the Power Rangers. I was saving my dad; he almost fell off the roof!
>
> AALIYAH: I saved my dad from getting electrocuted from a wire.
>
> DESHAWN: When I was a Power Ranger, I got in a robot and took the money away, from the bad guys.

Assuming Agency in Stories

Another way in which children personalized stories was to give themselves agency in stories, arguing what they would do or say if they were a certain character. These "I would" or "I wouldn't" statements allowed the children to insert themselves in a story and shape it, like clay, nearer to their own view of how things should proceed. For example, in Mrs. Martin's class during the reading of *Anansi and the Moss-Covered Rock* (Kimmel, 1988), Kevin asserted that he would be able to be a full-time trickster, unlike Anansi the spider, who is occasionally tricked himself: "If I was Anansi the spider I would trick all of 'em, but they wouldn't be able to trick me!" A more extended example of this type of response is the following excerpt from the discussion of *Wings* (Myers, 2000), a fantasy about a boy named Ikarus Jackson, who flies over rooftops with a beautiful pair of wings; most of the children in school (and even some of the teachers) shun him, however. On the 10th opening of this picturebook, the narrator, a little girl who sometimes feels ostracized herself, comments,

100   TEACHER [reading]: **Walking home from school, I knew how he felt, how lonely he must be. Maybe I should have said something to those mean kids.** What do *you* think she could have said to those mean kids?
101   KATRIN: "Why did you do that to that angel?"
102   JOE: I think she should have said, "Don't do that no more."
103   KEVIN: She should have said, "Everybody go back to your own, go back home and tell your parents what you all did."
104   KHALIL: She's probably going to call the cops for them . . . 'Cause my dad said, if I be bad he would call the cops on me.
105   AALIYAH: She should have said, "Why'd you do that? Each one of you are in a strange way. How come you guys laugh at somebody that strange just like you?"
106   KATRIN: "Keep flying!"
107   EDWARD: "Come down from there."
108   BELLA: She should have said, "Sorry."
109   AMANDA: "Keep your soul up and fly."

In this excerpt, at Mrs. Martin's invitation (100), the children generated some wonderful alternatives. Aaliyah's (105) and Amanda's (109) comments are especially poignant; Aaliyah points out that everyone is strange in one way or another, and Amanda offers encouraging spiritual advice.

Another example of a series of "I would" statements occurred during the reading of the Galdone (1975) *Gingerbread Boy* in Mr. Taylor's kindergarten class. In this case, Mr. Taylor (like Mrs. Martin) invited the responses, which tended toward the metaphysical:

TEACHER: What would you do if you saw a gingerbread boy running down the street? Rona?
RONA: Give him back to the little old woman and give him back to the little old man.
CALLIE: Give him a cookie! [student laughter]
TEACHER: Give him a cookie?
SAMPSON: He *is* a cookie! [emphatically] He can't eat *hisself*, 'cause he can't murdered hisself. He can't bite off his [own] head!
VIVIAN: I would run faster and faster as I can so I could catch him.

A third example of an extended "I would" or "I wouldn't" set of personalizations occurred during the reading of *Little Red Riding Hood* (Hyman, 1983) in Ms. Bigler-McCarthy's class. Unlike Mrs. Martin and Mr. Taylor, Ms. Bigler-McCarthy did not need to invite the children to voice their comments:

> TEACHER [reading]: "I'm going to Grandmother's. She is sick in bed, you know." "Is that so?" he [the wolf] murmured. "And what have you got in your basket?" "A loaf of bread, some sweet butter, and a bottle of wine."
>
> GORDON: I wouldn't do that, I would say, "oh nothing" [looking up innocently and whistling].
>
> TRENT: If I was Little Red Riding Hood, and um, the wolf asked me where grandma's was, I'd say, she's in New York, and a hundred miles [away].
>
> SEAN: If I were Red, I wouldn't care, I'd just go through the shortcut.

Controlling Story Characters

At some points, there were indications that the children considered characters to be protean creations whom the children could personally control. During the readaloud of Paul Galdone's (1985) version of *The Three Bears* in Ms. Bigler-McCarthy's class, there was a discussion about how old Goldilocks might be, given the fact that the illustrator had depicted her with missing front teeth:

> TEACHER: How old are children who are losing their teeth?
>
> SEAN: Twenty-nine?
>
> TRUDY: Real tiny babies.
>
> TEACHER: But there are children in here [the classroom] who have missing teeth. Do you think Goldilocks could be your age?
>
> GORDON: Let's *make* her our age!

For the children, then, stories were malleable, not immutably etched in stone. There was room in stories for *them*—their personalities, their choice-making, and their capabilities. Gordon felt free to become a co-author of *The Three Bears*. This recognition that stories could be controlled by the children led them to another way of following the personalizing impulse: envisioning themselves as the tellers of the entire tale, as in this comment by Krissy after the discussion of Hyman's (1983) *Little Red Riding Hood*: "We could make a story about Little Red Riding Hood, like a puppet show. We could make a puppet show about Little Red Riding Hood, after reading a whole bunch of stories about Little Red Riding Hood." Here, Krissy imagines giving herself (and her friends) agency, not *in* specific details or episodes of the story, but rather *over* the entire story. Krissy and her friends will personally own the story, and their story will stand alongside the "whole bunch of stories" about Red Riding Hood. As Sally commented during the reading of *Strega Nona* (dePaola, 1975), "*We* are retelling the tale again today."

Blurring Life and Story

Last, there were instances of personal response that indicated that the children were purposefully blurring the distinction between their lives and the world of the story. During the reading of *Swimmy* (Lionni, 1963) in Mr. Taylor's kindergarten class, Polly remarked, "We got fish right here; one's named Swimmy over there. The rest of the fish over there is the red fish." Polly was referring to Swimmy's different color (black), in contrast to the other fish in the story, who were red. Polly was able to connect a real fish, in the class aquarium, with the illustration in Lionni's book.

Another instance of this blurring of life and story, again in Mr. Taylor's class, occurred during the readaloud of *Red Riding Hood* (Coady, 1991), in which Lettie told the class of a dream she had had:

> LETTIE: I had a dream that I was Little Red Riding Hood. I was at, um, I, the wolf ate me up and then that's when, that's when my mom, that's when my grandmom got out, that's when somebody came to help me and my sister out.
>
> TEACHER: In your dream?
>
> KEYRON: Then that was a different version! [student laughter]
>
> JUAN: Who was the author? [student laughter]

This, for kindergartners, is an almost unbelievably sophisticated exchange. Lettie tells her dream, and this personal story—what would be more personal than a dream?—is interpreted by Keyron and Juan as yet another *Red Riding Hood* story to set alongside the other variants they already had heard (notice Keyron's and Juan's confident use of the metalanguage of stories—"version" and "author"). Juan's remark—"Who was the author?"—launches us into a metaphysical speculation about where our dreams come from: are we, in our waking lives, the authors of our own dreams? Or do we possess another identity or multiple identities, which are largely unconscious? An author controls what he or she writes, but did Lettie have the same control as the author of her dream? In any case, Juan's question suggests that the children thought of stories as malleable and of themselves as capable authors, whether waking or sleeping.

CHILDREN'S PERSONAL RESISTANCE TO STORIES

I found that personal response did not consist solely of drawing the story to the self in various ways; it could also represent a personal distancing from the story. My data suggest three principal ways in which children's personal responses indicated their resistance:

1. *Preferential or Categorical Resistance.* Children resist some stories after a cursory examination. They may literally judge a book by its cover by considering it too babyish: "I'm too old for that." Boys may reject a book because they consider it a "book for girls." Research shows that girls, on the other hand, are much more tolerant of books where a boy is the main character (Childress, 1985). A glance at the illustrations may convince some children that the book isn't for them; some kindergarteners didn't want to read Christopher Coady's (1991) version of *Red Riding Hood* because "the pictures are too scary." Children may also resist whole categories or genres of books ("I don't like stories that aren't real") or be quite narrow in their preference ("I only like books about trucks"). The shorthand for this type of resistance is, "I don't like stories like that."

2. *Engaged or Kinetic Resistance.* The second type of personal resistance is based on Möller and Allen's (2000) idea of "engaged resistance," which they developed to interpret some of the responses of a small group of fifth-grade African American and Hispanic girls to Mildred Taylor's (1987) *The Friendship.* Möller and Allen observed that these readers identified with characters in Taylor's evocation of friendships between white and African American individuals in rural Mississippi of the 1930s. However, the girls resisted the cruel and unjust events in the story, including racial intolerance and blatant discrimination. The girls said that although they valued the story, it was too emotionally draining and painful; they felt a sense of helplessness that was disturbing and uncomfortable for them. It is significant that these readers were students of color; Cai (2002) suggests that readers from non-hegemonic cultures may resist texts from fear and anger at the injustice in the story and its connection to the real world. However, this type of resistance may also be exhibited by readers from mainstream cultures. The shorthand for this type of resistance is "That may be how life is, but it's too painful, and I don't want to hear about it."

I also believe that this type of resistance is similar to Deanne Bogdan's (1990) concept of "kinetic response." Bogdan asserts that one of the ways in which readers evaluate literature is to judge it by their immediate emotional reaction to it—whether it "packs a[n emotional] whollop" (p. 126) for them or not. In the case of engaged resistance, there is a significant emotional effect, but the effect is painful and thus to be avoided. Young children, too, exhibit this type of resistance. In Mrs. Martin's kindergarten class, as the teacher read *Something Beautiful* (Wyeth, 1998), a few of the kindergarteners complained, "This story is just too sad—I like happy stories." This comment demonstrates more than dissatisfaction; it reveals the disjunction between what the children expect or believe about stories—in this case, that stories should be about pleasant experiences—and the content of *Something Beautiful*. The comment also suggests that the depictions of life in this piece of realistic fiction are, in a sense, *too* real for some of the children; they resist paying attention to these distressing features of reality.

This type of resistance raises the enormous question of what is proper fare for the young. Probably all of us would agree that young children should not be exposed to extreme, horrific words and images of violence, sexuality, or suffering. However, some of us, along with Maurice Sendak (1988), might argue that children know a lot more about the world than we often assume, and that they need opportunities to discuss their concerns, anxieties, and confusion in supportive situations with their peers and with compassionate, knowledgeable adults (Robertson, 1997).

3. *Exclusionary Resistance*. The third type of personal resistance to stories that is displayed by young children is based on issues of representation: *who* is represented in stories (and who is not represented), and *how* they are represented. The notion of "identifying" with story characters is complex; it can involve perception of similarities between readers and story characters, or perhaps the wish to be like them in some way. The research (for example, Nevel, 1999; Sims, 1983; Taylor, 1997; Towell, Schulz, & Demetrulias, 1997) is inconclusive about "the relationship between readers' cultural identity and their preferences for multicultural literature or identification with characters in the story" (Cai, 2002, p. 161). Nevertheless, most educators believe that it is important that children be able to "see themselves" in stories. This may be especially crucial for children whose racial, ethnic, and cultural identity is not that of the "culture of power" (Delpit, 1995, p. 24); however, as culture is not monolithic and is experienced differently by individual members of that culture (Smolkin & Suina, 1997), the presence of a character with a similar cultural background is no guarantee that identification will occur.

The shorthand for exclusionary resistance is, "I don't see myself—I am left out of this story!" Writing about a fourth- and fifth-grade discussion of *Maniac Magee*, Enciso (1994) records a Latina girl's comment about the book: ". . . there's a black part and a white part. Where would like Mexicans or Chinese or someone like that be?" (p. 524). This comment suggests that the student felt she was excluded from the world of the book. Although the world of children's literature has made advances in the quantity and quality of multicultural books since the publication of Nancy Larrick's (1965) influential essay, "The All-White World of Children's Books," there is still a long way to go before all children regularly engage with books that function as "mirrors" of their own experiences as well as "windows" onto the experiences of people different from them (Galda, 1998).

Children may also feel excluded when the characters they might potentially identify with are presented problematically. In *The Paper Bag Princess*, Robert Munsch's (1999) parody of the standard "prince-saves-princess-from-dragon" story, there is a lack of an "acceptable role" for boys (Altmann, 1994, p. 27) because Prince Ronald is a nasty, self-centered twit. Girls may identify with (and feel empowered by) Princess Elizabeth, but perhaps at the expense of boys. As Altmann observes, to merely turn the tables on gender roles—to invert the power equation—may be simply to perpetuate injustice. While the girls in Mrs. Martin's kindergarten class loved the ending of *The Paper Bag Princess*, the boys resisted it mightily. As Kevin declared, "I don't got no use for those stories—they's for girls!"

The type of literary understanding that is highlighted by all the types of personal responses in this category is the aspect that is valorized by all reader-response criticism: the reader's awareness of her own reactions, feelings, and personal associations with a text.

8

Transparent and Performative Responses

In this chapter, I describe two of the five major types of response that I found to characterize children's literary meaning-making in my research. I include them both in one chapter because the responses in both these categories were quite rare in the data: there are simply not that many of them to discuss. However, quantity is not indicative of quality; these two types of responses represent some of the most interesting and provocative data in my research. Another reason for presenting these two types of response in the same chapter is that, as I will argue in chapter 9, they represent two different, contrasting enactments of what I call the aesthetic impulse.

TRANSPARENT RESPONSE: ENTERING THE STORYWORLD

The rare responses in Category 4—Transparent Response—suggested that the children had entered the "secondary world" (Benton, 1992) of the story as, for the moment, they surrendered to the "power of the text" (Scholes, 1985) and had a "lived-through experience" (Rosenblatt, 1978/1994) of the story. Since their focus was on engaged reception of the story by active listening, their verbalizations represent, as it were, only the exposed tip of an iceberg. Thus, the very interiority of this lived-through experience, in studies based on the *verbal* responses of children, demands circumspection and a tentative stance when interpreting the data.

There was an inadvertent and spontaneous quality about these responses, which did not seem to have communicative intent, for example, Gordon's *sotto voce* comment (mentioned at the beginning of chapter 4) expressing his pessimism regarding Grace's ability to "be anything I want to be" in the readaloud of *Amazing Grace* (Hoffman, 1991) in Ms. Bigler-McCarthy's class. It is possible that the chunks of *silence* on the children's part were more indicative of their aesthetic reception and transparent stance than any verbal responses could be; yet, silence constitutes only negative evidence. Even so, every perceptive teacher knows when children are engaged with rapt

169

attention in a story, and when their silence indicates merely boredom or disengagement. Thus, I consider transparent response to be an important aspect of literary understanding, despite the rarity of the verbal utterances that indicate it.

Responses that seemed to be directed to an audience (the other children or the teacher) were not included in this category. However, this logic depended on the validity of my inference about a child's intention: did the utterance have communicative intent, or was it verbalized "inner speech" (Vygotsky, 1986)? In *Mufaro's Beautiful Daughters* (Steptoe, 1987), one of the characters (the lazy sister) declares vehemently, "I will be queen. I will be queen." Immediately after Ms. Bigler-McCarthy read this, several children I could not identify said quietly but just as vehemently, "No she won't! No she won't!" These responses were just barely audible on the audiotape. Their spontaneous immediacy, coupled with the low tone of voice in which they were spoken, seemed to indicate an engagement in the world of the story. Other spontaneous expressions of delight, disgust, caution, or fear included Krissy's comment, "Rotten girl!" after the teacher read Red Riding Hood's promise not to stray from the path on her way to see her grandmother; and Trent's voiced "Uh-oh" following the description of the huntsman's sighting of the wolf. (Both comments took place during the reading of the Hyman [1983] version of *Little Red Riding Hood*.)

Transparent response could be very simple, amounting to a spontaneous expression of emotion or production of a sound effect. These kinds of responses were prevalent in the reading of *Wiley and the Hairy Man* (Sierra, 1986), a retelling of a well-known Southern African American folktale; it's a rather frightening story, about a half-man, half-animal called the Hairy Man, who threatens Wiley, a young boy. Wiley must outwit the Hairy Man three times to be free from him forever. During this readaloud, Mrs. Martin read:

TEACHER [reading]: **The Hairy Man just grinned and drool rolled off his long, yellow teeth.**
MANY CHILDREN: Eiouuu!

In the same readaloud, Kevin whimpered, "I'm getting scared!" when the teacher read the Hairy Man's threat to the protagonist: **Wiley! W I-I-I-I-LEY! I'm a-coming to get you. . . . tonight!**

Transparent responses could be more linguistically complex, however. During the reading of *The Tale of Peter Rabbit* (Potter, 1902/1987) to several kindergarten classes, the children took Peter's plight very seriously. When they heard Potter's description of Peter being chased by Mr. McGregor, several children excitedly shouted, "Run, Peter! Run for your life!" and exclaimed "Thank *God* he didn't get killed!" when Peter was able to squeeze underneath the garden fence to safety. Similarly, children encouraged story characters, cheering them on, or warning them. During the readaloud of *Swimmy* (Lionni, 1963) in Mr. Taylor's class, for example, Latoya yelled, "Swim faster, Swimmy, swim faster!" During *Red Riding Hood* (Coady, 1991), Lottie warned the protagonist: "Don't talk to that wolf, girl! Why you so stupid?" These examples demonstrate children's propensities to "talk to" story characters directly, as if the children were in the storyworld with the characters.

In Mrs. Martin's kindergarten class, this propensity to address story characters directly (by warning, greeting, or conversing with them) constituted similarly rare but intense, important moments during readalouds. During the reading of the Coady (1991) version of *Red Riding Hood*, at the point in the story where the disguised wolf invites Red Riding Hood into her grandmother's bed, Kevin shouted, "Don't do it! Don't do it!" Perhaps the most amusing of these "audience participation" moments occurred during the readaloud of Steven Kellogg's (1997) *The Three Little Pigs*. In this version of the tale, the mother pig sets up a waffle business, which supports her three children. Upon meeting the three pigs, the wolf growls, "Howdy, Ham. Howdy, Bacon. Howdy, Sausage," and proceeds to try to catch them. Eventually, they are all rescued by their mother, who positions the waffle machine in the hearth of the fireplace just as the wolf leaps down the chimney. Thus, instead of landing in the pot of boiling water featured in other versions of the story, the wolf is turned into a "woofle," steaming the meanness out of him. At this climatic point in the story, Joe triumphantly yelled (presumably to the wolf), "*Now* who's gonna be the sausage?," indicating his understanding of the way the tables had turned.

Another variation of transparent response was to momentarily *become* one of the story characters and speak "in role" (Adomat, 2005; Edmiston, 1993), a type of comment Naisha made frequently enough that these responses seemed to constitute part of her individual response style. During the reading of *Leola and the Honeybears* (Rosales, 1999), Naisha pleaded pitifully, "Don't eat me!" at the point in the story when Leola (the Goldilocks figure) is confronted by the irritated bears. In this case, she was, of course, speaking as (or for) Leola, almost as an act of ventriloquism. Naisha displayed her ability to switch roles within her transparent response stance when, at the end of the story, the bears forgive Leola and send her home with a basket of food. At this point, Naisha placed herself in the bears' role, waved, and called sweetly, "Bye-bye, sweetheart; bye-bye!" In a much scarier story, *Wiley and the Hairy Man* (Sierra, 1986), Katrin voiced the thoughts of the Hairy Man as he threatened Wiley's mother: assuming a deep, threatening tone of voice, she growled, "I'm lookin' . . . for the boy." This ventriloquism was also in evidence during the reading of *Flossie and the Fox* (McKissack, 1986), a rural Southern story told to author Patricia McKissack by her grandfather. In this story, which has some elements of *Red Riding Hood*, young Flossie is asked to take some eggs to a neighbor's house, on the other side of a dark forest, where she meets a fox. Flossie pretends she doesn't know that the fox is indeed a fox, and frustrates him almost to the point of insanity by her refusal to believe any of the proofs he offers. When he says, "See, I have thick, luxurious fur," Flossie replies that he must be a rabbit. His long, pointed nose doesn't convince Flossie, either: she sniffs, "Come to think of it . . . rats got long pointed noses." At this point, Amanda chimed in, becoming Flossie: "Maybe you're a rat!" During the reading of the James Marshall (1987) version of *Red Riding Hood*, when Mrs. Martin read about the wolf eating Red Riding Hood, Donna commented in a deep voice, "Oh, that was delicious!" In these forms of transparent response, it seems that, in Georges Poulet's words, the children are experiencing "possession" by the author: "This I, who 'thinks in me' when I read a book, is the I of the one who writes the book" (Poulet, 1980, p. 46). These responses are also similar to the theory of "method acting" (Stanislavski, 1970), in which the ideal actor tries to feel the emotions of a character so deeply that the actor and the character become one.

Although transparent responses almost always occurred during dramatic moments of the story, these moments could also be less public. Rose was a child who very rarely spoke during story time; in fact, during all the readalouds that I observed in Ms. Bigler-McCarthy's class, she made only one audible utterance. This single response occurred during the reading of *Owl Moon* (Yolen, 1987), a gentle and quiet story about a little girl who goes owling with her father late at night. The catalyst for Rose's response was Alice's comparison of the image of a flying owl in *Owl Moon* to a similar image in *Owl Babies* (Waddell, 1992), which has already been mentioned in chapter 6. When Alice showed the illustration of the mother owl flying back to her babies, Rose said slowly, quietly, and with great emotional intensity, "Here she comes! Here she comes!" Rose was looking directly at the illustration as she spoke, not at any other child. The utterance was not picked up by the tape recorder, and if I had not been sitting beside her, I would not have heard it. My inference is that Rose was, for the moment, placing herself in the world of the story as one of the owl babies, and that her utterance was intended for herself alone, as she experienced the joy of the babies (who had been feeling frightened and abandoned) at seeing their mother return to their nest.

The type of literary understanding that responses in this category represent is the ability to position oneself in (or indeed, *inside*) the dynamics of the narrative to such an extent that the story and one's own life, for an evanescent moment, merge with and are transparent to each other. By their oral response (and perhaps mostly by their silence), children indicated that they were immersed in the storyworld—"lost in the book" (Nell, 1988). Thus, I am arguing that deep engagement in a story is in itself an aspect of literary understanding, one that has often been noted anecdotally by teachers (especially those in the primary grades), but that has not been theorized extensively or incorporated into a broader theoretical framework; the response, like many other types of response, is simply noted as one kind of interesting reaction young children display, without relating it to the complex and diverse matrix of responses children exhibit through their talk.

Transparent response may be interpreted by some as immature and naïve: it may seem that the children are behaving as if the story were "real," and the characters were actually alive. D. W. Harding (1962) and James Britton (1984) might say that the children were not yet able to assume the "spectator stance" that is appropriate for literature or other forms of "poetic language," and that they were inappropriately assuming a "participant stance" that is suitable only for real-life "transactive language," such as the language used when going to the bank, going shopping, or otherwise participating in the real world of day-to-day life. Yet what I find fascinating is that the children could move from this type of "in-the-storyworld" response to quite detached, analytical responses in the space of a few seconds. Their capacity for engagement and "entering in" (Ballenger, 1998, p. 63) the story did not seem to interfere with their ability to critique, analyze, and evaluate the text; rather, their transparent responses exhibited one element in an impressive range—an enviable and supple literary flexibility. Louise Rosenblatt might argue that they were demonstrating a deft, effortless, and dynamic movement back and forth along the efferent-aesthetic continuum.

PERFORMATIVE RESPONSE: THE TEXT AS A PLATFORM FOR CHILDREN'S CREATIVITY

Although the responses in Category 5—Performative Response—comprise only about 5% of the conversational turns, they are some of the most intriguing responses in all the data sets. In discussing Category 3, Personal Response, a type of personal response was described that was evidence for the children's understanding that stories were plastic and malleable, like clay. They personalized the story by talking about what they would do if they were a story character. In Category 5, this idea of malleability was carried by the children to an even higher level: the text was stretched and kneaded until it became the platform or "pretext" (O'Neill, 1995) for the children's own expressive creativity; responses in this category are aesthetically expressive, whereas the responses in Category 4 are aesthetically receptive. In other words, whereas in Category 4 the children seemed to surrender to the power of the text and were therefore manipulated by it, in Category 5 the tables were turned: the children manipulated the text and controlled it (occasionally to the extent of hijacking it). The responses in Category 4 seemed inadvertent and often just barely audible, since the intention was not to communicate but to represent the experience to oneself. The responses in Category 5, by contrast, were definitely intended for audience consumption: they constituted a performance, meant to be heard, seen, and appreciated by other children.

Ballenger's (1998) work with immigrant Haitian preschoolers is helpful in illuminating the difference between transparent and performative responses. Some of the responses (which she calls "entering in" the story, p. 63) she records seem similar to my category of transparent response—talking back to story characters, even rising up to punch out the monsters in a book, or sitting on top of a book to keep the monsters inside. However, other responses Ballenger reports as examples of "entering in" seem more akin to performative response, which I discuss in this section of the chapter: "they enter into the text and change it *at will*" (italics mine)—in other words, the children wrest control and take over the story for their own purposes. Ballenger ascribes some of this general stance toward books as part of the Haitian culture of storytelling, where tales may be changed and manipulated, and where audience participation is a critical part of the storytelling.

Performative responses were characterized by creativity, playfulness, wry humor, sly puns, or flights of fancy that seemed (at first blush, anyway) to have only a tangential relationship to what most adults might consider the proper and sensible story line. Thus, the responses were often mildly (or wickedly) subversive and transgressive; in some quarters, they would probably be considered totally off-task. They threatened to deconstruct the story into a totally free (and in some cases anarchic) play of signifiers. As such, their very existence depended on the liberal and tolerant atmosphere of the classroom; in a more conservative environment, these exotic blooms might have been quickly squashed. In the Introduction to this book, I have already mentioned kindergartner Keyron's amazing triple pun in response to the teacher's question, "What do you think this story—*Red Riding Hood*—might be about?": "Probably she read and she write a lot, and she live in the 'hood." In Mrs. Martin's kindergarten class, I found very few performative responses; this was almost certainly not due to her lack of toleration for them. Her class of children, at least in the year I studied them, seemed to prefer other types of response. Therefore, the examples I present in the rest of the chapter are from Ms. Bigler-McCarthy's first/second-grade class. It is possible that most children are developmentally ready to make such responses after kindergarten; however, Keyron's spectacular performative response belies any blanket generalizations we might make about the abilities of kindergartners in this area. It may not be so much that the children were developmentally unready, as that their culture was not one that valued performative response quite so much as the culture of the Haitian preschoolers in Ballenger's (1998) fascinating study. According to Ballenger's description, there were plenty of what I would call performative responses in her storybook readalouds. Or it may be that the kindergarten children in Mrs. Martin's class had already been socialized into more acceptable ways of "doing school."

As I explored the idea of children's performative responses, I began to consider other sections of data, such as the children's discussion of Goldilocks' missing front teeth during the readaloud of Galdone's (1985) version of *The Three Bears*, which has already been introduced. Pointing to Galdone's illustration of the broadly smiling Goldilocks, Joey blurted out: "Maybe right here she got punched in the face! [pause, about 2 seconds] Maybe *Kenny* punched her! [dissolving into giggles]." The class was delighted by this response, and a moment of chaos ensued as several children (mostly boys) began to throw fake punches at each other. Joey's remark was very knowing, sly, and ironic, because Kenny was notorious for getting into fights. There was an additional level of irony (possibly lost on everyone but Ms. Bigler-McCarthy and me), in that Joey himself had a rather pugnacious reputation. In this case, Joey deliberately (and cleverly) played with the fiction/reality distinction in a subversive way. His response was performative because he intended that his audience react—he even timed his "punch line"—and he was not disappointed.

Terry was an inveterate punster, and often made performative plays on words. His star performance occurred during the reading of *Black and White* (Macaulay, 1990), a winner of the Caldecott Medal that contains many images of bovines, when he declared, "Hey, Miss Bigler, it won the *Cow-decott Medal!*" Terry's classmate Charles also displayed a great number of performative responses. One of the most representative of these often brief but hilariously funny comments occurred during the reading of *Chicken Little* (Kellogg, 1985), which begins with a wanted poster for Foxy Loxy:

Teacher [reading]: **Wanted, Foxy Loxy, for kidnapping poultry and committing other dreadful crimes. Warning: Foxy Loxy is shrewd, rude, mean, and dangerous. If you see him, call the police immediately.**
Charles [laughing]: 1-800, dial 9-1-1!

Charles's performative responses were occasionally musical in nature, and he was the only child who reacted in this way during storybook readalouds. During the reading of *Chicken Little*, he responded to a portion of the text that described Foxy Loxy (dressed as a policeman) talking about taking Chicken Little and her friends to "headquarters":

CHARLES: Headquarters mean police.
TEACHER: Do you think headquarters might mean the police, Charles?
CHARLES: Or cops.
GORDON: Or it might mean, um:
CHARLES [singing]: Bad boys, bad boys, whatcha gonna do when they come for you?

After the readaloud, when asked about the source of this song, Charles said that it was the theme song of a television program called *Cops*. This response was an intertextual connection used in a performative manner. Another singing response occurred after the teacher read the title of the book *Bad Day at Riverbend* (Van Allsburg, 1995), when he broke into a chorus of "Down by the Riverside."

Charles commonly took on the role of characters in the story by speaking for them, but not "in role," as children assumed when ventriloquizing in transparent response: Charles gave characters his own distinctive voice. During the readaloud of *Piggybook* (Browne, 1986), for example, he responded to the description of Mrs. Piggott's daily chores with another incisive intertextual connection that had performative intent:

TEACHER [reading]: **As soon as they had eaten, Mrs. Piggott washed the dishes, washed the clothes, did the ironing, and then cooked some more.**
CHARLES: Cinderella, Cinderella! Get your butt down here!

We can be fairly certain that Charles had never heard a version of *Cinderella* in which the stepsisters speak to Cinderella in quite so colloquial a manner. Charles's response was his own signifying invention.

These performances were not all one-liners, however. An excerpt from the transcript of the small-group readaloud of *Amazing Grace* (Hoffman, 1991) was introduced earlier in chapter 4 to provide examples of all the categories for the children's talk. The following exchange occurred immediately after that part of the transcript in which Sally made the insightful quasi-thematic statement that "Grace put her mind to it, I guess, and she got chosen":

100   GORDON: You're Peter Pan [to the teacher] because you're wearing green! I'm Peter Blue! [He is wearing a blue shirt]
101   JULIE: I'm Peter White! [She is wearing white]

102 TERRY: [gets up and starts turning around, doing ballet movements]
103 JULIE: Terry, sit down! [laughing]
104 SALLY [gets up, too, and turns around]: I'm just stretching! [looking at the teacher mischievously]
105 TEACHER: OK, wait! [laughing]
106 TERRY: Now I'm a helicopter!
107 TEACHER: OK, wait, Julie, nobody's listening.
108 JULIE: Right here [showing tenth opening], this is the back [showing back cover].
109 TEACHER: Yes, I believe you're right. Good observation.
110 TERRY [speaking softly to the teacher]: Sometimes I do it in the house, it's fun, I like it.
111 [Sally, Julie, Gordon, and Terry all get up and start twirling around]
112 TEACHER: This story is causing people to want to get up and fly, I can tell! This story is a moving story, isn't it?

This vignette demonstrates how exhilarating performative responses could become for the children. Even Sally, who usually approached stories very seriously and had just responded to the theme of the story, is caught up (104) by the carnival begun by Gordon, Julie, and Terry. Julie attempts an analytical comment, pointing out that a part of an illustration in the body of the text recurs on the back cover (108), but abandons her within-the-text response to become a ballet dancer/helicopter with everyone else. The teacher is attempting to be "teacherly" and on track, but the children have kicked over the traces, as if to say, "What track? We don't care about your agenda." The children ignore the seriousness of the story and finally the teacher gives up.

Another example of an extended series of performative responses took place during the reading of *The Stinky Cheese Man and Other Fairly Stupid Tales* (Scieszka, 1992), which itself subversively plays with the conventions of the picturebook and the conventions of traditional stories. "Title page" is printed on the title page in huge letters; endpapers are inserted before the end of the story; the table of contents *falls* on all the characters, actually ejecting one story from the book; and the individual stories—like "The Princess and the Bowling Ball," "The Really Ugly Duckling," and "Little Red Running Shorts"—have bizarre twists of plot. Even the front dust jacket flap is out of control, and seemed to provoke the performances in the following excerpt:

100 TEACHER [reading front flap]: **Only 16.99! 56 action-packed pages. 75% more than those old 32-page "Brand-X" books. 10**

complete stories! 25 lavish paintings! New! Improved! Funny!
Good! Buy! Now!

101 TERRY: Why?

102 JULIE: It got a medal, too!

103 GORDON: "Why," just say, "why," just say "why," just say it.

104 TEACHER: What? OK, "Why"?

105 GORDON: How come? Because. Where? When? Who? [dissolves into giggles]

106 TEACHER [laughing]: OK. **New! Improved! Funny! Good!
     Buy! Now!**

107 TERRY: I don't wanna go "bye" now. I don't wanna go byebye now!

108 GORDON: Me neither!

109 ALL [waving frantically]: Bye-bye! Bye-bye!

110 TERRY: I don't want to go to the bathroom and be the stinky
     cheese man!

111 ??: [uproarious laughter]

112 SALLY [laughing]: Enough of this goofiness!

At 101, Terry interrogates the text: why should we buy the book, just
because it tells us to? Julie tries to keep us on track with her comment at
102, but the other children were having none of it. At 103 and 105, Gordon
sets up an imitative display of the stacatto language of the book, which the
teacher feeds into by rereading part of the text (106). At 107 and 110, Terry
makes moves that the deconstructive critic Geoffrey Hartman (Atkins, 1990)
would be proud of, punning and using the text as a springboard for his own
transgressive text-to-life connection. At 112, Sally brings us back to earth.

My one-to-one reading of *Changes* (Browne, 1990) with Terry elicited
a number of extended performative responses. *Changes* is a bizarre story in
which a young boy's mother and father leave him at home, telling him there
are going to be many changes in his life. The change turns out to be a new
baby sister; however, furniture and other parts of the house surrealistically
change into other forms before the father and mother return with the baby.
The fourth opening of *Changes* depicts a bathroom sink seemingly changing
into a person. On the verso of the double-page spread, the sink has developed
a nose and the drain has become a mouth; on the recto, eyes have appeared on the tops of the faucets, and the sink's porcelain pedestal has become
a gray flannel–clad leg with a shoe. Terry took these images as an invitation
to play. He pretended to turn on one of the faucets:

TERRY: You want some water to drink? Poooshhhh! Oh! No! Ouch!
Ouch! Oh no! It's *hot* water! [High-pitched voice, ending with a

strangled sound; clutches hand to his throat, sticks out his
tongue, with an agonized expression on his face]
TEACHER [laughing, playing along]: He wants some water to drink:
TERRY [giggling]: And he got some *hot* water. Oucha, oucha, oucha,
ouch! Ouch! I want some soda!

In this astonishing excerpt, Terry plays three roles: the tormenter of the
sink, the sink itself, and the narrator. He also throws in sound effects for
good measure. The tormenter asks the sink, "You want some water to drink?"
"Poooshhhh!" is the sound of the water being turned on. Then Terry becomes
the sink, its drain now a sensitive mouth: "Oh! No! Ouch! Ouch! Oh no!
It's hot water!" Terry then provides some narratorial commentary: "And he
got some *hot* water." Finally, he again becomes the poor sink: "Oucha, oucha,
oucha, ouch! Ouch! I want some soda!"

Terry gave a performative response to virtually every transformation
in *Changes*. When he saw the elephant's trunk protruding from the wall in
the 11th opening, he held his nose shut with his thumb and forefinger and
said, "The elephant's like, 'OOOOO! I can't talk this way! I can't get
through!'" On the 14th opening, the close-up illustration of the newborn,
crying with its mouth wide open and its round tongue protruding, provoked
this interpretation:

TERRY: Hey, that [the baby's tongue] looks kinda like he swallowed
a sucker. That, like the wrong way!
TEACHER [laughing]: Like the baby swallowed a lollipop the wrong way?
TERRY: The wrong way! He put the stick in first! "Oooh, gulp! I
swallowed a sucker!" [Holds throat and makes choking noises]

Terry thus used the entire text as a platform for his own carnivalesque ex-
travaganza. The sheer strangeness and wildness of this book seemed to
release, in Terry, an exhilarating torrent of performances.

There is a sense in which these more extreme performative responses
interrupted or disrupted the serious meaning-making that was the principal
activity in which the children were engaged; performative response could
represent a rupture (or even an eruption) of some kind. In Cynthia Ballenger's
(1998) experience, she was at first surprised and disturbed when the children would "enter into the text and change it at will" (p. 63). However,
another way of looking at these responses is to conceptualize them as expressively aesthetic acts on a high level. They represent a type of literary
understanding that sees the text as "a vessel of associations helplessly open
to the mastery of [our] response" (Grudin, 1992). Children used the text as
a platform for the expression of their own *sprezzatura* creativity, approaching

the text as what Cecily O'Neill (1995) calls a "pretext" for a spontaneous presentation. Extended performances in which several children joined in (represented by the examples above from *Amazing Grace* and *The Stinky Cheese Man*) are what I (following Bakhtin, 1984) call a "carnivalesque romp." According to Bakhtin, carnival has the following characteristics:

- "Official certainties are relativized, inverted, or parodied" (Dentith, 1995, p. 68); thus there is a subversive element to carnival.
- The common people assume roles of power usually held by their masters.
- The tone is frequently humorous, mocking, and outrageous: out of control.
- The body and bodily functions—particularly ones considered taboo— are celebrated.
- Creativity is expressed, not in the calm Apollonian manner, but rather in the wild Dionysian manner.

The children's responses have all of these carnivalesque qualities. They are playful; they don't take the text seriously, as something to understand, but rather as pretext for exuberance. The responses are often subversive, in keeping with the idea of carnival as a time to throw off or ignore dominating power structures. Children take control—wrest control, really, from both the text and the teacher—in order to respond with a high-spirited creativity that owes more to Dionysius than to Apollo. (I discovered belatedly that Lensmire [1994] also explored the application of Bakhtin's notion of "carnival" among third-graders, though in a writing workshop rather than as literary response.)

If, as I have argued, the findings of these studies indicate that the children were astute literary critics and displayed various types of literary understanding, the children's performative responses display their abilities as specifically *deconstructive* literary critics. Here I should note that my use of the term "performative" is the virtual opposite of what Douglas Barnes (1976) and Gordon Wells (1987, 1990) mean by "performance" and "performative." For these researchers, the terms refer to a procedural display or a disciplined reading behavior rather than the exuberant and transgressive bypassing of procedures and discipline.

In the next chapter, I explain performative response as an enactment of the expressive aspect of what I call the aesthetic impulse, just as transparent response is theorized as an enactment of the receptive aspect of the aesthetic impulse. I also recapitulate all five types of response, argue that they are instantiations of five types of literary understanding, and use them to construct a grounded theory of young children's literary understanding.

9

A Grounded Theory of the Literary Understanding of Young Children

In this chapter, the five types or aspects of literary understanding described in chapters 4 to 8 are synthesized to advance a theory of the literary understanding of young children. This theory does not aspire to be applicable to all ages and all types of literature; it is the literary understanding of picture storybooks that is here described because the picture storybook is the principal format through which most young children experience literature. Furthermore, the theory is based exclusively on verbal responses of children before, during, and after readalouds of picturebooks, because I believe this situation most clearly captures the dynamic, in-the-moment process of the construction of literary understanding, as distinguished, for example, from talk or writing after a book has been read in some literature discussion groups, book clubs, and literature circles. The theory is grounded in the sense that it arises from the data for the studies used in this book.

FIVE FACETS OF LITERARY UNDERSTANDING

Table 9.1 presents a visual summary of five aspects or facets of the literary understanding of young children. It is based directly on the typology of children's responses during the picture storybook readalouds that formed the data for this book. I am assuming that what children say can be categorized into five types of responses, and that these responses are in turn indicative of five aspects or facets of literary understanding. To summarize:

   1. *Analytical responses* indicate a type of literary understanding that is based on the making of narrative meaning through a discernment of story plot, setting, characters, theme, and style, as well as the use of illustrations to interpret these narrative elements, integrating words and pictures. Analytical literary understanding also involves discussing the picture storybook

TABLE 9.1. Five Facets of Literary Understanding: A Theoretical Model

TYPE OF RESPONSE	**A. STANCE** How children situate themselves in relation to text	**B. ACTION** What children do with texts	**C. FUNCTION** How texts function
1. Analytical	Within texts	Children analyze	Using texts as objects
Dealing with the text as an object or cultural product. Children stay within the text and make comments that reflect an analytical stance.			
2. Intertextual	Across texts	Children link or relate	Using texts as context
Relating the text being read to other cultural products. The text is reviewed in relation to other texts, and functions as an element in the matrix of interrelated contexts.			
3. Personal	From or to texts	Children personalize	Using texts as stimuli
Connecting the text to one's own life, moving either from life to the text or from the text to one's life. The text acts as a stimulus for a personal connection.			
4. Transparent	Through texts	Children merge with texts	Using texts as their identity
Entering the world of the story and becoming one with it. The storyworld becomes (momentarily) identical with and transparent to the children's world.			
5. Performative	On texts	Children perform or "signify"	Using texts as platforms
Entering the text-world and manipulating it for one's own purposes. The text functions as a platform for children's creativity, becoming a playground for a carnivalesque romp.			

Adapted from Sipe (2000a), p. 268. Used by permission of the International Reading Association.

as a cultural object produced by authors and illustrators, editors, and designers; exploring the meaning of specific words or phrases in a text; talking about the elements of visual design (color, shape, texture, line, and the portrayal of three-dimensional space) in the illustrations; and grappling with the distinctions between fiction and reality.

2. *Intertextual responses* are those in which children make links or connections between the picture storybook being read aloud and other books and "texts" in the broad sense of the word: television programs, commercials, and advertisements; music; paintings and commercial art; other texts of popular culture; and the art and writing of their own classmates.

3. *Personal responses* involve linking the text to one's own life by explicating how characters, actions, or situations are like or unlike the child's own life experiences or the experiences of others. They also include "I would" or "I wouldn't" statements indicating what children would say or do differently from the characters in the story; in this way, children demonstrate their ownership of the story.

4. *Transparent responses* indicate that for a transitory moment, the world of the text and the children's psychic worlds are transparent to each other: that children have entered the storyworld. They may (1) express spontaneous emotion as evidence of their deep engagement in the story; (2) talk back to the story characters, warning, evaluating, or cheering them on; or (3) assume the role of storybook characters, speaking in role as the characters.

5. *Performative responses* suggest that the children are playfully manipulating the story for their own creative purposes. Their intention in these types of responses is not to interpret the story, but rather to wrest control from both the text and the teacher who is reading the text. Their intent is frequently subversive, sly, ironic, or (from a more conservative perspective) "off-task" according to what most adults would consider to be a sensible comprehension of the story. Such responses are frequently humorous, out of control, and possess many of the characterstics of the carnivalesque.

The headings at the top of Table 9.1 (Stance, Action, and Function) indicate that each of the five facets of literary understanding may be viewed as (A) stances assumed by children; or as (B) actions performed by children; or in terms of (C) the various functions served by texts. The chart may therefore be viewed vertically, comparing and contrasting the five facets of literary understanding with each other, through a consideration of each of the three columns. The chart may also be viewed horizontally, giving a brief description of the stance, action, and function that together summarize each of the five aspects.

Stance: How Children Situate Themselves

Stance refers to how children situate themselves in relation to the text. In the analytical aspect of literary understanding (1), children situate themselves *within* the text, in order to engage in interpretation through a close reading, treating the text as a verbal icon susceptible to analysis and appreciation of an author or illustrator's craft. They do this close reading by interpreting the traditional elements of narrative: setting, characters, plot, tone, and theme. They also use both text and illustrations in a transmediative manner, interpreting the illustrations in terms of the words of the story, and interpreting the words of the story in light of the illustrations, in a continual "relaying" process. Children also utilize all the parts of the picturebook—including peritextual features such as the front and back covers, dustjacket, endpapers, half-title and title pages, and dedication page—in order to predict what will happen in the story, to begin to interpret the relationship of characters to one another, and to discern the general tone of the story. As the reading of the story proceeds, children confirm and disconfirm their hypotheses, and engage in chains of speculative reasoning and interpretation with each other and with the teacher. They discuss the style and tone of both the verbal text and the illustrations. They observe, describe, and interpret the ways in which the illustrations and verbal text are arranged on each double-page spread, and they speculate and fill in gaps about what might have happened between one double-page spread and the next, in the "drama of the turning of the page" (Bader, 1976). They adopt an analytical stance toward the illustrations, performing "visual semiosis" interpreting the various "codes" of color, line, shape, texture, and placement of objects and characters on the page, all in the service of interpreting the text.

In the intertextual aspect of literary understanding (2), children situate themselves *across* two or more texts, for the purpose of making interpretive links that are helpful in (a) understanding the book they are currently discussing, and (b) perceiving the ways in which stories (and other texts) "lean on other stories," connecting the world of stories, and understanding the text as part of the broad matrix of interconnected texts. They experience the truth of J. R. R. Tolkien's claim that "there are no new stories, only a 'cauldron of stories' into which we dip as we write" (quoted in Cairney, 1990, p. 478).

In the personal aspect of literary understanding (3), children are drawn *to* texts when they relate their own lives to the text; and they draw *from* texts when they relate the text to their own lives. They may see stories as mirrors of their own lives, or as windows onto new experiences (Galda, 1998). They may also draw away from the text by resisting elements of the story.

In the transparent aspect of literary understanding (4), children situate themselves psychologically so that for the moment, they live their lives *through* the story as it is being read. They become one with the character or characters in the story, or insert themselves intimately in the story. In this way, they become lost in the book, deeply engaged with the storybook characters and their actions.

In the performative aspect of literary understanding (5), children situate themselves *on* the text, as if the text were a platform, in order to express themselves creatively. In this stance, children have little interest in interpreting the story; the story becomes merely a springboard for their own creative energies. Their stance is ludic, festive, and frequently subversive. These are the five stances children may assume in relation to picture storybooks.

Action: What Children Do with Texts

Action refers to what children do with texts. They may (1) *analyze* a text as a self-contained unit, discussing and interpreting its structure, its characters, its plot, or its setting. They may also discuss the form and content of the illustrations, as well as the media used in producing them. Children may also relate the illustrations to the verbal text; "read" various illustrational conventions and codes; predict what may happen; or apply particular items of literary knowledge such as foreshadowing.

Another way in which children may interpret is to (2) *link or relate* several texts to each other. If enough texts are linked together, this may result in the ability to understand high-level generalizations about groups of texts. In this way, as they experience the connections among stories, children develop implicit theories of what constitutes a literary genre, such as fairy or folk tales, realistic fiction, or historical fiction.

Children may also (3) *personalize* texts, making them their own by relating them to their own lives; by using texts to understand or cope with some personal issue; by being challenged to alter their view of reality through their experience of the text; by seeing themselves as tellers of the same tale; or by telling what they would do if they were a storybook character. They may understand that stories can function as templates for thinking of their own lives in new ways, reinventing themselves in terms of their views of themselves, their goals, and their sense of purpose in life.

Children may also (4) *merge* with texts, becoming momentarily one with the story, so that their "third area" (Winnicott, 1974) or inner imaginative functions integrate receptively with the story to the extent that the storyworld and their third area are temporarily united.

Finally, children may (5) *perform* or "signify" (Gates, 1988; Lee, 1995) on texts, using texts as catalysts for their own flights of creative fancy. These are the various actions children may take in relating to picture storybooks.

Function: How Children Use Texts

Function refers to the various ways in which texts may be used. Texts may function as (1) discrete *objects* for children's analytic energies. Texts are viewed as aesthetic objects ("verbal icons") worthy of interpretation, in which every part of the text is considered as a part of an integrated aesthetic whole. Thus, children begin to develop an understanding of art: its nature, characteristics, and potentials.

Texts may also function (2) as elements in the larger *context* created by the connections among several texts. In this way, texts function as components in a complex pattern of interrelated texts. Children understand texts as part of a web of meaning that stretches across time, space, and other cultures.

Another way that texts function is as (3) *stimuli* for personal self-knowledge, growth, or empathy. In other words, texts may have certain affordances that resonate with certain children's personalities, emotions, or cognitive functions.

When (4) a child merges with a text intimately, the text and the child's "third area" become transparent to each other. In this way, a text may function as the momentary *identity* (or, to use a more postmodern phrase, the momentary *subjectivity* of the child). This is part of what we mean when we say that a child has "identified" with a story, or that a story has "resonated" with a child.

Finally, (5) a text may function as a *platform*, "pretext," or playground for the child's expressive creative performative response. These are the various functions served by texts of narrative literature.

The table may also be read horizontally, joining together each phrase from the three columns so that a complete sentence is formed. Thus, by addressing stance, action, and function, the sentences succinctly summarize each facet of literary understanding.

BLURRING THE CATEGORIES

Although Table 9.1 expresses the relationships among the various types of literary understanding by providing ways of comparing and contrasting them by the stance assumed by children, the actions performed by them, and by the various functions performed by texts, there is, nevertheless, a static quality to this representation that does not accord well with the dynamic and fluid nature of children's literary understanding. In this section, therefore, I argue that the facets or aspects of literary understanding are not rigidly distinct categories, hermetically sealed off from each other, but are rather porous to each other. Perhaps the best way to demonstrate this porosity is through the use of several concrete examples of children's talk that have already been discussed.

Piggybook (Browne, 1986) is a contemporary fantasy that tells the story of a family named Piggott, in which Mrs. Piggott does all the work while her husband and two sons do nothing but order her around. During the readaloud of this story, Charles responded to the portion of the text that describes Mrs. Piggott's labors:

TEACHER [reading]: **As soon as they had eaten, Mrs. Piggott washed the dishes, washed the clothes, did the ironing, and then cooked some more.**
CHARLES: Cinderella, Cinderella! Get your butt down here!

In the discussion of Performative Response, Charles's comment was called an *intertextual* connection with *performative* intent. Thus, at least two facets of literary understanding (the 2nd and 5th facets, respectively) were present in the response. Charles was clearly making a connection to another text or cluster of texts: the palimpsest of variants of the Cinderella story. It is equally clear that Charles was also using the story as a platform for an expressively playful performance; he was manipulating the story so as to insert this playfully humorous statement as he signified on the text.

The three other facets of literary understanding seem to be present, as well. Charles's comment is evidence of interpretive close reading: quite incisively so, for it reveals, implicitly, his *analytical* understanding of the relationships among the story characters, an understanding of such acuity that he is able to express these relationships in one pithy remark. Mr. Piggott and the two sons are indeed very much like the stepmother and stepsisters in *Cinderella*, as Mrs. Piggott is like Cinderella. Thus there is a suggestion of the first facet of literary understanding. From this perspective, Charles's remark is a complex metaphor.

Furthermore, it is highly unlikely that Charles has heard a variant of the Cinderella tale in which the stepsisters call to Cinderella with the words used by Charles. It therefore seems that Charles is *personalizing* by utilizing his own distinct voice; perhaps he is even remembering occasions when he was spoken to (or spoke) in this way. In this way, the third or personal facet of literary understanding may be present.

Finally, the immediacy with which Charles speaks and the incisive quality of his comment argue a participation in the world of the story and a momentary *merging* with the text (just prior to his comment) that is characteristic of the fourth aspect of literary understanding: he momentarily becomes one of the stepsisters, in an act of ventriloquism, assuming her identity. Thus, all five aspects of literary understanding may be present in this one moment, though some may be more immediately evident than others; Charles may be assuming multiple *stances* and performing multiple *actions*; and the text may have multiple *functions* for him as he makes this response.

Another example of the imbricated nature of at least some of the children's responses is the series of comments made by the children during the reading of the Marshall (1987) version of *Red Riding Hood*, in response to the teacher's question about what the wolf might be thinking when he first saw Red Riding Hood:

CHARLES: Yummy, yummy!
TRUDY: Yummy, yummy, here comes my dinner.
DON: There's my food floating in the air!
JULIE: I'm gonna jump out and eat her!
TRENT: [whistles—a real "wolf whistle"]
TEACHER: He's thinking, whewie, there's a pretty girl, huh?
TRENT: A pretty girl, and also delicious!

This vignette will be cited in chapter 10 as an example of a question by the teacher that encouraged a specific type of response—in this case, a performative response: the children are controlling, manipulating, and altering the text. However, these responses are more directly related to the plot of the story than other performative responses, which seem much more tangential to the story line. Although they are not using storybook language, the children do seem to be staying within the story, and their comments are interpretive, even analytical, in nature because they are considering what a character might be thinking. Don's comment, in particular, is probably the result of his analytical interpretation of the illustration on this page, which depicts no shadow under Red Riding Hood, so that it may look as if she is "floating in the air." Also, the children's knowledge of other versions of *Red Riding Hood* may be brought into play, so there is an intertextual element to their responses. By inserting themselves in the story, they are personalizing the story for themselves; and by giving their comments the form of first-person narration, they may be verbalizing their aesthetic, lived-through experience of the story.

These two examples were chosen to demonstrate the intricate interrelationships among all five facets of literary understanding; other examples could be chosen to demonstrate possible overlaps between pairs of facets. The point is that the facets may blur in some instances. It is therefore necessary to convey this quality of imbrication in the theoretical model, as well as the dynamic and fluid quality of the children's responses: their ability to move so quickly and easily from one facet of literary understanding to another.

THREE BASIC LITERARY IMPULSES

In this section, I relate the five categories or aspects of children's literary understanding by envisioning them as enactments of three foundational impulses the children followed as they responded during picture storybook readalouds.

The Hermeneutic Impulse (Categories 1 & 2)

In exploring the relationships among the five facets of literary understanding, I argued that both intertextual connections and within-text analysis seemed to have a primarily interpretive intent. Whether the children stayed within the text or related it to other texts, the principal focus of their talk was to understand the story. Interpretation can focus within the text itself, as children attempt to understand the text's form and content. Interpretation can also focus on the context, in other words, the world of texts outside the text under consideration. In this case, interpretation is a matter of forging links between the text at hand and the world of texts outside, as the text is placed or perceived in relation to other texts. These two facets of literary understanding might therefore be conceptualized as the two components of a single impulse, which I name the *hermeneutic impulse*: the basic impulse to grasp the meaning of the narrative, either from the standpoint of within or without the text. This impulse is most closely related to the New Critics' insistence on "close reading" of texts.

At the core of the *hermeneutic impulse* is the desire to master the text. Children construct meaning through the process of assimilation and accommodation (Piaget, 1985). Story grammars (Graesser, Golding, & Long, 1991) and schema theory (Anderson & Pearson, 1984) describe this taking-in of information and organizing it into preexisting cognitive structures, which are in turn modified, extended, and refined by this new information. The New Critics' concern with close reading, as well as the concerns of structuralism and narratology (Barthes, 1974; Genette, 1980; Todorov, 1977), relate to the analytical (within-text) pole of this impulse. The interest of archetypal criticism (Frye, 1957) and Russian Formalism (Propp, 1958) in the ways texts display common patterns or express common universal themes relates to the intertextual pole of this impulse. Other theoretical perspectives that concern themselves with context in various ways are the so-called "New Historicism"

(Veeser, 1989) and Marxist literary theory (Eagleton, 1983; Williams, 1977). The concern of New Historicists and Marxists is to place the text in the interpretive context of historical, sociocultural, and economically driven hegemonies. All of these theories have to do with mastering the text in one way or another, either from within it or from without.

The Personalizing Impulse (Category 3)

The tendency to want to personalize a story constitutes a second basic impulse. To draw the story to oneself in some way, and to use the story to inform (or even transform) one's own life: this urge is also a foundational impulse, which I name the *personalizing impulse*. This is the impulse to forge links between the concepts, assumptions, narrative trajectory, and thematic meanings evoked or invited by the text and the reader's (or listener's) own psychic world. On the one hand, we bring our own life experiences to bear on a text. What else, indeed, do we have to bring? These are life-to-text connections. On the other hand, the evoked concepts and meanings are another form of experience (a "virtual experience," in Suzanne Langer's [1953] terminology), and may thus be heuristic in informing or transforming our lives. The personalizing impulse therefore travels in two directions: "I am like [or not like] the text; it is like [or not like] me"; and it thus can inform or transform me. These are the dual preoccupations of the personalizing impulse.

At the core of the *personalizing impulse* is the desire to link or connect ourselves to texts. Some postmodern thinkers (Derrida, 1976) conceive of the human psyche as another text in the universe of texts; if we take this view, then the personalizing impulse collapses onto the hermeneutic impulse because connecting our lives to the text is a special form of intertextual connection. I do not take this view; on the contrary, I am enough of a believer in the "unified subject" or at least in common patterns of "subjectivity themes" (Broughton, 2002) to think that I am not merely a collection of continually shifting identities based on the linguistic and sociocultural discourses and situations I find myself in; in other words, I believe in what Jung called the Self. Thus, I think there is a valuable distinction between making a personal connection (1) between myself (and my world) and another text (and the storyworld of the text) and (2) between two or more texts that are "outside" my Self. In any case, unless we make the text our own, it remains distant and remote. Texts are dry bones and mere black specks (or strokes of color) on a page unless they are personalized. "A book exists only when a living mind recreates it and that recreation comes into being only through the full imaginative participation of a particular sensibility" (White, 1994, p. 376). The range of reader-response theories (Bleich, 1978; Fish, 1967, 1980; Holland, 1975; Iser, 1978; Poulet, 1980) is most centrally focused on the dynamics of the personalizing impulse: the meaning the text possesses for each reader. Theorists and researchers who speak of the life-transforming power of literature (Booth, 1988; McGinley & Kamberelis, 1996) or the ways in which literature can change our view of reality and impel us to social justice (Davies, 2003b; Harris, 1993), as well as those concerned with our abilities to resist or read against the text (Enciso, 1994; Sipe & McGuire, 2006c), are also centrally concerned with the personalizing impulse.

The Aesthetic Impulse (Categories 4 & 5)

I have also argued that the conceptual category called the Transparent was receptive in nature, whereas the conceptual category of the Performative was expressive in nature; moreover, that they both were manifestations of an aesthetic stance. These two facets of literary understanding might therefore be conceptualized as the two components of a single impulse, which I name the *aesthetic impulse*. In its receptive form, the aesthetic impulse results in the lived-through experience of a work of literature, as we aesthetically surrender, for the moment, to the power of the text. Aesthetic reception, however, must not be conceived of as merely passive, because it involves an active sensitivity and a reconstruction, as the world of the text, for the moment, merges with and becomes transparent to the children's own psychic world or "third area" (Winnicott, 1974). The aesthetic impulse, however, may also result in expression, as the reader (or listener) utilizes the experience of the text as a platform or launching pad for his or her own creative action. The power of the text, and the "entering in," rather than being something to which the reader surrenders, becomes instead the catalyst for creative expression. These are the two poles of the aesthetic impulse.

At the core of the *aesthetic impulse* is the desire to forget our own contingency and experience the freedom that art provides. Edmund White (1994), paraphrasing the German Romantic writer Schiller, writes that "Art educates us in freedom since it alone shows the human spirit untrammeled by compromising circumstance; art alone is pure play" (pp. 330–331). Not only does art show or embody this state; it also is the catalytic enabler for a state of untrammeled freedom in those who view it, read it, or otherwise experience it. There may be, *contra* White, other ways of reaching this state; it seems, for example, to be the goal of much philosophical and religious experience. Indeed, a philosophical distinction may help us here. The ancient Greeks distinguished between two types of time: *chronos* and *kairos*. Chronos represents time as an endless linear succession of instants; we locate ourselves along this line by talking of the past, the present, and the future. Kairos, on the other hand, is time without linearity. It is the eternal present, the meaningful and exhilarating moment when we feel that linear time is obliterated;

it is similar to the flow experience described by some psychologists (Csikszent-mihalyi, 1998). In the workaday world, the cycles of sleeping and waking, and the myriad routines of everyday living, we experience chronos. Art allows us to free ourselves from our own state of human contingency—to liberate ourselves from chronos. As we contemplate a painting or piece of sculpture or view dance and drama, as we read a novel or listen to a picture-book being read aloud, time ceases to be a dull and mechanical succession of instants. The aesthetic impulse is precisely the desire to turn chronos into kairos. Winnicott (1974) might say that our "third area"—our inner, imaginative cognitive functions—was the psychological site for the activation of this desire or impulse.

Susan Sontag's (1961) famous (not to say notorious) comment in *Against Interpretation*, that "In place of a hermeneutics, we need an erotics of art" (p. 14), expresses the emphasis of the aesthetic impulse. Sontag is making the point that it is the pleasurable *experience* of literature (and of all art) that is important, rather than the interpretation of it. Benton's (1992) concept of the "secondary world," and theories of pleasure (Barthes, 1975), focus on the dynamics of the receptive pole of the aesthetic impulse. Bakhtin's (1984) concept of the "carnivalesque"; Gates's (1988) concept of "signifying"; and theories of drama (Cole, 1992; Wolf, 1994) and play (Block & King, 1987; Garvey, 1977) all concern themselves with the expressive pole of the aesthetic impulse.

CONNECTIONS TO OTHER THEORETICAL MODELS

Several theories seem to be equally concerned with all three impulses. Louise Rosenblatt's transactional theory (1978/1994, 2004) has a reader-based component, and is thus deeply concerned with the personalizing impulse: literary meaning is, first of all, personal meaning. My "aesthetic impulse" and "hermeneutic impulse" bear some similarities to her aesthetic and efferent stances, respectively. However, there are some differences. Rosenblatt's aesthetic stance seems to partake equally of the *receptive* pole of my concept of the aesthetic impulse and of my personalizing impulse. For Rosenblatt, the "lived-through experience" of a work of literature (or any work of art) is private, interior, and personal: the "poem" is constructed inside the reader's psyche. Rosenblatt does not deal with the *expressive* pole of the aesthetic impulse, which results in the public expression of the reader's creativity. Rosenblatt's efferent stance corresponds in a similar way to my idea of the hermeneutic impulse. One expression of the efferent stance is to read in order to take something away from the text, as when we read a recipe in order to cook. Another expression of the efferent stance is literary analysis. The first of these expressions of the efferent stance—reading in order to take some-thing away—is not a part of my concept of the hermeneutic impulse, because the hermeneutic impulse is a literary impulse, and such a purpose is not a literary purpose at all. The second of these expressions of the efferent stance—literary analysis—is a part of my idea of the hermeneutic impulse. However, the hermeneutic impulse also consists of another pole, that of connecting the text to the wider world of cultural products and contexts. Rosenblatt seems to deal with this only glancingly.

Judith Langer's (1990, 1995) model of envisionment describes four stances readers may take relative to texts. "Being out and stepping in," in-volving the reader's mobilization of prior life experiences in order to under-stand a text, would seem to combine the personalizing and hermeneutic impulses. "Being in and moving through," referring to the reader's immer-sion in the text, is similar to the receptive pole of the aesthetic impulse. "Being in and stepping out," concerned with comparing the lives of characters in the story with one's own life, may be similar to the personalizing impulse. "Stepping out and objectifying experience" may be most closely related to the hermeneutic impulse.

Deanne Bogdan's (1990) concept of the "kinetic response" (defined as the type of response we make when we judge a literary work by whether or not it packs an emotional wallop for us) relates to the personalizing impulse. Her "spectator response" (concerned with the analysis of the text as an ob-ject) is similar to the analytical pole of the hermeneutic impulse. Bogdan's "stock response" "interprets and values a text solely according to whether the work in question seems to reinforce or countervail the welter of ideas, values, and feelings that go to make up the reader's conscious or unconscious worldview" (p. 124). Stock response thus seems to be another aspect of the personalizing impulse. Bogdan writes of the "apprehension of total form" that results from the combination of these three types of responses. In terms of my theory, the richest literary understanding results from the activation and the interaction of all three impulses. This dynamic quality of literary understanding is discussed in the next section.

THE DYNAMICS OF LITERARY UNDERSTANDING

Having explained the three basic literary impulses, I now present a visual representation of their interrelationships. These impulses may be concep-tualized as three defining planes or vectors of cognitive space, as shown in Figure 9.1.

The arrows in Figure 9.1 indicate that the planes or vectors of the three impulses rotate in the same way as the arms of a whirligig (a metaphor

FIGURE 9.1. The Dynamics of Literary Understanding

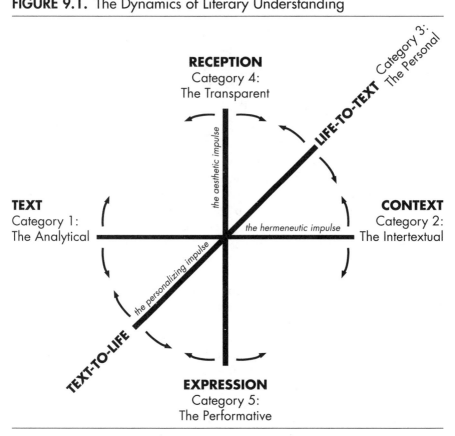

suggested by Dr. Theresa Rogers, personal communication, 1996). Unlike the arms of a whirligig, however, the impulses move independently of each other, thus overlapping each other at points as they rotate around the same pivot. In other words, a child's response at any given moment may indicate that two (or even all three) of the impulses are being followed. It is these instances that indicate the "blurring" of the conceptual categories, as in the examples discussed above. There are also times when the impulses are separately distinguishable, corresponding to the positions in which they are depicted in the diagram. The complex and dynamic interaction of the three impulses (and the 5 facets of literary understanding) are thus indicated. When one of the impulses (or one of the 5 facets of literary understanding, which constitute the arms of the whirligig) is absent, literary understanding is impoverished, because the richest understanding results from the interaction of all three impulses and all five facets.

The formal theoretical definition of literary understanding that is implied by this discussion may be stated as follows:

- The literary understanding of young children consists of five facets: the analytical, the intertextual, the personal, the transparent, and the performative.
- These five facets are the enactments of three basic literary impulses: the hermeneutic impulse, the aesthetic impulse, and the personalizing impulse.
- Literary understanding is the dynamic process whereby these three impulses are activated and dynamically interact with one another.

However, this literary understanding does not take place in splendid isolation in each child's mind: it has a social and cultural component, and is best developed in intense social interactions with expert others and peers. How may literary understanding be developed, encouraged, and enabled by teachers and by other children? What are other influences on how children develop literary understanding? In chapter 10, I describe several ways in which expert teachers in my studies assisted the construction of literary understanding for young children and address various other factors that may both constrain and enable response.

PART III

Teachers as Enablers of Children's Meaning-Making and Implications for Pedagogy and Further Research

In this final part of the book, I turn to the teachers' roles in helping children to interpret picture storybooks, and to develop their literary understanding. In chapter 10, I first forward an interpretation of that slippery term, "scaffolding," as it relates to the ways in which literary understanding was enabled in the studies upon which this book is based. I then present five conceptual categories of adults' talk that emerged from the analysis of the readaloud data, with numerous examples. Following this, I discuss the ways in which each category assisted in scaffolding the children's developing literary understanding. Teachers' questioning receives particular attention because of the power and control that questions exert over discussion.

One teacher's methods of reading and scaffolding puzzled me because her talk did not fit neatly into the typology of conceptual categories that was applicable to the teachers in the rest of the studies. I interpret kindergarten teacher Mrs. Martin as employing a style of story-*telling* rather than story-*reading*. After the discussion of adults as scaffolders of literary understanding, the chapter ends with a section devoted to children's enabling of the literary understanding of their peers.

Finally, chapter 11 discusses the many implications for teaching, particularly practitioners' handling of the storybook readaloud situation. The chapter also includes a reflection on the further research that might be done to extend and refine our grasp of young children's literary understanding.

10

Teachers' and Children's Roles in Enabling Literary Understanding

In chapter 2, I introduced Wood, Bruner, and Ross's (1976) idea of scaffolding as a part of the discussion on talk in the classroom, and related it to Vygotsky's theory of cognition, teaching, and learning, which had inspired it. In the time since Bruner and his colleagues introduced the term, the idea has been interpreted in various (and contradictory) ways.

WHAT IS SCAFFOLDING?

One crucial distinction is whether the task is understood as set by the teacher or the child. Early on, Searle (1984) commented, "Too often, the teacher is the builder and the child is expected to accept and occupy a predetermined structure" (p. 482). This understanding of scaffolding, which privileges the teachers' intentions and goals, continues in many models of comprehension instruction (e.g., Pressley, 2002), and is the basis for Pearson and Gallagher's (1983) "gradual release of responsibility" model, which assumes that the teacher sets and frames the task, ceding more power and control to the children over time as they become more expert. Other views of scaffolding are more child-centered. For example, Berk and Winsler (1995) list five components of scaffolding for young children: joint problem-solving; intersubjectivity (arriving at mutually shared meanings); warmth and responsiveness; keeping the child in the ZPD; and promoting self-regulation. Rogoff et al. (1993) use the term "guided participation" to describe adults' support and guidance of children, while actively involving them in their own learning.

Following are several assertions and assumptions that delineate my own take on scaffolding, specifically in relationship to what teachers say and do to assist children in their own literary meaning-making.

- First, I assume that scaffolding is not a univocal construct, but rather that it involves the teacher playing multiple roles (a term I prefer over the term "strategies" [e.g., Gallimore & Tharp, 1990; Pressley, 2002], which implies a more disembodied, less socially dynamic conception of what teachers do); and that each role will have a particular function in assisting children in constructing their own literary interpretations. These roles change from "moment-to-moment" (Clark & Graves, 2005) during the give-and-take of literary conversation.
- Second, I assume that in the case of picture storybooks, there are multiple interpretations, and that there is not necessarily one "best" interpretation that the teacher must scaffold "for" or "toward." Following Wolf, Carey, and Mieras (1996), this is my reason for preferring the term "interpretation" rather than "comprehension," which seems to imply a more text-centered approach that leads to one correct answer, a view that is not appropriate for literary fiction.
- Third, the proportion of teacher talk to student talk (especially the ways the teacher controls discussion by beginning new lines of discussion or by asking questions) may be indicative of the degree of intervention the teacher provides.
- Fourth, I do not believe scaffolding (as the gradual release of responsibility model seems to suppose) has the characteristics of a zero-sum game, where more power, control, or knowledge by the teacher necessarily implies less power, control, or knowledge by the children in the process of literary meaning-making. Rather, there is a synergy involved, where the teacher's astute assistance may result in more active participation in literary interpretation on the part of the children; in other words, the construction of literary meaning becomes a truly *shared* responsibility (Meyer, 1993).
- Fifth, scaffolding of literary interpretation depends partly on the nature of the text being read. The type of scaffolding appropriate for informational stories (for example, *The Carrot Seed* [Krauss, 1945], referenced in Clark and Graves, 2005) is not necessarily appropriate for the scaffolding of fictional texts like picture storybooks.
- Finally, the readaloud situation itself, with its implicit and explicit rules for participation and expectations for both teacher and students, provides a sociocultural context that is itself a form of scaffolding (Many, 2002; Palincsar, 1998).

FIVE CONCEPTUAL CATEGORIES FOR ADULT TALK

With this understanding of scaffolding, I now introduce five broad conceptual categories for the conversation that the adults in these studies contributed during the readalouds; all five categories are understood as roles that teachers played, and each of these roles had different scaffolding functions.

1. Readers

In Category 1 of the adults' talk, they functioned as *Readers* of the text. They read the words of the verbal text of the story, including the publishing information, book jacket flaps, and other information. They commented directly about the visual aspects of the text, pointing out various words ("yes, that word is 'changes'"). They essentially acted as tour guides for the book, pointing out various parts of the books ("here are the endpages"). This category comprised a little over a fourth of the adult conversational turns.

2. Managers and Encouragers

In Category 2, adults acted as both *Managers and Encouragers*. They managed the discussion by calling on children, asking children to wait, dealing with disturbances, or directing the children's attention to an item in the story or to another child's comment. They encouraged children with praise or with remarks or utterances that tended to continue the children's responses. This category comprised a little over a third of the adult conversational turns.

3. Clarifiers or Probers

In Category 3, the adults reacted to children's responses by acting as *Clarifiers or Probers*. They connected a child's remark to another remark by pointing out how it supported, extended, amplified, or contradicted what had been previously said. They asked for more information or explanation from the children. They asked questions to which they probably already knew the answer, or they asked general questions such as, "Do you have any predictions about what might happen?" They directed children's attention to an element of text or illustration in order to make a link to it later on, or they pointed out previous linkages that had been made. This category comprised about a fourth of the adult conversational turns.

4. Fellow Wonderers or Speculators

In Category 4, adults acted as *Fellow Wonderers or Speculators*. They questioned and wondered along with the children, putting themselves in the position of fellow seekers after sensible interpretations. They also acted as fellow players or performers, playfully contributing to the creative flight of the children's imaginations. This category comprised approximately 3% of the adult conversational turns for all the coded readalouds. This small percentage, consistent across all the studies, suggests that it was primarily the adults' *silence* that placed them in this role.

5. Extenders or Refiners

In Category 5, the adults acted as *Extenders or Refiners* of children's responses. They took advantage of "teachable moments," moments in the discussion at which new concepts or new interpretations could be introduced. They continued or amplified a child's thought. They summarized groups of responses so as to achieve closure in the discussion. They reminded children of what they already knew in order to make a generalization. This category comprised approximately 5% of the adult conversational turns for all the coded readalouds. The small percentage here, also characteristic of the teachers in all the studies, likely indicates their very sparing, selective use of this high degree of intervention.

EXAMPLES OF THE CATEGORIES OF ADULT TALK

The following excerpt from the transcript of the whole-group readaloud discussion of *Where the Wild Things Are* (Sendak, 1963) provides examples of each of the five categories for adult talk. The excerpt is from the middle part of the readaloud, and deals with some of the Wild Rumpus scene, in which the Wild Things cavort, with Max as their leader. The excerpt also includes the discussion about the double-page spread immediately after the Wild Rumpus scene, where Max is beginning to think about going home. The text of the book (which Ms. Bigler-McCarthy read) is in **bold** font, the numbers of the categories are in brackets, and the conversational turns are numbered, beginning with 100 (see Appendix C for a full listing of transcription conventions).

> 13th opening; a wordless page, showing Max and four Wild Things hanging from several trees by their hands. The background is light blue.
> 100   [3] TEACHER: What would you make up for this part, Joey?
> 101   JOEY: "They swing like monkeys."
> 102   ??: EE, EE, EE, EE! [monkey sounds]
> 103   JULIE: It looks like monkey bars.
> 104   [2] TEACHER: Oh, the trees look like monkey bars?
>
> 14th opening; another wordless page, showing Max and five Wild Things, walking or dancing in a line. Max sits astride the back of one of the Wild Things. The background is dark green and black.

105 [3] TEACHER: And into the next night.

106 KENNY: You could tell your own story!

107 [5] TEACHER: You could tell your own story even if there were words on the page.

108 JOEY: You could say it in your head.

109 KRISSY [disdainfully]: Your brain can't talk.

110 TERRY: You could think in your head with words.

15th opening; shows Max sitting on a three-legged stool in a striped tent, looking bored or pensive. Three Wild Things doze beside him. The eyes of the Wild Thing on the extreme left are half-open.

111 [1] TEACHER: "Now stop!" Max said and sent the wild things off to bed without their supper. And Max the king of all wild things was lonely and wanted to be where someone loved him best of all. Then all around from far away across the world he smelled good things to eat so he gave up being king of where the wild things are. [The children read along with this.]

112 JOEY: Miss Bigler, it looks like, on that one, he should be asleep, but his eyes are open.

113 GORDON: His nose is big, he looks like he's fat!

114 [4] TEACHER: Maybe he's a little bit tired, not quite falling asleep.

115 KRISSY: Or maybe he looks like he's old, like he's bored.

The Categories of Adult Talk

This excerpt was chosen because it provides examples of each of the five categories for adult talk within a small number of conversational turns. At 111, the teacher acts as the reader of the text; this conversational turn represents the simplest example of Category 1, the teacher as Reader.

At 104, the teacher responds to Julie's remark that Max and the Wild Things look like they are swinging from monkey bars. The teacher's comment, "Oh the trees look like monkey bars?," acts to acknowledge and praise Julie, and possibly to encourage her to continue to say more (although Julie did not, in fact, say anything else). The comment also acts as a managing device, in that it controls the discussion. This comment is therefore an example of Category 2, the teacher as Manager and Encourager.

At 100, the teacher asks a specific question to a specific child: "What would you make up for this part, Joey?" The opening she has just shown is wordless, so she is inviting Joey to make up his own words to go with the illustration. In other words, she is trying to elicit an interpretive response to the illustration. In 105, after she has shown another wordless double-page spread, the teacher clarifies the meaning of the illustration by providing a gloss; since the background of the illustration is dark, the teacher interprets this as an indication that the Wild Rumpus has continued into the night. These two conversational turns are examples of Category 3, the teacher as Clarifier or Prober.

At 114, the teacher adds her own speculative interpretive response to other speculations that Joey and Gordon have made concerning the Wild Thing on the extreme left of the double-page spread. Joey thinks that the Wild Thing "should be asleep, but his eyes are open." Gordon comments that the Wild Thing's nose is big and that "he looks like he's fat!" The teacher's comment indicates that she has joined this conversation as another participant who may add her own opinion. Her stance here as Fellow Wonderer or Speculator is an example of Category 4.

At 107, there is a brief and very subtle teachable moment. Kenny says, "You could tell your own story," because there are no words on the page. This is true, but the teacher takes advantage of this moment to comment that it is also possible to "tell your own story" when there *are* words on the page. She is acting as an Extender and Refiner of Kenny's response (Category 5).

It is clear that this teacher could move across the categories with great fluidity and flexibility; in this excerpt, she moved across all five categories in the short space of 16 conversational turns, 6 of which were her own. How were these various conversational turns on the part of adults related to the children's responses? In other words, what did the adults' moves help the children to do, and how was the children's understanding scaffolded? The following is an analysis of the same excerpt that, instead of simply instantiating the categories, seeks to answer these questions.

The Effects of Adult Talk

When adults probed for a response (as at 100), they almost invariably got one. In this instance (as my field notes for this readaloud show), Ms. Bigler-McCarthy utilized this type of probing question to engage the attention of Joey, who was prone to off-task behavior that irritated the other children. Her question, however, not only reengaged Joey; indirectly, it enabled the responses at 102 and 103, in which several children used Joey's speculation to make their own interpretive comments. The teacher's encouragement of Julie at 104, though it did not in this case result in further response from Julie, often did have this effect. It was also a simple way of giving the children the message that their responses were valuable. When Kenny remarked that "you could tell your own story" from the illustrations, the teacher made one of the implications of his comment clear: in this passing moment, she taught the children something extremely important. The message was that the children did not need to be bound to the words on the page. They could use their imaginations to tell their own story. This was a message of empowerment, ownership, and control for the children. Three children then amplified on the concept that Kenny and the teacher had developed together. Joey (now totally engaged) thought of one way "you could tell your own story": you could say it in your head. Joey's comment (108) shows that he had gotten the point of the teacher's teachable moment. Krissy's response (109) questioned the validity of Joey's comment, but Terry (110) supported Joey by rewording Joey's remark to make it clearer.

At 111, the teacher returned to being the reader of the story. Her own expressive reading constituted an interpretation of the story, so it was really the teacher's performance of the story (rather than the story itself) that the children were experiencing and to which they were responding. The adult reader was the lens through which the children saw the story. The teacher was quite willing to share the role of reader with the children, as shown by the way they read along with her. She knew that they were quite familiar with this story, and that it gave them pleasure to show their mastery of the story in this manner.

The teacher's last conversational turn (at 114) shows the way she was able to join the children's discussion without directing it. The fact that Krissy added her own speculation after the teacher's response demonstrates that the teacher's comment was taken as one in a series of equally probable speculations, rather than being the final word.

This excerpt is drawn from a readaloud in which Ms. Bigler-McCarthy was the principal "expert other." There were, of course, a number of other adults who conducted readalouds in other classrooms, and I was the reader for the small-group and one-to-one situations. However, the categories that are being discussed arose from a comprehensive analysis of all the data, and the patterns discussed below—the ways in which the adult's comments related to and scaffolded the children's responses—were discernible regardless of the adult who was reading. The next group of sections, then, seeks to lay out the various aspects of assistance represented by the five types of adult talk: if the children were indeed constructing their own view of literary understanding, how did adults provide the framework or scaffold for such a construction?

SCAFFOLDING PROVIDED BY CATEGORY 1: READER

The most basic scaffolding function fulfilled by adults when they read was to make the verbal text of the story available to the children, many of whom would not have been able to read it for themselves. The adults, in other words, mediated the story for the children by presenting it to them in an oral format that was accessible to them. In this view, storybook readalouds represented an accommodation to the children's zones of proximal development. Beyond this basic scaffolding function of reading aloud, however, there was evidence of other aspects of the scaffolding function displayed by the adults when they were acting as readers.

As readers of the story, the adults were tour guides or docents. A tour guide is a knowledgeable person who organizes the experience of those who are less knowledgeable about a particular place, so that they can get the most out of their experience. A docent in a museum has a similar function, pointing out aspects of the museum's collection that deserve special scrutiny. Tour guides and docents are therefore scaffolders of the experience of those they accompany. In their roles as readers, teachers also scaffolded the children's experience of the story by pointing out particular features of it. The simplest way we did this was to point out the parts of the book: "Here are the endpages"; "Here's the title page"; "This is the dedication page." By focusing attention on a particular part of the book, we conveyed the message that it was significant in some way. During the reading of *The Stinky Cheese Man* (Scieszka, 1992), for example, I pointed out the "endflaps" to the children and read them. In a later reading of *The Very Lonely Firefly* (Carle, 1995), Krissy pointed out that the back dust jacket flap duplicated the illustration that it covered. Ms. Bigler-McCarthy's repeated use of the word "endpages" in her readalouds drew the children's attention to this particular feature of picturebooks. Because Brad's attention had been drawn to the endpages, he was able to consider them as potentially meaningful, as shown by his comparison of endpages to the stage curtains for a play during the reading of *The Three Little Pigs* (Marshall, 1989), mentioned in the Introduction to this book.

As readers, Ms. Bigler-McCarthy and I interpreted and enacted the story. In mediating the text for the children, we added sound and expressive emotion to the silent words on the page. That the children were sensitive to this expressive reading is shown by their evaluation of Ms. Bigler-McCarthy's reading of a page of *The Whales' Song* (Sheldon, 1990). After Kenny's comment that "the colors are slow, and the words are slow, too," Ms. Bigler-McCarthy read the last page of the book in two ways: in a fast, clipped manner and a slow and dreamy manner. Mickey's reaction to the fast reading was, "It sounds yucky. 'Cause it doesn't sound like the book's supposed to be. You're reading it so fast that it sounds like you don't have any periods or commas in it." Our expressive reading was thus part of the scaffolding that enabled the children to respond with their own interpretation.

The ways in which Ms. Bigler-McCarthy and I divided the story into segments by our reading also scaffolded the children's experience. It was not often that we read even one complete page without children wanting to respond. During the reading of *Owl Moon* (Yolen, 1987), for example, the second opening of the book was handled in this way:

> TEACHER [reading]: **I could hear it** [the train] **through the woolen cap Pa had pulled down over my ears. A farm dog answered the train, and then a second dog joined in. They sang out, trains and dogs, for a real long time.**
>
> GORDON: How, how can they talk? How'd they understand?
>
> TEACHER: How'd they understand one another?
>
> GORDON: Yeah, but how could they know?
>
> TEACHER: How the train would whistle, and the dog would holler back at the whistle. And the train would whistle again, and the dog would holler back.
>
> GORDON: Oh.
>
> TEACHER [reading]: **They sang out, trains and dogs, for a real long time. And when their voices faded away it was as quiet as a dream. We walked on toward the woods, Pa and I.**

In this excerpt, the teacher read about half of the page before Gordon interjected a question. After the exchange with Gordon, the teacher reread the last sentence she had read before. This reading of short segments combined with rereading is a very common occurrence in the data; it represents the adult's desire to assist the children in following the story while also stopping whenever the children wished to make a comment. Resuming the reading automatically directed the children's attention back to the story.

SCAFFOLDING PROVIDED BY CATEGORY 2: MANAGER AND ENCOURAGER

In managing, the teachers tended to interpret on-task behavior very broadly, as shown by their tolerance for performative responses, extended personal connections, and other discussion that would probably be considered tangential to the narrative of the story by many adults. Indeed, the teachers encouraged these conversational detours in various ways because they believed that *they did not constitute detours for the children*, but were rather part of the literary understanding that they were constructing. Examples (already mentioned) of this tolerance are the children's performative response as twirling ballet dancers and helicopters during the reading of *Amazing Grace* (Hoffman, 1991) and Ms. Bigler-McCarthy's encouragement of Kenny's extended story about fleas during the reading of *The Napping House* (Wood,

1984). This broad interpretation of on-task behavior scaffolded the children's understanding by giving them the freedom to explore pathways that would almost certainly never have occurred to the adults. If this exploration threatened to obliterate the narrative entirely, we would redirect their attention to the text; however, the children, more often than not, did this themselves: a child would be sure to say, "Can we get on with the story?" if the discussion went on too long.

"There's starting to be some messing about" was Ms. Bigler-McCarthy's usual management statement when some children were clearly not paying attention. Management also included the sorting-out of whose turn it was to speak, because the children were eager and aggressive responders. I found that in a small group of five, the children were, if anything, more eager. The scaffolding function of these types of management was to reinforce the conventions of the readaloud situation and to encourage the children to listen to one another as well as to the teacher.

Ms. Bigler-McCarthy and I encouraged the children more directly, as well. The simplest type of encouragement was an acknowledgment: "Um-hmm" and "Uh-huh" occur quite frequently in the data. For example, during the 10 one-to-one readalouds of *The Tunnel* (Browne, 1989), the shortest set of transcripts, I used this type of conversational encourager an average of seven times for each readaloud. Restating or repeating a child's utterance was another common way of encouraging a child to amplify on what she had said:

> Krissy: I like the pictures.
> Teacher: Krissy, you like the pictures?
> Krissy: Yeah, ### it looks like watercolors.

Agreeing with and praising children's comments were also frequent methods of encouragement, evidenced during the reading of Dewan's (1994) *3 Billy Goats Gruff*:

> Teacher: And the sign says **Stop! Pay troll. Then go away.**
> Kenny: That's not fair!
> Teacher: That's *not* fair, is it?

and Bunting's (1991) *Fly Away Home*:

> Trudy: The bird could be watching over the boy, maybe it's his mother, turned into a bird.
> Teacher: Oh, that's a lovely idea. That's a beautiful idea.

These encouraging remarks by the adults helped to create an atmosphere of "warmth and responsiveness" that maximized "children's engagement with a task and willingness to challenge themselves," and that are an important aspect of scaffolding (Berk & Winsler, 1995, p. 29). Children are much more likely to become risk-takers in situations characterized by acceptance and encouragement.

A final way in which these types of comments scaffolded the children's response and developing understanding was to model the way people have a conversation in which everyone is respectful of the ideas and feelings of others, and in which everyone gets a chance to contribute if he or she wishes. Some of the children began to adopt the types of praise and encouragement offered by adults, as in the following example from Bunting's (1991) *Fly Away Home*:

> JIM: Kenny gots a good point. He [the boy in the story] might get caught, too.
> TRUDY: Yeah, I think you're right.
> KENNY: Maybe, maybe the kid gets the bird, and the bird, like, goes outside and gets free.
> TEACHER: The kid gets what?
> KENNY: Maybe the kid gets the bird, and walks out, out the door, to the outside, and, like lets the bird free.
> TEACHER: Oh, and sets the bird free.
> JIM: Kenny gots a good point, he might get caught, 'cause he might either get caught, or he'll miss the airport.

Here, Jim and Trudy used praise and agreement in the discussion about what would happen to the trapped bird and the homeless boy.

SCAFFOLDING PROVIDED BY CATEGORY 3: CLARIFIER/PROBER

In this category, the scaffolding provided by the adults took a more active and directive form. Adults initiated lines of inquiry through questions, encouraged particular types of response, and attempted to clarify and probe children's responses so as to draw out verbalizations that better expressed the children's thought. These attempts at clarification and probing not only allowed the children to better express what they were thinking, but also had the effect of helping the children develop their thought and to raise their literary understanding to higher levels.

It was not common for adults to initiate questions that were not the result of previous comments, but when they did so, the questions were almost always open-ended in nature. For example, after the reading of John Howe's (1989) version of *Jack and the Beanstalk*, the teacher asked a question about Jack's behavior: "Do you think that Jack made appropriate choices?" Children had differing opinions on Jack's character, and compared it to the character of the giant. Some children pointed out that Jack stole things, and the giant did not. Others pointed out that, according to Steven Kellogg's (1991) version of the tale, the giant had taken the gold, the magic hen, and the singing harp from some pirates, so the giant had stolen, as well. Sean thought the giant was greedy, whereas Jack and his mother were poor and needed the money. The discussion continued:

> KENNY: The pirates shouldn't have stole it either.
> CHARLES: It should go where it was at the beginning [before the pirates took it].
> TEACHER: The gold should go to where it was originally? That's kind of how I feel, too, Charles, that maybe he should have made another choice instead of taking it. But, then again, it is just a story.
> JOEY: He [Jack] should have thought before he made that choice.
> SALLY: He should have asked.

The point of the teacher's question was to provoke discussion and speculation, not to hit upon a correct answer. Children were allowed to reach their own conclusions. After the teacher read the title of John Steptoe's (1987) *Mufaro's Beautiful Daughters*, Joey asked, "Is this a Cinderella story?"

> TEACHER: What makes you ask that question, Joey?
> JOEY: 'Cause we've been reading Cinderella stories for a long time.
> TEACHER: I'll let you be the judge of that, OK? So when you think it is or isn't, you raise your hand and let me know, OK?

A common stem of many clarifying or probing questions was for the teacher to ask, "Why do you suppose . . . ?" During the reading of the Coady (1991) version of *Red Riding Hood*, after she showed the illustration of Red Riding Hood approaching the disguised wolf, the teacher asked, "Why do you suppose you can't see her face?" This question elicited a number of responses:

> JULIE: Because she's so far away from the bed.
> GORDON: Maybe she's just lookin' at the stars.

BRAD: Maybe she's backwards.
ROBERT: Maybe she's turned around.

Some probing questions were designed to elicit a specific *type* of response, though not a "correct" answer. The following was part of the discussion of James Marshall's (1987) version of *Red Riding Hood*, in response to the teacher's question, "What do you think the wolf might be thinking right now?"

CHARLES: "Yummy, yummy!"
TRUDY: "Yummy, yummy, here comes my dinner!"
DON: "There's my food floating in the air!"
TEACHER: What else? Julie?
JULIE: "I'm gonna jump out and eat her!"
TRENT: [whistles—a real "wolf" whistle]
TEACHER: He's thinking, whewie, there's a pretty girl, huh?
TRENT: "A pretty girl—and also delicious!"

Here the teacher's probe was intended to encourage performative responses, and the children obliged with some wonderfully inventive performances.

All of these questions show the various ways in which the teachers elicited responses. Questions (especially open-ended ones) were an important part of adult scaffolding, because they gave children the opportunity to examine aspects of the story that may not have otherwise been explored. The questions were heuristic in nature, focusing children's attention on particular points and structuring the situation so that their responses were enabled.

Another important form of clarifying and probing was what might be called "talking children through" a line of reasoning; this was the type of scaffolding in which the adult supplied the "hard bits," leaving the children to reason for themselves where possible. The following example is drawn from the readaloud of *The Napping House* (Wood, 1984), when the discussion turned to the changing point of view in the illustrational sequence. In this book, the viewer seems to look at the bed (present in each illustration) from an ever-increasing height. The children were struggling with this idea of changing point of view, as well as with the idea that objects seem smaller as we distance ourselves from them. The teacher reminded them of *Night in the Country* (Rylant, 1991), when they had also discussed this issue:

100   TEACHER: Do you remember the perspective of the book
        [*Night in the Country*] the way you were looking, how you felt
        you were looking from, in that book?

101   ?: From far away.

102   TEACHER: And how did you know you were supposed to be looking from far away in *Night in the Country*?

103   ?: 'Cause it showed a lot of background.

104   TEACHER: A lot of background [nodding]. And what else? How were the animals? Could you see the light in their eyes?

105   SEAN: When you were close up, they were big, and when you were far away, they were small.

106   TEACHER: Yes. When an illustrator wants to show that something's far away, then the object looks smaller. In this case, though, it looks like you are looking from above, and does it look like you're fairly close?

107   ??: Yeah.

108   TEACHER: Yes, so not only are you, it looks like you are going from the side, looking up high, you also seem to be looking closer as you do that.

109   CHARLES: If you had mice way over there in the corner, they'd look eensy-weensy, but when they come up, they'd get bigger.

110   TERRY: It's like you're standing on the floor, and then you kind of walk up the wall backwards.

111   TEACHER: Why would you do that?

112   TERRY: Because, first you are looking straight at it, and then you're starting to go up and you're looking down a lot.

113   TEACHER: Yes. Terry, you captured that perfectly. Thanks.

Here the teacher is scaffolding by encouraging, clarifying, and probing (with one instance of Category 5, Extending and Refining, at 106). After reminding the children of *Night in the Country* at 100, the teacher probes their understanding at 102 and 104 to elicit Sean's comment (105) about the relationship of distance and size. At 106, the teacher extends and refines his comment by defining it as a general principle of the conventions used by illustrators. At 109, Charles shows that he understands this general principle by providing his own example. At 110, Terry has visualized the changing point of view in the illustration sequence to the extent of being able to articulate an accurate metaphorical description of the process. Still not satisfied, the teacher (111) probes further, and Terry (112) articulates his understanding in more abstract terms. In this excerpt, the teacher's scaffolding questions and statements enabled the children to reach higher levels of understanding as well as to articulate what they already knew.

SCAFFOLDING PROVIDED BY CATEGORY 4: FELLOW WONDERER/SPECULATOR

The type of scaffolding represented by this category is the adults stepping back and allowing the children to function more independently. The adults wondered along with the children about the whys and hows of the story.

During the readaloud of *Owl Moon* (Yolen, 1987), the children initiated a series of predictions about the point of view that the illustration on the next page might take. Gordon felt that "it's probably gonna show the front of the owl, probably." Julie predicted that the back of the owl would be shown. The teacher joined the children in making a prediction:

> TEACHER: My prediction is that they're going to show the owl lifting off the branch and moving.
> ?: No.
> TEACHER: No? I might be wrong. I'm just going to make a guess.
> [12th opening; shows a front view of the owl, sitting on a branch]
> TEACHER: Oh. You were right, I was wrong.
> GORDON: I guess I was right!
> TEACHER: I guess you were.
> JULIE: Me and you are wrong.
> TEACHER: Yeah, but that's all right, because it's kind of fun to play the game of what might happen.

In this excerpt, by taking on the role of a fellow speculator, the teacher takes a risk and finds that her prediction was wrong. By doing so, she encourages the children to take similar risks, which is one of the features of good scaffolding. Also, the teacher has modeled the best way of acknowledging that she was incorrect in her prediction: simply acknowledge it without becoming upset, and treat it as a game in which you lose a turn. Julie joined the teacher in shrugging it off, making it more likely that she would not be inhibited from predicting in the future because she might be incorrect in her prediction.

The teacher's wondering stance was also useful in tossing the conversational ball back to the children, so as to encourage them to voice an opinion. In *Piggybook* (Browne, 1986), Mrs. Piggott leaves home for a few days because her husband and sons do not help with any of the work. The surreal illustrations show many objects in the household taking on a porcine appearance. The children were enchanted with these transformations:

> TRUDY: There's flowers, and they turned into pigs. Back here [turning to the previous page] they weren't. And there's a pig on

    the doorknob, here, too [pointing to doorknob on the 7th
    opening].
KENNY: Oh, this is, too! [pointing to light switch on 7th opening].
TRUDY: And pig wallpaper, too [turning to the 8th opening].
KRISSY: How does it do that?
TEACHER: Why, I wonder?
KRISSY: She said that they're pigs. So now they're turning into pigs!

Here, the teacher's wondering stance gave Krissy a chance to speculate further on why all these transformations were happening.

    The teachers were continually finding out new things about books from the children. One of their specialties was noticing details in illustrations that we, for all our experiences with the books, had never seen. During his one-to-one readaloud of *The Tunnel* (Browne, 1989), Terry noticed an image of a bird in one of the tree trunks. My simple acknowledgment, "You know, I never saw that bird before, Terry," assisted Terry in making a positive evaluation of himself as a responder to books. I did not have to feign my surprise, for despite studying the book and reading it to six children previously, I had not noticed Terry's discovery. Another positive effect of the teachers' wondering stance was the children's adoption of the same stance. Krissy was particularly prone to begin her responses with "I wonder why . . . ," and these wonderings provided opportunities for the children to speculate freely.

SCAFFOLDING PROVIDED BY CATEGORY 5:
EXTENDER/REFINER

It was in this category that the "teachable moments" described by Eeds and Wells (1989) were prevalent. The power of these teachable moments stemmed from the fact that they were stimulated by the children's comments and questions. In this sense, they were not plannable, because we could not predict what the children's responses might be. However, teachable moments *were* plannable in the sense that if we studied the book carefully before the readaloud and refined our *own* responses to it, we were more likely to see the potential in the children's comments because our own knowledge of the book was rich and extensive.

    Each teachable moment added a new item of knowledge to what the teachers came to call the children's "literary tool kit": the many types of literary knowledge that the children could then utilize in their construction of meaning and interpretation. Because new knowledge must be linked to what is already familiar to be of any use, the best way to add new items to the literary tool kit was to fasten onto something the children had said and extend or refine it.

An example of this process is the development of the children's idea of *foreshadowing* in a narrative. In the field notes and transcripts of readalouds, the first statement that can be construed as an understanding of the concept of foreshadowing occurred in the third week of November, during the read-aloud of *An Angel for Solomon Singer* (Rylant, 1992). The teacher had just removed the dust jacket of the book, with its color illustration, and showed the children the plain maroon front cover, with its stamped image of a coffee cup, the moon, and some buildings. Krissy wondered "why the author put that there?" Joey remarked, "It gives you a clue about what it's going to be about, maybe." At this point, the teacher did not choose to talk about foreshadowing. (It is quite possible that talk about "clues" had occurred before, but this is the first example in the data set.)

The next instance of talk about foreshadowing took place during the reading of Christopher Coady's (1991) dark version of *Red Riding Hood* in the second week of December. This excerpt has already been discussed in the section of chapter 4 dealing with the semiotic significance of color. The oval vignette on the title page of this book depicts a bare tree and a full moon tinged with red; red also suffuses the bottom curve of the oval. After Sean pointed out the "red strokes" over the moon and on the lower border of the vignette, Nicole connected the red with Red Riding Hood, and Mickey connected it with the blood in the story. The teacher extended and refined the children's responses with a teachable moment: "Do you think that might be something we call fore-shadowing, to let you know . . . Foreshadowing is what allows you to predict what might happen. Because when the illustrator and the author give you little clues to foreshadow what will happen next, and to let you know what will happen next." Charles summarized the idea: "It's a warning of blood from the wolf that's going to eat the grandma." This was the first time the teacher used the word "foreshadowing," but the concept had been built up gradually before this.

The next instance of the idea of foreshadowing in the readaloud data occurred in the third week of December, during the reading of Delamare's (1993) *Cinderella*. Included in the illustration of Cinderella running away when the clock strikes midnight is an image of an owl hovering overhead. Bill commented that "The owl is her fairy godmother," and went on to explain that maybe the fairy godmother turned into an owl to watch over Cinderella when she went to the ball. Bill's interesting idea seemed to be confirmed when, after the story was finished, the teacher returned to the vignette before the title page, which depicts the faces of Cinderella and three other figures, one of which is an owl:

TEACHER: I wanted to show you something that I thought about after Bill made his comment. Up here beside Cinderella, whose face does this look like?

?: The owl's.

TEACHER: The owl's. So it's from the very beginning.

RESEARCHER: You know, often when an artist presents a little
picture like that, even before the story begins, it has a lot to do
with what the story's going to be about. I think Bill's comment is
really interesting, because that explains the owl.

Here, Ms. Bigler-McCarthy remembered Bill's suggestion that the fairy
godmother transformed herself into an owl, and pointed out the presence of
the owl in the vignette: "So it's from the very beginning." Although I spoke
very rarely during readalouds with the whole group, I did, in this case, expand
on Ms. Bigler-McCarthy's comment by talking about illustrators using beginning vignettes to foreshadow what is going to happen.

That the children had internalized this concept is shown by the following excerpt from the small-group readaloud of *Piggybook* (Browne, 1986)
in mid-February. The children had been discussing the fascinating changes
of objects into pigs. Brad turned to the fourth opening, in which Mr. Piggott's
shadow has the appearance of a pig:

BRAD: This lets us know that they're gonna turn into pigs.

TEACHER: Do you think that's our first clue, Brad?

TRUDY: No.

??: Yeah.

TEACHER: I'm inclined to think that.

TRUDY: No, because [turning to second opening], look at the cereal.

In this excerpt, Brad used the same language that Ms. Bigler-McCarthy
and I had used: "this lets us know." Trudy added her speculation about foreshadowing by pointing out an even earlier instance of the appearance of pigs
in the book: on the cereal boxes on the breakfast table in the second opening.

This sequence of four vignettes from four different readalouds traces the
development of the concept of foreshadowing until children demonstrate that
it is a part of their literary tool kit. It is possible, even probable, that on the
days I was not in the classroom, the teacher had mentioned this concept several
more times; however, the data I have show that the adults had scaffolded this
element of literary understanding to the point where the concept could now be
used independently as an interpretive tool in making meaning from a story.

STORYTELLING: MRS. MARTIN'S STYLE
OF READING AND SCAFFOLDING

As I have explained above, Mrs. Martin's comments, questions, and general
participation in the storybook readalouds for her kindergarten class seemed

to be qualitatively different from the rest of the teachers in the studies. This puzzled me and the graduate students who were helping with the research, until we noticed that Mrs. Martin seemed to be drawing on a number of traditional story-*telling* techniques. We arrived at this hypothesis after hearing Mrs. Martin's introduction to *The Hatseller and the Monkeys* (Diakite, 1999), a West African folk tale retold and illustrated by Baba Wague Diakite. After Mrs. Martin read the title, she referred to the idea of "retelling," mentioned on the title page:

> Now when they say it is retold, that means it is a really old story. This man did not write this story. He is not the owner of these words. Somebody else made up the story a long, long time ago, and told it to children in Africa. There's storytellers in Africa. They tell stories to children, and when they grow up they tell their children, and when they came to America, they brought their stories with them. And they told them to children over here and now I am telling it to you.

We were struck by Mrs. Martin saying, "now I am telling it to you"; it seemed as if she were positioning herself as a storyteller, rather than merely the reader, the latest in a long human chain of storytellers who had told this story before. Thus, we began to research the theory and practice of storytelling, and came to the conclusion that this might be the key to Mrs. Martin's style of conducting readalouds.

Storytelling is an oral performance and is a "situated activity" (Bauman, 1986), in that "its form, meaning, and function [are] rooted in culturally defined scenes or events" (p. 3). Storybook readalouds with a class of children are an example of a situated activity: the teacher is the performer; the students are the audience; and the story (the picturebook) is combined in a communicative event. The characteristics of storytelling are defined by folklorists and anthropologists in the following ways:

- Storytelling is not primarily concerned with word-for-word repetition of a fixed text, but is a flexible means of communication (Heckler, 1996, pp. 22–23).
- Storytelling acknowledges and adjusts to the audience's responses (Birch, 1996, p. 107).
- The success of the storytelling depends upon the intimacy created between teller and listener (Harley, 1996, p. 130).
- The story is created by both the audience and the narrator (Martin, 1996, p. 143).
- In some cultures, storytelling is connected to song, dance, visual elements, and social interaction, becoming a multimedia performance (Price & Price, 1991, pp. 12–14).

Mrs. Martin displayed all of these qualities of storytelling in her picture storybook readalouds with the 21 African American children in her class, acting as a storyteller in 4 ways. She was the *Teller* of the story; she acted as a *Bridge* between the children and the story; as a *Flexible Adaptor* of the story, she let her reading be determined in part by her audience; and as an *Extender and Multiplier of Meaning*, she encouraged different kinds of responses to the story.

Teller

As the *Teller*, Mrs. Martin was relatively unconcerned with a word-for-word rendering of the story, departing in significant ways from the written text. She re-created the text, rather than simply reading what was written. She assumed ownership of the story, rather than being simply a mouthpiece for the written word. While the author's words were an important part of the readaloud, so were the teacher's own interpolations, expansions, and personalizations, all in the service of engaging the children with the story. Interactive and performative readaloud styles have been noted by previous researchers (Barrentine, 1996; Dickinson & Keebler, 1989; Hickman, 1981), but this teacher interpolated and wove her own comments, observations, and interjections into the text. In doing so, she acknowledged that she remained herself, in relationship to the tale and its culture. While a storyteller cannot say what it is like to belong to another culture not her own, she can speak of her own understanding of that culture, and in that way act as a mediator of understanding (Heckler, 1996, p. 29). Notice in the following example from *Something Beautiful* (referred to in chapters 6 and 7) how the words of the text, which are presented in bold, are enmeshed with the teacher's own creative comments. Also notice how the teacher integrates the illustration with the text:

> TEACHER: Well, let's see what she's going to do. I can see her washing something. . . . **and a sponge and some water. I pick up the trash. I sweep up the glass. I scrub the door very hard. When** *Die* **disappears, I feel powerful.** She says, "Oh, boy, look what I did! I took that nasty word off my door." And she cleaned up everything. **Someday I'll plant flowers in my courtyard. I'll invite all my friends to see.**

Bridge

As an emotional *Bridge*, the teacher involved the audience of children, and also involved herself in the story. She also valorized children's responses by seriously entertaining and engaging with children's responses, and assisted children in personalizing the story. During the lively reading of *There's a Monster Under My Bed* (Howe, 1990), Mrs. Martin read of the protagonist's fear.

> TEACHER [reading]: **What if there are more? More and more monsters coming to get me. Coming to munch me for a midnight snack!**
> ??: There's a lot of 'em/I can see them!
> TEACHER [continuing to read]: **Goodbye, Mom! Goodbye, Dad! Goodbye, Glen Oaks Elementary! Goodbye Mrs. Grover!** What do you think Glen Oaks Elementary is?
> ?: His school!
> TEACHER: Right, his school. If you were going to . . . if you were this person in this book you would be saying, "Goodbye [name of the children's school]! Goodbye, Mom! Goodbye, Dad! Goodbye, Mrs. Martin! Goodbye, Mrs. Rawley!"
> ??: Ohh! That's funny! [student laughter]

Here, as an emotional bridge, Mrs. Martin personalizes the situation. She brings the story close to the children by changing "Glen Oaks Elementary" to the children's own school and "Mrs. Grover" to her own name, adding the name of the classroom teacher aide, Mrs. Rawley, for good measure.

This kind of scaffolding encouraged children to insert themselves as well. The following example is taken from the readaloud of *Wiley and the Hairy Man* (Sierra, 1996).

> TEACHER: **"No thank you, Wiley. I'll just wait right here till you get tired or hungry."** He's saying, "That's okay, you know I can't climb up that tree, but you are going to have to come down sooner or later and I'm going to be waiting right here!" That's something my mother used to tell me when I was little.
> KATRIN: My mom used to tell me every day!

Mrs. Martin is demonstrating here her awareness that storytellers "are compelling when they find their own voice and speak with conviction and with attitudes which can make their points of view springboards for the audience" (Birch, 1996, p. 108).

Just as the teacher in the above example encouraged the children to engage emotionally with the story as a way to help them connect with the story, in the following example she helped them co-create their understanding of the story. This following vignette is from the readaloud of *The Magic Tree: A Folktale from Nigeria* (Echewa, 1999), an African folk tale:

> TEACHER: Okay. What do you think? How do they treat him?
> AMANDA: They treat him like a slave!
> TEACHER: They treat him like a slave. They ask him to do things over and over again, but they're not very nice to him. **Beginning very early in the morning when the first person in the village woke up, it was "Mbi, wake up so you can do this! Mbi, sleepyhead, wake up and do that!"**
> AMANDA: And they call him names.

Just as the teacher incorporated her own comments in with the text, in the above example she incorporated a child's response ("They treat him like a slave") into the reading of the text, also. In an example from *Strong to the Hoop* (Coy, 1999), the story of a young African American boy who tries to play in a neighborhood basketball game with some older boys, the teacher inserted her own life into the story:

> TEACHER: **I cut through the lane and bump into Marcus. It's like running into a rock.** Oh my goodness! **"You're too small. Get out of here or I'll push you out." I don't like his talking. Why can't he just shut up and play?** They are saying mean things to him, too. "You're too small!" And if you go to a real basketball game, and I go to a lot of basketball games, you'll see that the players are talking to each other, "Get him, get him, get him, run over here, guard, guard, guard him!" They are talking a lot of jive talk.

In this excerpt, Mrs. Martin is demonstrating that "[i]t is precisely the storyteller's work to explore a story and make a personal relationship with it" (Heckler, 1996, p. 29).

Flexible Adaptor

As a *Flexible Adaptor*, she, like a storyteller, let her storybook reading be determined, in part, by her audience. The following is taken from a reading of *The Adventures of Sparrowboy* (Pinkney, 1997), a fantasy picturebook in which a young African American boy sees a sparrow while delivering newspapers and imagines himself a superhero. In the fantasy, he seems to enter a comic book and acquire the ability to fly from the bird.

TEACHER: **RRRRRP!!! IS IT TOO LATE FOR THE SPARROW?**
How many think it's too late? (show of hands) Well, guess what?
"Hang on, little guy!" Here he comes! **"I don't get it. Why can't
you fly?"** Why can't he fly . . . . he's saying to the bird, "I don't
get it, why can't you fly?" Why? What is wrong. Why can't that
bird fly?

JOE: Because the bird gave him the powers.

TEACHER: How many think that's right? (show of hands) I don't
know. What do you think, Amanda?

AMANDA: It is right because that's a sparrow.

TEACHER: He gave his powers to the boy, you think?

AMANDA: Yes, and he doesn't have any, that's why he can't fly.

TEACHER: So what do you think he should do? What is Sparrowboy
going to do?

SEVERAL CHILDREN SPEAKING AT ONCE: Fly! / he gonna kill him /
and sparrow boy gonna give them back so he can get to fly.

TEACHER: Okay, let's see . . . you think he's gonna get his powers
back; let's see.

This readaloud evoked long conversations about superheroes in general,
but in this particular passage the teacher engaged with the children in wondering how this particular instance of power transfer was going to work out
for the boy and the bird. Her stance was one of co-wonderer; she followed
the children's conversational leading and included herself in their speculations ("Okay, let's see"). Together they built alternate story lines and ex-
perimented with the world of the tale. As Martin (1996) writes, "Stories must
be re-created, not just re-performed. If tellers let technical skills grow out
from their own experience, understanding, and inner seeing of the tale, the
telling that emerges tends to have the power to move an audience" (p. 146).

Extender and Multiplier of Meaning

As an *Extender and Multiplier of Meaning*, Mrs. Martin encouraged multiple ways of responding, including physical movement, sociodramatic play,
dramatic reenactments, and journal-writing as extensions of the readalouds.
She also encouraged the children to be co-creators of the story along with
her, acknowledging the children's suggestions even when these suggestions
seemed unlikely. In the following example, from the readaloud of *Wiley and
the Hairy Man* (Sierra, 1986), the teacher and children are thinking about
how the boy, who has climbed a tree, might escape the monster waiting for
him below. Isaac, Kevin and Edward responded with words, but Amanda
engaged in a dramatic response.

ISAAC: If he try to go home and get something to eat he's gonna eat him!

TEACHER: That's right, if he tries to go home you are going to be hungry and I'll be waiting for you! You will have to come down sooner or later! And I will be waiting right here. Oooh! **Wiley thought about that Hairy Man down there on the ground, and he thought about his hound dogs back home, and he came up with a plan.** What do you think the plan's going to be? Kevin?

KEVIN: The monster . . . the Hairy Man gonna go to sleep, and he ain't gonna hear him, and the boy gonna tippy-toe and untie the dog and he gonna wake up and the dog is gonna come and bite him.

TEACHER: Oooh! That's a good idea—he could wait for the Hairy Man to go to sleep and he could sneak down and they could come back and bite him! What do you think, Edward?

EDWARD: I think he's gonna kick him in his face!

TEACHER: Gonna kick him in the face! What do you think, Amanda?

AMANDA: When the hairy monster is not looking he'll say, "Oh, I'm walking down the street . . . " acting like there is somebody else coming and he'll look back and see and then he'll jump down and he'll go get his dogs and then he'll get back up and try to look to see if he's still there . . .

TEACHER: Oh, so he can act like somebody else is coming, and when he looks away, he'll sneak down?

AMANDA: Yes, and then his dogs . . . then he'll put some fire around his legs and he'll be burning up . . .

TEACHER: He'll be burning up, okay . . .

AMANDA: And the dogs will be barking.

In this example Amanda, inspired perhaps by the other children's stories, began to act out her scenario by pantomiming walking down the street, pretending to be occupied and then suddenly lighting out to get the dogs. This kind of dramatic response was not infrequent in the class, and included pretending to fight, dance, swoon, and kiss. Later in the same readaloud:

TEACHER: **The Hairy Man yelled, gnashed his teeth, and stomped all over the cabin.**

SEVERAL CHILDREN: I told you he was gonna do that!

TEACHER: **He grabbed that baby pig and stormed out the door into the swamp, knocking down trees as he ran.**

KATRIN: And he stomped his feet, and pulled his hair! [Children are stomping their feet]

The alternate stories offered by Kevin, Edward, and Amanda and Mrs. Martin's acceptance of them illustrate folklorist Barre Toelken's point: "Does it really matter after all that a story can have numerous meanings? Not at all, as long as we are ready and willing to deal with the delights of variety, ambiguity, suggestion, nuance, and culturally centered elements of meaning" (1996, p. 41).

The teacher's reading style is thus significant on several levels. First, it was dialogic in the Bakhtinian sense (Bakhtin, 1981, p. 349) of allowing for multiple, free, open-ended, and unresolved points of view in the readaloud literary discussion. Second, this style encouraged a remarkably free, open, and incredibly rich response to literature on the part of lower-socioeconomic-status African American kindergarten children who may not have participated regularly in interactive storybook readalouds prior to entering this classroom. Third, it incorporated elements of a traditional storytelling style, which may have encouraged this free and open participation. This may, in part, be because it is culturally congruent in a way similar to that discussed by McMillon and Edwards (2000) in their research on the reasons why a young African American boy who excelled in his Sunday School classes was not successful in his regular school classroom. In other words, Mrs. Martin's readaloud style may have played an important role in making her classroom culturally congruent to the children's home culture. Children who come from a culture that emphasizes oral language and storytelling (such as some urban African American children) may therefore be more highly engaged when a teacher employs such a readaloud style. Thus, this explication of Mrs. Martin's storytelling style has significant pedagogical implications for the ways in which teachers read to young children.

Sonia Nieto (2000) tells us that our curriculum "lets students know whether the knowledge they and their communities value has prestige within the educational establishment" (p. 96). If children believe that what they bring with them is valued by the teacher, they can feel free to apply whatever they know to the making of literary meaning, and can develop sophisticated ways of talking about what they read. In the social milieu of a readaloud, they also learn how meaning can be constructed in collaboration with others, peers as well as the teacher: that they can contribute to the creation of knowledge, not as passive recipients of knowledge from the teacher.

TYPES OF TEACHER QUESTIONS

As we have seen above, teacher questions are an important controlling and directing mechanism in a literary discussion (Commeyras, 1994; Gilles, 1994; Wollman-Bonilla, 1994). For this reason, it is important to further analyze the questions asked by the teachers. For the purposes of this analysis, I excluded the teachers' calling on students with an interrogative tone ("What do you think, Julie?") as well as instances where the teachers merely repeated what a student had said with an interrogative tone ("You think the bird will escape?") as generally representative of the managing/encouraging role. After I excluded these questions, I found that there were five other basic types of questions the teachers asked during the picturebook readalouds:

- *Invitations.* These questions invited children to look, reflect, interpret, or infer ("What's happening here?" "What do you think they are doing?" "Why do you suppose it says this is the 'true story'?" "Can anyone tell me something about the cover?").
- *Encouragements.* These questions encouraged the children to continue talking ("Anything else?" "Any other ideas?" "What else?"). These encouragements were general in nature, and seemed meant to continue the children's conversation in as nondirective a way as possible.
- *Probes.* These questions probed in order to clarify what a child meant ("Why do you feel bad for the wolf?" "Why do you think that?" "Is there another way you could explain that?"). With these questions, the teacher attempted to understand what a child had said, as well as to help the other children understand a child's point. This category also included questions that asked a child to prove his/her statement by a reference to the text ("How do you know that?").
- *Predicting questions.* These questions directly encouraged the child to speculate on what would happen next in the story ("What do you think they are going to do now?" "What do you think will happen?").
- *Factual questions.* These were questions to which the teacher already knew the answer (identified as such by him/herself), asked to confirm children's understanding of an event or situation in the story ("Who saved Red Riding Hood?" "Why do you have to be quiet when you go owling?").

Invitations for the children to reflect or interpret, general encouragement to continue talking, probing in order to clarify what a child said, and inviting children to predict comprised a high proportion of the teachers' questions, while less than a 10th of the questions were questions to which the teacher already knew the answer. As Nystrand (1997) points out, "This request for elaboration is not an attempt to push the student toward the 'right' answer, but an attempt to encourage the student to explore her own 'interpretive horizons'" (p. 83).

CHILDREN'S ENABLING OF THEIR PEERS' RESPONSE AND UNDERSTANDING

According to Vygotsky (1978), the role of "expert other" can be played by an adult or a more knowledgeable peer. In this section, the children's enabling and scaffolding of one another's literary understanding is discussed, and evidence for the social construction of meaning is presented.

One of the simplest ways in which the children scaffolded one another's literary understanding was to assist in explaining things in the verbal text or illustrations that were unclear to another child. For example, during one of the readalouds of *3 Billy Goats Gruff* (Dewan, 1994), the children talked about the background of the last illustration, which depicts the troll sitting on a planet in space:

KENNY: That's Mars. That's Jupiter.

KRISSY: And maybe this is the stars. I wonder why the author didn't go [traces a five-pointed star shape] like people usually go like that.

TEACHER: Oh, you mean why the author made the stars just like dots?

KRISSY: Yeah, because it looks like:

KENNY: It's because stars, when you look up in, in the sky, there's nothing but dots. Maybe really close it looks like stars.

In this excerpt, Krissy's characteristic "I wonder why" response queries why the stars in the illustrations don't have five points, like the ones she is accustomed to drawing. Kenny's explanation references reality rather than the conventions of illustration: the stars are far away, and so they look like tiny dots of light. Kenny is unsure what they would look like if the viewer were "really close," and he diplomatically suggests that stars could look like their conventional representations from a nearby vantage point.

The children also assisted one another by refining one another's hypotheses. The long list of hypotheses about the nature and purpose of the "slime" in *Bad Day at Riverbend* (Van Allsburg, 1995) has already been presented in chapter 4. In that example, the chain of reasoning that this series of hypotheses represents was described as a chain that the children built with one another. They reacted to and built upon one another's hypotheses. For example, after Jim's speculation that the slime had something to do with the rainbow, Krissy, Kenny, and Trudy all used his idea to come up with a quasi-scientific theory involving sunlight, water, and color. During the same readaloud, in a similar fashion, they constructed a theory about the origin and

production of the book, based on the fact that the back cover included a photograph of a man and a little girl with a cowboy hat that was similar in color
and shape to the cowboy hat worn by the little girl in the last illustration:

> KENNY: That's the girl that was coloring it, and she has the same
> cowboy hat on.
> KRISSY: Maybe she likes cowboys.
> JIM: She's coloring there, too. She's scribbling there, too.
> TEACHER: Um. Who do you think this might be here [pointing to the
> man in the photograph]?
> KRISSY: Her dad.
> JIM: The author.
> KENNY: The sheriff.
> TRUDY: It's her dad, and he's the author. This right here [showing
> back cover with the photograph], she's drawing her own picture,
> and this [showing the 14th opening, with an illustration of the
> girl in the same cowboy hat] is of the same girl.
> TEACHER: So you think this person here is the same as the one on the
> back cover?
> KRISSY: Except it looks like a cartoon, sort of. Maybe she's dream-
> ing about it, and after that, like, she made a book about it, and
> that's and after that, one day, um, her dad helped her, and he did
> the words, and she colored it, and made the other stuff.
> TRUDY: Her dad colored it, her dad drawed it, and she colored it.

Here, the reasoning proceeded ever nearer to the identification of the
man in the photograph as the author, the identification of the little girl in
the photograph with the girl in the story, and the way the book came about.
The children scaffolded one another's reasoning to arrive at a conclusion that
was quite possibly accurate.

The children challenged and changed one another's perceptions of reality through discussion during the readalouds. It has already been mentioned
that during the readaloud of *Amazing Grace* (Hoffman, 1991), Sally made a
sturdy declaration of her Native American heritage. At that time, Gordon
demonstrated a stereotypical understanding of Native Americans: he reasoned
that Sally couldn't be an Indian because "you didn't come from the Indian
places," perhaps the Southwest. When Sally retorted that "Just because you're
an Indian doesn't mean you have to come from an Indian place," Gordon
saw the force of Sally's argument and apologized. During the readaloud of
Amazing Grace to another small group, Krissy displayed her impatience with
white people calling African Americans "black." I had just read the text,
which stated that some of the children in the story told Grace that she couldn't

be Peter Pan because she was black. Krissy declared, "She's [Grace] not black, she's *brown*. White people, white people call brown people black people. And we're *not* black, we're brown. And I'm mixed up with white." (Krissy was biracial.)

In Part II, I mentioned at several points that at least some children seemed to have an identifiable set of "signature" responses. This individuality would appear to be of great significance in the social construction of meaning. When multiple viewpoints or perspectives were introduced into readaloud discussions, this multiplicity often resulted in a more full and rich discussion: clearly, the children's literary understanding was enriched by Jim's thoughtful generalizations, Sally's analytical abilities, Krissy's wondering stance and fascination with art media, and Charles's performative responses. Because various cultural, ethnic, and social backgrounds were represented in the classroom, this diversity also resulted in more stimulating conversations about books.

11

What's the Point of Literary Understanding? Implications for Practice, Research, and Beyond

The conversations between teachers and children in this book reflect a high potential for literary understanding—perhaps higher than the level that may be found in most classrooms and schools. In this last chapter, therefore, the potentials inherent in these "information-rich cases" (Patton, 2002) are discussed as a series of implications for classroom practice and further research.

PEDAGOGICAL IMPLICATIONS OF THE STUDIES

Reading stories aloud to children, though touted as an important element in the array of highly recommended classroom literacy practices, is seldom discussed in any detail. In the following sections, I discuss more specific suggestions for conducting storybook readalouds and encouraging a wide spectrum of responses, thereby realizing the full potential of this literacy practice.

Handling the Storybook Readaloud

In these studies, the storybook readaloud situation was highly structured, in the sense that several routines and rules (both explicit and implicit) organized it. The readalouds were frequent, usually occurring twice a day. They took place in a certain space in the classroom at predictable times. The children knew that they were free to comment at any time during the reading, that it was important to listen to the comments of others, and that a variety of comments were acceptable. They knew that making links to other books was valued, and that they could show books that related to the book being read aloud, because the classroom's collection of books was close at hand. The children were accustomed to detailed discussion about peritextual features before they heard the verbal text of the story, because the teachers allowed time for interpretation of these features. All of these routines and rules were useful in assuring that the readalouds were highly productive. The routinized nature of the situation enabled the building of "progressively richer knowledge structures" (Snow, Nathan, & Perlmann, 1985, p. 168).

Building a classroom community is an important concern for teachers (Peterson, 1992; Sergiovanni, 1994). In these studies, the storybook readaloud situation was one of the most important sites for the formation of a literary "interpretive community" (Fish, 1980) in the classroom. Children felt free to share and construct their literary competence in the context of a secure environment that encouraged—even valorized—speculation, wondering, spontaneous performative response, and provocative interpretations. Teachers may want to reflect on how their own storybook readaloud practices assist in the formation of a classroom interpretive community.

One aspect of the way readalouds were handled in these studies deserves special mention. About two-thirds of the children's conversational turns in these studies occurred during the reading of the story, whereas one-third of the turns occurred after the reading. Moreover, the *quality* of talk during the readalouds was also high. Allowing children to talk during the reading of the story may not be a common practice among teachers, however. In Hoffman, Roser, and Battle's (1993) study of storybook reading practices, the category of discussion *during* reading does not even occur—only discussion before and after; this may be a possible indication of how little it happens in classrooms.

Though this book (and the studies on which it is based) emphasizes interactive readalouds, there is no one best way to read stories to young children. However, if we *always* expect children to listen quietly to a story and to save their responses until the story is finished, we may be imposing our adult view of what constitutes the proper way of experiencing literature—a view that may not be particularly productive for young children. Because the children's responses in these studies were so often *of* the moment and *in* the moment, to hold the response to the end of the reading would have been, in many cases, to lose it. Also, certain types of responses manifested by the children occurred almost exclusively during the reading of the story. For example, intertextual responses, performative responses, predictions, and "talking back to the story" characteristically happened as the story was being read. These types of responses may simply not be in evidence if children are not allowed to comment during storybook readalouds.

In fact, talking as the story unfolds is one of the unique affordances of the storybook readaloud situation. In most literature circles, literature discussion groups, and classroom book clubs (Daniels, 2002; Eeds & Wells, 1989; McMahon, Raphael, Goatley, & Pardo, 1997), the discussion takes place only *after* the story is read. These literature discussion groups are certainly valuable, but storybook readalouds offer the possibility of evoking different types of responses. To allow children to talk freely during the reading of a story gives teachers a window on the children's process of making narrative meaning. In turn, this allows teachers the opportunity of scaffolding the children's meaning construction *as it is in the process of being constructed*, with all the "mucking around," false leads, backtracking, confirming, and disconfirming that this entails. Scaffolds are most useful as a structure is being built!

Encouraging a Variety of Responses

The data suggest that there were five types of responses made by children, responses that in turn were representative of five different types or aspects of literary understanding. In reflecting on their own classroom practice, teachers may want to consider how many of these types of response are manifested by their students. For example, if all the talk seems to be text-centered, personalizing responses may be modeled and encouraged. If, on the other hand, only personalizing responses are manifested, teachers may want to model and encourage analytical talk. There seems to be a range of types of literary understanding, and teachers can consider how they may increase their students' repertoires to include a greater portion of this spectrum. Because textual features may play a role in evoking particular types of response, teachers should consider choosing a variety of genres and formats. There is a great range of picturebooks available today, from the treatment of serious social problems—like *Fly Away Home* (Bunting, 1991) and *Amazing Grace* (Hoffman, 1991)—to the outrageous postmodern hijinks in *The Stinky Cheese Man* (Scieszka, 1992), to books like *Don't Let the Pigeon Drive the Bus* (Willems, 2003) and books with sparse text like *No, David!* (Shannon, 1998) that fairly cry out for very active involvement on the part of children. Teachers' knowledge of this ever-expanding range of possibilities is therefore crucial. If we limit children's experience to a few genres, we may be limiting their developing literary understanding.

Exploiting Every Part of the Picturebook

One of the unique affordances of picturebooks is the rich visual stimulation they provide. For example, all of these studies demonstrate the great potential of the peritext of picturebooks for making meaning, yet these features are often skipped or given short shrift. Children should be encouraged to explore this potential. The ways in which teachers *begin* a storybook readaloud should be carefully considered. In the studies represented in this book, the teachers and children discussed peritextual features, exploring the affordances of the book itself rather than teachers' own purpose-setting questions. This strategy may free children to construct their own interpretive trajectories, and it contradicts recommendations of more directive ways of preparing children to listen. Beginning a story with purpose-setting questions automatically puts the teacher in firm control, and it is possible that if this is the usual method of introducing a story, the children's sense of agency may be reduced or eliminated. There is no one best way to begin a picturebook readaloud, but teachers should certainly consider trusting the book to be its own best introduction; after all, all the introductory peritextual elements have been carefully designed and orchestrated to produce a total effect, and part of the purpose of this careful orchestration is precisely to *prepare* us to read the book. In literature-based basal reading series, almost all the peritextual elements are omitted, depriving children of the rich meaning-making and preparation that the peritext affords (Feathers & Bochenek, 2006; Reutzel & Larsen, 1995).

Similarly, the great importance of the illustration sequence in the total meaning of picturebooks should not be underestimated. In chapter 1, I emphasized that the illustrations act to fill in gaps in the text, and the text acts to fill in gaps in the illustrations. There is a synergy between text and illustrations: together, they have a potential for meaning that is more than the sum of their parts. In order to understand this special affordance of picturebooks, teachers should consider refining and extending their own understanding of art, illustration, and picturebook theory. Bang (2000), Kiefer (1995), Stewig (1995), and Doonan (1993) discuss principles of art, the conventions and semiotic codes of illustration, and picturebook theory in ways that are quite accessible to classroom teachers who may not have as rich a background in the visual arts as they might wish. If teachers are to enrich their students' aesthetic appreciation and understanding of the visual features of picturebooks, they must first possess their own appreciation and understanding. Once teachers begin taking a close look at the visual material in picturebooks, they will begin to learn from the children, because children tend to notice details that we adults would miss. In other words, teachers should plunge in and learn about visual semiosis alongside the children, rather than feeling that they need to be art experts before discussing these aspects of picturebooks. Articles that deal with specific picturebooks or picturebook authors (Larry, 1995; McClay, 2000; Neumeyer, 1990; Nodelman, 2001; Pantaleo, 2003b) or articles that review recent research about picturebooks (for example, Wolfenbarger & Sipe, 2007) may be helpful, as well as individual book chapters and articles (Nikolajeva & Scott, 2000; Sipe, 2001a, 2001b, 2002a, in press; Sipe & Brightman, 2005, 2006, Sipe & Ghiso, 2005; Sipe & McGuire, 2006a, 2006c, in press).

Because picturebooks consist of at least two related sign systems (the visual sign system of the illustrations and the verbal sign system of the written text), they can increase the ability to move among several sign systems. This type of understanding is important for children's use of such new textual entities as hypertext. Lemke (1993) comments that in illustrated informational texts and hypertext, there are "many possible pathways through the textworld"; this is equally true of picturebooks. Margaret Meek (1983) argues that "A picture book invites all kinds of reading and allows the invention of a set of stories rather than a single story" (p. 174). By according illustrations equal importance with the text, teachers encourage this diversity of interpretation, and also facilitate their students' abilities to integrate visual and verbal information.

Exploring Intertextual Connections and Story Variants

The research reported in this book suggests that intertextual connections are pivotal in enabling the children to make a great variety of interpretive moves, suggesting the importance of forging intertextual links. If these connections are not occurring as often as teachers think they should be, they can demonstrate and encourage children to make these connections by posing direct questions ("What other stories does this story remind you of?") and by explicitly referring to other books, television and video programs, and a wide variety of other texts in the course of the discussion. Children who do make links to other books and cultural products should be praised, and their responses may be probed to encourage intertextual analysis. Teachers may want to examine the eight ways in which intertextual connections were used by the children in these studies (described in chapter 6), comparing them with the ways in which their own students make use of such connections.

I found that there is a quantitative aspect to intertextual connections, in that after a certain number of stories are interrelated, a type of cognitive "critical mass" is achieved that allows the children to reach higher levels of abstraction and generalization about story theme and structure. Reading many stories to children allows them to more readily build up this critical mass. Reading many stories that are representative of the same genre might also result in rich classroom discussions.

Reading many variants of one story (like the multiple picturebook versions and variants of the *Cinderella* and *Rapunzel* stories described in chapter 6) allows children to increase their intertextual knowledge with the greatest ease. Variants are identifiable *as* variants precisely because they share many common elements of structure, character relationships, and themes. It may therefore be easier for children to forge intertextual links among different versions of the same story, even if they have little previous experience of literature. Thus, teachers may want to consider units of study in which many variants and versions of the same story are read and reread. In this way, they arrange their storybook readings so that children may begin to link stories together in a naturalistic way, without much explicit direction from the teacher. In my studies, I found that the teachers did not need to construct comparison/contrast charts in order to elicit this type of response (or that they constructed charts in response to the children's comments, rather than planning them as a teacher-initiated activity).

It should also be remembered that the children in these studies made links to many cultural products other than books. There were links to television programs, videos and movies, advertisements, and the art or writing of other children—the broad range of "textual toys" described so eloquently by Dyson (2003). The studies show that even the most vulgar elements of popular culture may be utilized by the children to achieve remarkably sophisticated and beautiful interpretations (remember, for example, Judy's use of the television program *Married With Children* in her sensitive interpretation of the bird in *Fly Away Home* [Bunting, 1991] as a symbol of the boy's deceased mother, discussed in chapter 6). Therefore, the literary understanding of the children may be best served if all their intertextual links (including some that the teacher may consider too low-brow) are honored, rather than valorizing only connections to other books. The making of links between the story and the art or writing of other children seems to be particularly important, so that children may see themselves as fellow authors and illustrators along with the authors and illustrators in books. Thus the children may internalize the idea that they, too, have agency and control in generating, refining, and critiquing texts (such as Sally's comment, "and *we* are retelling the tale again today," in response to the teacher's remark that *Strega Nona* was Tomie dePaola's (1975) version of an Italian folktale, in chapter 6).

The Crucial Roles of Teachers

Taken together, these studies provide evidence for the critical roles teachers play in enabling their students' development of literary understanding. There were five main ways in which teachers scaffolded the children's literary understanding: as readers, managers and encouragers, clarifiers or probers, fellow wonderers or speculators, and extenders or refiners. In addition, the style of one of the teachers, Mrs. Martin, seemed to be more like story-*telling* than story-reading. In all cases, however, teachers played an essential part in supporting and developing that understanding. Teachers may reflect on their own scaffolding roles and ask how their own comments, questions, and responses may assist children in reaching higher levels of literary understanding.

Questions

Because teacher questions are so powerful, it would be enlightening for teachers to audiotape themselves reading a story to the children, and to ascertain how many questions they ask and how many of those questions are ones to which the teacher already knows the answer. In other words, what are the quantity and quality of questions? It's well known that questions are a critical technique for controlling a discussion (Wollman-Bonilla, 1994). If there are too many questions (of any sort), the message given by the teacher is that she is the dominant force in the trajectory of the discussion. And if there is a high proportion of questions to which the teacher already knows the answer, this implies that the purpose of the discussion is actually to test and assess children's knowledge rather than to engage in the exploratory, "rough draft" talk that Douglas Barnes (1976) thinks is so valuable in developing children's higher-level thinking skills. Vernon-Feagans, Hammer, Miccio, and Manlove (2001) comment that none of the studies they examined found that African American or Hispanic parents engaged their children in question-asking routines, unlike in white, middle-class families where children were often asked questions to which adults knew the answer. As a result, children from nonmainstream cultures may experience difficulty attempting to answer the types of questions asked by their teachers. As demonstrated by Heath (1983) and Vernon-Feagans (1996), "Children may think that they are being tricked or may not understand why they are being asked a question with a known answer and may respond incorrectly" (p. 201). This is a powerful argument for teachers to speculate and interpret alongside the children.

Scaffolding

It is also crucial for teachers to consider their own theories of scaffolding in general: does scaffolding involve following the children's leads, or solely the teacher's own ideas of how the discussion should proceed? In other words, who controls the conversation, at what points, and for what purposes? The view of scaffolding presented in this book valorizes listening closely to the children and being willing to follow the conversational trajectories initiated by them, even when these trajectories may seem to be off task or contradictory to the teacher's own agenda for the story. As Newkirk and McClure (1992) mention, the children's talk frequently left them "in the dust," wondering what connection the conversation had with the story; however, they eventually understood the significance of the conversations. As Erickson (1986) and Yonge and Stables (1998) wisely remark, children always are on task, though that task may not be the one the teacher has in mind!

When I first began thinking about the methodology I would use in research about young children's literary understanding, I examined frameworks of discussion (for example, Chambers, 1993) that could be used to stimulate the children's thinking. These frameworks, while useful collections of provocative and open-ended comments and questioning techniques, did not prove necessary. In the overwhelming majority of cases, the teachers and I could follow the children's lead rather than directing the discussion. In this way, we could ensure that any new information we introduced was contextualized, making it more likely that children could assimilate it. Truly listening to the children (Paley, 1986) seemed to be the key. Teachers just beginning this process may want to seek more explicit direction (Fisher, Flood, Lapp, & Frey, 2004; McGee & Schickedanz, 2007), but of course there is no standard formula for a successful picture storybook readaloud.

Preparing to Read Aloud

This listening and following the children's lead did not, however, absolve us from thinking seriously about our readalouds beforehand. Indeed, we found that if we were going to perceive the potential of teachable moments in what the children said, we needed to have already considered the possibilities for meaning for ourselves. This points to the necessity for teachers to refine and extend their own literary taste and sensibilities. Perhaps we jump rather too quickly to the consideration of the ways in which we can "use" literature in classrooms, rather than first experiencing and understanding literature ourselves. If teachers are going to follow the lead of the children, there is a sense in which they must be in even greater command of literature (and even more sensitive to its potentialities) than if they were in total control of the discussion. If we are going to help children add items to their literary tool kits, then our own tool kits must be full.

Being Open to a Variety of Responses

These studies identified a particular type of response that was quite unexpected. Performative responses were not even seen *as* responses at first. The more the teachers and I examined these responses, the more intrigued we became with their creatively aesthetic qualities. What we learned from this experience was that the broader one's range of tolerance, the greater the diversity of children's responses resulted. A possible implication for teachers is to expand their conceptualization of what constitutes response to literature—"everything considered" (Hickman, 1983). This stance may place some teachers in an uncomfortable space, but being in uncomfortable spaces has the potential for being on the growing edge of practice. Who can predict what fascinating insights and literary interpretation can result from a seemingly off-task response by a child?

Identifying and Using Individual Response Styles

Throughout this book, I have mentioned, in passing, that certain children seemed to exhibit patterns of responses that highlighted their fascination with certain aspects of picturebooks. The studies suggest that at least some children, even children as young as kindergarten or first- or second-grade, may have styles of response that can be distinguished as unique and individual (Brightman & Sipe, 2006; Sipe, 1998c). There are several pedagogical implications of this finding. First, teachers should simply be aware of and on the lookout for manifestations of these individual styles in their students. What specializations or passions do individual children develop in regard to literature? Are there ways in which the child's response seems to express his or her identity theme or basic personality? Do children seem to try out styles of response, only to discard these approaches in favor of others, or does the style seem to be a fairly constant aspect of their literary meaning-making across different discourse structures (Santori, 2006)? Second, these individual styles may be understood and encouraged as elements of strength: as particularly well-developed aspects of children's literary understanding. In the studies, Gordon became our resident expert on illustration arrangement and "texture"; Krissy became our expert on illustrational media and style. Naisha frequently assumed the voice of storybook characters, making transparent responses. Jim was adept at summarizing and considering the "big picture" for a story, thus often producing quasi-thematic statements. Terry was the go-to person for proving a statement by going back and reading the actual words of the text. Literary understanding is a social construction, with children bringing their own unique perspectives, thus extending and refining one another's thought.

The idea of individual children's unique response styles also raises the question of whether particular cultural, ethnic, or racial groups may have characteristic styles of response, a question that has been raised recently in research. Latina children in Lopez-Robertson's (2005) teacher research study seemed to have a high proportion of personalizing responses, which I have called "stories on the story": the children wanted to tell extended stories about their own experiences that were sparked by an action or character in the storybook; however, each child's stories served varying purposes. Teachers should keep this possible propensity for particular responses in mind as they read with children, (1) valorizing and praising these types of responses and (2) encouraging other types of response to augment them, so that the children's literary understanding is both validated and extended.

FURTHER RESEARCH

The major theoretical construct of this book, that of literary understanding, is a part (and, as I have argued, a neglected part) of literacy learning in general. Research that makes clear the connections between literary understanding and the broader cognitive processes involved in learning to read and write, and that places the literary understanding of young children in the wider context of literacy learning, is therefore needed. The following are possible areas of investigation.

Extending Research on Literary Understanding

Meek (1988) asserts that texts teach what children need to learn. We know that narrative literature is highly motivating for children, but what other qualities make literature a powerful tool in learning to read? What are the crucial lessons in narrative that teach "how texts work" even as texts motivate children to continue to read? Clearly, this book has been concerned only with fiction in the form of picture storybooks; however, children should be exposed to a wide range of other genres. For example, what lessons do nonfiction and informational formats (Duke, 2000; Pappas, 1993) teach young children? What lessons do the various subgenres of the information book (Pappas, 2006) teach children? Furthermore, various literary texts, especially those with metafictive elements, exemplified in the "postmodern picturebook" (Pantaleo, 2002, 2004a, 2004b; Sipe, 2004), may well involve different types of scaffolding moves and more (or different) intervention, according to children's previous experience with these texts.

The connection between literature and writing is very powerful (DeFord, 1984; Sipe, 1993). Children with developed literary understanding may be children who are able to "write like readers" and "read like writers" (Hansen, 1987; Smith, 1984). The links between literary understanding and writing deserve more investigation, for as we expand our view of what constitutes literary understanding beyond the traditional "elements of narrative," this broader view may reveal more connections between literary understanding and the ability to write well. How, for example, would a child's aptitude for performative response impact on his or her ability to write forcefully and with strong rhetorical purpose? Of what use are intertextual connections in learning to present a cohesive argument? How does the development of the personalizing impulse assist children in generating written text that "speaks" to its readers? I believe that picturebooks, if discussed and reflected upon properly, are as influential and useful (and perhaps even more useful) in children's writing as the often violent, and essentially sterile, stereotypical, and formulaic models offered in popular culture.

We might hypothesize that children with developed literary understanding are children who are alive to the force and value of multiple interpretations of what they read, and who know how to engage in a critical exchange of views with their peers. What are the associations between literary understanding and this ability to consider multiple points of view when discussing the interpretation of texts?

What are the connections between literary understanding and the ability to read thoughtfully and inferentially? What are the associations between literary understanding and the ability to interrogate or resist a text, not accepting it at face value, but rather probing its underlying ideological assumptions?

Is the pleasurable surrender to the power of the text heightened by developed literary understanding? What are the connections between pleasure and literary knowledge? Rosenblatt argues that the purpose of analysis is to increase our pleasure, not destroy it; we should therefore consider whether our analyses of story structure and other narrative elements with children do in fact contribute to their pleasure and love of reading, or whether these exercises in analysis are simply deadening children's motivation.

How is transmediational skill—the ability to move easily among several different sign systems—developed by experience with picturebooks? How does this skill impact on children's use and understanding of hypertext and other alternative cyberformats for presenting text? How can children's art, drama, and other nonverbal responses be integrated with their verbal responses to (1) demonstrate their transmediational abilities and (2) refine and extend their literary understanding?

Further Examination of Storybook Readalouds

The storybook readaloud situation has been the object of more research than any other early literacy event because it is possible to view this situation from many different perspectives. The literary and aesthetic understanding that children develop during the storybook readaloud situation deserves more complete investigation. For example, we have some convincing evidence that storybook reading style not only varies across teachers (Dickinson & Keebler, 1989; Dickinson, McCabe, & Anastasopoulos, 2003; Dickinson & Tabors, 2001; Martinez & Teale, 1993; Morrow & Brittain, 2003; Reese, Cox, Harte, & McAnally, 2003), but that some reading styles impact more powerfully than others on later literacy ability (Allison & Watson, 1994; Brabham & Lynch-Brown, 2002; Dickinson & Smith, 1994). How do variations in storybook reading style impact on the development of literary understanding? What styles of storybook reading encourage or facilitate the development of particular types of response from the children? How do the types of discussion and response during storybook readaloud situations compare and contrast with the types of discussion and response that occur during literature discussion groups and literature circles?

Possible Additional Theoretical Frames

There are several alternative theoretical frames that could be brought to bear on the data in this study or similar data. In order to socially construct meaning, children must learn the skills of cooperation and the conventions of social discourse that involve several people. Perspectives from sociology and sociolinguistics, for example, might be useful in analyzing the ways in which children learned the rules and conventions of discussing literature, and the ways in which they developed tolerance for one another's opinions.

Play

When they discussed literature during storybook readalouds, the children were engaged in a pleasurable and sophisticated form of linguistic play, and their imaginations were highly engaged. Performative and transparent responses were perhaps the most obvious indication of this linguistic play; however, all the forms of response were evidence of deep engagement and children's delighted participation in what they evidently regarded as a pleasurable game. Analysis could therefore profitably be framed with theories of play (Fox, 2003; Kantor & Fernie, 2003; Rowe, 1998; Scarlett, 2005; Winnicott, 1974).

Drama

Theories of drama for young children (Adomat, 2005; Edmiston, 1993) may also be useful. Edmiston (1993) writes that

> As readers, we may go inside a book as we become characters, empathize with them, and critique their actions. However, when we talk about literature, we are always outside our world of the story and are no longer experiencing it except in retrospect. Even if we relive a moment as we share it with a friend, neither of us are inside the story as we talk about it. (p. 256)

However, this is not the case in the theory I present, which is based on in-the-moment experiences of the children as the picture storybook is in the process of being read aloud, perhaps as close as we can come to a "lived-through" experience that is individual and personal and at the same time intensely social. Thus, when children talk about literature in this way, they can position themselves either inside or outside the story (in Edmiston's terms), depending on which of the literary impulses they are enacting as they listen to and talk about the story.

Gender

The data for my studies suggest that boys spoke more often than girls, and that they (with some notable exceptions) tended to dominate the discussions. A gendered analysis, of the type developed by Davies (2003a, 2003b, 2004) with preschoolers, by Gallas (1998) with primary children, or adapted from Anderson's (2002), Lewis's (1997), and Evans's (1996) work with older students, would be useful in understanding the ways in which gender affected the nature of the discussion and the responses. Did the boys tend to focus on actions in the story, while the girls focused on characters' feelings, as some researchers have suggested (Cherland, 1992, 1994)? Or is this a possible perpetuation of a stereotype (Evans, 1996)? How do young boys and girls who do not conform to the heteronormative rules of gendered behavior (Blackburn, 2003) interact and respond during storybook readalouds? Would a readaloud group of all girls or all boys generate a different type of discussion (Evans, 1996)? What types of gendered responses are generated by fairy tales, which tend to reflect the patriarchal hegemony (Marshall, 2004), and how do these responses differ from the gendered responses generated by contemporary realistic fiction? Specific chapters in Nikolajeva (2005) and Wolf (2004) provide excellent starting points for bringing feminist literary perspectives to bear on children's responses.

Race and Culture

Analysis of readaloud data with a central focus on culture, race, class, and ethnicity (Cross, 1993; Perkins, 1992) could be illuminating as well. The possible relationship between the African American use of "signifying" (Gates, 1988; Lee, 1995) and some features of performative response has been suggested. Are African American students from certain socioeconomic levels more likely to engage in and appreciate performative response to literature than their European American peers? If this is so, how does the possible suppression of these types of responses in traditional classroom situations impact on these children's engagement in discussion about books? Also, how does the teacher's style of storybook reading differentially affect various cultural, ethnic, and racial groups? Recent research (mentioned above in the pedagogical implications) has shown that some Latina children's individual response styles were characterized by a high proportion of personal stories (Lopez-Robertson, 2005), and this is another possible relationship between ethnicity/culture and response. Since the studies on which this book is based did not include a significant proportion of Asian Americans or Hispanic Americans, it is possible that different types of response or different proportions of the same responses might be identified. We have a great deal to learn about how culture, race, ethnicity, and socioeconomic status both enable and constrain response to literature, and thus shape literary understanding. Cynthia Ballenger's (1998) insightful study of preschool Haitian children reveals first her puzzlement and frustration with what I would call performative and transparent responses, and then her gradual acceptance of them as an important part of the children's style of response. We need more studies like this, with the addition of stronger theoretical frames to place these types of response in broader contexts. Critical literary theory of various types has been incisively applied to children's literature (though not solely to picturebooks) by McGillis (1996) and Wolf (2004), whose work could provide additional starting points for applying such lenses to children's responses.

Poststructuralist Theories

My explication of performative response has relied heavily on some poststructuralist theories that emphasize the infinitely deferred meaning in texts and their lack of transparency to reality, as well as the ways in which texts (and children) can be subversive and playful. In postmodern picturebooks such as *Bad Day at Riverbend* (Van Allsburg, 1995), there may be further ways in which poststructuralist theories can be applied both to the analyses of such books as well as to children's responses. Glasheen (2007), for example, critiques standard theories of text–picture relationships in relation to *Bad Day at Riverbend*, pointing out that none of these theories can be satisfactorily "applied to a picturebook whose text and illustrations are initially intended to confound the reader" (p. 3) and thus do not represent the unity/synergy of the visual and the verbal emphasized by so many theorists. In other words, the relationship of text and pictures in this book goes well beyond Nodelman's (1988) concept of an ironic relationship, and into a deliberately subversive mode. In *Bad Day*, text and pictures continually destabilize each other until the closing pages, when the illustration alone reveals the solution to the mystery of the book—that a child has been coloring the pages: "though the concept of a coloring book is not new to these students [the two second-graders who were Glasheen's informants], a book about the characters of a coloring book is!" (p. 3). McGillis's (1996) discussion of poststructuralist theories as applied to children's literature may provide additional insights, especially for picturebooks that refuse to conform to standard conventions.

The Importance of Longitudinal Studies

Longitudinal studies of the developing literary understanding of the same children over 2 or more years, though time-consuming and labor-intensive, would be extremely useful. Cox's (1994) research with children from kindergarten through third grade seems to be one of the very few studies that is truly longitudinal in nature. Such longitudinal studies would assist us in understanding how literary understanding develops over time. How, for example, are new elements added to the literary tool kit? Are these elements utilized in more complex ways? Is there increasing evidence of personalizing response to literature, or evidence of the life-transforming power of literature over time? Do children tend to make more generalizing and thematic statements as they develop literary understanding? Does individual response style hold steady over time, or are various styles and modes of response tried out by children, laid aside, or taken up again? Are certain types of response (for example, performative response) in evidence in the first years of school, only to disappear or go underground in later years?

Testing the Application of the Conceptual Categories and Grounded Theory

The conceptual categories of children's responses in these studies and the grounded theory that arose from them need to be tested across many cases in order to validate, extend, and refine them. Do the five facets of literary understanding and the hermeneutic, aesthetic, and personalizing impulses seem to apply to the literary responses of other young children? What modifications or refinements are necessary in order to characterize the literary responses of slightly younger or older children? How would the use of other literary genres or formats affect the formulation of conceptual categories for children's response? Would other readaloud styles used by teachers result in different conceptual categories or suggest a different configuration of impulses?

This study used only high-quality picturebooks (defined by their mention in standard texts of children's literature, public recognition in the form of medals and awards and favorable reviews). If low-quality literature were read to children, would their literary understanding enable them to critique these books? Landes (1983) found that young children displayed a preference for the original version of *Peter Rabbit* over simplified versions with less distinguished illustrations: the children were actually irritated by the dumbed-down versions. This research is provocative, but such studies are rare.

The Role of Intertextual Connections

The findings of my studies suggest the pivotal and crucial role played by intertextual connections in the children's developing literary understanding. Are there other ways in which intertextual connections function to assist children in interpreting, predicting, summarizing, or evaluating literature?

Is there more evidence for the concept of a "critical mass" of intertextual connections in other classroom situations? Is it generally true that exposing children to many variants and versions of the same tale is the easiest way to facilitate the formation of intertextual links? What are the long-term effects (in terms of critical thinking, abstract reasoning, and the ability to compare and contrast ideas and situations) of an early emphasis on helping children to forge intertextual links?

The Visual Potentials of Picturebooks

It is puzzling that the visual aspects of picturebooks have not been the object of more empirical research, given that these visual aspects share equally with written text in telling the story and affording potential meaning-making. Senior researchers in the field of literacy have called for "broadening the lens" of what we conceptualize as literacy (Flood & Lapp, 1995). Included in their broader vision is the role of aesthetic response, with specific mention of picturebooks. The "verbo-centric" nature of Western intellectual life is gradually being challenged by the "new literacies" that are based much more on visual meaning-making than was the case in the past. Reading and discussing picturebooks with young children would seem to provide an ideal way of assisting them to integrate both visual and verbal sign systems, as well as to negotiate multiple pathways through hypertext and other nontraditional texts. Picturebooks may be an important bridge in this process.

The ways in which young children learn to exploit the meaning potential of the peritextual features of picturebooks deserve more examination. Peritextual semiosis proceeded quite intensely for the children in my studies, and contributed significantly to their meaning-making, but empirical research has thus far paid little attention to these important features of picturebooks.

Another possible line for further research is to pay particular attention to the children's interpretation of page turns in picturebooks. A page turn represents a necessary gap in text and pictures. For example, the second opening of *Where the Wild Things Are* (Sendak, 1963) depicts Max chasing the family dog with a fork. When the page is turned to the third opening, Max is shown in his bedroom with a frown on his face. Children could be encouraged to speculate on what might have happened *between* the two openings. The gaps in page turns are not always as dramatic as this one— some are much more subtle—but there is always at least a slight rift in the narrative when a page is turned (Bartow, 2007). A picturebook is not a movie, where there is often continuous action. Even in a movie, there are breaks in scene and changes in perspective, so gaps are always present. But in a picturebook, after every double-page spread, we are exposed to what Barbara Bader calls "the drama of the turning of the page" (1976, p. 1). According to author/illustrator Steven Kellogg (2003), the turning page

> gives the illustrator the chance to utilize the elements of surprise to advance the movement of the story, and to deepen the involvement of the viewer in much the same way that the theatrical director uses the revolving stages or the rising curtain between the scenes and acts of a play. (para. 7)

For this reason, page turns might be a powerful site for investigating children's cognitive integration of text and pictures, as well as their ability to make high-level and subtle inferences.

The learning of illustrational codes and conventions deserves a great deal more attention from researchers. The children in this study learned a variety of these codes, but there are many others (Moebius, 1986) that could be researched. The ways in which these codes are dependent on cultural knowledge and norms need investigation. In our increasingly multicultural society, how might children's understanding of these codes both conflict with each other and be modified by their diverse interpretations?

The Pleasure of Children's Literature

I have suggested that the theorization of the pleasure children take in literature has not been well-developed, and that even reader-based theories (which might be expected to address this issue) rarely discuss pleasure in a serious way (Touponce, 1996). If it deals with pleasure at all, the discourse of literacy tends to approach it crabwise and obliquely in theories of "attitude," "affect," or "motivation" (Matthewson, 1994; McKenna, 1994) that, for all their care and hard thought, seem curiously sterile, missing the target at which they are aiming. Research could focus on the ways in which children express their pleasure in literature, with the goal of developing a grounded theory of the literary pleasure of young children that would conceptualize that intense pleasure more directly. A possible beginning to this exploration would be to attempt to apply Barthes's (1975) distinction between "pleasure" (*plaisir*) and "bliss" (*jouissance*) to the literary experience of young children. It would seem that children do experience both types of literary pleasure: the pleasure of mastery and the pleasure of being overwhelmed, puzzled, and enthralled.

Researchers might also investigate the particular pleasures afforded by the activation of what I call the hermeneutic, the personalizing, and the aesthetic impulses. In Aristotelian terminology, what is the "proper pleasure" afforded by the hermeneutic impulse? Perhaps it is based on the satisfaction of confirming or disconfirming one's interpretation, and the knowledge that at least in this small corner of the world, we have achieved control and mastery (of a text, if not of life). Perhaps the proper pleasure of the personalizing impulse is to exult in breaking down the seemingly intransigent wall between ourselves and the rest of the world: to see ourselves as intimately connected to the web of life, not as strangers alienated from everything around us. And might the pull of the aesthetic impulse be in the direction of freedom from the continuous and burdensome contingencies of time and space, and the possibility of being universalized?

There are those, I know, who might consider these observations more appropriate fare for an adult class in philosophy than for children; yet my studies convince me that the intellectual, emotional, and social sensitivities of children are marvelous and boundless. Children are a lot less innocent and naive than we assume (Sendak, 1993). In a world where many children are unprotected from vicious and demoralizing experiences, and where they may feel existential despair, dread, and anxiety just as intensely as adults, these issues are eminently relevant for them, and the experience of literature and the development of literary understanding may be an empowering and affirming force in their lives.

The Usefulness of Storybook Readalouds for Silent Children

In these studies, the readaloud situations in the large and small groups were characterized by a fast-paced, energetic discussion in which many diverse comments were made in a short space of time. We might raise the question of what type of thinking would be enabled and stimulated by this rapid-fire situation, and what type of thinking might be hampered or constrained by it. In short, was the situation depriviliging for children who may have needed more time to process their thoughts, and who could not easily follow a discussion that jumped from point to point? (R. Donelson, personal communication, 1996). In their research on "silent sixth-grade students," Jones and Gerig (1994) found that language arts classes that were evaluated by teachers as successful (because of the lively nature of the discussion) may have had a negative effect on the more silent students: "These language arts classes were ability grouped, and the class discussions were particularly fast paced and competitive. The competitive atmosphere may have contributed to silent students' decision not to participate in class discussion" (p. 175). Studies that focus on the behavior of the less vocal students during storybook readalouds are therefore needed. Such students' literary understanding may be more fruitfully investigated in situations that are less competitive and allow more time for response to develop.

Effects of Rereading on the Development of Literary Understanding

Barthes (1974) humorously remarks that the rereading of books "is tolerated only in certain marginal categories of readers (children, old people, and professors)" (p. 16). Various researchers have found important gains in literacy learning for children who have been exposed to multiple rereadings of texts (Martinez & Roser, 1985; McCarrier, 1991, 1992; McGee & Schickedanz, 2007; Morrow, 1988; Yaden, 1988). We might also ask what effects multiple readings of the same text have on the development of literary understanding. Arizpe and Styles (2003) as well as Belfatti (2005) found that rereading Anthony Browne's (1994) *Zoo* had the effect of enriching the children's responses, raising their thinking to higher levels of abstraction. Both Hickman (1981) and Kiefer (1982) argue that time is needed to develop and deepen response; revisiting stories after an initial exposure may provide this element of time. Strickland (2001) points out that "even with limited resources, teachers must make books accessible to children, especially those they had read aloud, as those are the books to which children naturally gravitate to *revisit* on their own" (p. 330, italics mine). Literary critical perspectives on rereading, for example, Calinescu's (1993) *Rereading*, may prove helpful in this line of research.

The Ideology of Children's Literature

I have touched on the issue of the ideological and political assumptions of children's literature, though it is clear that all children's literature is deeply inscribed by these assumptions (Stephens, 1992). How do children learn to discern the implicit ideology in books? How can texts function to heighten children's awareness of social issues, and engage their "moral imagination" (Coles, 1989) so that they can strive for social justice? How does literature assist children in envisioning other possible selves and other possible worlds? It would seem that literature and the other arts can provide a source of ideas for socially transforming society. Literary critics such as Wayne Booth (1988) have done much to rehabilitate the idea that literature can (and should) have a profound ethical and moral effect.

The ability to imagine a different society may be partly based on the ability to impose a new narrative construction on the social facts at our disposal: to tell a *different story*. If this is the case, then reading stories to children is a profoundly political, transformative action, which research can explore. Finally, although all literature is freighted with ideology, some literary genres may forefront this ideology more sharply. For example, *Fly Away Home* (Bunting, 1991) and *Something Beautiful* (Wyeth, 2002) seemed to elicit provocative discussions by children, and true critical questioning about issues relating to injustice and inequality in society. Realistic fiction, then, may provide young children with greater opportunities to discuss these issues than other genres.

BEYOND LITERACY: WHAT GOOD IS LITERARY UNDERSTANDING, ANYWAY?

This book has argued that children as young as kindergarten and first and second grade can demonstrate impressive literary critical abilities. But why would we want young children to be literary critics? Why would we want to encourage the development of literary understanding? In addition to the important role it may play in becoming literate, the significance of literary understanding may reach even beyond its connections to literacy. During the past four decades, thinkers from many academic disciplines have pondered the meaning that stories can have for our lives. Knowledge of narrative may be a way—perhaps a primary way—of structuring reality itself: an "organizing device" (Langer, 1953, p. 261). According to many cognitive psychologists and anthropologists (Bruner, 1980, 1986, 1990; Geertz, 1973; Wolf & Heath, 1992), the experience of "story" may be one of the most powerful ways we have of imposing order and meaning on the world. We know that experience shapes language (and literature), but language (and literature) can also shape experience. Various writers in the human sciences and the humanities (Hardy, 1978; Mitchell, 1981; Polkinghorne, 1988; White, 1980) have argued that narrative is a crucial factor in the formation of identity and the constitution of what Jung called the Self, to the extent that the human mind may be understood as a mechanism for turning the raw data of day-to-day experience—the "booming, buzzing confusion" of life (James, 1890)—into narratives, thereby rendering reality understandable and meaningful (Ricoeur, 1980). According to some psychoanalysts (Spence, 1982), one of the main ways we cope with an event or a situation is by turning it into a story. For Shklovsky (1966), literature frees us from the tyranny and enervating dullness of the quotidian, rendering the familiar strange, and the strange familiar. Literature thus allows us to perceive our lives, the lives of others, and our society in new ways, expanding our view of what is possible, serving as a catalyst to ignite our capacity to imagine a more just and equitable world. To understand stories and how they work is thus to possess a cognitive tool that not only allows children to become comprehensively literate, but also to achieve their full human potential.

Appendix A:
The Research Studies for This Book

There are two principal studies on which this book is based. The first was a 7-month study of one combined first- and second-grade public school classroom (with 27 children) in a working-class community adjacent to a large Midwestern city. I spent 3 to 4 days per week in this classroom, where the teacher read aloud to the children twice a day. Twenty-three children were European American, including eight with Appalachian heritage; three were African American; and one was Native American. About 23% of the children qualified for the district's free/reduced-price lunch program. The school as a whole was committed to a philosophy of informal schooling, with an emphasis on activity-based learning and thematic integration of subjects, and had been using literature in creative ways for over 20 years. The teacher, Ms. Bigler-McCarthy (a European American), was very knowledgeable about children's literature, and relied on trade books to teach literacy. The classroom was print-rich and contained many children's books. The purpose of the study was to describe in detail the literary understanding of these children, and ways in which the teacher scaffolded their oral responses. Data consisted of field notes, interviews with the teacher, and audiotaped storybook readalouds to (1) the entire class; (2) two groups of five children each; and (3) one-to-one readalouds with individual children. The findings were based on data from a total of complete transcriptions of 59 readalouds of a variety of genres, including fantasy, traditional tales, and contemporary realistic fiction.

The second main study that is the foundation for this book was a 9-month study with 21 African American kindergarten children in a public school in a large Eastern city. 95% of the children qualified for free or reduced-price lunch. I (a European American man) and two research assistants (one European American woman and one Japanese American woman) spent 4 to 5 days per week in this classroom. The teacher, Mrs. Martin (a European American), had 10 years of experience, was a doctoral student in literacy, and read to the children twice a day. The purpose of the study was to describe the ways in which the children developed literary understanding through examination of their oral responses to storybook readalouds, one-to-one conversations with children during free-choice time, and spontaneous and planned sociodramatic play. In this study, the major data consisted of complete transcripts of 42 readalouds. The selection of picture storybooks emphasized literature by and about African Americans, though other types of picturebooks were also used.

In addition to these two main studies, there are three studies that provided supplemental data:

- A 10-month study (13 visits) in a public school kindergarten classroom (26 children) in a large Eastern city. Twenty-five children were African American and one child was Puerto Rican, and all qualified for the district's free/reduced-price lunch. The teacher, Mr. Taylor (a European American), had 3 years' experience and was a master's student in literacy; he was concerned to maintain a print-rich classroom, and emphasized children's writing. The purpose of the study was to describe the literary responses of these children to storybook readalouds of traditional literature and fantasy, and the teacher's scaffolding roles as he read aloud to the children. Data consisted of field notes, interviews with the teacher, and completely transcribed audiotapes of 13 readalouds.

- A 2-month study (10 visits) in a combined first-second grade (20 children) in an independent school in a large Eastern city. The experienced teacher, Mrs. Zigler (a European American), was a doctoral student in literacy. Children represented a diversity of ethnicities and socioeconomic statuses. The purpose of the study was to describe the ways in which the children developed an understanding of the structure of a traditional tale through the intertextual connections they made while hearing a succession of five different picturebook variants of one traditional story from various cultures. Data thus consisted of field notes and complete transcriptions of five readaloud discussions.

- A study in 15 kindergarten and first-grade classrooms in public schools in a large Eastern city. The purpose of the study was to describe a wide range of responses by urban (primarily African American) children to Beatrix Potter's (1902/1987) classic story, *The Tale of Peter Rabbit*, and to examine the various ways in which the children interpreted the story and its relevance to their own lives. Three of the teachers were European American and 12 teachers were African American. Data consisted of field notes and complete transcriptions for 15 readalouds.

These studies are not a hodgepodge of different methods and questions; they cohere with and complement one another in the following ways:

- All of the studies involved aspects of young (K–2) children's literary understanding and classroom teachers' scaffolding of that understanding.
- The overwhelming majority of the participants were not children of privilege, though there was a representation of a variety of ethnic, racial, and socioeconomic backgrounds. Many of the children were African American, living in urban environments.
- Children's oral response to picture storybooks read aloud by classroom teachers was the focus of all the studies. Discussion by teachers and students before, during, and immediately after the readalouds was transcribed, and these transcriptions formed the foundational data for each study, along with field notes. Response to literature in nonschool settings may comprise a different set of speech genres (Bakhtin, 1986) than response in classrooms: thus, I focused only on school-based literary discussions.
- The teachers in each case were experienced and knowledgeable about literature written for children, particularly picture storybooks. They were skilled in scaffolding children's literary understanding. Additionally, the physical arrangement of the classrooms was quite similar, with comfortable book corners conducive to reading aloud, and hundreds of books readily available, within an arm's length, if the children wanted to refer to another book during the storybook readaloud. In all cases, the children sat on a small carpeted area, and were physically close to the teacher and the book.
- The books utilized were all picture storybooks, in various genres (realistic fiction, fantasy, magical realism, traditional literature, and historical fiction), including a significant quantity of culturally relevant literature. All were works of narrative fiction (that is, there were no nonfiction/informational books). The rationale for the exclusion of informational books was that children's responses to these types of books have been shown to be qualitatively different from their responses to narrative fiction.
- All of the studies were qualitative and naturalistic (taking place in classrooms during readalouds of picture storybooks, a commonly occurring literacy practice in all those classrooms), and were descriptive and interpretive. Data analysis for all the studies was based on standard qualitative content analysis techniques (Bogdan & Biklen, 2006; Patton, 2002). The unit of analysis was the conversational

turn—what was said by one speaker before another speaker responded (Sinclair & Coulthard, 1975). This unit of analysis was chosen because it reflects changes in who has the floor in a discussion (Edelsky, 1981), and is thus a powerful indicator of the dynamic, back-and-forth nature of a discussion—the interactive quality I wanted to capture. The analysis relied heavily on the three-stage procedures described by Strauss and Corbin (1998): (1) identifying conceptual labels for each conversational turn; (2) grouping these conceptual labels into a manageable number of robust conceptual categories; and (3) relating these categories to one another to arrive at a formulation of the "core category," which answered the question of what constituted literary understanding on the part of the children and the question of what constituted scaffolding by the classroom teachers.

In summary, the book lays out a grounded theory of the literary understanding of young children (K–2) that is based on the analysis of 101 completely transcribed picture storybook readalouds in two different sites, in classrooms with children of a variety of ethnic, racial, and socioeconomic backgrounds; field notes; and interviews. The two principal studies are supplemented by 33 readaloud transcripts from 3 additional studies.

Appendix B:
A Glossary of Picturebook Terminology

bleed When the illustration extends to the very edge of the page, with no white space or border, it is said to "bleed." When the illustration extends to all four edges of the page, this is called a "full bleed." An example of a full bleed is the Wild Rumpus scene, stretching over three double-page spreads, in Sendak's *Where the Wild Things Are*. An illustration can bleed to one, two, three, or all four edges.

borders Illustrators often design a border for their illustrations in a picturebook. Sometimes (as in many of Jan Brett's picturebooks) the border is used to tell more of the story, or to tell a parallel story.

continuous narration Joseph Schwarcz's term for the use of several separate illustrations on the same page (a montage) that indicate motion, action, or the sequence of time. A good example is the four panels in Maurice Sendak's *In the Night Kitchen* that depict Mickey flying higher and higher.

cross-hatching Fine parallel lines, usually in black, that are crossed with another set of parallel lines to produce the effect of shading. Cross-hatching also gives an illustration a feeling of energy or vibrancy.

cut-out An illustration that has no frame, but that simply appears against the background. An example is the title page of *Where the Wild Things Are* by Maurice Sendak, which shows Max in the act of menacing two monsters. Motion and freedom are suggested by the lack of a frame.

double-page spread Picturebooks are planned as a series of facing pages called double-page spreads or openings. An illustrator may choose to spread the illustration over both pages of an opening. This is called a double-page spread illustration.

dust jacket The thick paper wrapper around the outside of the picturebook. Sometimes the dust jacket's illustrations are the same as the illustrations on the front and back cover. In some cases, the front and the back cover have different illustrations or are simply plain cloth or heavy board.

edition The *trade edition* of the book contains the fullest expression of the art of the picturebook, containing a dust jacket, endpages, etc. The *library* *edition*, which has a stronger binding, frequently omits the dust jacket, reproducing the same illustration on the front cover. The *paperback edition* omits the dust jacket and frequently omits the endpages and/or illustrations on the back cover of the book.

endpages   Also called *endpapers*. The first pages one sees when opening the picturebook, and the last pages one sees at the end of the book before closing it. Endpages are like stage curtains, framing the performance of a play. The color and/or design of the endpages are chosen to coordinate in some way with the rest of the book. In some cases, as in Steven Kellogg's *Jack and the Beanstalk*, the illustrator uses the endpages as an additional space to tell the story. The endpages consist of the "pastedown," attached to the inside of the front or back cover, and the "flyleaf," the other half of the endpage that is opposite the pastedown.

establishing shot   In filmmaking terminology, a film sequence that shows the overall terrain in which the action will take place. Picturebooks often include an establishing shot in the first illustration. The title page of *Rosie's Walk* by Pat Hutchins shows the entire barnyard in which the action will take place.

fold and gathers   Before the picturebook is bound, all the printed pages are gathered and folded so that reviewers can see what the finished book will look like. Often abbreviated "F and G's."

frame   In a picturebook, the illustrations are frequently surrounded by an illustrated border or by white space, giving the impression of a framed picture. Sometimes part of the illustration may "break the frame," seemingly breaking out of and overlapping the straight edge of the illustration.

front matter   The "fine print," indicating the publishing information and copyright information, as well as the Library of Congress classification, a very brief summary, and the ISBN number. Sometimes, there is a note about what artistic medium was used in the illustrations. This information is occasionally located at the back of the book, in which case it is usually simply termed the "publishing information."

glossy/matt (or matte) paper   If the paper used in the picturebook is shiny and smooth, it is glossy. If it is dull, it is matt (sometimes spelled "matte"). "Glossy paper gives colors a glistening clarity, but it is distancing partially because the light shines equally through all the colors and creates an overall sheen that attracts attention to the surface of a picture and therefore makes it more difficult for us to focus on specific objects depicted" (Perry Nodelman, *Words About Pictures*, 1988, p. 47). On the other hand, matt paper or rougher stock invites our touch and our sensuous interaction, as in Chris Van Allsburg's *Jumanji*.

gutter   When the book is opened, the middle groove where the pages are bound. If an illustration spreads over both pages the illustrator must make sure that important parts of the illustration (like a character's head) do not cross the gutter.

half-title page   At the beginning of the picturebook, a page with only the title of the book (see *title page*).

home-away-home   A frequent structural device in children's literature. The main character begins at home, in familiar surroundings; then goes away and has some sort of adventure; and then returns home. Examples of this type of story are Beatrix Potter's *Peter Rabbit* and Maurice Sendak's *Where the Wild Things Are*.

hue   A pure color, such as red, blue, green, purple, etc., without any addition of white or black.

illustrational sequence   In a picturebook, the illustrations do not stand alone, but in an ordered sequence. As in a motion picture, this sequence conveys meaning, chronological order, and the narrative.

irony   In a picturebook, the illustrations never tell us exactly the same thing that the text does, and the text never tells us exactly the same things as the illustrations. There is therefore the possibility for irony: the text may comment ironically on the illustrations, or vice versa. In *Rosie's Walk*, the illustrations are an ironic commentary on the flat, rather uninteresting text, which merely tells us that Rosie takes a walk. The illustrations indicate that a fox is trying to capture Rosie; this is never mentioned in the text.

jacket flaps   The parts of the dust jacket that fold over the front and back covers. Frequently, the front jacket flap contains a summary of the book, and the back jacket flap contains information about the illustrator and the author.

matt (or **matte**)   A term for a dull surface on a piece of paper or the medium used in an illustration. See *glossy*.

medium (plural, *media*)   The paints or other materials (tissue paper, real objects, etc.) the illustrator uses to produce the illustrations.

montage   In laying out a page of a picturebook, an illustrator may choose to include several illustrations on the same page. This is known as a montage. In Peter Spier's *Noah's Ark*, several of the pages contain four or five separate illustrations.

motif   A recurring element in the illustrations or text of a picturebook, for example, the triangular shapes reminiscent of witches' hats that occur throughout the illustrational sequence of Anthony Browne's version of *Hansel and Gretel*.

narrative trajectory   The plot is not an emotionally even or flat sequence of actions; some actions increase our emotion, and some diminish our emotion. We could graph the plot as a rising and falling line, with a high point or climax. This whole sequence is known as the narrative trajectory.

opening   In a picturebook, the pages are rarely numbered. Thus, there is a difficulty in referring to a particular illustration or page. The "first opening" is the two facing pages where the text of the book begins, and the openings are numbered after this.

page break   The picturebook is carefully planned as a series of facing pages ("openings" or "double-page spreads"). When we turn from one opening to another, these gaps are also carefully planned, and are known as page breaks. The reader/viewer is invited to make inferences about what happens in the page break from one opening to another.

peritext   Gerard Genette's term for anything in a book other than the printed text. This would include the dust jacket, front and back covers, endpages, title page, etc. In a picturebook, the peritext conveys a great deal of meaning, and should be as closely examined as the body of the text.

point of view   An illustration is planned from a certain point of view, so that viewers feel themselves to be in a certain position in relation to the scene in the illustration. We can seem to look down on a scene, or seem to be placed below the scene, or on a level with it. In *Jumanji*, Chris Van Allsburg frequently varies the point of view in his illustrations, adding to the surreal or disorienting effect.

recto   The right-hand side of a page opening (or double spread). See *verso*.

shade   A pure color to which black has been added, to darken it.

signature   In a picturebook, a single large sheet of paper is usually printed with 8 book pages on one side and 8 book pages on the other side. When this large sheet is folded and cut, it is called a signature. Most picturebooks have two signatures, or 32 pages.

spine   The bound edge of the book, which is frequently reinforced with an extra strip of cloth or cardboard.

stock   The type of paper used in the picturebook. We can speak of glossy or matt (matte) stock, or stock of various weights, colors, and thicknesses. See *glossy/matt (matte) paper*.

synergy   "The production of two or more agents, substances, etc., of a combined effect greater than the sum of their separate effects" (*Shorter Oxford English Dictionary*). In relation to picturebooks, this term refers to the fact that the illustrations and the verbal text of the book combine together to produce an effect that is greater than the sum of their parts. The total effect of the picturebook depends on the perceived interactions between the text and the illustrations.

stamping   An image or letters are sometimes pressed into the front or back cover of a picturebook by a heavy metal die. If the image is simply stamped without any color, it is called "blind stamping"; if it is pressed in gold or another color, it is called "foil stamping."

text box   The text of a picturebook may simply be printed below or above the illustrations, in a plain white space. The designer may also choose to print the text directly on the illustration. Also, the text may be printed in a box placed on top of part of the illustration. This is known as a text box. In *Outside Over There*, Maurice Sendak uses text boxes in several openings.

texture   An illustration may appear to have a smooth or rough surface, depending on the technique that is used to produce it. Paper itself can have a smooth or rough texture.

tint   A pure color to which white has been added to lighten it. In watercolors, water is added instead of white.

title page   The page that indicates the title of the book, the author, the illustrator, and (usually) the publisher and the city in which the book was published. The *half-title page* (if present) contains only the title of the book.

trompe l'oeil   An illustration that looks so realistic that it fools the eye, looking three-dimensional and real. In John Scieszka's *The Book That Jack Wrote*, the picture frames are *trompe l'oeil*.

typography   Illustrators or designers choose the typeface, or font, that is used for the text, the title, and other printed portions of the book. The typography coordinates in some way with the meaning of the text and the overall look of the book. For example, very modern typography would look out of place in Margaret Hodges' *St. George and the Dragon*, an old tale.

value   The proportion of darkness or lightness in a color. Lighter colors are higher in value and darker colors are lower in value.

verso   The left-hand side of a page opening (or double spread). See *recto*.

vertical moment   An important or emotionally charged moment in the plot of a story. Vertical moments in *Snow White* include the three times the wicked queen attempts to poison the young girl.

vignette   A small illustration used to break up a section of text or otherwise decorate a page. The round illustrations on the last page of Maurice Sendak's *In the Night Kitchen* and the back cover are examples.

wash   Watercolor or ink that has been much diluted with water, producing a pale effect. Oil paints may be diluted with a great deal of turpentine, and are similarly pale.

Appendix C:
Transcription Conventions

Description	Symbol	Example
An unknown child is speaking	?:	?: It's an African tale.
Several unknown children are speaking	??:	??: Yeah!
Unintelligible speech (one word)	#	Ken: She looks like a # witch.
Unintelligible speech (multiple words)	###	Ken: I had a garder snake and I ###, and my dad ranned over it.
Reading the text of the book	**bold**	Teacher: Let me read that again. **They spent all their time going to the Palace Disco.**
Page turns	[ ]	[4th opening] [title page] [front cover]
Nonverbal behaviors	[ ]	[nods] [makes muscle pose with arms]
Overtalking (two or more people talking at once)	/ //	Teacher: She doesn't seem to be too/clever, does she? Terry: Yeah, she probably// doesn't know much.
Run-on talking (another person begins talking with no pause)	:	Teacher: Our book today: Gordon: Is by James Marshall.
Loud talking	ALL CAPS	I'd probably just go POW and karate chop him!
Emphasized word	*italics*	She really *does* look like a witch!
Representations of sounds	attempted phonetic representation	Ewww! Oooh! Um-hmm.

Children's Literature References

Berenzy, A. (1995). *Rapunzel*. New York: Henry Holt.

Browne, A. (1986). *Piggybook*. New York: Alfred A. Knopf.

Browne, A. (1989). *The tunnel*. New York: Alfred A. Knopf.

Browne, A. (1990). *Changes*. New York: Alfred A. Knopf.

Browne, A. (1994). *Zoo*. New York: Alfred A. Knopf.

Bunting, E. (1991). *Fly away home*. New York: Clarion.

Carle, E. (1984). *The very busy spider*. New York: Philomel.

Carle, E. (1995). *The very lonely firefly*. New York: Philomel.

Carle, E. (1999). *The very clumsy click beetle*. New York: Philomel.

Carter, D. (1999). *Wil'hemina Miles: After the stork night*. New York: Farrar, Straus and Giroux.

Coady, C. (1991). *Red Riding Hood*. New York: Dutton Children's Books.

Cole, B. (1986). *Princess Smartypants*. New York: G. P. Putnam's Sons.

Cole, B. (1987). *Prince Cinders*. New York: G. P. Putnam's Sons.

Collier, B. (2000). *Uptown*. New York: Henry Holt.

Coy, J. (1999). *Strong to the hoop*. New York: Lee & Low.

Crews, D. (1998). *Bigmama's*. New York: Harper Trophy.

Delamare, D. (1993). *Cinderella*. New York: Green Tiger Press.

dePaola, T. (1975). *Strega Nona*. New York: Prentice-Hall.

Dewan, T. (1994). *3 billy goats gruff*. New York: Scholastic.

Diakite, B. W. (1999). *The hatseller and the monkeys*. New York: Scholastic.

Drescher, H. (1994). *The boy who ate around*. New York: Hyperion.

Echewa, R. O. (1999). *The magic tree: A folktale from Nigeria*. New York: Morrow Junior Books.

Egielski, R. (1997). *The gingerbread boy*. New York: HarperCollins.

Galdone, P. (1975). *The gingerbread boy*. Boston: Houghton Mifflin.

Galdone, P. (1978). *Cinderella*. New York: McGraw-Hill.

Galdone, P. (1985). *The three bears*. New York: Clarion.

Grimm, J. (1972). *Snow White and the seven dwarfs* (R. Jarrell, Trans.). New York: Farrar, Straus and Giroux.

Grimm, J. (1988). *Dear Mili* (R. Manheim, Trans.). New York: Farrar, Straus.

Grimm, J. W. (1992). *Rapunzel*. New York: Ideals Children's Books.

Grimm, W. (1997). *Rapunzel*. New York: North South Books.

Helldorfer, M. C. (1999). *Silver Rain Brown*. Boston: Houghton Mifflin.

Hesse, K. (1999). *Come on, rain!* New York: Scholastic.

Hodges, M. (1984). *Saint George and the dragon*. Boston: Little, Brown.

Hoffman, M. (1991). *Amazing Grace*. New York: Dial.

Howe, J. (1989). *Jack and the beanstalk*. Boston: Little, Brown.

Howe, J. (1990). *There's a monster under my bed*. New York: Aladdin.

Huck, C. (1989). *Princess Furball*. New York: Greenwillow.

Hutchins, P. (1968). *Rosie's walk*. New York: Simon & Schuster.

Hyman, T. S. (1983). *Little Red Riding Hood*. New York: Holiday House.

Isaacs, A. (1994). *Swamp Angel*. New York: Dutton Juvenile.

Jiannan, F. (1996). *Hou Yi shoots the suns*. Beijing: Dolphin Books.

Katz, K. (1999). *The colors of us*. New York: Henry Holt.

Kellogg, S. (1985). *Chicken Little*. New York: Morrow.

Kellogg, S. (1991). *Jack and the beanstalk*. New York: Morrow.

Kellogg, S. (1997). *The three little pigs*. New York: Morrow Junior Books.

Kimmel, E. A. (1988). *Anansi and the moss-covered rock*. New York: Scholastic.

Kitamura, S. (1997). *Lily takes a walk*. London: Happy Cat Books.

Krauss, R. (1945). *The carrot seed*. New York: Harper & Row.

Lionni, L. (1963). *Swimmy*. New York: Alfred A. Knopf.

Louie, A. L. (1982). *Yeh-Shen: A Cinderella story from China*. New York: Philomel.

Lowell, S. (1994). *The three little javelinas*. New York: Scholastic.

Macaulay, D. (1990). *Black and white*. Boston: Houghton Mifflin.

Marshall, J. (1987). *Red Riding Hood*. New York: Dial.

Marshall, J. (1988). *Goldilocks and the three bears*. New York: Dial.

Marshall, J. (1989). *The three little pigs*. New York: Dial.

Martin, R. (1992). *The rough-face girl*. New York: Scholastic.

Mayer, M. (1987). *There's an alligator under my bed*. New York: Dial.

McKissack, P. (1986). *Flossie and the fox*. New York: Dial.

Munsch, R. (1999). *The paper bag princess*. New York: Scholastic.

Myers, C. (2000). *Wings*. New York: Scholastic.

Nolan, D. (1987). *The castle builder*. New York: Macmillan.

Olaleye, I. (2000). *In the rainfield, who is the greatest?* New York: Scholastic.

Perrault, C. (1993). *The complete fairy tales of Charles Perrault* (N. Philip, Trans.). New York: Clarion.

Pinkney, J. B. (1997). *The adventures of Sparrowboy*. New York: Simon and Schuster.

Pinkney, J. B. (2000). *Cosmo and the robot*. New York: Greenwillow.

Pinkney, S. L. (2000). *Shades of black: A celebration of our children*. New York: Scholastic.

Potter, B. (1902/1987). *The tale of Peter Rabbit*. London: Warne.

Raschka, C. (1993). *Yo! Yes?* New York: Scholastic.

Rosales, M. (1999). *Leola and the honeybears: An African American retelling of Goldilocks and the three bears*. New York: Cartwheel.

Rylant, C. (1982). *When I was young in the mountains*. New York: Dutton Juvenile.

Rylant, C. (1991). *Night in the country*. New York: Macmillan.

Rylant, C. (1992). *An angel for Solomon Singer*. New York: Orchard.

Sabuda, R. (2003). *Alice's adventures in Wonderland: A pop-up adaptation*. New York: Little Simon.

Sabuda, R. (2005). *Winter's tale*. New York: Little Simon.

Scieszka, J. (1992). *The Stinky Cheese Man and other fairly stupid tales*. New York: Penguin.

Sendak, M. (1963). *Where the wild things are*. New York: HarperCollins.

Sendak, M. (1981). *Outside over there*. New York: Harper & Row.

Sendak, M, Yorinks, A., & Reinhart, M. (2006). *Mommy?* New York: Scholastic.

Shannon, D. (1998). *No, David!* New York: Scholastic.

Sheldon, D. (1990). *The whales' song*. New York: Dial.

Sierra, J. (1986). *Wiley and the hairy man*. New York: Dutton.

Singer, H. L. (1994). *The swan princess*. New York: Scholastic.

Slobodkina, E. (1947). *Caps for sale*. New York: Addison-Wesley.

Stanley, D. (1995). *Petrosinella: A Neapolitan Rapunzel*. New York: Econo-Clad Books.

Steptoe, J. (1987). *Mufaro's beautiful daughters: An African tale*. New York: Lothrop, Lee, & Shepard Books.

Taylor, M. (1987). *The friendship*. New York: Puffin.

Van Allsburg, C. (1990). *Just a dream*. Boston: Houghton Mifflin.

Van Allsburg, C. (1993). *The sweetest fig*. Boston: Houghton Mifflin.

Van Allsburg, C. (1995). *Bad day at Riverbend*. Boston: Houghton Mifflin.

Waber, B. (1972). *Ira sleeps over*. Boston: Houghton Mifflin.

Waddell, M. (1992). *Owl babies*. Cambridge, MA: Candlewick Press.

Wiesner, D. (2006). *Flotsam*. New York: Clarion Books.

Willems, M. (2003). *Don't let the pigeon drive the bus!* New York: Hyperion.

Wood, A. (1984). *The napping house*. San Diego: Harcourt Brace & Co.

Wyeth, S. D. (1998). *Something beautiful*. New York: Doubleday.

Yolen, J. (1987). *Owl moon*. New York: Philomel.

Yorinks, A. (1986). *Hey, Al*. New York: Farrar, Straus and Giroux.

Yorinks, A. (1990). *Ugh*. New York: Farrar, Straus and Giroux.

Zelinsky, P. (1997). *Rapunzel*. New York: Dutton.

Zolotow, C. (1962). *Mr. Rabbit and the lovely present*. New York: HarperTrophy.

Zolotow, C. (1995). *The old dog*. New York: HarperCollins.

References

Adams, M. J., & Collins, A. M. (1979). A schema-theoretic view of reading. In R. O. Freedle (Ed.), *New directions in discourse processing* (pp. 1–22). Norwood, NJ: Ablex.

Adomat, D. (2005, December). *Outside, inside, and all around the story: Struggling first-grade readers construct literary understanding through dramatic response to literature.* Paper presented at the National Reading Conference, Miami, FL.

Allison, D., & Watson, J. (1994). The significance of adult storybook reading styles on the development of young children's emergent reading. *Reading Research and Instruction, 34*(1), 57–72.

Altmann, A. (1994). Parody and poesis in feminist fairy tales. *Canadian Children's Literature, 20,* 22–31.

Anderson, D. D. (2002). Casting and recasting gender: Children constituting social identities through literacy practices. *Research in the Teaching of English, 36,* 371–427.

Anderson, R. (1984). Role of the reader's schema in comprehension, learning, and memory. In R. Anderson, J. Osborn, & R. Tierney (Eds.), *Learning to read in American schools: Basal readers and content texts* (pp. 243–257). Hillsdale, NJ: Lawrence Erlbaum Associates.

Anderson, R., & Pearson, P. D. (1984). A schema-theoretic view of basic processes in reading comprehension. In D. Pearson (Ed.), *Handbook of reading research, Vol. I* (pp. 255–291). New York: Longman.

Anderson, R. C., Hiebert, E. H., Scott, J. A., & Wilkinson, I. A. B. (1985). *Becoming a nation of readers: The report of the Commission on Reading.* Washington, D.C.: National Institute of Education.

Applebee, A. (1978). *The child's concept of story: Ages two to seventeen.* Chicago: University of Chicago Press.

Aristotle (1997). *The Poetics* (M. Heath, Trans.). New York: Penguin Classics.

Arizpe, E., & Styles, M. (2003). *Children reading pictures: Interpreting visual texts.* New York: RoutledgeFalmer.

Arnheim, R. (1969). *Visual thinking.* Berkeley and Los Angeles: University of California Press.

Arnheim, R. (1974). *Art and visual perception: A psychology of the creative eye.* Berkeley and Los Angeles: University of California Press.

Arnheim, R. (1986). The images of pictures and words. *Word and Image, 2,* 306–310.

Atkins, D. G. (1990). *Geoffrey Hartman: Criticism as answerable style.* New York: Routledge.

Auden, W. H. (1968). *Secondary worlds*. London: Faber.

Bader, B. (1976). *American picturebooks from Noah's ark to the beast within*. New York: Macmillan.

Bakhtin, M. M. (1981). *The dialogic imagination* (K. Brostrom, Trans.). Austin: University of Texas Press.

Bakhtin, M. M. (1984). *Rabelais and his world* (H. Iswolsky, Trans.). Cambridge, MA: MIT Press.

Bakhtin, M. (1986). *Speech genres and other late essays* (C. Emerson & M. Holquist, Trans.). Austin: University of Texas Press.

Ballenger, C. (1998). *Teaching other people's children: Literacy and learning in a bilingual classroom*. New York: Teachers College Press.

Bang, M. (2000). *Picture this: How pictures work*. Boston: Little, Brown.

Barnes, D. (1976). *From communication to curriculum*. Hardmondsworth: Penguin.

Barrentine, S. J. (1996). Engaging with reading through interactive read-alouds. *The Reading Teacher, 50*, 36–43.

Barry, A. M. (1997). *Visual intelligence: Perception, image, and manipulation in visual communication*. Albany: State University of New York Press.

Barthes, R. (1974). *S/Z: An essay* (R. Miller, Trans.). New York: Hill and Wang.

Barthes, R. (1975). *The pleasure of the text* (R. Miller, Trans.). New York: Hill and Wang.

Barthes, R. (1985). *The responsibility of forms: Critical essays on music, art, and representation* (R. Howard, Trans.). New York: Hill and Wang.

Bartow, K. (2007). *The (untold) drama of the turning page: The role of page breaks in understanding picturebooks*. Unpublished manuscript.

Bauman, J. F., & Bergeron, B. S. (1993). Story map instruction using children's literature: Effects on first-graders' comprehension of central narrative elements. *Journal of Reading Behavior, 25*, 407–437.

Bauman, R. (1986). *Story, performance, and event: Contextual studies of oral narrative*. New York: Cambridge University Press.

Beach, R. (1993). *A teacher's introduction to reader-response theories*. Urbana, IL: National Council of Teachers of English.

Beck, I. L., & McKeown, M. G. (2006). *Improving comprehension with questioning the author: A fresh and expanded view of a powerful approach*. New York: Scholastic.

Beck, I. L., McKeown, M. G., Hamilton, R. L., & Kucan, L. (1997). *Questioning the author: An approach for enhancing student engagement with text*. Newark, DE: International Reading Association.

Belfatti, M. A. (2005). *Revisiting Anthony Browne's Zoo: Young children's response to literature with repeated read-alouds*. Manuscript submitted for publication.

Bellack, A. A., Kliebard, H. M., Hyman, R. T., & Smith, F. L. (1966). *The language of the classroom*. New York: Teachers College Press.

Benton, M. (1979). Children's responses to stories. *Children's Literature in Education, 10*, 68–85.

Benton, M. (1992). *Secondary worlds: Literature teaching and the visual arts*. Buckingham, UK: Open University Press.

Benton, M., Teasey, J., Bell, R., & Hurst, K. (1988). *Young readers responding to poems*. New York: Routledge.

Berger, J. (1977). *Ways of seeing*. New York: Penguin.

Berk, L. E., & Winsler, A. (1995). *Scaffolding children's learning: Vygotsky and early childhood education*. Washington, DC: National Association for the Education of Young Children.

Berlin, I. (1986). Verification. In H. Adams & L. Searle (Eds.), *Critical theory since 1965* (pp. 698–708). Tallahassee: University of Florida Press.

Birch, C. (1996). The storyteller as narrator. In C. L. Birch & M. A. Heckler (Eds.), *Who says?: Essays on pivotal issues in contemporary storytelling* (pp. 106–128). Little Rock, AR: August House Publishers.

Black, J. B., & Wilensky, R. (1979). An evaluation of story grammars. *Cognitive Science, 3*, 213–230.

Blackburn, M. (2003). Exploring literacy performances and power dynamics at the loft: Queer youth reading the world and the word. *Research in the Teaching of English, 37*, 467–490.

Blackburn, S. (1994). *The Oxford dictionary of philosophy*. New York: Oxford University Press.

Bleich, D. (1978). *Subjective criticism*. Baltimore: Johns Hopkins University Press.

Bleich, D. (1980). Epistemological assumptions in the study of response. In J. P. Tompkins (Ed.), *Reader-response criticism: From formalism to post-structuralism* (pp. 134–163). Baltimore: The Johns Hopkins University Press.

Block, J., & King, N. (Eds.). (1987). *School play: A sourcebook*. New York: Teachers College Press.

Bloom, H. (2003). *A map of misreading* (2nd ed.). New York: Oxford University Press.

Bloome, D., Puro, P., & Theodorou, E. (1989). Procedural display and classroom lessons. *Curriculum Inquiry, 19*, 263–291.

Bogdan, D. (1990). In and out of love with literature: Response and the aesthetics of total form. In D. Bogdan & S. Straw (Eds.), *Beyond communication: Reading comprehension and criticism* (pp. 109–137). Portsmouth, NH: Heinemann.

Bogdan, R., & Biklen, S. K. (2006). *Qualitative research for education: An introduction to theories and methods* (5th ed.). Boston: Allyn & Bacon.

Booth, W. C. (1988). *The company we keep: An ethics of fiction*. Berkeley: University of California Press.

Brabham, E., & Lynch-Brown, C. (2002). Effects of teachers' reading-aloud styles on vocabulary acquisition and comprehension of students in the early elementary grades. *Journal of Educational Psychology, 94*(3), 465–473.

Bressler, C. E. (2007). *Literary criticism: An introduction to theory and practice* (4th ed.). Upper Saddle River, NJ: Pearson Prentice Hall.

Brewer, W. F., & Lichtenstein, E. H. (1981). Event schemas, story schemas, and story grammars. In J. Long & A. D. Baddeley (Eds.), *Attention and performance IX* (pp. 363–379). Hillsdale, NJ: Lawrence Erlbaum Associates.

Brightman, A. E., & Sipe, L. R. (2006, December). *First-graders' individual literary response styles during picturebook readalouds*. Paper presented at the National Reading Conference, Los Angeles, CA.

Britton, J. (1984). Viewpoints: The distinction between participant and spectator role language in research and practice. *Research in the Teaching of English*, *18*, 230–331.

Britton, J. (1993). *Literature in its place*. Portsmouth, NH: Heinemann.

Brooks, C. (1965). *Modern poetry and the tradition*. New York: Oxford University Press. (Original work published 1939)

Brooks, C. (1968). *The well-wrought urn: Studies in the structure of poetry*. London: Methuen. (Original work published 1947)

Brooks, C., & Warren, R. P. (Eds.). (1943). *Understanding fiction*. New York: Appleton-Century-Crofts.

Broughton, M. A. (2002). The performance and construction of subjectivities of early adolescent girls in book club discussion groups. *Journal of Literacy Research*, *34*, 1–38.

Bruner, J. (1980). The narrative construction of reality. *Critical Inquiry*, *7*, 1–21.

Bruner, J. (1986). *Actual minds, possible worlds*. Cambridge, MA: Harvard University Press.

Bruner, J. (1990). *Acts of meaning*. Cambridge, MA: Harvard University Press.

Cai, M. (2002). *Multicultural literature for children and young adults: Reflections on critical issues*. Westport, CN: Greenwood Press.

Cairney, T. (1990). Intertextuality: Infectious echoes from the past. *The Reading Teacher*, *48*, 478–484.

Cairney, T. (1992). Fostering and building students' intertextual histories. *Language Arts*, *69*, 502–507.

Calinescu, M. (1993). *Rereading*. New Haven: Yale University Press.

Campbell, J. (1972). *The hero with a thousand faces*. Princeton: Princeton University Press.

Carrington, V., & Luke, A. (2003). Reading, homes, and families: From postmodern to modern? In A. van Kleeck, S. A. Stahl, & E. B. Bauer (Eds.), *On reading books to children: Parents and teachers* (pp. 231–252). Mahwah, NJ: Lawrence Erlbaum Associates.

Cazden, C. (1988). *Classroom discourse: The language of teaching and learning*. Portsmouth, NH: Heinemann.

Cazden, C. (1992). *Whole language plus: Essays on literacy in the United States and New Zealand*. New York: Teachers College Press.

Cech, J. (1983–84). Remembering Caldecott: "The Three Jovial Huntsmen" and the art of the picture book. *The Lion and the Unicorn*, *7/8*, 110–119.

Chambers, A. (1985). *Booktalk: Occasional writing on literature and children*. New York: Harper & Row.

Chambers, A. (1993). *Tell me: Children, reading, and talk*. South Woodchester, Stroud, Glos. UK: Thimble Press.

Cherland, M. (1992). Gendered readings: Cultural restraints upon response to literature. *The New Advocate*, *5*, 187–198.

Cherland, M. (1994). *Private practices: Girls reading fiction and constructing identity*. New York: Taylor and Francis.

Childress, G. T. (1985). *Gender gap in the library: Different choices for girls and boys*. Top of the News, *42*(1), 69–73.

Cianciolo, P. (1984). 1984 illustrations in children's books. In Z. Sutherland & M. C. Livingston (Eds.), *The Scott Foresman anthology of children's literature* (pp. 846–884). Glenview, IL: Scott Foresman.

Clark, K. F., & Graves, M. F. (2005). Scaffolding students' comprehension of text. *The Reading Teacher, 58,* 570–580.

Clifford, J. (1988). Introduction. *Reader, 20,* 1–6.

Cochran-Smith, M. (1984). *The making of a reader.* Norwood, NJ: Ablex.

Cole, D. (1992). *Acting as reading: The place of the reading process in the actor's work.* Ann Arbor: The University of Michigan Press.

Coles, R. (1989). *The call of stories: Teaching and the moral imagination.* Boston: Houghton Mifflin.

Commeyras, M. (1994). Were Janell and Neesie in the same classroom? Children's questions as the first order of reality in storybook discussions. *Language Arts, 71,* 517–523.

Cooney, B. (1988). *Remarks made at a symposium, "Ways of saying, ways of knowing": Art for all ages.* The New England Reading Association Annual Conference, Portland, ME.

Cox, C. (1994, April). *Young children's responses to literature: A longitudinal study, K–3.* Paper presented at the American Educational Research Association Meeting, New Orleans, LA.

Cox, C., & Many, J. (1992). Reader stance towards a literary work: Applying the transactional theory to children's responses. *Reading Psychology, 13,* 37–72.

Cross, L. B. (1993). *Narrative styles in African-American children: The effects of SES and reading stories to children.* Unpublished doctoral dissertation, University of Maryland, College Park, MD.

Csikszentmihalyi, M. (1998). *Finding flow: The psychology of engagement in everyday life.* New York: Basic Books.

Culler, J. (1975). *Structuralist poetics: Structuralism, linguistics and the study of literature.* Ithaca, NY: Cornell University Press.

Daniels, H. (1994). *Literature circles: Voice and choice in the student-centered classroom.* York, ME: Stenhouse.

Daniels, H. (2002). *Literature circles: Voice and choice in book clubs and reading groups* (2nd ed.). York, ME: Stenhouse.

Davies, B. (2003a). *Frogs and snails and feminist tales: Preschool children and gender* (rev. ed.). Cresskill, NJ: Hampton Press.

Davies, B. (2003b). *Shards of glass: Children reading and writing beyond gendered identities* (rev. ed.). Cresskill, NJ: Hampton Press.

Davies, B. (2004). *Gender in Japanese preschools: Frogs and snails and feminist tales in Japan.* Cresskill, NJ: Hampton Press.

DeFord, D. E. (1984). Classroom contexts for literacy learning. In T. E. Raphael (Ed.), *The contexts of school-based literacy* (pp. 162–180). New York: Random House.

Delpit, L. (1995). *Other people's children: Cultural conflict in the classroom.* New York: New Press.

DeLuca, G. (1984). Art, illusion, and children's picture books. *Children's Literature Association Quarterly, 9,* 21–25.

de Man, P. (1982). *Allegories of reading: Figural language in Rousseau, Nietzsche, Rilke, and Proust.* New Haven: Yale University Press.

Dentith, S. (1995). *Bakhtinian thought: An introductory reader.* London: Routledge.

Derrida, J. (1976). *Of grammatology* (G. Chakravorty Spivak, Trans.). Baltimore: Johns Hopkins University Press.

de Saussure, F. (1983). *Course in general linguistics.* London: Duckworth. (Original work published 1916)

Dewey, J. (1987). *Art as experience.* The collected works of John Dewey (Ed. J. A. Boydston), Vol. 10. Carbondale, IL: Southern Illinois University Press. (Originally published 1934)

Dickinson, D., & Keebler, R. (1989). Variation in preschool teachers' styles of reading books. *Discourse Processes, 12,* 353–375.

Dickinson, D., McCabe, A., & Anastasopoulos, L. (2003). A framework for examining book reading in early childhood classrooms. In A. van Kleeck, S. Stahl, & E. Bauer (Eds.), *On reading books to children: Parents and teachers* (pp. 95–113). Mahwah, NJ: Erlbaum.

Dickinson, D., & Smith, M. (1994). Long-term effects of preschool teachers' book readings on low-income children's vocabulary and story comprehension. *Reading Research Quarterly, 29,* 105–122.

Dickinson, D., & Tabors, P. (Eds.). (2001). *Beginning literacy with language: Young children learning at home and school.* Baltimore, MA: Paul H. Brookes.

Dillon, D., & Searle, D. (1981). The role of language in one first grade classroom. *Research in the Teaching of English, 15,* 311–328.

Dimino, J., Gersten, R., Carnine, D., & Blake, G. (1990). Story grammar: An approach for promoting at-risk secondary students' comprehension of literature. *Elementary School Journal, 91,* 19–32.

Dixon, C. N., Frank, C. R., & Green, J. L. (1999). Classrooms as cultures: Understanding the constructed nature of life in classrooms. *Primary Voices, K–6, 7,* 4–8.

Dooley, P. (1980, October). The window in the book: Conventions in the illustration of children's books. *Wilson Library Bulletin,* 108–112.

Doonan, J. (1993). *Looking at pictures in picture books.* Stroud, Glos., UK: The Thimble Press.

Duke, N. K. (2000). 3.6 minutes per day: The scarcity of informational texts in first grade. *Reading Research Quarterly, 35,* 202–224.

Dyson, A. H. (1989). *Multiple worlds of child writers: Friends learning to write.* New York: Teachers College Press.

Dyson, A. H. (1997). *Writing superheroes: Contemporary childhood, popular culture, and classroom literacy.* New York: Teachers College Press.

Dyson, A. H. (2001). Writing and children's symbolic repertoires: Development unhinged. In S. B. Neuman & D. K. Dickinson (Eds.), *Handbook of early literacy research, Vol 1* (pp. 126–141). New York: Guilford Press.

Dyson, A. H. (2003). *The brothers and sisters learn to write: Popular literacies in childhood and school culture.* New York: Teachers College Press.

Eagleton, T. (1983). *Literary theory: An introduction.* Oxford: Blackwell.

Eco, U. (1979). *The role of the reader: Explorations in the semiotics of texts*. Bloomington: Indiana University Press.

Edelsky, C. (1981). Who's got the floor? *Language in Society, 10*, 383–424.

Edmiston, B. (1993). Going up the beanstalk: Discovering giant possibilities for responding to literature for drama. In K. E. Holland, R. A. Hungerford, & S. B. Ernst (Eds.), *Journeying: Children responding to literature* (pp. 250–266). Portsmouth, NH: Heinemann.

Edwards, A. D. (1979). Patterns of power and authority in classroom talk. In P. Woods (Ed.), *Teacher strategies: Explorations in the sociology of the school* (pp. 237–253). London: Croom Helm.

Eeds, M., & Peterson, R. (1991). Teacher as curator: Learning to talk about literature. *The Reading Teacher, 45*, 118–126.

Eeds, M., & Wells, D. (1989). Grand conversations: An exploration of meaning construction in literature study groups. *Research in the Teaching of English, 23*, 4–29.

Enciso, P. E. (1992). Creating the story world: A case study of a young reader's engagement strategies and stances. In J. Many & C. Cox (Eds.), *Reader stance and literary understanding: Exploring the theories, research, and practice* (pp. 75–102). Norwood, NJ: Ablex.

Enciso, P. (1994). Cultural identity and response to literature: Running lessons from *Maniac Magee*. *Language Arts, 71*, 524–533.

Erickson, F. (1986). Tasks in times: Objects of study in a natural history of teaching. In K. K. Zumwalt (Ed.), *Yearbook of the Association for Supervision and Curriculum Development* (pp. 131–147). Washington, DC: Association for Supervision and Curriculum Development.

Evans, K. S. (1996). A closer look at literature discussion groups: The influence of gender on student response and discourse. *The New Advocate, 9*, 183–196.

Feathers, K., & Bochenek, J. (2006). How do basal and original stories compare?: Primary grade students take a closer look. *Michigan Reading Journal, 39*(1), 9–15.

Fish, S. (1967). *Surprised by sin: The reader in "Paradise Lost."* New York: Macmillan.

Fish, S. (1980). Literature in the reader: Affective stylistics. In S. Fish, *Is there a text in this class? The authority of interpretive communities* (pp. 21–67). Cambridge: Harvard University Press. (Original work published 1970)

Fish, S. (1980). *Is there a text in this class? The authority of interpretive communities*. Cambridge, MA: Harvard University Press.

Fisher, D., Flood, J., Lapp, D., & Frey, N. (2004). Interactive read-alouds: Is there a common set of implementation practices? *The Reading Teacher, 58*, 8–17.

Fitzgerald, J., & Spiegel, D. L. (1983). Enhancing children's reading comprehension through instruction in narrative structure. *Journal of Reading Behavior, 15*, 1–17.

Flinders, D. J., & Eisner, E. W. (1994). Educational criticism as a form of qualitative inquiry. *Research in the Teaching of English, 28*, 341–357.

Flood, J., & Lapp, D. (1995). Broadening the lens: Toward an expanded conceptualization of literacy. In K. Hinchman, D. J. Leu, & C. K. Kinzer (Eds.), *Perspec-*

tives on literacy research and practice (pp. 1–16). Chicago: National Reading Conference.

Flynn, E. (1983). Complementarities: Reading research and theories of response. *Reader, 10,* 37–44.

Fox, C. (2003). Playing the storyteller: Some principles for learning literacy in the early years of schooling. In N. Hall, J. Larson, & J. Marsh (Eds.), *Handbook of early childhood literacy* (pp. 189–198). Thousand Oaks, CA: Sage.

Frye, N. (1957). *Anatomy of criticism: Four essays.* Princeton: Princeton University Press.

Frye, N. (1964). *The educated imagination.* Bloomington, IN: Indiana University Press.

Gadamer, H. G. (1986). Truth and method. In H. Adams & L. Searle (Eds.), *Critical theory since 1965* (pp. 840–855). Tallahassee: University of Florida Press.

Galda, L. (1982). Assuming the spectator stance: An examination of the responses of three young readers. *Research in the Teaching of English, 16,* 1–20.

Galda, L. (1990). A longitudinal study of the spectator stance as a function of age and genre. *Research in the Teaching of English, 24,* 261–278.

Galda, L. (1998). Mirrors and windows: Reading as transformation. In T. W. Raphael & K. H. Au (Eds.), *Literature-based instruction: Reshaping the curriculum* (pp. 1–11). Norwood, MA: Christopher-Gordon.

Galda, L., Ash, G. E., & Cullinan, B. E. (2000). Children's literature. In M. L. Kamil, P. B. Mosenthal, P. D. Pearson, & R. Barr (Eds.), *Handbook of Reading Research, Vol. III* (pp. 361–379). Mahwah, NJ: Erlbaum.

Galda, L., & Beach, R. (2001). *Response to literature as a cultural activity. Reading Research Quarterly, 36,* 64–73.

Gallas, K. (1998). *"Sometimes I can be anything": Power, gender, and identity in a primary classroom.* New York: Teachers College Press.

Gallimore, R., & Tharp, R. G. (1990). Teaching mind in society: Teaching, schooling, and literate discourse. In L. C. Moll (Ed.), *Vygotsky and education: Instructional implications and applications of sociohistorical psychology* (pp. 175–205). Cambridge: Cambridge University Press.

Garvey, C. (1977). *Play.* Cambridge, MA: Harvard University Press.

Gates, H. L. (1988). *The signifying monkey: A theory of African-American literary criticism.* New York: Oxford University Press.

Geertz, C. (1973). *The interpretation of cultures.* New York: Basic Books.

Genette, G. (1980). *Narrative discourse* (J. E. Lewin, Trans.). Ithaca, NY: Cornell University Press.

Genette, G. (1997). *Paratexts: Thresholds of interpretation* (J. E. Lewin, Trans.). Cambridge: Cambridge University Press.

Genette, G. (1998). *Palimpsests: Literature in the second degree* (C. Newman & C. Doubinsky, Trans.). Omaha: University of Nebraska Press.

Ghiso, M. P., & McGuire, C. E. (2005, December). *"The illustrations will tell us what he's up to": Teacher mediation of picturebooks with sparse verbal text during whole-class readalouds.* Paper presented at the National Reading Conference, Miami, FL.

Gibson, J. J. (1979). *The ecological approach to visual perception*. Boston: Houghton Mifflin.

Gilles, C. (1994). Discussing our questions and questioning our discussions: Growing into literature study. *Language Arts, 71*, 499–508.

Gilmore, P., & Glatthorn, A. A. (1982). *Children in and out of school*. Washington, DC: Center for Applied Linguistics.

Glasheen, G. (2007). *Might as well read it backwards: The subverted text-picture relations in Bad Day at Riverbend*. Unpublished manuscript.

Golden, J. (1990). *The narrative symbol in childhood literature: Explorations of the construction of text*. New York: Mouton de Gruyter.

Golden, R., & Rumelhart, D. (1993). A parallel distributed processing model of story comprehension and recall. *Discourse Processes, 16*, 203–237.

Goldstone, B. (1999). Brave new worlds: The changing image of the picture books. *The New Advocate, 12*, 331–344.

Gombrich, E. H. (1969). *Art and illusion: A study in the psychology of pictorial representation* (2nd ed.). Princeton, NJ: Princeton University Press.

Gombrich, E. H. (1972). The visual image. *Scientific American, 227*, 82–96.

Graesser, A., Golding, J. M., & Long, D. L. (1991). Narrative representation and comprehension. In R. Barr, M. Kamil, P. Mosenthal, & P. D. Pearson (Eds.), *Handbook of reading research, Vol. 2* (pp. 171–205). New York: Longman.

Green, J. L., & Wallat, C. (Eds.) (1981). *Ethnography and language in educational settings*. Norwood, NJ: Ablex.

Grey, M. (2006). Acceptance speech for 2005 Boston Globe Horn Book Awards, Picture Book. *The Horn Book Magazine, January/February*, 17–20.

Grudin, R. (1992). *Book: A novel*. New York: Penguin.

Gumperz, J. J. (1986). Interactional sociolinguistics in the study of schooling. In J. Cook-Gumperz (Ed.), *The social construction of literacy* (pp. 45–68). London: Cambridge University Press.

Hade, D. D. (1988). Children, stories, and narrative transformations. *Research in the Teaching of English, 22*, 310–325.

Hall, S. (1990). *Using picture storybooks to teach literary devices*. Phoenix, AZ: Oryx Press.

Halliday, M. A. K. (1975). *Learning how to mean: Explorations in the development of language*. London: Edward Arnold.

Hansen, J. (1987). *When writers read*. Portsmouth, NH: Heinemann.

Harding, D. W. (1962). Psychological processes in the reading of fiction. *British Journal of Aesthetics, 2*, 133–147.

Hardy, B. (1978). Narrative as a primary act of mind. In M. Meek, A. Warlow, & G. Barton (Eds.), *The cool web: The pattern of children's reading* (pp. 12–23). New York: Athenaeum.

Harker, W. J. (1992). Reader response and cognition: Is there a mind in this class? *Journal of Aesthetic Education, 26*, 27–39.

Harley, B. (1996). Playing with the wall. In C. L. Birch & M. A. Heckler (Eds.), *Who says?: Essays on pivotal issues in contemporary storytelling* (pp. 129–140). Little Rock, AR: August House Publishers.

Harms, J., & Lettow, L. (1989). Book design: Extending verbal and visual literacy. *Journal of Youth Services in Libraries, 2*, 136–142.

Harris, V. (1993). From the margin to the center of curricula: Multicultural children's literature. In B. Spodek & O. Saracho (Eds.), *Language and literacy in early childhood education* (pp. 123–140). New York: Teachers College Press.

Harste, J., Short, K., & Burke, C. (1988). *Creating classrooms for authors.* Portsmouth, NH: Heinemann.

Heath, S. B. (1983). *Ways with words: Language, life and work in communities and classrooms.* New York: Cambridge University Press.

Heckler, M. A. (1996). Two traditions. In C. L. Birch & M. A. Heckler (Eds.), *Who says?: Essays on pivotal issues in contemporary storytelling* (pp. 15–34). Little Rock, AR: August House Publishers.

Hickman, J. G. (1979). *Response to literature in a school environment, grades K–5.* Unpublished doctoral dissertation, The Ohio State University, Columbus, OH.

Hickman, J. (1981). A new perspective on response to literature: Research in an elementary school setting. *Research in the Teaching of English, 15*, 343–354.

Hickman, J. (1983). Everything considered: Response to literature in an elementary school setting. *Journal of Research and Development in Education, 16*, 8–13.

Higonnet, M. (1990). The playground of the peritext. *Children's Literature Association Quarterly, 15*, 47–49.

Hirsch, E. D. (1973). *Validity in interpretation.* New Haven: Yale University Press.

Hoffman, J. V., Roser, N. L., & Battle, J. (1993). Reading aloud in classrooms: From the modal to a "model." *The Reading Teacher, 46*, 496–503.

Holland, N. (1968). *The dynamics of literary response.* New York: Oxford University Press.

Holland, N. (1975). *5 readers reading.* New Haven: Yale University Press.

Iser, W. (1978). *The act of reading: A theory of aesthetic response.* Baltimore: The Johns Hopkins University Press.

James, W. (1890). *The principles of psychology.* New York: H. Holt and Co.

Jameson, F. (1972). *The prison-house of language: A critical account of structuralism and Russian formalism.* Princeton, NJ: Princeton University Press.

Johnson, T. (1992). Emerging reading. In L. O. Ollila & M. Mayfield (Eds.), *Emerging literacy: Preschool, kindergarten, and primary grades* (pp. 71–99). Boston: Allyn & Bacon.

Jones, M. G., & Gerig, T. M. (1994). Silent sixth-grade students: Characteristics, achievement, and teacher expectations. *Elementary School Journal, 95*, 169–182.

Jung, C. G. (1934–5). *The archetypes and the collective unconscious: Vol. 9. The collected works of C. G. Jung.* Bolligen Series 20. Princeton: Princeton University Press.

Kantor, R., & Fernie, D. (2003). *Early child classroom processes.* Cresskill, NH: Hampton Press.

Kellogg, S. (2003). *Steven Kellogg.* Retrieved March 15, 2007, from http://www.stevenkellogg.com/page2.html

Kiefer, B. (1982). *The response of primary children to picture books.* Unpublished doctoral dissertation, The Ohio State University, Columbus, OH.

Kiefer, B. (1993). Visual criticism and children's literature. In B. Hearne & R. Sutton (Eds.), *Evaluating children's books: Aesthetic, social, and political aspects of analyzing and using children's books* (pp. 73–91). Urbana, IL: Graduate School of Library and Information Sciences.

Kiefer, B. Z. (1995). *The potential of picturebooks: From visual literacy to aesthetic understanding.* Englewood Cliffs, NJ: Prentice-Hall.

Kiefer, B., Hepler, S., & Hickman, J. (2006). *Charlotte Huck's children's literature* (9th ed.). New York: McGraw-Hill.

Knobel, M. (1993). Simon says see what I say: Reader response and the teacher as meaning-maker. *The Australian Journal of Language and Literacy, 16,* 295–306.

Kress, G., & van Leeuwen, T. (2006). *Reading images: The grammar of visual design* (2nd ed.). London: Routledge.

Kümmerling-Meibauer, B. (1999). Metalinguistic awareness and the child's developing concept of irony: The relationship between pictures and text in ironic picturebooks. *The Lion and the Unicorn, 23,* 157–183.

Landes, S. (1983). Teaching literary criticism in the elementary grades: A symposium. In J. P. May (Ed.), *Children and their literature: A readings book* (pp. 161–164). West Lafayette, IN: ChLA Publications.

Langer, J. A. (1990). The process of understanding: Reading for literary and informative purposes. *Research in the Teaching of English, 24,* 229–260.

Langer, J. A. (1995). *Envisioning literature: Literary understanding and literature instruction.* New York: Teachers College Press.

Langer, J. A., & Close, E. (2001). *Improving literary understanding: Through classroom conversation.* State University of New York at Albany: National Research Center on English Learning and Achievement Website: http://cela.albany.edu/env.pdf.

Langer, S. (1953). *Feeling and form.* New York: Scribner's.

Larrick, N. (1965). The all-white world of children's books. *Saturday Review, 11,* 63–65, 84–85.

Larry, C. (1995). The art of tradition: Nancy Ekholm Burkert's illustrations for *Snow White and the Seven Dwarfs. Journal of Children's Literature, 21,* 20–26.

Lather, P. (1986). Issues of validity in openly ideological research: Between a rock and a soft place. *Interchange, 17,* 63–84.

Lee, C. (1995). A culturally based cognitive apprenticeship: Teaching African American high school students skills in literary interpretation. *Reading Research Quarterly, 30,* 608–630.

Lehman, B. A., Freeman, E. B., & Allen, V. G. (1994). Children's literature and literacy instruction: "Literature-based" elementary teachers' beliefs and practices. *Reading Horizons, 35,* 3–23.

Lemke, J. (1993, December). *Multiplying meaning: Literacy in a multimedia world.* Paper presented at the National Reading Conference, Charleston, SC.

Lensmire, T. (1994). Writing workshop as carnival: Reflections on an alternative learning environment. *Harvard Educational Review, 64,* 371–391.

Lewis, C. (1997). The social drama of literature discussions in a fifth/sixth-grade classroom. *Research in the Teaching of English, 31,* 163–204.

Lewis, D. (1990). The constructedness of texts: Picture books and the metafictive. *Signal*, 62, 131–146.

Lewis, D. (1992). Looking for Julius: Two children and a picturebook. In K. Kimberly, M. Meek, & J. Miller (Eds.), *New Readings* (pp. 50–63). London: A & C Black.

Lewis, D. (1996). Going along with Mr. Grumpy: Polysystemy and play in the modern picturebook. *Signal*, 80, 105–119.

Lewis, D. (2001). *Reading contemporary picturebooks: Picturing text.* London: RoutledgeFalmer.

Lopez-Robertson, J. (2005, December). *Young Latinas' response styles during literature discussions: Personal life stories as meaning-making devices.* Paper presented at the National Reading Conference, Miami, FL.

Lunn, J. (2003). The picture book: A commentary. In A. Hudson & S. A. Cooper (Eds.), *Windows and words: A look at Canadian children's literature in English* (pp. 185–190). Ottawa, Ontario, Canada: University of Ottawa Press.

Madura, S. (1995). The line and texture of aesthetic response: Primary children study authors and illustrators. *The Reading Teacher*, 49, 110–118.

Madura, S. (1998). An artistic element: Four transitional readers and writers respond to the picture books of Patricia Polacco and Gerald McDermott. In T. Shanahan & F. V. Rodriguez-Brown (Eds.), *National Reading Conference Yearbook*, 47, 366–376.

Mailloux, S. (1982). *Interpretive conventions: The reader in the study of American fiction.* Ithaca, NY: Cornell University Press.

Makaryk, I. R. (1993). Introduction. In I. R. Makaryk (Ed.), *Encyclopedia of contemporary literary theory: Approaches, scholars, terms* (pp. vii–ix). Toronto, Ontario, Canada: University of Toronto Press.

Maloch, B., & Duncan, D. (2006, December). *"Big loud voice. You have important things to say": The nature of student initiations during one teacher's interactive read-alouds.* Paper presented at the National Reading Conference, Miami, FL.

Mandler, J. M., & Johnson, N. S. (1977). Remembrance of things parsed: Story structure and recall. *Cognitive Psychology*, 9, 111–151.

Many, J. E. (2002). An exhibition and analysis of verbal tapestries: Understanding how scaffolding is woven into the fabric of instructional conversations. *Reading Research Quarterly*, 37, 376–407.

Many, J., & Wiseman, D. L. (1992). The effect of teaching approach on third-grade students' response to literature. *Journal of Reading Behavior*, 24, 265–287.

Marantz, K. (1977). The picturebook as art object: A call for balanced reviewing. *The Wilson Library Bulletin*, 148–151.

Marshall, D. G. (1993). *Contemporary critical theory: A selective bibliography.* New York: The Modern Language Association of America.

Marshall, E. (2004). Stripping for the wolf: Rethinking representations of gender in children's literature. *Reading Research Quarterly*, 39, 256–270.

Martin, R. (1996). Between teller and listener: The reciprocity of storytelling. In C. L. Birch & M. A. Heckler (Eds.), *Who says?: Essays on pivotal issues in contemporary storytelling* (pp. 141–154). Little Rock, AR: August House Publishers.

Martinez, M., & Roser, N. (1985). Read it again: The value of repeating readings during storytime. *The Reading Teacher, 38*, 782–786.

Martinez, M., & Roser, N. (1991). Children's responses to literature. In J. Flood, J. Jensen, D. Lapp, & J. Squire (Eds.), *Handbook of research on teaching the English language arts* (pp. 643–654). New York: Macmillan.

Martinez, M., & Roser, N. L. (2003). Children's responses to literature. In J. Flood, D. Lapp, J. R. Squire, & J. M. Jensen (Eds.), *Handbook of research on teaching the English language arts* (2nd ed., pp. 799–813). Mahwah, NJ: Erlbaum.

Martinez, M., Roser, N., & Dooley, C. (2003). Young children's literary meaning making. In N. Hall, J. Larson, & J. Marsh (Eds.), *Handbook of early childhood literacy* (pp. 222–234). Thousand Oaks, CA: Sage.

Martinez, M., & Teale, W. (1993). Teacher storybook reading style: A comparison of six teachers. *Research in the Teaching of English, 27*(2), 175–199.

Matthewson, G. (1994). A model of attitude influence upon reading and learning to read. In R. B. Ruddell, M. R. Ruddell, & H. Singer (Eds.), *Theoretical models and processes of reading* (4th ed.) (pp. 1131–1161). Newark, DE: International Reading Association.

May, J. (1995). *Children's literature and critical theory: Reading and writing for understanding.* New York: Oxford University Press.

McCarrier, A. (1991, December). *The role of talk during multiple readings of the same storybook.* Paper presented at the National Reading Conference, Palm Springs, CA.

McCarrier, A. M. (1992). *Supporting literacy learning in at-risk children: A case study of an urban kindergarten.* Unpublished doctoral dissertation, The Ohio State University, Columbus, OH.

McClay, J. (2000). "Wait a second . . .": Negotiating complex narratives in *Black and White. Children's Literature in Education, 31*, 91–106.

McCloud, S. (1994). *Understanding comics.* New York: Harper.

McCormick, K. (1988). "First steps" in "Wandering Rocks": Students' differences, literary transactions, and pleasures. *Reader, 20*, 48–67.

McGee, L. (1992a). An exploration of meaning construction in first graders' grand conversations. In D. Leu & C. Kinzer (Eds.), *Literacy research, theory, and practice: Views from many perspectives* (pp. 177–186). Chicago, IL: National Reading Conference.

McGee, L. (1992b, December). *First graders' responses to literature in grand conversations: Exploring shared meaning construction.* Paper presented at the National Reading Conference, San Antonio, TX.

McGee, L. (1992c). Focus on research: Exploring the literature-based reading revolution. *Language Arts, 69*, 529–537.

McGee, L. (1995). Talking about books with young children. In N. Roser & M. Martinez (Eds.), *Book talk and beyond: Teachers and children respond to literature* (pp. 105–115). Newark, DE: International Reading Association.

McGee, L., Courtney, R., & Lomax, R. (1993, December). *Supporting first graders' responses to literature.* Paper presented at the National Reading Conference, Charleston, SC.

McGee, L., Courtney, L., & Lomax, R. (1994). Supporting first graders' responses to literature: An analysis of teachers' roles in grand conversations. In C. K. Kinzer & D. J. Leu (Eds.), *Multidimensional aspects of literacy research, theory, and practice* (pp. 517–526). Chicago, IL: National Reading Conference.

McGee, L. M., & Schickedanz, J. A. (2007). Repeated interactive read-alouds in preschool and kindergarten. *The Reading Teacher, 60,* 742–750.

McGillis, R. (1996). *The nimble reader: Literary theory and children's literature.* New York: Twayne Publishers.

McGinley, W., & Kamberelis, G. (1996). "Maniac Magee" and "Ragtime Tumpie": Children negotiating self and world through reading and writing. *Research in the Teaching of English, 30,* 75–113.

McKenna, M. (1994). Toward a model of reading attitude acquisition. In E. H. Cramer & M. Castle (Eds.), *Fostering the love of reading: The affective domain in reading education* (pp. 18–40). Newark, DE: International Reading Association.

McMahon, S. I., Raphael, T. E., Goatley, V. J., & Pardo, L. S. (Eds). (1997). *The book club connection: Literacy learning and classroom talk.* New York: Teachers College Press.

McMillon, G. T., & Edwards, P. A. (2000). Why does Joshua "hate" school . . . but love Sunday school? *Language Arts, 78,* 111–120.

Meek, M. (1983). *Achieving literacy.* London: Routledge and Kegan Paul.

Meek, M. (1988). *How texts teach what readers learn.* South Woodchester, Stroud, Glos., UK: The Thimble Press.

Meek, M. (1992). "Children reading-now." In M. Styles, E. Bearne, & V. Watson (Eds.), *After Alice* (pp. 172–187). London: Cassell.

Mehan, H. (1979). *Learning lessons: Social organization in the classroom.* Cambridge, MA: Harvard University Press.

Meyer, B., & Rice, G. E. (1984). The structure of text. In P. D. Pearson (Ed.), *Handbook of reading research, Vol 1* (pp. 319–351). New York: Longman.

Meyer, D. K. (1993). What is scaffolded instruction? Definitions, distinguishing features, and misnomers. In D. J. Leu & C. K. Kinzer (Eds.), *Examining central issues in literacy research, theory, and practice. 42nd Yearbook of the National Reading Conference* (pp. 41–53). Chicago: National Reading Conference.

Meyer, L. A., Wardrop, J. S., Stahl, S. A., & Linn, R. L. (1994). Effects of reading storybooks aloud to children. *Journal of Educational Research, 88,* 69–85.

Miall, D. S., & Kuiken, D. (1994). Beyond text theory: Understanding literary response. *Discourse Processes, 17,* 337–352.

Miller, J. H. (1992). *Illustration.* Cambridge, MA: Harvard University Press.

Mitchell, W. J. T. (1981). *On narrative.* Chicago: University of Chicago Press.

Mitchell, W. J. T. (1994). *Picture theory: Essays on verbal and visual representation.* Chicago: University of Chicago Press.

Moebius, W. (1986). Introduction to picturebook codes. *Word and Image, 2,* 141–158.

Moll, L. C. (Ed.). (1990). *Vygotsky and education: Instructional implications and applications of sociohistorical psychology.* Cambridge: Cambridge University Press.

Möller, K., & Allen, J. (2000). Connecting, resisting, and searching for safer places: Students respond to Mildred Taylor's *The Friendship*. *Journal of Literacy Research*, *32*, 145–186.

Morrow, L. M. (1988). Young children's responses to one-to-one readings in school settings. *Reading Research Quarterly*, *23*, 89–107.

Morrow, L. M., & Brittain, R. (2003). The nature of storybook reading in the elementary school: Current practices. In A. van Kleeck, S. Stahl, & E. Bauer (Eds.), *On reading books to children: Parents and teachers* (pp. 140–158). Mahwah, NJ: Erlbaum.

Moss, E. (1990). A certain particularity: An interview with Janet and Allen Ahlberg. *Signal*, *61*, 20–26.

National Reading Panel. (2000). *Report of the National Reading Panel: Teaching children to read*. Washington, DC: National Institute of Child Health and Human Development, U.S. Government Printing Office.

Nauman, A. (1994, December). *Reader-response theory: What it is and what it does*. Paper presented at the National Reading Conference, San Diego, CA.

Nell, V. (1988). *Lost in a book: The psychology of reading for pleasure*. New Haven: Yale University Press.

Neumeyer, P. F. (1990). How picture books mean: The case of Chris Van Allsburg. *Children's Literature Association Quarterly*, *15*, 2–8.

Nevel, L. A. (1999). *Students' transactions with multicultural poetry in the high school classroom: A case study*. Unpublished doctoral dissertation, Georgia State University.

Newkirk, T., & McClure, P. (1992). *Listening in: Children talk about books (and other things)*. Portsmouth, NH: Heinemann.

Nieto, S. (2000). *Affirming diversity*. White Plains, NY: Longman Publishing Group.

Nikolajeva, M. (2002). *The rhetoric of character in children's literature*. Lanham, MD: Scarecrow Press.

Nikolajeva, M. (2003). Visual and verbal literacy: The role of picturebooks in the reading experience of young children. In N. Hall, J. Larson, & J. Marsh (Eds.), *Handbook of early childhood literacy* (pp. 235–248). London: Sage.

Nikolajeva, M. (2005). *Aesthetic approaches to children's literature: An introduction*. Lanham, MD: Scarecrow Press.

Nikolajeva, M., & Scott, C. (2000). The dynamics of picturebook communication. *Children's Literature in Education*, *31*, 225–239.

Nikolajeva, M., & Scott, C. (2001). *How picturebooks work*. New York: Garland.

Nikola-Lisa, W. (1994). Play, panache, pastiche: Postmodern impulses in contemporary picture books. *Children's Literature Association Quarterly*, *19*(1), 35–40.

Nodelman, P. (1988). *Words about pictures: The narrative art of children's picture books*. Athens, GA: University of Georgia Press.

Nodelman, P. (2001). Private places on public view: David Wiesner's picture books. *Mosaic*, *34*, 1–16.

Nodelman, P., & Reimer, M. (2002). *The pleasures of children's literature* (3rd ed.). New York: Allyn & Bacon.

Novitz, D. (1976). Conventions and the growth of pictorial style. *British Journal of Aesthetics*, *16*, 324–337.

Nystrand, M. (1997). *Opening dialogue; Understanding the dynamics of language and learning in the English classroom*. New York: Teachers College Press.

O'Connor, M., & Michaels, S. (1996). Shifting participant frameworks: Orchestrating thinking practices in group discussion. In D. Hicks (Ed.), *Discourse, learning, and schooling* (pp. 63–103). New York: Cambridge University Press.

Ocvirk, O. G. (2006). *Art fundamentals: Theory and practice* (10th ed.). Boston: McGraw-Hill.

O'Neill, C. (1995). *Drama worlds: A framework for process drama*. Portsmouth, NH: Heinemann.

Paivio, A. (1986). *Mental representations: A duel coding approach*. New York: Oxford University Press.

Paley, N. (1992). Postmodernist impulses and the contemporary picture book: Are there stories to these meanings? *Journal of Youth Services in Libraries, 5,* 151–162.

Paley, V. G. (1986). On listening to what the children say. *Harvard Educational Review, 36,* 122–131.

Palincsar, A. S. (1998). Keeping the metaphor of scaffolding fresh—A fresh response to C. Addison Stone's "The metaphor of scaffolding: Its utility for the field of learning disabilities." *Journal of Learning Disabilities, 31,* 370–373.

Pantaleo, S. (2002). Grade 1 students meet David Wiesner's three pigs. *Journal of Children's Literature, 28* (2), 72–84.

Pantaleo, S. (2003a). "Godzilla lives in New York": Grade 1 students and the peritextual features of picture books. *Journal of Children's Literature, 29,* 66–77.

Pantaleo, S. (2003b). The art of playful parody: Exploring David Wiesner's *Tuesday. The Dragon Lode, 22*(1), 42–50.

Pantaleo, S. (2004a). The long, long way: Young children explore the fabula and syuzhet of *Shortcut. Children's Literature in Education, 35*(1), 1–20.

Pantaleo, S. (2004b). Young children interpret the metafictive in Anthony Browne's *Voices in the Park. Journal of Early Childhood Literacy, 4,* 211–233.

Pantaleo, S. (2005). Young children engage with the metafictive in picture books. *Australian Journal of Language and Literacy, 28,* 19–37.

Pappas, C. (1993). Is narrative primary? Some insights from kindergartners' pretend readings of stories and information books. *Journal of Reading Behavior, 25*(1), 97–129.

Pappas, C. (2006). The information book genre: Its role in integrated science literacy research and practice. *Reading Research Quarterly, 4,* 226–250.

Pappas, C., Kiefer, B., & Levstik, L. (1999). *An integrated language perspective in the elementary school: An action approach* (3rd ed.). New York: Longman.

Patton, M. Q. (1990). *Qualitative evaluation and research methods* (2nd ed.). Newbury Park, CA: Sage.

Patton, M. Q. (2002). *Qualitative research & evaluation methods* (3rd ed.). Thousand Oaks, CA: Sage.

Pearson, P. D., & Gallagher, M. C. (1983). The instruction of reading comprehension. *Contemporary Educational Psychology, 8,* 317–344.

Peirce, C. S. (1931–1958). *Collected papers of Charles S. Peirce* (Vols. 1–8). (C. Hartshorne & P. Weiss, Eds.). Cambridge, MA: Harvard University Press.

Perkins, F. D. (1992). *Response patterns of third-grade African-Americans to culturally conscious literature.* Unpublished doctoral dissertation, University of Alabama at Birmingham, Birmingham, AL.

Peterson, R. (1992). *Life in a crowded place: Making a learning community.* Portsmouth, NH: Heinemann.

Peterson, R., & Eeds, M. (1990). *Grand conversations: Literature groups in action.* New York: Scholastic.

Piaget, J. (1985). *The equilibration of cognitive structures: The central problem of intellectual development.* Chicago: The University of Chicago Press.

Polkinghorne, D. (1988). *Narrative knowing and the human sciences.* Albany: State University of New York Press.

Poulet, G. (1980). Criticism and the experience of interiority. In J. P. Tompkins (Ed.), *Reader-response criticism: From formalism to post-structuralism* (pp. 41–49). Baltimore: The Johns Hopkins University Press.

Pressley, M. (2002). *Reading instruction that works: The case for balanced teaching* (2nd ed.). New York: Guilford.

Price, R., & Price, S. (1991). *Two evenings in Saramaka.* Chicago: The University of Chicago Press.

Propp, V. (1958). *Morphology of the folktale.* Minneapolis: University of Minnesota Press.

Ransom, J. C. (1941). *The new criticism.* Norfolk, CT: New Directions.

Raphael, T. E., & McMahon, S. I. (1994). Book club: An alternative framework for reading instruction. *The Reading Teacher, 48,* 102–116.

Reese, E., Cox, A., Harte, D., & McAnally, H. (2003). Diversity in adults' styles of reading books to children. In A. van Kleeck, S. Stahl, & E. Bauer (Eds.), *On reading books to children: Parents and teachers* (pp. 37–57). Mahwah, NJ: Erlbaum.

Reutzel, R., & Larsen, N. (1995). Look what they've done to real children's books in the new basal readers! *Language Arts, 72,* 495–507.

Richard, O. (1969). The visual language of the picture book. *Wilson Library Bulletin,* 436–447.

Richards, I. A. (1964). *Practical criticism.* London: Routledge. (Original work published 1929)

Richter, D. (1989). *The critical tradition: Classic texts and contemporary trends.* New York: St. Martin's Press.

Ricoeur, P. (1980). Narrative time. *Critical Inquiry, 7,* 169–190.

Robertson, J. P. (1997). Teaching about worlds of hurt through encounters with literature: Reflections on pedagogy. *Language Arts, 74,* 457–466.

Rogoff, B., Mosier, C., Mistry, J., & Goncu, A. (1993). Toddlers' guided participation with their caregivers in cultural activity. In E. A. Forman, N. Minick, & C. A. Stone (Eds.), *Contexts for learning* (pp. 230–253). New York: Oxford University Press.

Rogoff, B., & Wertsch, J. (Eds.). (1984). *Children's learning in the zone of proximal development.* San Francisco: Jossey Bass.

Roller, C. M., & Beed, P. L. (1994). Sometimes the conversations were grand, and sometimes . . . *Language Arts, 71,* 509–515.

Rorty, R. (1967). *The linguistic turn.* Chicago: The University of Chicago Press.

Rosenblatt, L. (1964). The poem as event. *College English, 26,* 123–128.

Rosenblatt, L. M. (1982). The literary transaction: Evocation and response. *Theory into Practice, 21,* 268–277.

Rosenblatt, L. (1985). Viewpoints: Transaction versus interaction—A terminological rescue operation. *Research in the Teaching of English, 19,* 96–107.

Rosenblatt, L. (1986). The aesthetic transaction. *Journal of Aesthetic Education, 20,* 122–128.

Rosenblatt, L. (1994). *The reader, the text, the poem: The transactional theory of the literary work.* Carbondale: Southern Illinois University Press. (Original work published 1978)

Rosenblatt, L. (1996). *Literature as exploration* (5th ed.). New York: Modern Language Association of America. (Original work published 1938)

Rosenblatt, L. (2004). The transactional theory of reading and writing. In N. J. Unrau & R. B. Ruddell (Eds.), *Theoretical models and processes of reading* (5th ed.) (pp. 1057–1092). Newark, DE: International Reading Association.

Roser, N. L., & Martinez, M. G. (Eds.). (1995). *Book talk and beyond: Children and teachers respond to literature.* Newark, DE: International Reading Association.

Rowe, D. W. (1994). *Preschoolers as authors: Literacy learning in the social world of the classroom.* Cresskill, NJ: Hampton Press.

Rowe, D. W. (1998). The literate potentials of book-related dramatic play. *Reading Research Quarterly, 33,* 10–35.

Sadoski, M., & Paivio, A. (1994). A dual coding view of imagery and verbal processes in reading comprehension. In R. B. Ruddell, M. R. Ruddell, & H. Singer (Eds.), *Theoretical models and processes of reading* (4th ed.) (pp. 582–601). Newark, DE: International Reading Association.

Santori, D. (2006, November). *Children's individual response styles across participation structures.* Paper presented at the National Reading Conference, Los Angeles, CA.

Scarborough, H. S., & Dobrich, W. (1994). On the efficacy of reading to preschoolers. *Developmental Review, 14,* 245–301.

Scarlett, W. G. (Ed.). (2005). *Children's play.* Thousand Oaks, CA: Sage.

Scharer, P. (1991). Moving into literature-based reading instruction: Changes and challenges for teachers. In S. McCormick & J. Zutell (Eds.), *Learning factors/teacher factors: Issues in literacy research and instruction* (pp. 409–421). Chicago, IL: National Reading Conference.

Scharer, P. (1992). Teachers in transition: An exploration of changes in teachers and classrooms during implementation of literature-based reading instruction. *Research in the Teaching of English, 26,* 408–445.

Scharer, P., & Detwiler, D. (1992). Changing as teachers: Perils and possibilities of literature-based language arts instruction. *Language Arts, 69,* 186–192.

Scharer, P. L., Freeman, E. B., Lehman, B. A., & Allen, V. G. (1993). Literacy and literature in elementary classrooms: Teachers' beliefs and practices. In D. J. Leu

& C. K. Kinzer (Eds.), *Examining central issues in literacy research, theory, and practice* (42nd Yearbook of the National Reading Conference) (pp. 359–366). Chicago: National Reading Conference.

Scholes, R. (1982). *Semiotics and interpretation.* New Haven: Yale University Press.

Scholes, R. (1985). *Textual power: Literary theory and the teaching of English.* New Haven: Yale University Press.

Schwandt, T. A. (1994). Constructivist, interpretivist approaches to human inquiry. In N. K. Denzin & Y. S. Lincoln (Eds.), *Handbook of qualitative research* (pp. 118–137). Thousand Oaks, CA: Sage.

Schwarcz, J. (1982). *Ways of the illustrator: Visual communication in children's literature.* Chicago: American Library Association.

Schwarcz, J., & Schwarcz, C. (1991). *The picture book comes of age.* Chicago: The American Library Association.

Searle, D. (1984). Scaffolding: Who's building whose building? *Language Arts, 61,* 480–483.

Sebeok, T. A. (1994). *Signs: An introduction to semiotics.* Toronto: University of Toronto Press.

Selden, R., & Widdowson, P. (1993). *A reader's guide to contemporary literary theory* (3rd ed.). Lexington: University of Kentucky Press.

Sendak, M. (1988). Caldecott Medal acceptance speech. In M. Sendak, *Caldecott & Co.: Notes on books and pictures* (pp. 145–155). New York: Farrar, Straus & Giroux.

Sendak, M. (1993). *Maurice Sendak talks about "We Are All in the Dumps with Jack and Guy."* Promotional literature for *We Are All in the Dumps.* New York: HarperCollins.

Sergiovanni, T. (1994). *Building communities in schools.* San Francisco: Jossey-Bass.

Shine, S., & Roser, N. L. (1999). The role of genre in preschoolers' response to picture books. *Research in the Teaching of English, 34,* 197–254.

Shklovsky, V. (1966). Art as technique. In L. Lemon & M. Reis (Eds.), *Russian formalist criticism: Four essays* (pp. 3–24). Lincoln: University of Nebraska Press.

Short, K. G. (1990). Creating a community of learners. In K. Short & K. Pierce (Eds.), *Talking about books: Creating literate communities.* Portsmouth, NH: Heinemann.

Short, K. G. (1992). Researching intertextuality within collaborative classroom learning environments. *Linguistics and Education, 4,* 313–333.

Short, K. G., & Pierce, K. M. (Eds.). (1990). *Talking about books: Creating literate communities.* Portsmouth, NH: Heinemann.

Siegel, M. (1995). More than words: The generative power of transmediation for learning. *Canadian Journal of Education, 20,* 455–475.

Sims, R. (1983). Strong black girls: A ten year old responds to fiction about Afro-Americans. *Journal of Research and Development in Education, 16,* 21–28.

Sinclair, J. McH., & Coulthard, M. (1975). *Towards an analysis of discourse: The English used by teachers and pupils.* London: Oxford University Press.

Sipe, L. R. (1993). Using transformations of traditional stories: Making the reading-writing connection. *The Reading Teacher, 47,* 18–26.

Sipe, L. R. (1998a). How picture books work: A semiotically framed theory of text–picture relationships. *Children's Literature in Education*, 29(2), 97–108.

Sipe, L. R. (1998b). Learning the language of picturebooks. *Journal of Children's Literature*, 24, 66–75.

Sipe, L. R. (1998c). Individual literary response styles of first and second graders. *National Reading Conference Yearbook*, 47, 76–89.

Sipe, L. R. (2000). "Those two gingerbread boys could be brothers": How children use intertextual connections during storybook readalouds. *Children's Literature in Education*, 31, 73–90.

Sipe, L. R. (2001a). A palimpsest of stories: Young children's intertextual links during readalouds of fairytale variants. *Reading Research and Instruction*, 40, 333–352.

Sipe, L. R. (2001b). Picturebooks as aesthetic objects. *Literacy Teaching and Learning: An International Journal of Early Reading and Writing*, 6, 23–42.

Sipe, L. R. (2002a). Contemporary urban children respond to Peter Rabbit: Making a text culturally relevant. In M. Mackey (Ed.), *Beatrix Potter's Peter Rabbit: A children's classic at 100* (pp. 3–18). Lanham, MD: The Children's Literature Association and the Scarecrow Press.

Sipe, L. R. (2002b). Talking back and taking over: Young children's expressive engagement during storybook readalouds. *The Reading Teacher*, 55, 476–483.

Sipe, L. R. (2004, December). *What is "postmodern" about postmodern children's picturebooks?* Paper presented at the National Reading Conference, San Antonio, TX.

Sipe, L. R. (in press). Learning from illustrations in picturebooks. In D. Fisher & N. Frey (Eds.), *Picture This! The Role Visual Information Plays in Literacy Learning*. Association of Supervision and Curriculum Development.

Sipe, L. R., & Bauer, J. T. (2001). Urban kindergartners' literary understanding of picture storybooks. *The New Advocate*, 14, 329–342.

Sipe, L. R., & Brightman, A. E. (2005). Young children's visual meaning-making during readalouds of picture storybooks. *National Reading Conference Yearbook*, 54, 349–361.

Sipe, L. R., & Brightman, A. E. (2006). Teacher scaffolding of first-graders' literary understanding during readalouds of fairytale variants. *National Reading Conference Yearbook*, 55, 276–292.

Sipe, L. R., & Ghiso, M. P. (2005). Looking closely at characters: How illustrations support children's understandings. In N. Roser & M. Martinez (Eds.), *What a character! Character study as a guide to literary meaning-making in grades K–8* (pp. 134–153). Newark, DE: International Reading Association.

Sipe, L. R., & McGuire, C. E. (2006a). Picturebook endpapers: Resources for literary and aesthetic interpretation. *Children's Literature in Education*, 37, 291–304.

Sipe, L. R., & McGuire, C. E. (2006b, November). *Young children's meaning-making from picturebook peritexts.* Paper presented at the National Reading Conference, Los Angeles, CA.

Sipe, L. R., & McGuire, C. E. (2006c). Young children's resistance to stories. *The Reading Teacher*, 60(1), 6–13.

Sipe, L. R., & McGuire, C. E. (in press). *The Stinky Cheese Man* and Other Fairly Postmodern Picturebooks for Children. In S. Lehr (Ed.), *Shattering the looking glass: Challenge, risk, and controversy in children's literature.* Norwood, MA: Christopher-Gordon Publishers.

Sloan, G. D. (1975). *The child as critic* (1st ed.). New York: Teachers College Press.

Sloan, G. D. (2003). *The child as critic: Developing literacy through literature, K–8* (4th ed.). New York: Teachers College Press.

Smith, F. (1984). Reading like a writer. In J. M. Jensen (Ed.), *Composing and comprehending* (pp. 47–56). Urbana, IL: ERIC Clearinghouse in Reading and Communication Skills and National Conference on Research on English.

Smolkin, L. B., & Suina, J. H. (1997). Artistic triumph or multicultural failure? Multiple perspectives on a "multicultural" award-winning book. *The New Advocate, 10,* 307–322.

Snow, C. E. (1983). Literacy and language: Relationships during the preschool years. *Harvard Educational Review, 53,* 165–189.

Snow, C. D., Burns, M. S., & Griffin, P. (Eds.). (1998). *Preventing reading difficulties in young children.* Washington, DC: National Academy of Sciences–National Research Council Commission on Behavioral and Social Science and Education, U.S. Department of Education.

Snow, C. E., Nathan, D., & Perlmann, R. (1985). Assessing children's knowledge about book reading. In L. Galda & A. D. Pellegrini (Eds.), *Play, language, and stories: The development of children's literate behavior* (pp. 167–181). Norwood, NJ: Ablex.

Solomon, M. (2003). Publishing children's picture books: The role of design and art direction. In A. Hudson & S. A. Cooper (Eds.), *Windows and words: A look at Canadian children's literature in English* (pp. 191–200). Ottawa, Ontario, Canada: University of Ottawa Press.

Sontag, S. (1961). *Against interpretation and other essays.* New York: Doubleday.

Spence, D. (1982). *Narrative truth and historical truth: Meaning and interpretation in psychoanalysis.* New York: W. W. Norton.

Spiegel, D. L., & Fitzgerald, J. (1986). Improving reading comprehension through instruction about story parts. *The Reading Teacher, 39,* 676–682.

Spiro, R. J., Coulson, R. L., Feltovich, P. J., & Anderson, D. K. (1994). Cognitive flexibility theory: Advanced knowledge acquisition in ill-structured domains. In R. B. Ruddell, M. R. Ruddell, & H. Singer (Eds.), *Theoretical models and processes of reading* (4th ed.) (pp. 602–615). Newark, DE: International Reading Association.

Stake, R. (1994). Case studies. In N. K. Denzin & Y. S. Lincoln (Eds.), *Handbook of qualitative research* (pp. 236–247). Thousand Oaks, CA: Sage.

Stanislavski, C. (1970). *An actor prepares.* New York: Theatre Arts Books.

Stein, N. L., & Glenn, C. G. (1979). An analysis of story comprehension in elementary school children. In R. O. Freedle (Ed.), *New directions in discourse processing* (pp. 53–110). Norwood, NJ: Ablex.

Steiner, W. (1982). *The colors of rhetoric.* Chicago: The University of Chicago Press.

Stephens, J. (1992). *Language and ideology in children's fiction.* London: Longman.

Stevenson, D. (1991). "If you read the last sentence, it won't tell you anything":

Postmodernism, self-referentiality, and *The Stinky Cheese Man*. *Children's Literature Association Quarterly, 19*, 32–34.

Stewig, J. W. (1995). *Looking at picture books*. Fort Atkinson, WI: Highsmith.

Stott, J. (1983). Teaching literary criticism in the elementary grades: A symposium. In J. May (Ed.), *Children and their literature: A readings book* (pp. 160–172). West Lafayette, IN: ChLA Publications.

Stott, J. (1987). Spiralled sequence story curriculum: A structuralist approach to teaching fiction in the elementary grades. *Children's Literature in Education, 18*, 148–163.

Strauss, A., & Corbin, J. (1998). *Basics of qualitative research: Techniques and procedures for developing grounded theory* (2nd ed.). Thousand Oaks, CA: Sage.

Straw, S. (1990). Conceptualizations of communication in the history of literary theory. In D. Bogdan & S. Straw (Eds.), *Beyond communication: Reading comprehension and criticism* (pp. 49–66). Portsmouth, NH: Heinemann.

Strickland, D. S. (2001). Early intervention for African American children considered to be at risk. In S. B. Neuman & D. K. Dickinson (Eds.), *Handbook of early literacy research, Volume 1* (pp. 322–332). New York: Guilford Press.

Suhor, C. (1984). Towards a semiotics-based curriculum. *Journal of Curriculum Studies, 16*, 247–257.

Suleiman, S., & Crosman, I. (Eds.) (1980). *The reader in the text*. Princeton: Princeton University Press.

Sutherland, Z., & Arbuthnot, M. H. (1991). *Children and books*. New York: HarperCollins.

Sutherland, Z., & Hearne, B. (1977). In search of the perfect picturebook definition. *Wilson Library Bulletin*, 158–160.

Taylor, G. S. (1997). Multicultural literature preferences of low-ability African American and Hispanic American fifth-graders. *Reading Improvement, 34*, 37–48.

Teale, W. H. (2003). Reading aloud to young children as a classroom instructional activity: Insights from research and practice. In A. Van Kleeck, S. A. Stahl, & E. R. Bauer (Eds.), *On reading books to children: Parents and teachers* (pp. 114–139). Mahwah, NJ: Lawrence Erlbaum Associates.

Thompson, J. (1987). *Understanding teenagers' reading: Reading processes and the teaching of literature*. New York: Croom Helm.

Todorov, T. (1977). *The poetics of prose*. Ithaca, NY: Cornell University Press.

Toelken, B. (1996). The icebergs of folklore: Misconception, misuse, abuse. In C. L. Birch & M. A. Heckler (Eds.), *Who says?: Essays on pivotal issues in contemporary storytelling* (pp. 35–63). Little Rock, AR: August House Publishers.

Tolkien, J. R. R. (1938/1964). *Tree and leaf*. London: Unwin Books.

Tompkins, J. P. (Ed.). (1980). *Reader-response criticism: From formalism to poststructuralism*. Baltimore: The Johns Hopkins University Press.

Tough, J. (1977). *Talk for teaching and learning*. London: Ward Lock.

Touponce, W. F. (1996). Children's literature and the pleasures of the text. *Children's Literature Association Quarterly, 20*, 175–182.

Towell, J. H., Schulz, A., & Demetrulias, D. M. (1997). *Does ethnicity really matter in literature for young children?* (ERIC Document Reproduction Service No. ED 412 571)

Trites, R. (1994). Manifold narratives: Metafiction and ideology in picture books. *Children's Literature in Education, 25*, 225–242.

Uspensky, B. (1973). *A poetics of composition* (V. Zavarin & S. Wittig, Trans.). Berkeley: University of California Press.

Vandergrift, K. E. (1980). *Child and story: The literary connection.* New York: Neal-Schuman Publishers.

van Kleeck, A., Stahl, S. A., & Bauer, E. R. (Eds.) (2003). *On reading books to children: Parents and teachers.* Mahwah, NJ: Lawrence Erlbaum Associates.

Veeser, H. A. (Ed.). (1989). *The new historicism.* New York: Routledge.

Vernon-Feagans, L. (1996). *Children's talk in classrooms and communities.* Cambridge, MA: Blackwell.

Vernon-Feagans, L., Hammer, C. S., Miccio, A., & Manlove, E. (2001). Early language and literacy skills in low-income African American and Hispanic children. In S. B. Neuman & D. K. Dickinson (Eds.), *Handbook of early literacy research* (pp. 192–210). New York: Guilford Press.

Vygotsky, L. (1978). *Mind in society: The development of higher psychological processes.* Cambridge, MA: Harvard University Press.

Vygotsky, L. S. (1986). *Thought and language.* Cambridge, MA: The MIT Press.

Walmsley, S., Fielding, L., & Walp, T. (1991). *A study of second-graders' home and school literary experiences* (Report Series 1.6). Albany, NY: Center for the Learning and Teaching of Literature, The State University of New York.

Ward, J., & Fox, M. (1984). A look at some outstanding illustrated books for children. *Children's Literature Association Quarterly, 9*, 19–21.

Waugh, P. (1984). *Metafiction: The theory and practice of self-conscious fiction.* New York: Routledge.

Wells, G. (1986). *The meaning makers: Children learning language and using language to learn.* Portsmouth, NH: Heinemann.

Wells, G. (1987). Apprenticeship in literacy. *Interchange, 18*, 109–123.

Wells, G. (1990). Talk about text: Where literacy is learned and taught. *Curriculum Inquiry, 20*, 369–405.

Wertsch, J. V. (1985). *Vygotsky and the social formation of mind.* Cambridge, MA: Harvard University Press.

Wertsch, J. V. (1991). A sociocultural approach to socially shared cognition. In L. B. Resnick, J. M. Levine, & S. D. Teasley (Eds.), *Perspectives on socially shared cognition* (pp. 85–100). Washington, DC: American Psychological Association.

Whalen-Levitt, P. (1986). Breaking frame: Bordering on illusion. *School Library Journal, 32*, 100–103.

White, E. (1994). *The burning library: Writings on art, politics, and sexuality, 1969–1993.* London: Chatto & Windus.

White, H. (1980). The value of narrativity in the representation of reality. *Critical Inquiry, 7*, 5–27.

Wiencek, J., & O'Flahavan, J. (1994). From teacher-led to peer discussions about literature: Suggestions for making the shift. *Language Arts, 71*, 488–498.

Williams, R. (1977). *Marxism and literature*. New York: Oxford University Press.

Wimsatt, W. K. (1954). *The verbal icon: Studies in the meaning of poetry*. Lexington: University of Kentucky Press.

Wimsatt, W. K., & Beardsley, M. C. (1954a). The affective fallacy. In W. K. Wimsatt, *The verbal icon: Studies in the meaning of poetry* (pp. 21–39). Lexington: University of Kentucky Press.

Wimsatt, W. K., & Beardsley, M. C. (1954b). The intentional fallacy. In W. K. Wimsatt, *The verbal icon: Studies in the meaning of poetry* (pp. 3–18). Lexington: University of Kentucky Press.

Winnicott, D. W. (1974). *Playing and reality*. London: Tavistock/Routledge.

Wiseman, D. L., Many, J., & Altieri, J. (1992). Enabling complex aesthetic responses: An examination of three literary discussion approaches. In C. K. Kinzer & D. J. Leu (Eds.), *Literacy research, theory, and practice: Views from many perspectives* (pp. 283–289). Chicago, IL: National Reading Conference.

Wolf, S. A. (1994). Learning to act/acting to learn: Children as actors, critics, and characters in classroom theatre. *Research in the Teaching of English, 28*, 7–44.

Wolf, S. A. (2004). *Interpreting literature with children*. Mahwah, NJ: Lawrence Erlbaum.

Wolf, S. A., Carey, A. A., & Mieras, E. L. (1996). "What is this literachurch stuff anyway?": Preservice teachers' growth in understanding children's literary response. *Reading Research Quarterly, 31*(2), 130–157.

Wolf, S. A., & Heath, S. B. (1992). *The braid of literature: Children's worlds of reading*. Cambridge, MA: Harvard University Press.

Wolfenbarger, C., & Sipe, L. R. (2007). A unique visual and literary art form: Recent research on picturebooks. *Language Arts, 84*, 273–280.

Wollman-Bonilla, J. (1994). Why don't they "just speak"? Attempting literature discussion with more and less able readers. *Research in the Teaching of English, 28*, 231–258.

Wood, D. J., Bruner, J. S., & Ross, G. (1976). The role of tutoring in problem solving. *Journal of Child Psychology and Psychiatry, 17*, 89–100.

Yaden, D. (1988). Understanding stories through repeated readalouds: How many does it take? *The Reading Teacher, 41*, 556–560.

Yolen, J. (1981). *Touch magic: Fantasy, faerie and folklore in the literature of children*. New York: Philomel.

Yonge, C., & Stables, A. (1998). "I am It the clown": Problematising the distinction between "off-task" and "on-task" classroom talk. *Language and Education, 12*, 55–70.

Index

About the Author

Lawrence R. Sipe is an associate professor in the University of Pennsylvania's Graduate School of Education, where he has been a member of the program in Reading/Writing/Literacy and the Language and Literacy in Education Division since 1996. His Ph.D. in children's literature and emergent literacy was completed at The Ohio State University. He also studied for a master's degree in Psychology of Reading and Special Education at Temple University, a B.S. in Elementary Education from Bloomsburg State College, and a B.A. in English Language and Literature from the University of Chicago. His 19 years of school-based experience include teaching in a one-room school (grades 1–8) for 2 years; a multigrade (K–2) classroom for 4 years; and doing professional development in language arts, special services, and preschool education with primary and elementary school teachers for a school district in Newfoundland, Canada, for 13 years. His chief research interests are in literature written for children and adolescents, and the responses of young children to picture storybooks.